720.9 PRI

university college
for the creative arts

at canterbury, epsom, farnham
maidstone and rochester

**Maidstone,** Oakwood Park, Maidstone, Kent, ME16 8AG 01622 620120

This book is to be returned on or before the last date stamped below.
Fines will be charged on overdue books.

-3 FEB 2009

0 3 DEC 2009

2 6 MAR 2010

-9 NOV 2010

WITHDRAWN

FROM STOCK

FRANCESCA PRINA AND ELENA DEMARTINI

# 1000 Years
## of World Architecture

An Illustrated Guide

Thames & Hudson

First published in the United Kingdom in 2006 by
Thames & Hudson Ltd,
181A High Holborn,
London WC1V 7QX

www.thamesandhudson.com

© 2005 by Mondadori Electa spa, Milan

© L. Barragán, P. Behrens, W. Gropius, A. Loos, L. Mies Van der Rohe, J. Nouvel, J.J. Oud, D. Perrault, G. Rietveld, O.F. Wagner, F.L. Wright, by SIAE 2005
© Foundation Le Corbusier, by SIAE 2005

British Library Cataloguing-in-Publication Data
A catalogue record for this book is available from the British Library

ISBN-13: 978-0-500-34229-9

ISBN-10: 0-500-34229-6

Printed and bound in Spain

**To the reader**

This book is composed of two sections, the Guide followed by the references section.

*The Guide* is composed of 148 subjects, each presented on a pair of facing pages; in addition, 36 outstanding works of architecture are discussed in separate entries, also presented on facing pages. Each of these two-page entries bears a title, giving the date and location, beneath a coloured band indicating the style; on the pages dedicated to masterpieces the coloured band goes all across the top and bottom of the pages.

| | |
|---|---|
| ▬ | Romanesque |
| ▬ | Gothic |
| ▬ | Renaissance |
| ▬ | Baroque and rococo |
| ▬ | Historicist |
| ▬ | 20th century |
| ▬ | Masterpieces |

*Some pages include boxed articles with in-depth information on important people or subjects.*

*The references* offer further information on the subjects covered in the Guide, including biographies of the architects and artists, a glossary of special terms and an index of names, places, and works.

*On the cover*
*Front:* A selection of images from throughout the book.
*Back:* Photo Edwin Smith.

pages 14–15
*Gallery with Views of Modern Rome,* detail, 1759, Louvre, Paris

pages 384–85
Foster and Partners, detail of the dome of the Reichstag, Berlin, 1995–99

*Art coordination*
Dario Tagliabue

*Layouts*
Sara Salvi

*Editorial coordination*
Caterina Giavotto

*Editing*
Milena Archetti

*Picture research*
Elena Demartini

*Technical coordination*
Mario Farè

*Quality control*
Giancarlo Berti

*English translation*
Jay Hyams

*Typesetting*
Michael Shaw

# Contents

# Overview

### Ancient, modern, classical

We see works of architecture while walking in the street, and images of buildings appear on television, in films, and in pictures in books and magazines, but that familiarity with architecture is hardly more than superficial. Architecture offers itself to us in an apparently immediate way, as an object of daily use; but architecture has been subject to a continuous evolutionary process, one that reveals the historical development and cultural preferences of many generations.

The identification of historical styles is of primary importance when organizing a work about the history of art, whether that work deals with research or interpretation. What later generations see as the outcome of a logical evolution may in fact have resulted from a complex process involving groups or individuals that would be difficult to decipher. Furthermore, the fragmentary nature of the architectural patrimony that has survived across time, including the comparatively short time of more

recent constructions, the gaps and contradictions in the sources, and the often sudden and unpredictable changes in taste and judgment have given the concept of historical epochs a certain ambiguous frailty; each generation places itself in a certain specific relationship to history, rejecting or re-evaluating all the various traditions of the past. The style known as Gothic offers a primary example

Parthenon, Athens,
447–30 BC

of this. Before the various revivals of the Gothic in the 18th and 19th centuries, the style was looked upon negatively, considered the product of a barbarous and obscure age. In much the same way, the architects of the early modern movement condemned and rejected historicist eclecticism; later, the 20th-century version of 'modern' architecture involved the outright rejection of the functionalism and rationalism of the early half of the century in favour of a sudden re-evaluation of historicism, and not merely for its importance in making academic comparisons but for its direct application, as in the designs by many 'postmodern' architects. The subject of what is modern architecture is as contentious today as it was in the past.

The term *modern* was first used, at the end of the 5th century, to distinguish the characteristics of the Christian present from the Roman – and pagan – past. The term thus expresses the self-awareness that the people of a period come to by comparing themselves to an earlier tradition; they see themselves as the result of a transition from what was ancient to what is now new. This kind of self-awareness is most famously an aspect of the Renaissance, the period that we see as the beginning of our modern age, but there have been other such periods, such as the age of Charlemagne, the 12th century, the age known as the Enlightenment – in fact, all those periods in which Europeans have become aware of living in a new epoch because of a change in their relationship to the past, to antiquity. In this process *antiquitas* assumes the role of model, and only with Enlightenment positivism – meaning with a belief in progress as a constant, ongoing process, with increasing knowledge leading to continuous improvements in society and morality – did the role performed by the classical works of the ancient world change, thus changing the way later epochs measured themselves as 'modern.' For as styles became obsolete, whatever was 'modern' maintained a subtle relationship with the classical, and up until the Industrial Revolution, that meant a reference to antiquity. Beginning with the new European order that came about in the Middle Ages, with the various states beginning to come into definition, Europeans, from the age of the Carolingian renaissance to that of the Gothic, looked back more and more often to the ancient tradition. Humanism and the Renaissance offered a new interpretation of antiquity, based on a greater knowledge of the sources and a point of view that reflected the scientific and rational spirit that eventually replaced the supremacy of theology. The reference to the ancient generated the dualism of the modern age, with an art called classical on one side, and on the other a technique increasingly based on science and thus open-minded. It is a dispute that 20th- and 21st-century architecture has sought to resolve through the more complete application of technique.

Any historical perspective simplifies the complex events of which architectural works are material expressions. Many buildings considered revolutionary at the time of their construction had been forgotten or were being referred to as 'classics' within only a few decades. An historical view must also be prepared to accommodate the notion of 'mutations': destruction and reconstruction; partial or total transformation; construction periods so long they come to involve changes in shape and design, leading to overlapping styles; restorations. In this context the survival of any one building must be seen as accidental, and at the same time every building assumes documen-tary value as being typical of a period or as being an orig-inal creation based on plans and formal concepts that changed over the course of history.

## Architecture as the representation of space

You cannot close your eyes to architecture; it constitutes the urban fabric, is part of our lives as citizens, and is the sign of human presence on the landscape. We cannot deny its existence, but we face certain objective difficulties in approaching it, beginning with the physical impossi-bility of moving buildings from place to place so as to display and study them, the way we do with paintings and sculpture.

The specific character of architecture, that which dis-tinguishes it from the other arts, is that it expresses itself by way of a three-dimensional vocabulary that includes humans; it comes with an internal space that cannot be completely represented in any form and that can be under-stood and experienced only through direct experience. So

**Basilica of Maxentius,
Rome, *c.* 308**

it is that space itself becomes the protagonist of the architectural reality.

The reality of an architectural object is not limited to the three dimensions of perspective but exists in an infinite number of perspectives, at least as many as the possible points of view. In painting and sculpture the 'fourth dimension' is a quality representative of the object, but in architecture the 'fourth dimension' is created by humans, who, moving around inside and outside the building experience it from different points of view. Even so, architecture goes even farther: the enclosed space cannot be defined in dimensional terms but is a constituent phenomenon of the character of architecture.

The spatial experience of architecture extends out into the city, in the streets and squares; while every building can be fully defined as a work of architecture, the building itself does not end with that definition and must be considered also in terms of its relationship to its surrounding space.

It is also abundantly clear that many themes apparently unrelated to the subject of architecture – bridges, urban components and embellishments, the decoration of façades, gardens – contribute to the formation of urban spaces. At the same time every building is composed of a plurality of values – economic, social, technical, functional, artistic, spatial, and decorative – and is the sum of all of them; thus space itself, although it is the foundation of architecture, is not sufficient to define it.

A complete history of architecture is therefore the history of all those multiple coefficients that together form the reality of building activity across the centuries, and these include more or less the full range of human interests, from social concerns – the economic situation, the desires of the people who paid for the buildings or had them built – to intellectual matters – not only what groups and individuals were, but what they aspired to be – and to the technical aspects of a building in relation to the figutive and aesthetic world to which all the arts contribute. Taken together, such factors make up the setting within which a work of architecture comes into existence. Sometimes it is a materialization of the supremacy of a ruling class, sometimes of a religious myth; it might reflect a collective ambition, or perhaps a technical discovery, or nothing more than a new style. It is also the product of the coexistence and the balance of all the components of the civilization in which it stands.

## The ages of space: a brief review of Western architecture, from antiquity to the late Middle Ages

For a long time following the end of the ancient world, specific knowledge of 'Greek art' was lost, for it had been assimilated by Roman culture so thoroughly that it had become part of the generic concept of 'ancient art'. Only very slowly did awareness of its autonomous reality take shape, a process that began in the Renaissance and, at least initially, took place more in literary and philosophical fields than in those related to the arts, eventually reaching a passionate rediscovery in the 18th century through the efforts of Winckelmann. The mythical and suprahistorical concept that made Greek art the model of perfection, a style to be imitated but never equalled, has since then had an enormous weight on Western culture, a result most of all of the exemplary formative value that the middle-class secular world of 19th-century Europe assigned to the study of the classics, highly esteemed for

**Mausoleum of Santa Costanza, Rome, *c.* 350**

Western architecture, affecting the perception of Gre
architecture and its many variants. It is a concept that go
no farther than the orders, meaning column styles, a
the temple as the ideal building, and thus it ignores oth
typologies as well as urban structures. There can be
doubt but that the Parthenon is a work of genius and th
it makes an impression on all who see it. So it has be
that at certain moments in history when architecture h
seemed bereft of original inspiration, architects ha
turned to the past and have borrowed from the forms
the past symbolic or functional themes to use in the
buildings. Hence, for example, the neo-classicism of t
19th century – excellent examples are the Walhalla
the Propylaeum in Munich by Klenze – in which Gre
art was used to breathe life into monumental underta
ings and decorative notions.

As for ancient Rome, the multiformity of its buildi
programmes, the monumental scale of so many of
public buildings, the technical expertise in the use of t
arch and the vault, the use of concrete, and the maste
ful handling of gigantic structures – from cisterns
aqueducts to the huge spatial conceptions of basilicas
baths – present a different concept of architecture, o
with a highly scenographic awareness. Ancient Ron
also displayed such a fecund inventiveness that its buil
ings compose a sort of morphological encyclopaedia
architecture. In Rome, technical demands, which becan
more pressing given the monumental scale of imperi
buildings, helped in the adoption of the social theme
the basilica, the place of human action according to a ph
losophy and a culture that broke with the perfect equ
librium of the Greek ideal to make structures that we
psychologically richer and more suitable to serve t
rhetorical needs of grandeur. The Roman architecture
the 1st century AD presents a complete catalogue of t
architecture of the European and Mediterranean civ
lization, a veritable infinity of motifs and ideas fro
which to draw. It is certainly true that Rome absorbe
architectural ideas from all the territories that fell subje
to it, so it is equally true that the architectural languag
of Rome did not include the genesis of every one of t
later spatial conceptions. Before the Romans adopte
them, the arch had been used in Egypt and the vault
the Orient; but from the point of view of architectural hi
tory it is of fundamental importance to emphasize th

the way they make ethics coincide with aesthetics. So
great was the effect of this on architectural production
that Greek art was made to perform a singular role; in
Greek culture, the subject of 'form', understood as an
expression of meaning, came to assume a central role in
the rational translation of the complexity of the world of
nature or the ethical concept of the human and the divine.
However, this recognized centrality of 'form' led to a profound process of 'formalization', resulting in an academic
and rigidly formalistic concept that has been applied to
the field of architecture more than to any other; a fine
example of this is the continuity over time of the model
of the Greek temple. From the discovery of the treatise by
Vitruvius, the only surviving work on architectural theory from the ancient world, to its 19th-century academic
formalization, the theory of the architectural orders
became a sort of supra-historical rule in building. This
interpretation runs through all of the classical school of

me adopted elements that were – because of their spatial conception, scale, and their intention or meaning – completely different. Roman official architecture is dominated by symmetry and the absolute autonomy of spaces, emphasized by the thickness of walls. This monumental grandeur was an expression of the authority of Rome, a symbol of the overarching presence of its power. The measure of Roman architecture is the scale of that original myth, the fact of its existence, and the nostalgia it awakened later. This is why when classical-academic architects or eclectic architects turned to Roman architecture, they did not treat it the way they treated Greek architecture – which they turned to only for decorative elements or ornaments for façades – and instead took far more; the 'Roman style' has been used for the interiors of big American banks and for the immense marble halls of train stations, meaning works that are made impressive by their size. So it is that Roman architecture is also used to meet the needs of building programmes in need of symbolic architecture, with rhetorical buildings that express the imperial and mythical themes of military and political supremacy.

The Christians drew the form of their temple from the encyclopaedia of Greek and Roman architecture. In the name of humanity, they produced the Roman Catholic space, and in doing so achieved a functional revolution: the Christian church, a place of communion and prayer, is related to the Roman basilica because that

structure had been made as a place to serve the social theme of assembly. The Christians reduced the size of the basilica to serve the needs of their more intimate religion, creating a structure based on the measure of the human believer. This transformation meant changes in the overall arrangement of the church's elements, based on the spiritual path taken by humans. The bilateral symmetry of the Roman basilica was broken by eliminating one of the two apses and by relocating the main entrance to one of the two shorter sides, resulting in a building with a single longitudinal axis. The entire layout, the spatial concept of the interior, and thus all of the decoration too was configured on the basis of one dramatic measure: the route of the faithful from the entrance to the altar. This

architectural solution, with its revolutionary importance, resulted in a longitudinally arranged space in which the rhythm of the rows of columns indicates the route to be taken and makes the believer a participant, indeed an integral part. The Greeks achieved a human scale in their structures by way of the proportional relationship between the column and the height of a human; the Christian world based its structures on the basis of the spiritual journey taken by humans. The same dynamic conquest is also clear in buildings with a central-plan layout, from the space of the Pantheon – centred uniformly without gradations of light and shadow and marked off by powerful walls – to that of the temple of Minerva Medica – a splendid example of the period of Rome's

ecadence, when Roman thinking became more intro-
rted and reflective, adopting ideas from the Orient
riched with atmospheric motifs – to that of the mau-
leum of Santa Costanza, the ring-shaped area of which
eates a new spatial articulation, a dialectic between
ght and shadow that eliminates walls and suggests a
urality of directional possibilities.

The early Christian basilican theme was exalted and
rther elaborated in the Byzantine period, during which
e longitudinal scheme was imbued with the urgency of
dynamic acceleration. The central-plan buildings from
e Justinian age – the Hagia Sophia in Constantinople,
Vitale at Ravenna – employ the same spatial layout and
e same attitude, negating the vertical relationships

and accentuating the sense of radial directions. In the
Hagia Sophia the dilation of space typical of Byzantine
architecture is achieved by way of enormous exedrae
and by wall surfaces that have a sense of sweeping outward toward the exterior in a centrifugal movement.
Even in S Vitale, although its structure goes against the
usual Catholic arrangement, the spatial intent is that of
expanding the octagonal shape, denying the geometric
form by way of the splendid mosaics covering the walls,
transforming them into a glittering surface, a soft, thin,
and superficial material. The Byzantine space, perenni-
ally in expansion, is a space in which the dynamic element is revealed through the use of shining planes, vast,
luminous surfaces. This represented a new inspiration

**Torhalle, Lorsch, 767–74**

Palatine Chapel,
Aachen, 796–805

*Opposite*
**Westwerk of the
church of Corvey,
*c.* 873/85–1150**

suitable to a univocal spirituality, dogmatic and abstract; it was a new message that was heard most clearly in the 12th and 13th centuries – with St Mark's in Venice and the Martorana church at Palermo – and that was echoed in all of the East. The centuries of the late Middle Ages – barbaric and pervaded by civil strife and invasions – are considered, despite their apparent decadence, an age of formation during which certain vigorous and original creations laid the substratum for the development of Western awareness. So it is that the history of architecture can make out the seeds of Romanesque architecture, and the spatial concepts that were to be developed between the 11th and 12th centuries, in far earlier and far cruder structures. The pre-eminent architectural subject of this period was the church, with all creative energies, both artistic and artisanal, developed in terms of church-building. The iconographic and structural elements that stand as the most original expressions of

the architecture made during these centuries are t[ ] raising of the presbytery area, the installation of [ ] ambulatory following the nave around the apsidal ar[ ] and the thickening of the walls, with the visual accent ation of the relationships between weights and loa[ ] bearing structures. All of this was accomplished usi[ ] rough materials – bricks and hewn and unhewn ston[ ] – applied with great expressive effectiveness, and it w[ ] related to the negation of Byzantine space, to the inte[ ] ruption of horizontal lines, and to the break with the u[ ] vocal rhythm along the longitudinal axis. Raising t[ ] presbytery area meant breaking the perspective vision the interior space of the church; the installation of [ ] ambulatory meant articulating the building, making [ ] a more complex organism to the detriment of a unita[ ] spatial vision; thickening the walls and replacing surfa[ ] chromatics with rough, natural material meant ove[ ] turning the spatial concept and its decorative attribute builders left the centrifugal dynamism of the Byzanti[ ] model to return to the solid construction of the Lat[ ] model. Over the period of the Carolingian renaissan[ ] the Christian basilica was gradually transformed into t[ ] medieval church, and although the original layout w[ ] maintained – a nave and two aisles, apse, roof, with f[ ] thicker walls, fewer windows and less light, with t[ ] columns replaced by piers – the result was a massi[ ] structure based on the poetics of a closed and shadow space. In the 8th century, despite the progressive 'Roma[ ] ization' of Europe, as seen in the organization of loc[ ] churches, use of the liturgy, and the expansion of t[ ] Benedictine Rule, the centre of gravity of Western cu[ ] ture was transferred away from Rome and over the Al[ ] with the creation of the Carolingian Empire. Carolingi[ ] architecture, a court art made for an elite that sought fuse the classical Roman cultural tradition with t[ ] Christian spiritual civilization, is notable for a high[ ] important typological-structural innovation destine[ ] to have widespread use in the centuries to come, most all in the French-German area: the invention of oppo[ ] ing choirs. The result was a radical alteration in t[ ] visual reading of the church building, which went fro[ ] being a simple one-directional structure to having do[ ] ble, even multiple, directions. There was then the intr[ ] duction of the westwork, introducing an element of fi[ ] ural ambiguity. This highly original symbolic structu[ ]

s being used by builders in the empire as early as the
nstruction of the Rhine cathedrals. Following the dis-
egration of the Carolingian empire it took more than
entury for the vitality of this art to find new stimulus
d new development. The Holy Roman Empire made
forms of Western art its own, amplifying their stately
d sacred attributes.

## is book

en before Rome fell, in AD 476, the Western and East-
empires were separate, and the clashes and quarrels
ween them, the differences in their forms of Christ-
worship, their renouncing of each other's institu-
ns, even their use of different languages – Latin and
eek – resulted in a political, economic, cultural, social,
d religious division that had a direct impact on archi-
ture. The process of the 'Romanization' of the West-
regions and that area's awareness of its separate iden-
helped in the formation of a single European cultural
ty that proved itself capable of overcoming differences
d assimilating diverse components thanks to a dynamic
cess of economic and political development. For this
son, at least up to the 20th century, this book pays
st attention to works of architecture made in Western
rope, examining those areas where the architectural
ture of Europe saw the formation of what can be
ed its support structure. The principal characteristics,
jor developments, and regional features in architec-
al history over a period of a thousand years are cov-
d in this book; these aspects are organized and ana-
ed by way of a chronological review of styles designed
help the reader understand major developments.

Ranging as it does from installations that involve
ge expanses of territory to the minute details of domes-
life, architecture must make use of an interdisciplinary
proach and a wide variety of resources from many
ds. It is necessary to recognize the many ways in which
hitecture is closely related to other fields of knowledge.
thin the limits of a basic synthesis, this history of
hitecture offers a nearly comprehensive panorama of
evolution of Western architecture, from the Middle
es to today. By no means is this guide complete – that
uld be impossible – but it is designed to provide
ough information and enough starting-points for fur-
er investigation to awaken the reader's curiosity.

# Early Romanesque architecture in Europe
## Late 10th–middle 11th century

### On the threshold of a new millennium

Western Europe went through a period of cultural reorganization in the 11th century that involved experiments with new ideas and revivals of the past. The classical, early Christian, and Byzantine elements that had nourished Carolingian art were blended with contributions from Islamic art and that of the ancient East. Early Romanesque architecture ranged among these elements in search of its formal identity. The emblematic structure in this process was the church. Since churches were built to serve the specific requirements of the liturgy, their construction changed as those needs changed. The relationship between an architectural form and its meaning was reflected in the arrangement of the internal areas of churches, which was based on the complementary relationship between the plastic mass of the building and its atmospheric mass. The early Romanesque saw the overcoming of Byzantine models and the abandonment of the formal language of classical antiquity. The column was replaced by the pillar; spaces previously left empty were filled with thick walls, forming compact masses; and the elevation of walls was divided into three or even four levels (arcade, gallery, triforium, and clerestory). The major structural change, a result of advances in construction techniques, was the progressive ability to cover churches with vaulted ceilings. The need to enlarge the choir and to alter the arrangement of the presbytery led to revolutionary changes in the eastern ends of churches. The adoption of the choir with ambulatory, in combination with the transept and the crossing tower, led to a variety of spatial articulations. The achievement of visual, perspective, and chiaroscuro effects in the interior resulted in the creation of an articulated structure on the exterior, with varying combinations of volumes decorated with stylistic elements from late antiquity, such as pilaster strips, hanging arches, and blind arcades.

**Abbey of St Martin-du-Canigou, 1001–9, 1026** Changes in construction methods made possible the use of masonry vaulting in early Romanesque churches. Experiments had been made with such vaulting in southwestern regions of Europe as early as the late 10th century. Both of the two small churches at St Martin-du-Canigou in the French Pyrenees, making use of a technique that had never been forgotten throughout the early Middle Ages, have a nave and two aisles covered by a barrel vault of Roman ancestry. The early Romanesque buildings of southern Europe tend to be small, low, and narrow, with structure robust enough to permit the stone vaults to extend their full length, with small windows and thus shadowy naves. These early experiments required the partition of the internal space and the adjustment of supporting structures.

**...thedral, Trier, 1039–66**
...e western end of the ...hedral presents the new way ...composing the external ...rts by way of the ...mbination of different ...chitectural elements drawn ...m the Romanesque-...rmanic culture. The western ...cade becomes a true ...chitectural subject: the *...stbau* of Trier is perhaps the ...ost majestic of the German ...rly Romanesque. The ...stern apse, the four towers, ...d the niches and loggias ...ened in the walls in a refined ...stem of interconnections are

all notable for their rich and differentiated articulation. The *Westbau* was an evolution of the westwork of the Carolingian double-choir church and gave churches a double-ended form that became typical primarily in German-language areas.

**Ste Gertrude,
Nivelles, *c.* 1046**
This church in Nivelles, Belgium, reflects the Carolingian preference for spaces with differentiated proportions and for the use of architectural cubes. It

illustrates the process of structural diversification of churches with the related changes in support elements. The use of the transverse arch interrupts the visual sequence of the arcade, dividing the nave into two areas, a sort of early sketch of the system of bays of the mature Romanesque.

# Ottonian and Salian architecture

## c. 955–1070

### The lands of the Holy Roman Empire

The renewed splendour of the empire in Germany was reflected in the revival of ecclesiastical building activity. In terms of both architectural style and decoration, these buildings were a natural development of Carolingian art, with a greater amplification of the stately and spiritual aspects. The changes they present resulted from changes in the uses of churches. There were changes in the liturgy, but most of all there was the increasingly widespread veneration of relics, which led to the multiplication of altars. A consequence of this was the structural and also visual enlargement of the choir; at the same time, given the loss of its previous political and civil functions, the west-work of the church was transformed into a *Westbau*, giving the building a double-ended bipolarity and eliminating the single-perspective axis. The articulation of the spaces transformed the Carolingian juxtaposition of volumes into a new system of connections and architectural integrations that favoured a substantially unitary monumental image. The Ottonian church was based on a rigorously geometric concept, and in its most mature form the area of the crossing became an isolated compositional module. This is stately and solemn architecture, designed to reflect the ideology of imperial power, with preference given to linguistic choices that heighten the essential sense of the structure, with effects of impressive majesty.

**St Cyriakus, Gernrode, 961, 1118–52**
Gernrode introduced numerous innovations to the earlier tradition. Its interior already reflects a new concept of space that cares little for wall ornamentation in order to stress the geometric schematics of the square as module.

**St Maria im Kapitol, Cologne, 1040–49**
St Maria represents the successful resolution of the architectural problem of placing a rectilinear body atop a square one, in this case applying a nave with its two aisles to an older central-planned structure. Each of the apses is enveloped in an ambulatory giving the east end of the church a trefoil shape.

**...hedral, Speyer,
...un 1024**

... colossal nave of Speyer
...ents architectural ideas
... went against the flat
...tinuity of Ottonian walls
... introduced the division
...ays. The isolated crossing
...er and the growing
...ortance of the interior
...s are elements that were
...ecome typical in the next
...od, while the use of
...quity-style details gives
...nse of the ceremonial
...ity of the architecture
...mperial Rome. Medieval
...esiastical architecture
...hes one of its heights in
...cathedral of Speyer, part
...e long process of
...sformation of the early
...istian basilica into the
...manesque church.

**...antaleon, Cologne, end
...—early 11th century**

... westwork of St Pantaleon,
...posed of a central tower
...nded westward by a two-
...ey portico flanked by
...ers, expresses the full
...arity of reworkings of
...external articulation,
...hasized by monumental
...ster strips and round
...es. It represents the
...age from the Carolingian
...work to the *Westbau*, the
...sive western structure of
...nian architecture.

# St Michael, Hildesheim
## 1010–33

The Benedictine abbey of St Michael, founded in 996 and rebuilt in a monumental style during the early Romanesque period, between 1010 and 1033, by Bishop Bernward and the architect Goderamnus, is the most successful example of the double-ended bipolarity of Ottonian churches. Restored to the splendour of the past by careful restoration work to remedy the damages of World War II, it is a basilica with a nave and two aisles covered by a roof with a crypt and towers. It is symmetrical both longitudinally and crosswise and is based on two analogous poles because of the presence of two equal transepts, one to the east and one to the west, and two apsidal choirs of identical height that emphasize the crossing points between the longitudinal axis and those transversal. From the compositional point of view, the adoption of the square geometric module at the isolated crossing gives the entire building order and geometric clarity and makes it of a type that was to serve a fundamental role in the later Romanesque. The supporting piers and columns are arranged following an alternating system, a 'dactylic' rhythm – the so-called Saxon rhythm, destined for great success in this area during the Romanesque period – and the positions of the piers mark the corners of square modules. The elevation of the wall is divided in two levels, arcade and clerestory, separated by a tall, flat, and bare section of wall, a characteristic of Ottonian architecture. Abundant light comes in the windows, giving the interior a clear and diffused brightness, increased by the white and red of the voussoirs, which highlight the focal points of the crossings and the outlines of the arcades. The extraordinary perfection of the proportions, achieved through the strict application of mathematical principles, along with the symbolic number four, and the way the individual parts work together harmoniously give the church a rare beauty.

Bishop Bernward is known to have left the church a copy of Vitruvius's *De architectura* in his will; perhaps the master builder Goderamnus made use of this work when he designed this building with its Vitruvian proportions. St Michael is a reliquary-church that fixed for a long time the most common type of Saxon church and at the same time codified the principles that were to characterize in an important way the later developments in the German Romanesque.

m the exterior, the double-
ed nature of the building
bundantly clear in the
trast of the two enormous
umes joined by the
gitudinal body of the nave;
 further pronounced in the
jection of the arms of the
 transepts. The geometric
ity and architectural
balance of the distribution of
these elements, as well as the
precise definition of the
volumes in a composition
based on architectural blocks,
are made clear in the two
square towers over the crossing
and in the four stair turrets,
octagonal at bottom and
round at the top to terminate
in cones, that rise on each
gable end of the transepts.
Placing the entrances on the
long sides goes against the
axial arrangement of the
basilica, already negated by
the double-choir layout; the
progression from west to east,
from main entrance to altar,
has been abandoned.

### The early Romanesque in northern France

The creation in 911 of the duchy of Normandy, which settled the Normans, was not accompanied by an immediate reawakening in building activity; with the possible exception of the ruins of the small church of St Pierre at Jumièges, nearly a century had to pass before the first signs appeared of the buildings that were to later become of fundamental importance to the history of architecture.

In fact, over the course of the 11th century Normandy became a very important architectural laboratory, a sort of 'experimental workshop' in which new building techniques were created. The changes in the architectural language are well represented by the ruins of the abbey church of Bernay, begun in the second decade of the 11th century, in which the so-called *mur épais* – a sort of gallery built within the thickness of a wall at the height of the windows – was employed for the first time. But many other buildings, although in ruins, are representative of this evolution, presenting themes that proved of fundamental importance to the evolution of Western architecture, from the two-tower façade of Jumièges to the ambulatory of the longitudinal body in the cathedrals of Bayeaux and Coutances, to the tripartite choir and blind triforium of Bernay to the crypt surrounded by an ambulatory with three radiating chapels of the cathedral of Rouen. At the same time, St Martin at Tours presents a first version of the choir with ambulatory and radiating chapels, anticipating a style that reached its greatest expression in the churches built along pilgrimage routes at the end of the 11th century and into the 12th.

Throughout the 11th century, the territories of the French crown contiguous to Normandy – the so-called Royal Domain, including Ile-de-France, Champagne, and Picardy – remained substantially faithful to the imperial Ottonian and Salian culture, acting as a sort of peripheral zone and thus also an area for the diffusion of the early Romanesque basilican layout with a flat roof topped by towers and characterized by the accentuated articulation of the walls, as at St Germain-des-Prés in Paris (the oldest surviving Parisian church), St Etienne at Vignory, and St Rémi at Reims.

**Notre-Dame, Jumièges, 1040–67**
Jumièges presents a primit façade with two towers, the so-called harmonic façade that would become comme in Gothic cathedrals.

**St Etienne, Vignory, 1050**
St Etienne introduces new spatial elements that are purely Western: the elevati of the nave is pierced by a *clair étage*, a false gallery open over the aisles.

**St Rémi, Reims, 1005–49**
The division of the elevation into three levels marks a step toward the early Gothic cathedral. Construction of the vaults involved raising the walls and also introducing engaged columns, balancing the clear horizontal articulation of the church with a rhythmic vertical arrangement.

# The early Romanesque in Catalonia and southern Burgundy

## 10th–11th century

### The Pyrenees as connection

The territory lying between the course of the Loire River and that of the Douro is a highly distinct landscape of great originality in terms of early Romanesque architecture. Catalonia was the site of very lively architectural activity, a result of the encounter with the Mozarabic tradition and its application in combination with the figurative styles of Burgundy and Lombardy. A spatial typology was developed that became of fundamental importance to the history of European architecture: the hall church, or *Hallenkirche*, which although already encountered in terms of westworks and crypts, became a profoundly original concept when it was used as the principal space of the church. The result was a construction made entirely of stone with thick, compact walls, interior spaces in semidarkness, with no sharp distinction made between the total space of the nave and the partial spaces of the bays. These buildings were without internal sculptural decoration, and the articulation of the exterior was limited to simple framing of the surfaces with pilaster strips and hanging arches that confer dynamism and a sense of the picturesque.

Of all the regions of France, it was Burgundy that demonstrated the greatest originality in architectural creations. Some works, most of all Cluny, indicate efforts to meet precise functional and formal needs along with the application of great technical skills. Even so, Burgundian architecture must be seen in close relation to early Romanesque Catalan architecture; we find, in fact, stone barrel vaults and often the hall layout. The hall church was the dominant typology, but alongside it another classical form of medieval architecture was making its way, destined to have a widespread application in southern France and northern Spain in the late 11th and 12th centuries: the single-nave church covered by a barrel vault or dome.

**St Philibert, Tournus, 1008–1120**
The longitudinal body of the church of St Philibert is one of the most surprising creations of the early Romanesque in Burgundy. The powerful round pilasters that give such unusual height to the aisles and the transverse barrel vaults supported by diaphragm arches produce an effect similar to that of the later hall churches with domed vaults. This was an aesthetically daring but structurally functional measure that permitted, despite the great height, the opening of windows and thus direct illumination.

**S Vicente, Cardona, 1029–**
While not a *Hallenkirche* strictly speaking, Cardona brings all the elements of ▮ southern early Romanesqu ▮ to technical and formal maturity. The external fron ▮ are animated by blind arch ▮ of a clear Lombard derivation; the architectur ▮ of the interior develops a coherent and compact structure that is bare, sever ▮ and essential. On the crossing, which acts as a module for the entire composition, is a dome on ▮ squinches that, on the exterior, becomes the cent ▮ of the church around whic ▮ the masses of the apse and transept are organized.

**...nastery church,**
**...edro de Roda, *c.* 1022**

...ngular structure for the
...enean region, S Pedro de
...da descends from French
...uitaine and Burgundian
...mples with the adoption
...blind nave with barrel
...lts buttressed by
...drant vaults on the aisles,
...ansept with 'orientated'
...pels, and an archaic
...bulatory choir without
...pels. The wall
...angement and the
...orative elements belong
...he Mozarabic tradition.
...rs of free-standing and
...erimposed columns,
...ated in front of piers,
...all the classical use of
...ated columns and are
...d here as individual
...hitectural elements to
...hlight plastic values and
...rk off the rhythm of the
...ucture; this use marks a
...p in the column's loss of
...traditional support
...iction. The presence of a
...h stylobate and of capitals
...ved with palmettes or
...erweaving locates the
...lding within the sphere of
...rebirth of monumental
...man sculpture. The
...erall effect of the forms
...alls Hellenistic
...hitecture or, in general,
...t of late antiquity, just as
...re seems to be a direct
...erence to the typology of
...me's papal basilicas.

# Mozarabic architecture in Spain
## 10th–early 11th century

### Sacred architecture between Islam and Christianity

Considered the last autonomous cycle of Iberian artistic culture before the unifying process of the Romanesque, Mozarabic architecture constitutes a fundamental chapter in the history of early medieval architecture. Only a very small group of churches survives – including Berlanga, Mazote, Lebeña, S Millán de la Cogolla – from among the many that were built between the end of the 9th and the first seventy years of the 10th century. Inserted between the architecture of the Asturian court and the early Romanesque of Catalonia, in a borderland between Islamic and Christian kingdoms, Mozarabic art (*Mozarab* is from *Mustarib*, meaning 'arabicized') was made by Christian populations living under Arab domination who were permitted by the Moors to practise their religion and build their own churches. More broadly speaking, the concept of Mozarabic is applied to the art of the 10th and early 11th centuries that developed in the three kingdoms of Castile, Aragon, and León; this art was a result of the monastic communities that had fled northward to escape Arab repression and of the migration of master builders moving north for the same reason. As the product of exiled communities, Mozarabic architecture reveals the ways and forms of the native countries of its creators, most of all Andalusia. The influence of the Islamic centres of Toledo and Cordova is clear, but it is blended with artistic styles from the communities that had emigrated to the Christian kingdoms. The resulting architecture is simple and shows the strong influence of Arabian art, as in the adoption of the horseshoe arch, in the particular shape of the front of the presbytery, quite often shaped like a mihrab, in the use of *alfiz* framing, particularly around arches, in the *ajimex* shape of windows and doors, and the use of intersecting ribbed vaults. The plans of Mozarabic churches present certain elements, such as multiple horseshoe-shaped, rectangular, or semicircular apses; in the elevation, the horseshoe shape is often applied to the arcades, and there is then the technique of using medium-size squared stones. From the structural point of view, Mozarabic churches have a very sturdy vault covering that ensures solidity to the building. Initially, simple forms were used, like barrel vaults with transverse arches or cross arches, but more complex systems came into use later, such as the canopy vault with pitched sections at S Tomás de las Ollas or the vault with mesh ribs at S Millán de la Cogolla.

**S María, Lebeña, c. 930**
In this small church with a rectangular plan, a longitudinal barrel-vaulted nave with aisles is fitted together with transverse bodies of different heights using a reticulated division of space similar to that employed in mosques. However, the distinction between the smaller side areas and the area of the nave is not made distinct enough in terms of size and structure, and the result can be said to have failed.

**Monastery church, S Miguel de Escalada, near León, 913**
Built by the abbot Alfonso, the church has a nave and transept separated by a sanctuary screen, similar in function to a Byzantine iconostasis, which runs all around to wrap the space in a unitary rhythm that brings to light the figurative qualities and the pleasant synthesis between the essential bareness of the surfaces and the volumes. The series of arcades set upon columns is clearly reminiscent of early Christian and Byzantine basilicas. The arrangement of the presbytery, composed of three separate circular-plan rooms covered with spherical vaults opened in the enormous width of the wall and thus not visible from the exterior, is quite singular.

**S Baudelio, Berlanga,
10th century**
The hermitage of S Baudelio
is composed of a complex
and varied articulation of
internal space, centred on an
enormous central column
that supports palm-shaped
ribbed vaults, with a
porticoed tribune with highly
original forms that create a
strongly symbolic space.

# Between renewal and tradition
## First half 11th century

**The early Romanesque in northern Italy**

Until the 10th century, the church architecture of southern Europe remained faithful to a style leading back to the tradition of late antiquity; so it was that the early Christian basilica, with neither transept nor western body, survived throughout the Middle Ages. However, in the area of the Po River, which extends across all of northern Italy except for Venice and the lagoon, the Lombard master builders had long since developed – and spread over the Alps – certain elements characteristic of the Romanesque architectural language, while at the same time carrying on their own translations of the style, but without following it to its logical conclusions and arriving at the forms developed elsewhere. So it was that by the middle of the 11th century, Spanish and French master builders in Catalonia, Aquitaine, and Burgundy were making the first churches entirely vaulted in stone, while Lombard architects had still not moved beyond churches with a basilican layout covered by timbered roofs. Nor did the Lombard architects catch up until the last decade of the 11th century. Because of the absence of the transept, Italian architecture of this period did not address the compositional problem presented by the crossing, where the nave and transept intersect. The motifs typical of the exterior configuration of churches built on the northern side of the Alps – the westwork and its transformation into a western body surmounted by a tower, along with the groups of towers located at the site of the crossing – were adopted only rarely in Italy, where preference was given to a simple façade that externally reflected the internal longitudinal articulation. There were, however, certain isolated examples of towers flanking the apse – as at Ivrea Cathedral or S Abbondio at Como – or even isolated monumental towers, detached from the body of the church, such as at Pomposa, near Ferrara, or in the towered façade of S Maria del Tiglio at Gravedona, near Lake Como. At the same time, by way of that process of osmosis that from time immemorial has transferred ideas back and forth across the Alps, certain motifs and typologies used in northern Europe showed up in the area of the Po River valley, such as the apse with ambulatory, which appears in S Stefano in Verona (early 11th century), or the front transept, which can be seen in S Carpoforo at Como (*c.* 1025).

**S Maria Assunta, Torcello,** *c.* **1008**

The persistence of the early Christian tradition of wall that seem to hover in space atop long rows of columns reappears at Torcello. The nave is set apart from the presbyterial space – on the other side of the Holy Door of the iconostasis – by the chromatic device of the beautiful pavement in *opus sectile*. The continuity of early Christian sensibilities in S Maria reflects its Venetian background – in the iconostasis and in the of golden proportions, as already adopted in S Eufemia at Grado in Friuli – as much as its Byzantine background as in the mosaics and the plastic decorations, probably salvaged from elsewhere.

**S Maria Maggiore, Lomello,** *c.* **1025**

The Lombard area was not without elements that prefigured the coming Romanesque style. In S Maria Maggiore the wooden roof is supported by transverse arches, which by connecting the vertical walls represent the first elements in the future vaults. Lanfranco was to adopt this method at Modena about one century later.

28

**...Maria, Pomposa,
...d-11th century**

...the architecture of the
...rmanic empire, and to a
...tain extent in that of the
...nch crown's Royal
...main, the configuration of
...façade was dominated by
...development of the
...rolingian westwork or by
...decomposition – façades
...h one or more towers, the
...ertion of a narthex,
...lonnaded towers – but the
...aracteristic trait in Italy
...s the isolated bell tower,
...und or square, and not
...corporated in the body of
...e church. Much attention
...nt into the architectural
...coration of such towers.
...e façade of the basilica of
...Maria at Pomposa in
...nilia-Romagna has a
...rtico with three arches that
...e richly decorated with
...ajolica, terracotta, and
...rved stone. There is also an
...pressive bell tower that
...tes to the middle of the
...th century. It is divided
...to nine floors marked off
...decorative pilasters and
...nd arches, a decorative
...otif destined to become
...despread, notably during
...e early Romanesque period
...southern Italy, and to
...ntinue through all of the
...th century. The tower
...ows lighter as it moves
...ward through the increase
...the openings and their
...ht. The tower of Pomposa
...the most beautiful example
...the early Romanesque in
...ly. This typology, created as
...symbol of the power of the
...ligious community, was to
...joy great success in all of
...ly and resulted in authentic
...asterpieces in the 12th,
...th, and 14th centuries at
...nice, Modena, and Pisa.

# The mature Romanesque
## c. 1070–1170

### Forms and typologies

The Romanesque had reached maturity by the late 1060s. There was the more or less total adoption of the vault covering, symbolic of the progress made in construction techniques but also a deliberate stylistic choice, and experiments were being made in certain constructive and formal aspects of churches, such as systems for articulating the walls, which were still divided in bays with an elevation on several levels. This articulation was no longer applied exclusively to the nave but was being extended to all of the church, to the walls of the transepts, the presbytery, the apses, even the exterior.

The changes in church architecture were related to precise figural purposes: to welcome, shelter, and embrace the faithful in a setting both stately and dignified, designed along perspective lines to give a sense of depth, all culminating in the ambulatory apse. Church interiors were a complex and densely moulded material characterized by strong chiaroscuro contrasts that reinforced the plastic outlines of the columns and increased the sense of layered atmospheric density and spatial depth. From the structural point of view, this was made possible through the adoption of the system of bays taken as spatial units; they were no longer divisions, marked off by transverse arches, of a unitary space, but were rather spatial bodies that were added one to the next, an addition of cells in a rigidly symmetrical order. The isolated crossing had become a normal element that constituted the fulcrum of the building, conferring order and measure. The wall itself went through a transformation. It was now structured as a plastic mass that could be disassembled and into which space could enter by way of openings in its surface, sometimes creating internal galleries along which people could move. By then, the pier had taken the place of the column almost everywhere; in Italy, ornamentation and wall sculptures became more common, but without suffocating the architectural function of the wall. Some expressions of Romanesque architecture seem inseparable from their natural setting. Outstanding examples are the abbey of Mont-St-Michel in Normandy, suspended between earth and water, the basilica of Ste Foy at Conques, set atop a steep cliff in the Auvergne, or the cathedral of Trani, Italy, overlooking the Adriatic, its bell tower serving as a welcome beacon to sailors.

**Monastery church, Murbach, c. 1130**
The longitudinal parts of the church were knocked down in the 18th century, but it has a choir with a flat termination, typical of the area of the Upper Rhine, flanked by two side choirs, the so-called stepped, or 'Benedictine', choir adopted from Cluny. Two towers, also typical of the landscape of northern Europe, dominate the gables of the transept. The external walls begin to lose their weight in the elegant articulation of the tall, narrow blind arcades and in the strongly splayed windows. The area of the Upper Rhine is known for its use of the local yellow sandstone, which produced highly evocative effects in walls; the great freestones set in place with skill increase the building's monumental character.

**Cathedral, Santiago de Compostela, begun c. 1075**
Final goal of the pilgrimage routes to the tomb of the apostle saint, Santiago de Compostela, despite its monumental size, repeats in large part the building models of the period: a basilica with a nave and two aisles with galleries, transept and choir with ambulatory. Because of the absence of direct illumination of the nave, the enormous space is immersed in a half-light that brings out the severe articulation of the architecture. The choir alone is crowned by windows, which cast an almost mystical illumination on the tomb of St James.

**Notre-Dame-la-Grande, Poitiers, c. 1130–45**

The final twenty years of the 11th century and the opening years of the 12th are of great importance in terms of ecclesiastical architecture throughout France. Many of the architectural works were distinguished by novel methods, both in terms of typology as well as decoration. Important innovations are to be found on the exterior of Notre-Dame, beginning with the motif of the large blind arcades, which reflect the interior arrangement the building, and the profusion of sculptural decoration. What is most surprising about the façade, however, is how it inaugurates the motif of three strongly splayed and closely related porches, a motif that was later adopted in Gothic cathedrals.

# Normandy and the Anglo-Norman area
## c. 1066–1130

**The mature Romanesque astride the Channel**
The geographical area involved in the diffusion of Norman architecture expanded from the Continent of Europe across the Channel with the Norman Conquest of 1066 and maintained a substantially unitary architectural culture. Even so, the development of this historical cycle set off along an anomalous route in France. After having reached, in Jumièges, a building type structurally predisposed to receive an entire covering in vaults, Norman architecture turned back, refusing to take the step to vaults, and the churches of Normandy had to wait nearly sixty years for a definitive operation. The two great Benedictine abbeys of Caen – St Etienne and La Trinité – were given their stone vaults only between 1125 and 1130. In these building types Norman architecture on the Continent reached full maturity both in the development of the typologies and in the formulation of an architectural language applicable to individual elements, from the harmonic façade to the crossing tower, from the arrangement of the choir to the various uses of the *mur épais*.

The conquest of 1066 led to the introduction of Continental building types and architectural forms to England. Anglo-Norman architecture did not develop in precisely the same way as the Continental version of the Norman style, as is made plain by comparison of the systems used for covering the naves. The innovation adopted at Durham – ribbed vaults, repeated at Caen about a quarter of a century later – was not embraced in England, and English master builders continued to build large basilican churches roofed with timber. Anglo-Norman churches differed further from their Continental cousins by their increased size, with greatly elongated naves and transepts. The elevation of their walls is traditionally divided into three levels, and the walls themselves are high and strongly structured, the horizontal perspective sweep of the nave augmented by deep, structurally modulated arcades and galleries, with a 'Norman gallery' running in front of the windows, and massive, bundled piers, all these elements together creating effects of enormous, stately grandeur. The exterior fronts vary greatly, with outstanding examples of singular originality; the most frequently used motif is the great central window, which can occupy most of the façade.

**St Etienne, Caen, begun 10**
Built by William the Conqueror in expiation for his marriage to his cousin Matilda of Flanders, St Etienne presents all the forms typical of Norman architecture. It is a basilica with galleries with engaged columns that rise the full length of the elevation, a greatly elongated nave and transept, a 'Norman gallery' located along the clerestory wall, and an internal colonnade. The continuous line of the arcade, gallery, a clerestory windows continu into the bays of the transep and is thus an expression o the process of harmonizing internal spaces that was the taking place in churches and that, when connected to the ribbed vault, is a prefiguration of the forms of the Gothic cathedral.

**Cathedral, Ely, 1090–1130**
The nave of Ely Cathedral achieves full figurative qual in the sweeping perspective flight of its high walls mark off in a tight rhythm and modelled by the sharp definition of the plastic ma Hence the sequence of deer modulated arcades, the twinned openings in the gallery, the presence of the 'Norman gallery' in front of the clerestory windows, the presence of engaged semicolumns that rise to th roof. However, the structur system of English cathedral similar to that of Franco-Norman churches built before 1130, does not take final step in terms of the ro which is still a concave decorated ceiling.

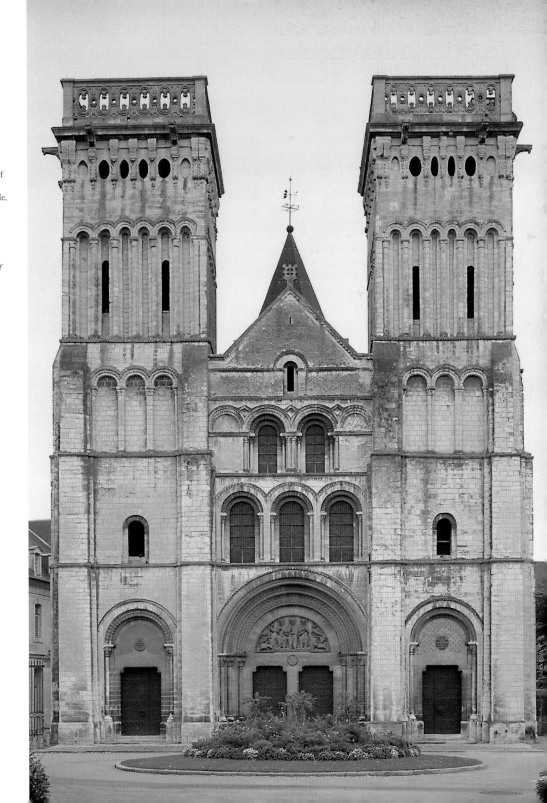

**a Trinité, Caen,**
**egun 1060–65**
uch like its twin building,
Etienne, the ex-convent of
Trinité presents the pure
rm of the two-tower façade,
hich in the abstraction of
e cubic volumes and the
rfect balance between the
wers and the transverse
dy, was to be developed
roughout the 12th century
become common in the
rly Gothic cathedrals of
rthern France.

# Durham Cathedral

## 1093–1133

Within the sphere of Norman architecture, Durham Cathedral is the link that joins the French architectural, linguistic, and technical tradition to the innovative skills of English builders. Along with Speyer and Cluny III it represents one of the first great entirely vaulted constructions of the mature Romanesque. The original organism of the cathedral was composed of a large, elongated longitudinal body with a nave and two aisles divided by arcades with alternating supports, with a gallery, wide transept – double and projecting – and a triple choir. Its chronological history illustrates the basic steps in the creation of a church building entirely vaulted in its complete and definitive form. The architectural form of this work is that of a building with Romanesque traits – except for the conformation of the vaults – in the structural use of very thick walls and in the powerful sense of the plastic mass of the cylindrical pillars and the enormous piers. Between 1099 and 1104, the first great pointed rib vault was made in the choir: an innovation both linguistic and technical-constructive destined to lighten and raise the heavy Romanesque walls in an anticipation of the characteristics and forms of Gothic architecture. The application of the type of vault used at Durham also marks the moment in which the problem of providing solidity to the roof was transformed into a more general construction problem, that of guaranteeing stability to the entire structure. The arched buttresses hidden in the galleries already have the shape of flying buttresses and serve the function of flying buttresses located to support central vaults. The breadth and size of the impressive nave balances the solidity of the mass, most of all the great height of the arcades and the height of the vaults.

The façade with two towers and the massive crossing tower increase the building's sense of grandeur, while the longitudinal extension of the northern flank fully reveals the 143 metres of length of the nave. Durham is located – with its monastery and castle – on the natural defence of a cliff overlooking the Wear River. This elevated position accentuates the impression of power and solidity of Norman architecture along with the spirit of the Romanesque in England.

The bays, unique for their type, are rectangular in shape with their longitudinal sense highly accentuated; every bundled pier alternates with a round pillar. For the first time, the lozenges, spirals, and zigzags typical of Norman decorations are incised on the trunks of the pillars, emphasizing their mass and giving them a majestic alternating rhythm that gives this masterpiece of Romanesque architecture a solemn dignity.

# Pilgrimage churches
## 11th–12th century

### The route to Santiago de Compostela

The pilgrimage churches located along the routes that cross the Pyrenees to reach Santiago de Compostela in Galicia (burial place of the apostle James) represent some of the major creations of French Romanesque architecture during the 11th and 12th centuries. In a church, the crypt and other relics are located in the choir-presbytery area, and the necessity of making this area available to the faithful is at the heart of the pilgrimage church. As an architectural type, the pilgrimage church came into being to serve the increasingly numerous crowds of the faithful visiting certain churches, an aspect of the enormous growth in the veneration of relics, with the consequent multiplication of minor altars. The basic plan of these churches is that of a vaulted basilica, but with several important alterations: the adoption of the chevet (apse, ambulatory, and radiating chapels); the blind nave, which gives greater importance to the gallery as a secondary means of moving crowds through the church; the transformation of the transept into a large transverse body with three large aisles; the extension of the nave's aisles to reach and encircle both the choir and the transept so as to move pilgrims along a clearly arranged route.

In addition to the cathedral of St James at Compostela, the most important pilgrimage churches were Ste Foy at Conques, St Sernin at Toulouse, Moissac, St Etienne at Nevers, and La Madeleine at Vézelay. The roads that led to these sites involved pilgrims in prayer and expiation but also in cultural and commercial exchanges.

Aside from changes in the ambulatories, transepts, and galleries – with minor altars arranged so that pilgrims could visit them without disturbing services at the main altar – certain areas of pilgrimage churches were imbued with symbolic value, such as portals and capitals, which were animated using an extraordinary figurative repertory that emphasized cosmic order and the providential nature of creation and redemption. The route to Santiago became a figural image of the route of the soul to God and was thus experienced by the pilgrim in a spirit of total dedication, and the several stops were marked by churches of ancient foundation, renewed and enlarged in an evocative encounter between human builder and created cosmos. Other than Santiago de Compostela, two other destinations were of primary importance: the Holy Sepulchre at Jerusalem and the tomb of St Peter at Rome.

**Pórtico de la Gloria, Santiago de Compostela, 1168–88**
The construction of the cathedral of Santiago de Compostela, which began in 1075 at the behest of King Alfonso VI, meant the importation to Spain of the French architectural model and its adoption in even the smallest detail, ignoring local traditions. The enormous size of this church, one of the most important of the pilgrimage churches, is the direct result of the enormous crowds of pilgrims visiting the tomb of St James, the apostle of Christ who had arisen to protect Christian Spain. A statue of the saint (seated and resting on his pilgrim's staff) decorates the trumeau of the double door of the Portico of Glory, a work by Master Matthew. It welcomes the pilgrim while at the same time emphasizing the important symbolism of the site at which one enters the cathedral. The tympanum, repeating stylistic motifs similar to those used in Burgundy, presents the themes of the Last Judgment and the Apocalypse.

**Ste Foy, Conques, mid-11th century**
This is the oldest of the pilgrimage churches still preserved. It represents the achievement, albeit on a reduced scale, of the perfect organic coherence and full expressive harmony of the blind-nave church. The austere but rich exterior articulation reveals the double arrangement, both horizontal and vertical, of chapels around the ambulatory of the choir and the apse toward the crossing tower in a superimposition of volumes typical of Romanesque art.

**St Etienne, Nevers,
begun 1063**
The gradual perfection of
the various elements of
church architecture led to
the desire to provide direct
illumination of the nave.
St Etienne, although
remaining a barrel-vaulted
church with galleries,
manages to satisfy this desire
through the marked
heightening of the nave
which permits the opening
of windows in the area above
the gallery. This wall/vault
passage, which gives the
elevation of the church three
levels, manages to preserve
the clarity and sense of
structural essentiality
that characterize
pilgrimage churches.

**St Sernin, Toulouse,
1060–1150**
St Sernin is the largest and
most varied development
of the building typology
established at Conques. The
exterior of the eastern end
of the church reveals the
striking verticality created by
the arrangement by height of
the various volumes, running
from the radiating chapels to
the choir and apse to
culminate in the great tower-
lantern, the result of a 17th-
century reworking by
Viollet-le-Duc.

# Benedictine monastic architecture
## between luxury and obedience
### 11th–12th century

## Cluniacs and Cistercians

The emotional impact of medieval architecture was based on its ability to translate the promise of eternal life into stone. At the base of all the architectural manifestations was the ability to depict, as described in John's Book of Revelation, the celestial Jerusalem, the city of salvation reflected in the organization of monasteries.

Three great complexes mark the history of medieval Benedictine monasticism: the mother abbey of Monte Cassino, Cluny, and Citeaux. Beginning in the 9th century these were structured architecturally around a cloister, an element of novelty that from then on became the fulcrum for all monasteries.

Founded in 909 by William, duke of Aquitaine, the Cluniac order became well known for its artistic expressions and kept up to date on technical innovations in Romanesque architecture. The order saw the liturgy as the focal point of monastic life. It was celebrated with an astonishing magnificence that was applied to all the ceremonial apparatus and in particular to the furnishings of churches, which gleamed with gold, enamel, and light to exalt the glory of God. As a result, the order needed increasingly large and luxurious spaces, suitable sites for choral singing and the multiplication of minor altars reserved for private Masses.

In open polemic with the luxurious interiors of Cluniac churches, Bernard of Clairvaux, 11th-century founder of the Cistercian order, made restrictive rules concerning the monasteries of the order. 'Let nothing remain in the house of God that knows of pride or superfluity or that can in any way compromise the poverty that the monks have wed as custodian of their virtue.' So it was that a Cistercian church, understood as a building constructed to serve the specific function of *oratorium*, presents characteristics of intentional and profound austerity, translated in a severe and rigorous clarity of forms and simplicity of solutions. Renouncing all figurative excess meant banning the construction of towers as well as the use of paintings, sculptures, furnishings, or stained glass to decorate church interiors. The clear separation between living spaces and work areas guaranteed the isolation of the church and the cloister from the places of access of the profane world.

**Abbey church, Fontenay, 1139–47**
Erected under the direct control of Bernard of Clairvaux, Fontenay was modelled on the blind-nave churches of southern Europe and is an expression of the spirit of austerity demanded by the order's founder. The stately nave, enormous and deep, is covered by pointed barrel vaults. The church is composed of this one long, uninterrupted space, engulfed in a half-light broken only by shafts of light from the side spaces and the windows at the far end.

**Abbey church, Alpirsbach, 1099–1125**
The 'Hirsau school' of architecture was based on the abbey church at Hirsau, which became a model for others. That church can be said to apply to architecture the spiritual principles of the Benedictine reform by returning to the style of original Christianity and reproposing a columnar basilica with a flat wooden ceiling. A peculiar characteristic of these buildings, which include the beautiful church of Alpirsbach, is the sharp spatial distinction of the first bay of the longitudinal body of the nave from the choir – the so-called *chorus maior* – transliterating in architecture its liturgical functions, strictly reserved for the monks. Alpirsbach is completely without sumptuous decorations, while the 'boxlike' proportions of the nave seem to increase the sense of monumentality.

**Abbey church, Cluny, begun in the 10th century**

The Benedictine abbey of Cluny II, thanks to the typological and compositional innovation of a second transept to increase the church's capacity, is the most grandiose layout of all the Middle Ages. With a nave and doubled aisles and an ambulatory choir with radiating chapels, a large narthex, and seven towers, it is such a monumental structure that the involvement of the great abbots – but most of all Peter the Venerable – was probably decisive in both its planning and execution. The church was demolished, with the exception of the southern wing of the transept, around 1810. Its originality resides not only in the extraordinary complexity of the whole, which is reflected in the multiplication of the visual effects and the perspective effects of the interiors, but also in the way the height of the nave is greatly increased in comparison to its width, in the general adoption of the pointed arch and pointed vaults, in the introduction of the system of direct illumination, and in the different sizes of the various structures, in which the great height of the arcade drastically reduces the portion of wall above it, with the consequent elimination of the gallery. This is a monument in which the necessity of obtaining the highest formal quality in image and the maximum spatial, perspectival, and chromatic-chiaroscural effects has perfected the division of the interior of pilgrimage churches, resulting in a work of extraordinary power that already presents in a nutshell many of the essential traits of the Gothic cathedral.

# Burgundy
## *c.* 1100–50

### The mature Romanesque in central France

The mature Romanesque appeared in Burgundy between the end of the 11th century and the middle of the 12th, with its own regional variant of the vaulted basilica in the important pair of churches called Paray-le-Monial–Cluny III. These buildings, which are based on the earlier churches with barrel vaults of the Tournus type, make clear the maturation of the local language and the progressive clarification of the proportions. The pointed barrel vault was divided into bays, and the windows, formerly opened within the vault, were now located in an upper area of the wall, in an articulation of classical beauty but also great originality. Of course, this was by no means the first time the wall had been articulated on several levels, for it had been anticipated in the Carolingian 'Torhalle' of Lorsch as well as in the western façade of Trier Cathedral. Walls and piers are covered with fluted pilasters and classical mouldings in a perfect formal balance that is unique on the panorama of Romanesque architecture, a system of articulation with an ancient flavour that probably drew its inspiration from the Roman remains in the region. The articulation of the nave continues in the same way in the transept and choir, achieving that continuity and homogeneity of internal spaces that prefigures the Gothic cathedral. The persistence of the barrel-vault system, with its strong lateral thrust, despite the pointed arches of the nave arcade and vault, did not permit the development of wide, spacious naves like those of the Rhineland or Lombardy; the barrel-vaulted churches of Burgundy are tall and narrow.

**St Lazare, Autun, 1120–46**
Diocesan see, as well as daughter of Cluny III, of which it is a faithful reproduction, St Lazare was built by Bishop Etienne de Bâgé. Aesthetically very similar to its model, it appears more easy-going in the treatment of details, with open references to classical elements. The substitution the engaged semicolumns with fluted pilasters, in all probability based on the Corinthian orders of the Roman Porte d'Arroux in Autun, gives the space a sense of stately solemnity. The western double door, with its trumeau and tympanum sculpted by Gislebertus with the *Last Judgment*, dates to between 1130 and 1135 and is one of the high-points of Romanesque sculpture.

**Abbey church, St-Benoît-sur-Loire,** *c.* **1073**
The most singular 11th-century monument in central France stands along the Loire River, the abbey church of St-Benoît-sur-Loire. The arrangement of the choir seems to indicate the desire to add a second, smaller transept, leading to the notion that St-Benoît should be considered an anticipation of the basilican church with two parallel transepts, distinct and projecting, as in the later Cluny III. The west façade has a massive tower, a grand dominating mass of ashlar masonry made following forms of great plastic and structural rigour.

**Notre-Dame, Paray-le-Monial, first half 11th century–1090**

Founded by St Hugh, abbot of Cluny, Paray-le-Monial presents – in the basilican layout with a nave and two aisles, a projecting transept, high tower-lantern over the crossing, and façade with two towers – a sort of 'reduced-scale' version of the mother church. Thus like Cluny, it clearly differentiates the wall from the vault by way of a cornice, the horizontal extent of which is compensated by the arched form of the barrel vault that gives the narrow space a sense of vertical tension. The elevation is divided into three levels, with an arcade of tall, pointed arches, a blind triforium, and a clerestory that provides light through small windows. The cornices that divide the three levels and the fluted pilasters of the compound piers create a complex rectangular system of horizontal and vertical lines that gives an impression of abundance and splendour in the treatment of the surfaces that has nothing whatsoever to do with the Rhineland or with Norman ways of closing off space.

# Church of the Madeleine, Vézelay
## 1104–1215

Dedicated to Mary Magdalene – it held her relics –
and an important pilgrimage centre, in fact the
departure point for one of the four French 'roads'
to Santiago de Compostela, the Church of the
Madeleine at Vézelay was built in three distinct
phases: the nave and aisles between 1104 and
c. 1132, the two-storey narthex between 1135 and
1151, and the transept and Gothic choir between
1190 and 1215. Its builders carried on the process
of simplification, aimed at giving churches a simple
and essential structure; in particular, they eliminated
the triforium/gallery. A masterpiece of Burgundian
Romanesque, La Madeleine clearly differs from the
so-called Paray-le-Monial–Cluny III churches in its
rejection of the barrel vault and the use of a system
similar to that of the Rhineland or Lombard area
in the adoption of transverse vaults – without,
however, using a system of supports and adopting
instead a rapid series of rectangular bays visually
marked off by round archivolts. The result represents
the perfect, definitive model of the basilica with a
nave and two aisles, with raised, sharply defined
transverse vaults in both the nave and the aisles,
tall transverse arcades with engaged columns,
direct illumination that highlights the building's
chiaroscural values, and simple and reduced exterior
buttresses. The power of the resulting image is based
on the regular cadence of the transverse vaults,
which form a steady framework and stand out
against the pale background of the bare walls. The
harmony of the spatial proportions and the plasticity
of the division of the walls by means of a heavy
horizontal cornice give the church a rare beauty.
There is also the use – in both the transverse arches
and the extradoses of the arcade arches – of
voussoirs that alternate in colour between red-brown
and white; and friezes and ribbons of decoration
emphasize with great decorative qualities the various
architectural parts – from the arcades to the
windows to the various levels of the elevation –
giving the entire structure a brilliantly clear legibility.

The sculptural decoration
of the portals, lintels, and
capitals is of exquisite
workmanship at Vézelay;
along with the sculpture at
Autun, it represents one of
the high points of European
Romanesque sculpture in the
first half of the 12th century.
The figuration of the portals
centres on themes of the
Pentecost, the descent of the
Holy Spirit, and the
departure of the apostles
to announce the good news,
in an intensely dynamic
composition of great
visionary force; a figuration
of particular importance
during a period of crusades
when it was the proclaimed
duty of every Christian to
spread the gospel.

**The mature Romanesque between France and Spain**
In the geographic area that spans southern France and
northern Spain, new building typologies, including
entirely vaulted basilicas, had been in use since as early
as the dawn of the 11th century. This situation became
consolidated and generalized over the course of the
12th century. The hall church was the most frequently
encountered architectural typology. Its style had been
standardized. Its general characteristics were still those
that had been established in the early Romanesque
period: a closed body composed of a nave and two aisles
of more or less the same height covered by barrel vaults
and illuminated with indirect lighting. Around the end
of the 11th century the uninterrupted barrel vault gave
way to divisions by way of transverse arches. By installing
a more forceful connection between the vault and its
support these arches contrasted the longitudinal sweep
of the nave and identified the bays as the dominant
structural element in the architectural order. The early
Romanesque configuration of the three parallel barrel
vaults, with effects of strong spatial division, was still
quite widespread in the 12th century, but there was no
lack of diversification, usually given by the use of areas
of barrel vaults, transverse vaults, or cross vaults on the
aisles. The hall churches and single-nave churches were
highly individual spatial and architectural organisms
and reveal particular solutions applied to the façade,
which was treated as a wall articulated so as to reflect the
internal divisions of the church. Towers were not given
great importance in this region. Like the development
of the western body of the church, they were often given
little attention; even so, there was no lack of towers,
such as the gigantic one of St Front at Périgueux, along
with isolated towers of surprising fantasy, such as those
of the cathedral of Le Puy.

The southwestern regions of France boast around
sixty single-nave domed churches, such as at Périgueux
and Le Puy. This is the apex of the internal Romanesque
space: a hemispherical dome rises over every bay, a
structure that makes the additive composition of the
space more visually effective. Domed churches were
typical of Aquitaine in the 12th century, but they also
appeared in other areas, such as Puglia, in southern
Italy, in the great round crossing towers at Salamanca,
and in the highly particular case of St Mark's in Venice.

**Cathedral, Jaca,
consecrated 1063**
The small cathedral of
Jaca presents a system of
alternating supports that is
completely unusual within
the panorama of Spanish
architecture of the period:
large piers alternate with
columns with finely carved
capitals. The semicolumns
set against the piers amplif
the architectural articulatio
while the vaults are from th
Gothic period.

**S Isidoro, León,
consecrated 1063**
The collegiate church of
S Isidoro presents the
architectural conformation
that is considered most
typical of Spanish churches
a closed organism, robust
and compact, with thick,
continuous walls and sever
simple forms. What makes
the church singular is the u
of the space between the ci
wall and the front of the
church, which is the site of
the chapel of the rulers of
León, the so-called Panteó
de los Reyes (1054–67).

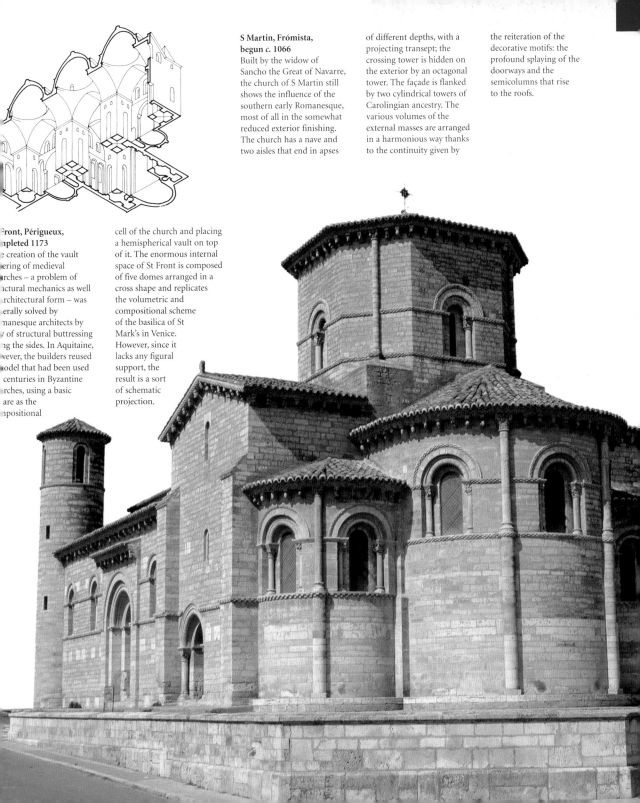

**S Martin, Frómista,
begun _c._ 1066**
Built by the widow of
Sancho the Great of Navarre,
the church of S Martin still
shows the influence of the
southern early Romanesque,
most of all in the somewhat
reduced exterior finishing.
The church has a nave and
two aisles that end in apses
of different depths, with a
projecting transept; the
crossing tower is hidden on
the exterior by an octagonal
tower. The façade is flanked
by two cylindrical towers of
Carolingian ancestry. The
various volumes of the
external masses are arranged
in a harmonious way thanks
to the continuity given by
the reiteration of the
decorative motifs: the
profound splaying of the
doorways and the
semicolumns that rise
to the roofs.

**Front, Périgueux,
mpleted 1173**
e creation of the vault
ering of medieval
rches – a problem of
ctural mechanics as well
rchitectural form – was
erally solved by
manesque architects by
y of structural buttressing
ng the sides. In Aquitaine,
wever, the builders reused
odel that had been used
centuries in Byzantine
rches, using a basic
are as the
npositional
cell of the church and placing
a hemispherical vault on top
of it. The enormous internal
space of St Front is composed
of five domes arranged in a
cross shape and replicates
the volumetric and
compositional scheme
of the basilica of St
Mark's in Venice.
However, since it
lacks any figural
support, the
result is a sort
of schematic
projection.

**The mature Romanesque in northern Italy**

Because of ongoing exchanges with France and northern and central Europe, the great architecture made in the northern Italian area composed of Lombardy and the Po Valley between the 11th and 12th centuries is part of the European Romanesque culture. This architecture was developed not only in the major cities of the area – Milan and Pavia – but also along the roads leading south to Rome. Fully vaulted churches came into being here between 1090 and 1120, clearly late compared with other areas of Western Europe; however, the Milanese masters introduced an element – the rib – that was of revolutionary importance both from the aesthetic and the structural points of view. The rib was created to rationalize the structure and to differentiate between its support functions and the functions of the vaulting cells. The characteristic traits of northern Italian Romanesque architecture are the use of the cross vault, the preservation of the gallery, apses with dwarf galleries, and large pediments on façades. Also, in the major churches of the Po Valley the crypt tends to come into an increasingly close spatial relationship with the upper church, coming to occupy almost the entire transept. This arrangement was adopted in the late 11th and 12th centuries at Modena, at S Zeno in Verona, and in Venice and was to also find fortune in southern Italy.

The Pavian churches of S Michele and S Pietro in Ciel d'Oro present the transformation of the façade into the so-called screen façade, a kind of frontal wall that when placed in front of the longitudinal basilican body hides the true profile of the nave. Such screen façades were in use until the 15th century. Apses built with dwarf galleries show up in great numbers in Lombardy, as they do in the Upper Rhine; the first datable example, and also one of the most pleasing, is at S Maria Maggiore at Bergamo, from c. 1137. Square shapes had a strong influence on builders in the Lombard area and show up in the construction of numerous ecclesiastical buildings, among them S Salvatore at Almenno, S Lorenzo at Mantua, the old cathedral of Brescia, and the Santo Sepolcro in the S Stefano complex at Bologna, all from the 11th century.

**St Mark's, Venice, 1063–94**
A unique case in the history of western Europe, St Mark's remained substantially extraneous to developments in Romanesque church architecture and in fact draws instead on a Byzantine model, the basilica of the Apostoleion (Holy Apostles) at Constantinople, rebuilt in the 6th century. Indeed, St Mark's has much in common with 6th-century Byzantine constructions: on a Greek-cross scheme the enormous piers and intermediate colonnades form a grand rhythm that culminates in the stately, perfect shape of the spheri[c] dome. The play of light on the marbles and gold-background mosaics of the interior give the masonry masses and surfaces pictor[ial] values, eliminating all sens[e] of spatial depth.

**S Ambrogio, Milan, begun 1080**

This church represents a magnificent exception within the panorama of northern Italy; S Ambrogio is in fact a hall church with galleries, in keeping with the typology of the 'blind-nave' pilgrimage churches. The modification of its proportions diminishes the effects of vertical momentum and gives it a low and wide conformation, more or less without illumination. The magisterial and highly original sloping façade with its arcaded loggia corresponds perfectly to the internal articulation. The narthex has an axial position similar to that in certain Rhineland constructions, thus repeating the axial character of ancient Roman buildings and the atriums of early Christian architecture.

**Cathedral, Modena, 1099–c. 1110**

The typology, construction methods, arrangement of the internal spaces, and the stylistic elements and decorative details inaugurated at Milan were adopted in the cathedrals of the Emilian area. The cathedral of Modena, made by the Lombard architect Lanfranco, gives an original form to the Romanesque vocabulary. Doing without the vault covering, it imposes a rhythmic vision on spaces and surfaces without structural weaving and without making direct reference to support or constructive functions. On the exterior, the projecting forms of the façade provide a precise reflection of the interior structure, while a continuous strip of arches wraps the front exterior in an agile rhythm that unifies the church's façade, sides, and apse. The gallery, which can be used only where it moves along the apses, represents an interesting phase of development in the dwarf gallery from the Rhine area.

# Central and southern Italy
## c. 1060–1130

### Italian regionalism

The Tuscan Apennines form the borderline between the Po area, site of major developments in Lombard Romanesque architecture, and central-southern Italy, where regional forms flourished during the same period. Several factors distinguish Tuscan Romanesque architecture from that of Lombardy during the same period. These include different ideological premises as well as vocabulary and aesthetic differences. Structural elements were interpreted differently, as were the values given to plastic forms in the use of smooth planes and the harmony of geometric relationships. Tuscany's autonomous architectural creativity evolved from two centres. First was Florence, with its baptistery and S Miniato al Monte; second was the school founded around the cathedral of Pisa, a school that went through extraordinary development both qualitatively and quantitatively over the course of the 12th century. A common feature of both is the use of polychromatic marble dressing, most of all on external surfaces, which, when connected to the use of blind arcades, distinguishes the Romanesque style in Tuscany, as in the Badia of Fiesole, the parish church of Empoli, and S Giovanni Fuorcivitas at Pistoia.

Outside the Tuscan area, the panorama of Romanesque architecture in central Italy offers little in terms of important undertakings or typological or linguistic originality. The rejection of stone vaults, and with them the concept of the architectural work as an organic system, was the distinguishing trait of this architecture until the middle of the 13th century. This rejection constituted an almost insurmountable barrier to the adoption of new ideas, and it was reflected in the persistence of the traditional basilican shape with columns or piers and a roof covering. The city of Rome, in the passive repetition of the early Christian–Constantinian basilican model, was immobilized in a period of conservatism, only slightly influenced by ideas arriving from the Lombard architectural culture, of which the only visual and vital sign was the reworking of bell towers. The fact that this stagnation continued throughout the entire Romanesque period cannot be justified as a reflection of the will to express religious fervour through the replication of the architectural forms of the original church. The only vaguely supportive element is the output of Roman marble workers, which did not waver from its skilful replication of the classical style and thus remained in perfect harmony with the late antique forms of the city's churches.

Another cultural centre that remained faithful to the conservative repetition of the basilican type was the abbey of Monte Cassino, reconstructed by Abbot Desiderius in 1066–71. Its T-shaped ground plan, with the dominant presence of a transept high over the naves, was to be repeated by the builders of the great Campagna churches of Salerno (1077–1175), Amalfi (begun 1060), and Ravello (1086).

The far southern regions of Italy shared the persistence of Byzantine architectural culture, often veined by Arabic influences; 'Latin' ideas were grafted onto this architectural culture by the spread of Benedictine monastic architecture, both of the Cassino type and the Cluniac.

**San Miniato al Monte, Florence, 1028–62**
The Benedictine church of San Miniato is constructed in a way similar to what Lanfranco devised for the Cathedral of Modena: an alternating system of piers and columns supports a transverse arch that supports the trussed roof and accentuates the division in bays. However, the structure of the building makes its statement in the volumetric synthesis of the interior space into a crystalline solid. Thus the chromatics of the inlays give linear definition to the planes, transforming the thick Romanesque walls into continuations of the graphic design. The highly refined dressing in geometric motifs that covers the walls further emphasizes the architectural elements. The selection of colours, the white and grey with the addition of a pale sand colour for the sandstone capitals and the horizontal lines, creates a sacred setting with a triumphal character, to which the small, round-arched windows contribute a quiet light, uniformly diffused.

# Campo dei Miracoli, Pisa

## 1063–1350

In 1063 Pisa defeated the Arabs at Palermo and enjoyed hegemony over the western Mediterranean. The abundant spoils permitted construction of a new cathedral designed first by Buscheto and then by Rainaldo (responsible for the enlargement of the naves and the working of the façade).

This monument's exceptional character is revealed in the fullness of its form, located at the centre of the large space following precise relationships with the other architectural objects in the complex: the baptistery, tower, and cemetery. The external volume is given a sense of harmonious articulation by an uninterrupted band of blind arcades – embellished by marble inlays – that embraces every side of the cathedral, the transepts, and the choir. The play of chromatic effects and the rhythm of the surfaces culminates in the splendid sandstone façade; the upper part represents one of the most successful solutions that Romanesque architecture provided for the problem of giving a harmonic front to the body of a church: the flat wall of the façade disappears, sculpted into four rows of open galleries that give a chromatic and luminous interpretation of the Lombard loggia.

The spatial distribution of the cathedral's interior is unusual in terms of the area where the transept meets the nave. There is no crossing and reciprocal spatial confluence; instead, a clear separation is created by the continuity of the walls of the nave, which isolate the side spaces. Doing so seems to establish a spatial and perspective separation between the great longitudinal basilica and the two smaller transversal bodies; perhaps the original idea was to create a multiple church with varied perspectives. The echo of the great early Christian columnar churches of Rome is tempered by the sense of height, accentuated by the point of the triumphal arch, by the strong relief of the capitals, each topped by a projecting abacus, and by the figural string-course.

Thus motifs drawn from the classical tradition (columns and capitals), those from the early Christian tradition (the basilican layout), and those from the Byzantine East (the pointed arch, the elliptical dome, and the alternation of black and white marble) blend harmoniously and in a singular way with the spatial proportions of the Western Romanesque.

The structure of the baptistery, designed by Deotisalvi in 1153, is inserted in a harmonic relationship with the cathedral in a way that reflects the climate of refined decoration and the learned elaboration of a variety of stylistic stimuli. Designed as a large cylindrical volume set down in front of the church on the same axis of symmetry, related to the cathedral itself and in a direct line to it, the baptistery is externally marked off by a rhythm of blind arches and is richly decorated with motifs drawn from the ancient and Byzantine traditions. The famous bell tower develops the theme used by Rainaldo on the façade of the church in an absolutely original way. Begun in 1173, perhaps by Bonanno, it was completed only near the end of the 13th century because the work had been gradually slowed by the subsidence of the ground.

The builders of the tower adopted the same figurative themes and architectural elements used in the cathedral and the baptistery, associating them in a similar arrangement and achieving the same outstanding result, amplified and made more effective by the multiplication of the visual effects of transparency and perspective and the chiaroscuro variations by the perforations in the cylindrical tower.

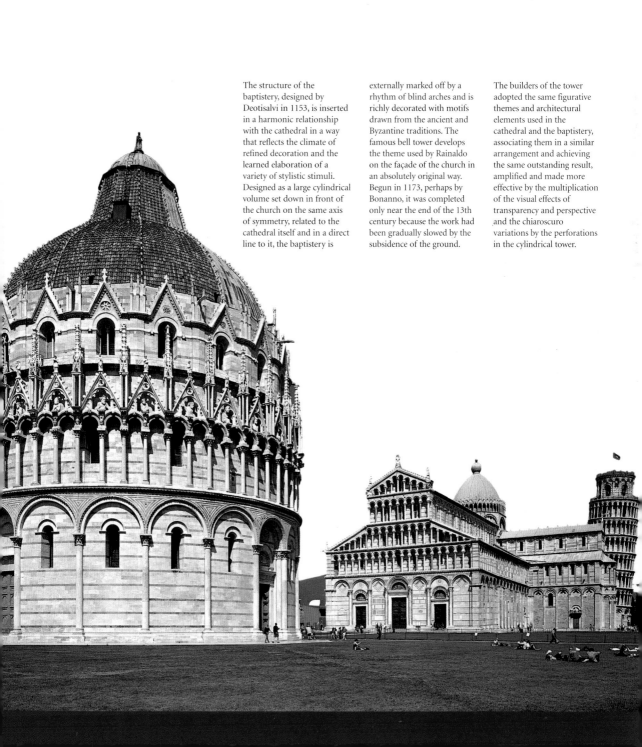

# Arab-Norman Sicily

## *c.* 1130–1200

**Northern conquerors under the Mediterranean sun**

Following two centuries of Arab domination, Sicily was brought back into the world of Western culture when it was conquered by the Normans. On their arrival, the Normans found that the architectural culture of the island reflected the influence of both Byzantine forms and the linguistic and decorative styles of Islam. The conquerors succeeded in carrying off the astonishing feat of assimilating these well-developed formal expressions and then applying them in a figural syncretism expressed in numerous works of great artistic quality. The dominant architectural theme of 12th-century Sicilian architecture is that of giving the greatest importance possible to the crossing, understood as the central nucleus of the church layout. This was done through the use of perspective and chiaroscuro effects, including arcades so wide and high that they give the visual sense of blending with the space above them. Elements more characteristic of the early Romanesque began showing up in this area around the middle of the 12th century: the rich, sometimes exaggerated articulations of exteriors, and in particular of apses; the tendency toward a centralized spatial configuration; the use of a Byzantine-style star vault; the taste for decoration with stone inlays; and 'stalactite vaults' with mannerist effects. The extraordinary variety and varying provenances of these decorative elements – Byzantine,

Islamic, Catalan-Provençal – reveal the eclectic traits of a profoundly courtly art.

Just as important were certain secular structures, which in terms of number and typological variety find no equal in mainland Italy: the palace, the suburban villa, the pavilion, and the cloister, such as the Torre Pisana in the Palazzo dei Normanni in Palermo, and the summer residence, such as the Ziza and Cuba palaces, which present cubic architectural forms in an axial and symmetrical arrangement of undoubted Islamic derivation.

**Cathedral, Monreale, 1174–89**
Begun under the Norman king William II, the cathedral of Monreale is an impressive complex designed as a grand symbol of absolute power and of the magnificence of the Norman monarchy. It blends heterogeneous elements in a work of great fascination and balance. This masterpiece of Norman syncretism has its fitting complement in the attached cloister.

**S Giovanni degli Eremiti, Palermo, begun 1142**
The earliest such monument to so clearly display its Arab heritage, the church of S Giovanni degli Eremiti bears the traits of Arabic art in its details while also revealing Byzantine influence. It is covered with five hemispherical domes that sit atop a closed and compact cube with flat articulations composed of interweaving pointed arches

### Palatine Chapel, Palermo, 1132–43

The Palatine Chapel resolves the compositional problem of the application of a dome to a longitudinal body, combining the model of the nave-with-two-aisles columnar basilica with a presbytery crowned by a dome with an octagonal drum. Its Arabic heritage is visible in the treatment of the walls, in the arches, and in the pendentives. Also of Islamic heritage is the wooden ceiling with stalactite and honeycomb carvings, a style that began in North African mosques and that was to find greater decorative application in the later covering of the Alhambra in Granada.

### Cathedral, Monreale, 1174–89

The Arabic contribution appears clear in the sharp insertion of the architectural volumes and in the colouristic fantasies that enliven the apsidal area, with an unbroken fabric of interwoven arches and cornices.

# German-language areas
## c. 1070–1170

**Between the traditional and the new**

Beginning around 1070 the Holy Roman Empire went through a period of political instability that had a profound impact on the history of German architecture. The Ottonian tradition remained solidly anchored to its historical and cultural roots, enlarging the gap between the ideological and socio-political conception of the courtly and stately imperial basilicas and the new image of the Romanesque church. In fact, the German-speaking lands were the last to accept the architectural methods of the mature Romanesque along with its principles, styles, and language. The passage to the Romanesque basilica still meant in large part the abandonment of the timber roof covering and its replacement by the vault. The first German abbeys and cathedrals built with stone vaults or transformed to receive them date to post 1080, but until the first half of the 12th century and even later the cultural trends tied to traditional methods had a strong influence on building activity, leading to the large-scale production of buildings still composed of the basilican layout with a roof supported by columns.

At the same time the group of great Rhine cathedrals – Speyer, Mainz, the abbey church of Maria Laach, and later the cathedral of Worms – held firm to the German layout with facing choirs and side entrances. Doing so meant they were prevented from taking advantage of the greater visual impact of a church interior when its entrance looks along an axis, and instead they had to accept only a partial vision, gradual and fragmentary.

Even so, while the builders that remained faithful to the conservative styles continued to apply Ottonian forms in the creation of church interiors, they experimented with new formal styles in the arrangement of the volumes and the exterior fronts. The building conceived as a plastic mass of stone was transformed into the contrast of two large bodies, square and overlapping, thus accentuating the values of geometric purity and structural essentiality. In that way, although 12th-century German architecture still refused to accept the concept of the church as a structural organism covered by vaults, it arrived at the formal experimentation of the Romanesque along another route, that of the aspiration to give the exterior appearance of ecclesiastical structures an importance and quality comparable to the treatment of the interiors.

**Sankt Godehard, Hildesheim, 1133–72**
Over the course of half a century, this church developed the elements characteristic of Ottonian architecture. In fact, the church presents a typology based on a collection of traditional elements – and a French-style ambulatory choir with chapels.

**Abbey church, Maria Laach near Coblenz, begun 1093**
The beauty of this church's exterior is augmented by two groups of towers that rise to the east and west, emphasizing the building's double-ended shape. However, the decoration of the façade in thin calligraphic outlining provokes an almost double-vision between the architectural volumes and their ornamentation.

**Cathedral, Mainz, 1110–37**
The cathedral of Mainz was rebuilt (two earlier versions had burned down) during the stylistic phase of the German Romanesque, characterized by a particular focus on the composition of exterior fronts. The shape of the impressive east end of the cathedral shows great qualities of plastic values highlighted by the red colour of the stone; the contrast between the bare and powerful walls, framed by two Ottonian-type cylindrical towers, and the pierced wall of the central apse creates a stately and solemn presence.

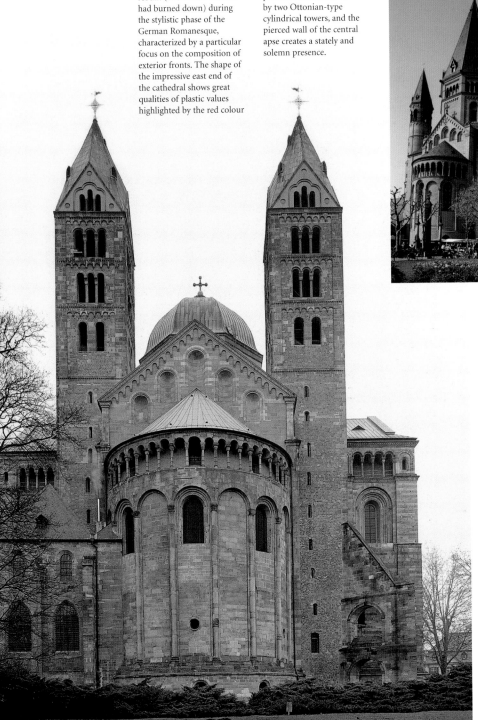

**Cathedral, Speyer, 1082–1106**
The transformation of the cathedral of Speyer marks the moment in which the empire's culture fully complied with the structural and figurative concepts of the Western Romanesque; the cathedral also displays the tendency of the German Romanesque to assign great importance to exterior fronts. While accentuating certain aspects typical of Carolingian and Ottonian architecture, such as the use of large volumes made to contrast with one another, it also adds elements of a Lombard flavour, such as the pilasters, arches, hanging arches, galleries, and loggias. Its varied and dynamic architectural complex rises atop a simple, compact layout; the block composed of the transept and the choir with towers finds its opposite number in the western body.

55

# Between Romanesque and Gothic

## 1170–1250

**Central-southern France**

In some areas of France the final expressions of Romanesque art took place in parallel with the affirmation of Gothic architecture. Among these areas was Burgundy, which continued to apply the architectural system that led back to the Paray-le-Monial–Cluny III churches; however, the use around 1200 of ribbed groin vaults over the nave in place of barrel vaults permitted the creation of spaces with greater width, leaving behind the narrow verticality of preceding structures. A second group of buildings, quite widespread in southwestern Europe, made reference to the typology adopted in the Cistercian abbey of Fontenay, enlarging the single nave with its barrel vault by way of rows of chapels. There was yet a third group, which includes the Cistercian abbey church of Pontigny and St Philibert at Dijon. It uses the longitudinal body of Vézelay as its model, and reworks that scheme to simplify it.

By around 1200, however, the Romanesque seems to have lost its drive even in Burgundy, and Burgundian builders began to adopt the forms of the early Gothic from nearby Champagne. The new choir of Vézelay, the church of Notre-Dame at Dijon, and the cathedrals of Auxerre, Chalons-sur-Saône, Geneva, and Lausanne present a new system that appears typically 'Burgundian' and is easily recognizable because of certain motifs, including the great open atrium, borrowed from Autun and Vézelay. The interiors are primarily distinguished by the lightness of the structures; by the use of a double shell composed of two thin walls at different heights, with windows opened in the outer one; and by internal passages in front of the aisle windows of the central nave.

With these buildings from the first half of the 13th century, Burgundian architecture made itself an important link between the areas of the early Romanesque and the Gothic of the Royal Domain.

**Notre-Dame, Dijon, portico, 1220–40**
The church of Notre-Dame, a masterpiece that makes use of all the Burgundian elements, has a wide, deep portico with three entry arches topped by two tiers of arches that recall similar Tuscan motifs from Pisa to Lucca.

**Abbey church, Fécamp, after 1168**
Late Norman churches did not abandon the 'thick-wall' building technique, with the consequent heaviness of the entire structural system. The abbey church of Fécamp, despite the presence of acute arches and angular projections, preserved the traditional robustness of the Romanesque framing and became a model of later constructions in the region.

*Opposite*
**Church of the Madeleine, Vézelay, choir, 1185**
The choir at Vézelay represents one of the first 'incursions' in Burgundy of the Gothic architecture of the Ile-de-France. Luminous and light, it announces its 'modernity' in the sharp linearism obtained through the use of narrow columns that support the ribbing of the vaults and surround the piers of the ambulatory. Equally innovative is the removal of the upper parts of the dividing walls among the radiating chapels, which permits the free passage of light.

# The late Romanesque in Germany

## c. 1150–1230

### The Rhineland

The history of the German Romanesque reflects the evolution of a long cultural process and involves certain traits and methods particular to the German world, including complex autonomous artistic activities and trends. This architecture came into being when French Gothic was in its early phases, but despite the ease of cultural exchanges between the two countries, what was happening in France did not have a determinant influence on ecclesiastical buildings in Germany, which long maintained the forms and types of the Romanesque-Ottonian tradition. The vigorous flourishing of the late Romanesque in the Rhineland coincided with the period of the Swabian dynasty, and the architecture expressed the same realistic vision, the same attachment to worldly things and earthly life. These same feelings are vividly presented in chivalric poetry, in the lyrics of the minnesingers, and in the personality of Frederick Barbarossa. The architecture of the Upper Rhine developed in the shadow of the great imperial cathedrals; the cathedrals of Worms and Mainz were given their definitive appearance, while that of Speyer underwent changes, including the insertion of the late-Romanesque domes on its towers. The great works of the end of the 12th century and first half of the 13th remained faithful to the use of vertical supports, which gave them a powerful rhythm particularly suitable to their monumental forms. The Upper Rhine did not share the freedom of ornamentation found in the Lower Rhine, nor was there the wealth of articulation obtained through the division of the nave into three or four levels and the decomposition of the apsidal wall by way of an internal gallery. Instead, the upper area showed a decided tendency to monumentality and formal rigour, accentuated by the use of the local sandstone, of a stupendous red tonality. The architecture of the exteriors repeated the German imperial tradition of the building conceived as a massive block of masonry – a grouping of contrasting square shapes – dominating the surrounding area.

By the 1230s, German Romanesque culture was showing signs of exhaustion; so it was that Gothic forms were introduced and applied to traditional typologies, but without adopting the entire mechanical-support system behind Gothic architecture.

**Gross St Martin, Cologne, 1150–72, 1185–1200**
The influence of St Maria im Kapitol led to various buildings that tend to give the crossing a central position. Gross St Martin has a three-apsed eastern body surmounted by a gigantic tower that becomes the body of the church.

**Holy Apostles, Cologne, 1190–1219**
The tendency to make the crossing the site of a vertical installation of volumes associated with a central-plan layout is here tempered by a layout hinged on the vertical axis of the lantern and balanced by an Ottonian-type western mass.

**athedral, Worms,
1000–1200**

he last of the great Rhine
thedrals to be built, Worms
resents the scheme
eviously adopted at Speyer
d maintains the typology
the two facing choirs. The
arked concentration of
astic effects is revealed in
e western body, with the
erlapping of two octagonal
odies set at different depths
d framed by two bell
wers, all of it animated by
eat dynamism.

**Cistercian church,
Heisterbach, 1202–37**
Because of the richness of
its decoration, this church
represents one of the heights
of late Romanesque
Rhineland art. The surviving
ambulatory choir shows
Burgundian schemes adapted
to local models. The vaults
are divided by ribbed folds,
an element that anticipates
the Gothic star vault and
palm vault, as in those of
Early English Gothic.

# The late Romanesque in Italy
## Mid-12th–13th century

**Conservatism and heterogeneity**

Not all areas of Europe enjoyed the kind of architectural dynamism found in the Rhineland and Burgundy, and late Romanesque architecture was primarily conservative. In Italy, most of all in the central and southern regions, this conservatism showed up primarily in the flat roofs given to basilicas, a custom that held on throughout the 13th century. Vaulted churches were more or less unknown in those regions, the few that did come into existence being the work of Cistercian builders and thus completely extraneous to any local tradition. The majority of the basilicas with flat coverings faithfully carried on the traditional style of the mature Romanesque, so they can be dated only on the basis of the decorative details that enriched the later phase of the Romanesque, from the moulding of cornices and ribs to the refinement of cubic capitals. However, in the late 12th century the vault covering, usually set on a system of vertical supports, spread across northern Italy, and during the 13th century forms borrowed from France appeared, such as round arches and sexpartite vaults, although these were applied without ever achieving the dynamism and articulation that their use generated to the north of the Alps. Furthermore, the simple arrangement of the eastern bodies of churches still predominated in Italy, although transepts and isolated crossings had begun showing up more and more often. The heterogeneous nature of this phenomenon is an expression of Italy's highly stratified society and greatly varied patronage. Rome was still the reference point for those seeking to revive the ancient past, and such movements often hoped for the ideological and political vindication of the city's patrimony. At the same time, the position of extreme conservatism of papal patronage crystallized the local architecture in the tired repetition of late antique models.

Alongside all these conservative buildings, there were also some original works, most of them located in northern Italy, which had assumed a role in the forefront of the late Romanesque art of Europe. There are the singular hall churches of Piedmont, such as S Bernardo and S Marco at Vercelli, and also the cathedral of Molfetta in Puglia, where the typology of the hall church is blended with that of the domed church, resulting in a structure that is unique to medieval architecture.

**thedral, Piacenza, 22–50**

longitudinal body and ir covered by sexpartite lts make the cathedral of cenza a completely new sibility on the Italian horama. The height of the asters and the arches gives impression of an interior ce structured like a hall. e the cathedral of Pisa, the atral nave extends without erruption to beneath the ssing tower; the arches ated at that bay rise higher in the others and open on all transept that has a ver ceiling than that of nave. The planimetric iations and differences in ght increase the play of ces, and the combination ween the basilican layout the longitudinal body and t of the hall of the nsept give the church a ly original character.

**Cathedral, Casale Monferrato, consecrated 1107**

The portico of Casale Monferrato is configured like a high, spacious interior, covered by a single vault and surrounded on three sides by smaller areas. The scheme of the vault is singular and quite innovative in terms of the panorama of the late Romanesque in Lombardy: flat parallel ribs intersect at right angles forming giant round arches supporting thin walls joined by vaults. The creation of a space so high and extended, surrounded by smaller spaces, reveals great originality. The old idea of the westwork is here revived in a completely original version that recalls the *Westchorhallen* of the Lower Rhine region and the Meuse.

**Baptistery, Parma, begun 1196**

The baptistery presents a soaring octagonal body articulated externally in six floors of galleries, some of them open through the use of a double wall. Famous for the sculptures by Benedetto Antelami, it can be considered one of the outstanding creations of the late Romanesque. The architecture of the Po area was enriched with new modulations in the original reworking of the motif of loggias and reached evocative, diaphanous effects thanks to the constructive technique using contrasting tonalities and double walls. The monumentality of the layout and the presence of an architrave motif within the blind arcades at the base and repeated in the four orders of the loggias shows an unequivocal vein of classicism.

# The late Romanesque in Spain

## *c.* 1150–1300

### The cimborios

Between the second half of the 12th century and the early 13th the Arabs were driven farther and farther south, and cities like Tarragona, Saragossa, Coimbra, and even Toledo and Seville were reconquered by Spain's Christian kingdoms and once again returned to form part of the history of Western architecture. The numerous ecclesiastical buildings undertaken from then on, even if geographically relevant, broke free from traditional Catalan architecture to work out completely new and original forms: the cathedral of Tarragona (after 1171), the old one of Salamanca, Zamora, and Toro are all basilicas with cruciform layouts with ribbed cross vaults, massive and heavy in form with pillars with ponderous basements and large ogival arcades that create a spatial connection between the naves and aisles similar to that of *Hallenkirche*. The walls are smooth, without articulation, interrupted only by ogival windows; the transverse arches, the ribbing, and the keystones are massive, while splendid figural capitals enliven the interiors. A characteristic of this style is the round, domed towers called *cimborios*, which rise over the crossing in a triumphant and fanciful profusion of plastic forms.

Beside the basilicas with ribbed cross vaults, a second group of constructions – including Vilabertrán, Besalú, and several Cistercian churches, such as Poblet – are instead firmly rooted in the earlier tradition, meaning the old Catalan model of the barrel-vaulted hall church. In these, the new stylistic taste was expressed only in formal details, while the spatial layout remained more or less unchanged, whether the hall was covered by a vault on high bundled pillars, as at La Coruña, or had a gallery, as in the cathedral of Coimbra. Similar considerations apply to the basilican-type churches covered with barrel vaults, often with windows on only one side, the most important of which is the cathedral of S Maria in Seo de Urgel. There were plenty of constructions that differed from the usual typologies, such as at Torres del Rio, where the simple octagonal central-plan layout is varied by a star vault with flat ribs of Islamic derivation.

Among all these many different expressions, one must not forget the especially important choir of the cathedral of Avila, which in certain senses seems to anticipate that of Vézelay and is externally shaped like a single circular block, not unlike the wall of a medieval city, which surrounds the ambulatory and the radiating chapels. Probably motivated by defensive reasons, this solution is also an expression of the desire for closed forms that is typical of the Spanish late Romanesque.

**Cathedral, Zamora,
*c.* 1151–74**
Around the middle of the 12th century, in the southern part of the kingdom of León, a region only recently won back from the Moors, the cathedrals of Zamora and Salamanca were built, along with the collegiate church of Toro. All three present a series of concordances, the most outstanding of which is the presence of the extraordinary towers called *cimborios*. An isolated case in the Spanish Romanesque, these towers, with their surprising architecture, are considered a regional particularity. The *cimborio* of the cathedral of Zamora has a highly complex exterior articulation, with four cylindrical towers located along the diagonal axes of the drum and flat bodies projecting along the transverse axes. The presence of miniature arcades, small domes, and cornices gives the exterior of the tower the appearance of a microarchitecture brought to large scale. These elaborate structures should not be taken as mere decoration, however, for they also serve a structural function: the angular tower located exactly above the pendentives, not only contribute to providing lateral support for the tower but neutralize the diagonal thrust of the dome.

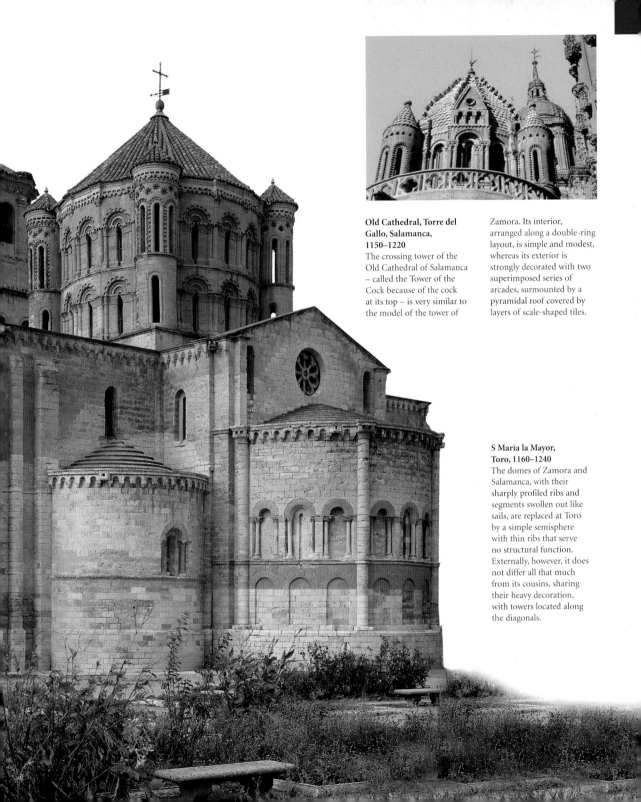

**Old Cathedral, Torre del Gallo, Salamanca, 1150–1220**
The crossing tower of the Old Cathedral of Salamanca – called the Tower of the Cock because of the cock at its top – is very similar to the model of the tower of Zamora. Its interior, arranged along a double-ring layout, is simple and modest, whereas its exterior is strongly decorated with two superimposed series of arcades, surmounted by a pyramidal roof covered by layers of scale-shaped tiles.

**S María la Mayor, Toro, 1160–1240**
The domes of Zamora and Salamanca, with their sharply profiled ribs and segments swollen out like sails, are replaced at Toro by a simple semisphere with thin ribs that serve no structural function. Externally, however, it does not differ all that much from its cousins, sharing their heavy decoration, with towers located along the diagonals.

### The timber church

The conversion of Norway to Christianity began around the end of the 10th century and ended shortly after the year 1000 with the unified kingdom established by Olaf II. As a result of these late dates, Norway has only a few surviving church buildings from the Romanesque period: the cathedral of Stavanger, the cathedral of Trondhiem, and the ruins of the cathedral of Bergen. Even so, Norway made a significant contribution to Scandinavian art during the Romanesque period thanks to the *stavkirke* ('stave church'), a type of wooden church that exists only in northern Europe. Several hundred of these were built between the 11th and 12th centuries, and they once spread across the entire Scandinavian territory, but only twenty-five have been preserved. Stave churches are a typology of church in which the combination of the masses and the architectural bodies is completely original to Scandinavia, while the construction of the naves, the arcades resting on cylindrical pillars, the wooden vaults, the articulation of the planes, and the elevation of various kinds of towers – clearly adapted to wooden constructions – are borrowed from the churches of southwestern Europe. The walls are made of wooden planks positioned upright between corner posts that reach up to the trusses of the ceiling. A series of rounded arches surrounds the exterior of the building, while the roofs are located at differing levels, one over the next. The most important examples are the *stavkirker* of Urnes (*c.* 1060, 1130–50), Lom (from the 11th century and modified around 1630), and Borgund (*c.* 1150). Comparison of Urnes with Borgund reveals the passage from a simple style to a more articulated version with heavier decoration and greater refinement in the proportions. The exterior of Borgund is richly decorated with inlays; the portals and cornices bear wooden sculpture – animals, vines, dragon heads, runic inscriptions – typical of the Romanesque figural repertory.

**...ddal, 1242**
...e *stavkirke* of Heddal,
...ilt in 1242, is the largest of
...e surviving Norwegian
...ve churches. With its three
...ll towers and sixty-four-
...rt articulated roof on
...eral levels, it is considered
...rue 'wooden cathedral'.

*...pposite*
**...rnes, c. 1060**
...rnes, the oldest Norwegian
...*vkirke*, is an elegantly
...mple building with a
...ofile composed of four
...scending levels. It is
...thout external decoration
...cept for the crowning that
...ns along the roof ridges.

**Borgund, c. 1150**
The *stavkirke* of Borgund
is the only one that has
remained unchanged since
the Middle Ages. Dedicated
to the apostle Andrew, whose
X-shaped cross appears in
the balustrade, it has a very
simple interior, without
decorations and illuminated
only by the few small
openings in the upper part
of the walls. Twelve wooden
columns support the central
part of the nave and the roof.
The interior structure of the
roof is composed of a system
of narrow beams and rafters
so thin they are hardly visible
in the half-light, making the
church even more graceful.

### The Holy Sepulchre as model

Nearly all the central-plan buildings of Romanesque architecture belong to the style's mature or late phase. They are based on the model of the Palatine Chapel at Aachen. Even so, some westworks present in a certain sense an architectural concept similar to the central-plan constructions (double-choir structures, in fact, sensibly modify the longitudinal body of the basilica, for which reason they have been called 'centralizing'), much like the three-conch plan of the churches of Cologne that blend choir and transept in a unitary composition. Central-plan structures are often designed to serve precise functions. Good examples are the baptistery, which particularly in Italy can assume truly monumental dimensions (Florence, Cremona, Parma, Pisa), and the church of the Holy Sepulchre, which usually follows the archetypical model of Jerusalem (Segovia, Oxford, or Neuvy-Saint-Sépulcre). Certain architectural types are often associated with precise regions. The simple circular chapel with apse is particularly widespread in central-eastern Europe, with its true centre in Bohemia; the circular chapel with four supports, sometimes articulated in two floors, or quadrangular structures with apses or towers, are found in Jutland, the Baltic islands, and Denmark, as at Kalundborg; in Provence and Italy one encounters the simple octagonal structure without secondary spaces based on the tradition of late antiquity; circular forms with ambulatory are relatively rare and are limited almost exclusively to northern Italy (S Salvatore at Almenno, Bologna, Mantua, Asti), although there are some important examples in northern Europe, including the Palatine Chapel of Kobern in the Rhineland. The Greek cross is adopted most of all in chapels dedicated to the Holy Cross, such as at Trier or Montmajour, although there are important examples at St Mark's in Venice and St Front at Périgueux. Finally, there is the cloverleaf layout that was adopted in Swabian architecture around 1150, which prefers harmonious forms and classical-type proportions (the chapel of Schwarzrheindorf and the chapel of All Saints at Regensburg), and the square layout with four supports used most of all in castle chapels and at Germigny-des-Prés.

**Baptistery of S Giovanni, Florence, c. 1070–1230**
Florence's octagonal baptistery makes clear reference to classical Roman architecture in a sort of 'Florentine proto-Renaissance' that integrate with the green-and-white-marble intarsia with its pu elementary geometric form Critics attribute the occasional discontinuities between the architectural and decorative forms to the long duration of the work.

**Church of the Templars, Tomar, end 12th century**
This highly original church with its ambulatory that surrounds the innermost chapel and ribs connecting the central body to the outer wall, is shaped like a copy of the Holy Sepulchre in Jerusalem and is notable for the contrast between the fortified structure of the exterior and the elegance of the interior. Since the Knights Templar were defenders of the Holy Land and pilgrims, this church represents the obvious attempt to transfer the symbolic building to Iberia soil, where the Christian reconquest took place unde the sign of the apostle Jame

*Opposite*
**Santo Sepulcro, Torres del Rio, end 12th–early 13th century**
Located along the pilgrimage route leading from Navarre to Santiago, the Holy Sepulchre of Torres del Rio has a simple octagonal layout without a central chapel. The dome, which culminates in a lantern on the exterior, is shaped like a star vault with flat interwoven ribs clearly derived from Islamic prototypes; it is illuminated by light that enters the narrow slits located at the base of the ribs. Torres del Rio makes clear the syncretic and international character of much 12th-century Spanish architecture. The central-pl layout is dedicated to the Holy Sepulchre and thus relates to the idea of crusad against Islam, the exterior o the church presents forms typical of pilgrimage churches, but all of this is surmounted by a dome modelled on the mihrab of the mosque of Cordova.

## The glory of a military aristocracy

The church was the primary symbolic structure on the artistic landscape of the Middle Ages, a period in which more or less the same social structure could be found from the Baltic all the way to Sicily.

There was, however, another face to that period, the one composed of castles and fortified places in general. Castles were originally constructed to defend borders and communication routes, but they later became the central hubs for vast territories; as administrative headquarters, the castle was the means by which the military aristocracy controlled its holdings. But castles were also fortified residences for the feudal nobility, whether rural or urban. The fragmentary nature of feudal power in the medieval period explains the extraordinary number of castles, and they remained active as long as the economic and social realities demanded.

Just as ecclesiastical architecture adopted completely innovative forms at the beginning of the second millennium, secular architecture, too, took off along new routes during that period. Over the centuries, beginning with the late medieval stronghold, the castle underwent changes due to developments in defensive and offensive techniques as well as increasing demands for greater comfort. In the first Romanesque phase, the turreted fortress was built in wood and surrounded by a bastion and moat; the stone tower became the model for later castles, which aside from the purely defensive structures, such as the fortified tower, watch tower, and circle of walls, did not lack an area set aside for living quarters, the sign of a marked social change. The French donjon and Anglo-Norman keep did more than merely satisfy security needs, for they also became recognized symbols of power. At the centre of the castle stands the isolated, powerful keep, its form somewhat simple: Swabian architecture showed a preference for pentagonal towers with glacis on the sides exposed to assaults, as in the castle of Altenwied in the Rhineland. In northwestern France, most of all in Norman territory, there was a greater wealth of forms, such as the octagonal fortress with side towers of Houdan from the first quarter of the 11th century. The adoption of the circular or octagonal shape represents a step ahead in defensive measures. Efforts were made to eliminate all dead ground while at the same time limiting the surfaces attackers could aim at. With the exception of certain fortified tower-homes of northwestern France and England, no European castle has survived in its original Romanesque form.

**Pont Valentré, Cahors, 1306–55**
By the 11th century, the bridges built by the Romans were no longer adequate to support the increased circulation of people and goods in the countryside and around cities and were often in a poor state of repair. Work began to replace them with new stone bridges, and by the middle of the 12th century these had become more architecturally daring.

**White Tower, London, begun 1078**
The powerful White Tower, built on the banks of the Thames to defend the city of London, is both fortress and royal palace, prison and government seat, centre of the English monarchy and symbol of the power of William the Conqueror, making it an example of the multiplicity of forms and functions of a keep.

**Vor Frue Kirke, Kalundborg, 1170–90**
A singular structure on the panorama of fortified buildings is the church-fortress of Kalundborg in Zealand, Denmark. Built of red brick with a central Greek-cross plan, it is composed of a central tower and four corner towers and was built to symbolize the recent conversion of the country to Christianity. Atop every polygonal apse rises a powerful polygonal tower; the important centre of the structure is highlighted by a taller quadrangular tower.

# The fortified city
## 12th–13th century

### The city-fortresses of Europe

Quite often, the Romanesque European city was built on the ruins of a Roman city that had been reduced to the state of bare subsistence by time and barbarian invasions. From the urbanistic point of view, these cities were laid out following completely different criteria, a tangible sign of a profoundly changed reality that was often composed of raids and sieges, making it necessary to devote great attention to a city's defences, meaning its walls. In many cases, increases in population required new walls, resulting in concentric rings around the historic centre. Most Romanesque cities were shaped like a closed circle, with an irregular street network; they were protected by walls, and the number of gates opened in the walls was limited, with each one protected by towers and gates. The castle, as a building within the city, stood, when possible, on a corner of the urban perimeter in an elevated position, often surrounded by a supplementary ring of walls as well as a moat.

The first cities laid out according to a plan were built in France during the reigns of Louis VII and Louis IX; between the 11th and the 12th centuries, the Midi was the scene of the proliferation of the so-called fortified manors, new fortified towns created to establish royal presence and to defend the territory. Topographical conditions and political necessities were of primary importance in determining the urban structure of these fortified centres. The fortress city atop a hill could dominate the surrounding territory, as is the case with Carcassonne in the Languedoc and the castle of Caernarfon in Wales; some were located to benefit from the protection of water, such as a river or swamp, as at Aigues-Mortes in Camargue, the town from which the French army set off on the Crusades, which has an irregular rectangular layout and towered walls, gates, and a rectangular network of streets.

**nteriggioni, 13th century**
lt by the Sienese to block
expansion of Florence,
fortified town of
nteriggioni reflects the
roughly Italian situation

in which cities, proud of
their civic autonomy,
undertook building activities
in the surrounding territory
as a means to protect
themselves against the

territorial expansion of
nearby rival cities. The
foundation of new
settlements no longer
followed only military
objectives but also involved

the population and
organization of dependent
areas. The result of this
attempt by cities to control
the surrounding countryside
was the proliferation of small

centres – castles, fortified
towns, 'new holdings' – that
had no chance of expanding,
so that central and northern
Italy is today densely covered
by small towns.

*posite*

**cassonne, 12th–13th century**
e fortress city of the
counts of Carcassonne
ame a Cathar stronghold
der Simon de Monfort and
sed to the French crown in
6. It is defended by two
s of concentric walls with
kways, crenellations, and
brasures. The defensive
ect is completed by
merous towers that serve
erent uses. Used as a rock
rry early in the 19th century,
rcassonne was completely
ored by Viollet-le-Duc in
2–79 and represents today
most complete example of
edieval fortified city.

**Avila, 12th century**
The only city to preserve its
Romanesque walls intact,
Avila was given its powerful
defensive works because of
its geographic location, on
the border of a territory that
was continuously attacked
by Arabs. The city is
surrounded by walls built
on an irregular rectangular
layout with eighty-eight
defensive towers, making it
one of the major works of
Castilian fortification of the
12th century.

# Gothic architecture
## 1144–14th century

### Forms and types

Around the middle of the 12th century, a new artistic sensibility with new architectural principles began spreading from the cathedrals of northern France. The Romanesque church gave way to an organism that replaced the construction system based on thick load-bearing walls in favour of a structure – called a skeletal system – that freed itself of all superfluous parts by identifying the forces acting on the interior – the thrusts of the vaults and the weight of the roof and walls – so as to direct them along predetermined routes. This transformation took place over the course of little less than a century and began in the Ile-de-France, where the desire to build very high naves resulted in close attention to the technical and formal aspects of construction. This preference for high naves, inherited from certain architectural currents of the Romanesque – from Cluny to the great Ottonian cathedrals – became the central compositional element of churches, leading to a new way of perceiving space and articulating it following a geometric division marked off by the vertical forms of pillars running to full height and pointed arches. As part of the 'skeletal web', the ribs of the vaults form an arched framework that concentrates the thrust from above and transfers it to points that are externally reinforced by rampant arches, which are in turn counterbalanced by flying buttresses that transfer the thrust of the weight to the ground. From the formal point of view, the upward soaring of the interior structure, the bay used as a module to create the internal space, the articulation of the walls, and the great expanses of windows result in the dissolution of the walls, replaced by a 'diaphanous system'. The autonomy of the parts is reduced in favour of greater spatial fusion, and the multiplicity of visual lines results in evocative effects of expansion. This agile and elastic structure frees the walls from their load-bearing function, making possible the broad expanses of windows with polychrome glass that bring rays of coloured light into the church interior, filling that space with its mutable shadings.

This light, so different from the half-light of Romanesque churches, became the fundamental element in the figurative theory of Gothic architecture, which uses light physically and metaphorically to reveal the logical and constructive procedures – arranged in accordance with the scholastic thinking of the period – that support the construction of the cathedral. In the view of medieval theology, the Gothic cathedral was an expression of cosmic order and a symbolic image of the immaterial substance of God reflected in the harmony of the building's proportions and its luminosity. The spires, pinnacles, and towers of the façade – arranged according to the principles of the golden section – accentuate the prevalence of the vertical, symbolic of the tension toward the divine; the door of the sky is illuminated, and it illuminates the interior thanks to the insertion of a great rose window, a true mystical membrane between the light of God and the heart of the faithful.

The Gothic cathedral is also an expression of the new urban civilization that created it. These upwardly soaring, enormous, breathtaking churches were seen as reflections of the ideal image the period had of itself. Such was the fundamental incentive behind these buildings, and it led to ever more ambitious constructions.

The imprint that Gothic left on the later figurative and architectural culture of Europe was the cause of heated critical debate, and beginning with Italian humanism in the 15th century many thinkers took a negative view of the apparently anticlassical aspects of the Gothic. The *maniera dei Goti* ('style of the Goths') was looked down upon as arbitrary and barbaric, but by the baroque great architects – most of all Borromini and Guarini – were making out the technical qualities and the formal originality of Gothic structures, and the romantics of the 19th century embraced the Gothic wholeheartedly, looking at it with renewed fondness and re-evaluating its broad expressive horizon, thanks to figures like Ruskin and Viollet-le-Duc.

**Cathedral, Amiens, begun 1220**
The structure of the Gothic nave according to Viollet-le-Duc.

## Notebook of Villard de Honnecourt, 1220–40

*The notebook of Villard de Honnecourt contains about 250 drawings that represent the principal theoretical and practical aspects of the professional training of a medieval architect, from carpentry work to the functioning of worksite machines, from sculptural models to those for the hewing of ashlars to geometric and proportional problems worked out with the square and compass. Through the use of a design technique based primarily on the application of the geometric and proportional schemes worked out* ad triangulum *and* ad quadratum, *Villard reveals in his designs the rational spirit he saw governing creation, a spirit the artist was called upon to imitate.*

**...thedral, Laon,
...ade, 1190–1205**

...on has a 'harmonic façade,'
... surface of which is
...ided into three different
...els. The area of the entry
...rtals is moved forward by
...ans of a deep portico,
...s pushing back the level
...the towers and giving the
...ade a sense of
...onomous spatiality
...entuated by the colossal
...nensions of the openings
...d the enormous central
...e window, the fulcrum of
... composition. The
...aroscural and volumetric
...iculation of the façade is
...riched with details and
...plodes in the extraordinary
...ventiveness of the towers.

**...ht
...thedral, Soissons,
...uthern transept, 1180**
...e particularly interesting
...thern transept of the
...hedral of Soissons, with its
...vation divided into four
...els, is considered one of the
...st examples of the mature
...thic. There is still a very
...ong sense of horizontality, a
...ult of the regular divisions
...the triforium and the
...rnices that interrupt the

bodies of the columns rising
toward the vault. The use of
the double-wall system
amplifies the sense of opening
up the walls, creating an airy
and luminous grid.
The visual meeting between the
traditional four-level elevation
of the transept with the three
levels of the choir was
borrowed from contemporary
experiments at Chartres, a fact
that emphasizes the radical
nature of Chartres.

**The origins of Gothic**

The architecture of France's Royal Domain was the source of the building methods of the mature Gothic, for the builders there sought to increasingly accentuate the articulation of their structures while at the same time seeking greater evanescence of forms, with effects of transparency and luminous space. Fifty years of experimentation produced results that were anything but homogeneous, from the cathedrals of the Paris region, which either had no transept or had transepts that projected only slightly, to the Picardy cathedrals of Noyon and Soissons, with complex layouts and large transverse bodies. The common denominator of these structures is the urge to achieve the greatest possible height, which in the more important examples translates into an elevation with four levels, justifying the presence of a triforium with the need to counterbalance the thrust of sexpartite vaults; the continuity between the nave, transept, and choir resulted in interiors of great elegance and astonishing effects of harmonization. The fusion of the double-wall system borrowed from Anglo-Norman architecture with the linear grid led to stratified structures of incredible lightness and transparency. The builders at Laon and Paris experimented with other technical and formal novelties; at Notre-Dame the vaults of the nave are supported by flying buttresses visible above the roofs, while Laon reinterpreted the Anglo-Norman technique of the *mur épais* by progressively stripping away the exterior wall, creating a 'telescopic' effect. These experiments were the precursors of the ponderous plasticism of the buttresses and rampant arches of the cathedral of Chartres.

**Wall rhythm of the Gothi[c] cathedral:** Comparison in[?] of the elevations of the ma[in] naves of Noyon, Laon, Par[is] Chartres, Reims, and Ami[ens]

**Cathedral, Noyon, nave, begun mid-12th century**
The linearity of the primit[ive] French Gothic reached its culmination at Noyon. Al[so?] maintaining sexpartite rib[bed] vaults on alternating supp[orts] the sense of double walls i[n?] bays and the feeling of ver[?] are visually enhanced by including fully four levels i[n] the elevation and introduc[ing] bundles of small upward-r[?] columns in the choir. The [?] the *mur épais* in the trifori[um] produces new effects of lig[ht] and transparency. The elev[ation] of the transept reveals the complexity of thought beh[ind] the construction, for in or[der to?] increase the luminosity fro[m] bottom upward, the windo[ws] on each level are positione[d at] a different depth, moving progressively inward as the[y?]

*Opposite*
**Abbey, St Denis, choir with ambulatory, 1144**
The new choir of St Denis [with?] a double ambulatory with radiating chapels, elegant r[ib?] vaults, and walls opened by large-scale windows – repr[esents] the first layout characterize[d by] the concentration of the we[ight] and thrusts on relatively th[in?] isolated columnar support[s;] use of light creates a sense [of?] expansion and vertical tens[ion.] The construction is related [to] the powerful personality of [?] Abbot Suger, promoter of [an] aesthetic doctrine accordin[g to] which a great urban struct[ure] should coincide with the concept of beauty and the elevation of the spirit.

# Chartres Cathedral
## 1194–c. 1221

The cathedral of Chartres represents the true prototype of the Gothic cathedral characterized by a longitudinal body with a nave and two aisles and an elevation on three levels – arcade, triforium, clerestory – crossed by a short transept and ending in a deep presbytery with ambulatory and radiating chapels. Work began rebuilding the cathedral in a sumptuous style almost immediately after the fire of 1194, which had left only the crypt and western façade of the earlier church, and it came to a conclusion c. 1221. The rectangular bays are covered by quadripartite ribbed cross vaults resting on alternating cylindrical and polygonal elements that may have been used, since they were no longer necessary, to avoid excessive monotony. The result is a continuous and serried rhythm that exalts the effect of verticality of the space emphasized by a plastic accentuation of the structural system: the revolutionary *pilier cantonné*, used here for the first time, confers a sensible material concreteness. The great windows, made possible by the use of the exterior buttresses, propose an innovative design based on a pair of lancet windows and a round window inscribed in an arcade. Such are the enormous dimensions that the nave is clearly higher than the aisles, thus increasing in an exponential way the sense of grandeur and monumentality. Work began on the façade of Chartres in the 1220s. The heads of the transept end in a richly decorated projecting atrium above which a series of fine lancet windows connects to rose windows, creating an extraordinary luminous surface that opened the way for the later transepts of St Denis and Paris.

The Chartres formula – the abolition of galleries, the enlargement of the clerestory, the rectangular bay, the quadripartite vaults, and engaged columns – enjoyed immediate success. It presents a simple and clear response to the need for the rationalization of the building processes, conferring a new grandeur on buildings.

In the shadow of this great structure, leading thinkers like Theodoric of Chartres and William of Conches further identified the Gothic aesthetic, according to which the *anima mundi*, the living energy of creation, was reflected in the articulated tension of the architectural structures and in the varied and curious repertory of their sculptural decorations.

The use of buttresses led to the abandonment of the graduated external profile in favour of an elevation on two levels, simple but majestic. The composition of the volumes is repeated in the sequence of the tall, massive buttresses that repeat on the exterior the rhythm of the internal bays. The weight of the vaults is passed to the buttresses by way of double arches and arcades of radial colonettes. The greater liberty made possible by the buttressing of the vaults thanks to rampant arches and the consequent abolition of tribunes permitted the master of Chartres to organize the interior spaces of the nave in a highly original way. He made a building that seems classical in the harmony of its proportions, as is clear in the elevation, where the arcade and the clerestory are given the same value. At the same time, the new liturgical demands for visual participation of the faithful in the celebration of the Eucharist, as established in the final years of the 12th century, led to a new concept of the choir: the luminous space of the apse became the preferred setting for the liturgy and for polyphonic singing.

## The great cathedrals
### 1195–1230

### The classic Gothic in France

The architectural evolution of the cathedral from early to late Gothic was accompanied by an increased exaltation of light and the related opening of the walls through the use of stained glass. Builders were immediately drawn to the flying buttresses that made this opening possible, and their awareness of the powerful structural implications of these buttresses is indicated by the rapid spread of their use in increasingly elaborate and complex variations. In the largest constructions they are used in overlapping groups arranged in series; they are supported by increasingly powerful buttresses topped by pinnacles and spires that radically transform the exterior appearance of the structure, breaking up the volumes in a sort of perspective kaleidoscope or a replication of the rhythmic modulation of the interior bays. There were equally important interior changes, for the use of flying buttresses made it possible to increase the height of the nave to the maximum technically possible without having to use tribunes above the aisles; the partition of the nave now reached its mature form, articulated on elevations with three levels of great size thanks to the elimination of the gallery.

It was in the two great worksites of Bourges and Chartres, where work began around the same time in the middle of the 1190s, that the potentials for improvement made possible by the removal of the tribune – uncomfortable and hardly functional – were exploited to achieve a new monumental appearance full of balance and harmony among the parts and the whole. These aspirations, pursued through the use of simple, musical relationships not unlike the thinking in the contemporary culture of the church's patrons, impregnated with neo-Platonism and Augustinian ideas, justified the definition 'classical Gothic'.

The cathedrals of Chartres, Bourges, Reims, and Amiens also experimented in the use of the so-called *pilier cantonné*, which permitted the central column to rise without interruption to the vault, augmenting the vertical sense and accelerating the compositional rhythm.

The monumental concept of the great cathedrals is an expression of the ascent to the French throne of the Capetian Philip II, and the spread of the Gothic across Europe is related to the growing influence of French politics and culture over the course of the 13th century.

**Cathedral, Reims, 1211–1427**
The choir at Reims – with a single ambulatory – has five radiating chapels, the wall of which, like the wall of the aisles, has a passage at the height of the windows that reveals its thickness. The windows form a single ogival opening completely pierced to permit even light to spread, increasing the sense of serene equilibrium. At no other place does Gothic architecture achieve an equally exact correspondence between exterior projection and interior space and at the same time the maximum unity of expressive clarity.

**Cathedral, Bourges, begun 1195**
The absence of the transept permitted the architect of Bourges to externally configure the aisles as two stepped bodies that wrap the apse without interruption. The regular succession of the thin and airy flying buttresses, rigorously conforming to the pyramidal structure of the mass, is the means by which a strongly unitary and compact exterior volume is achieved. Unlike the widespread application of the Chartres formula, the Bourges type of choir had only a limited following, most of all in peripheral areas.

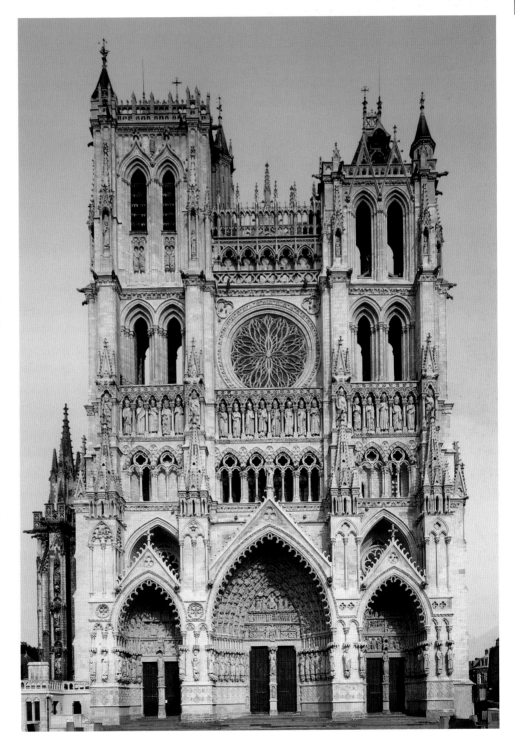

**Cathedral, Amiens,**
**façade, begun 1220**
In the façade of Amiens
the architect Robert de
Luzarches repeated forms
already tried at Paris,
assuming as the main focus
the great central rose
window located in a
position tangential to the
main interior keystone.
However, the unusual
proportions of the nave,
most of all its extreme
height, placed the rose
window in a very high
position on the façade, while
the lower area of the façade
with the portals is connected
to the height of the
triforium by way of two
superimposed galleries – an
ambulatory and the kings'
gallery – that further
emphasize the close
relationship between the
exterior and the interior. In
keeping with the effort to
lighten the structure as much
lightness as possible,
Luzarches greatly
diminished the depth of the
façade, which no longer
takes up the width of a bay,
as at Chartres or Reims;
instead, he placed enormous
projecting buttresses before
the two towers, and in them
opened the side portals.
The result is a highly
articulated front – cut by
deep shadows and loaded
with elements at different
levels – in sharp contrast
with the severe simplicity
of the interior areas.

# Rayonnant Gothic

## c. 1230–1350

### The Rayonnant style in France

The new designs applied to the windows at Reims and Amiens marked the beginning of an innovation in the Gothic style that is called *rayonnant* on the basis of the radiating design of the piercing of the rose windows. The figurative meaning of the architectural elements underwent a profound change. The expression of monumentality by way of ponderous masses was abandoned in favour of an incorporeal approach that reduced forms to the interweaving of lines on planes and in space without transforming in any radical way the structure of the Gothic church, which continued to follow the model set by Chartres in terms of both layout and elevation. What changed was the series of supports that compose the interior view; the vertical tension is brought to extremes, everything becomes more linear, without depth in the treatment of surfaces and visually without weight. Once again the cathedral of St Denis was among the avant-

garde. In the reconstruction of its choir, the new types of column – dense clusters of colonettes similar to a moulding or a rib – transformed the design of the nave into a purely graphic display. Builders also concentrated on the design of the stone frameworks that form and decorate the openings of the windows, making them gradually more elaborate, while on the exterior all forms of extreme gigantism were eliminated in favour of large but balanced proportions. The Rayonnant formula spread with surprising speed until around 1340, when it was interrupted by the recurrent outbreaks of the plague and the darker moments of the Hundred Years' War. The end of dynastic continuity with the ascent to the French throne of the house of Valois in 1328 greatly reduced the aura of sacredness surrounding the king and brought back much of the feudal favouritism, leading to a decrease in the creation of religious architecture and an increase in military and civil buildings, both royal and public.

**Cathedral, Reims, c. 1250**
Designed by Bernard de Soissons, the façade of Rei presents a row of narrow sculptural pediments abov three deep-set portals. The depth and potential darkn of these openings is ingeniously offset by the use of stained glass in the tympana of the portals in place of the usual sculptur Reims presents a summary all the earlier forms, but it also new and original in th way it matches contrasting forms and uses them to create a unitary compositi

**Ste Chapelle, Paris, 1241/42–48**
Paris was the leading centr for the elaboration of the Rayonnant language, which reached its apex at Ste Chapelle, perhaps designe by Pierre de Montreuil to hold the relics that Louis I had acquired at Constantinople. The extraordinary airiness of t upper area is made possibl by both the solidity of the external buttresses and the recourse to ingenious technical artifices. The refined quality of the architecture is matched by the rich decorations, the u of colour, and the marvello polyphony of the sparkling multicolour light that ente through the enormous stained-glass windows. Ste Chapelle carries the 'skelet structure' to extremes in terms of the technical possibilities of Gothic architecture: the walls disappear, replaced by a more or less continuous expanse of stained glass.

**Cathedral, Beauvais,
begun 1284**
What was perhaps the worst
accident involving Gothic
architecture took place in
1284 when the choir of
Beauvais Cathedral, begun
1225 and completed in
1272, gave in to a strong
wind and collapsed. Put
simply, the structure was too
tall. This mishap marked the
end of an epoch, and from
then on builders and patrons
alike abandoned the
aspiration for ever-higher
structures, which had
been the outstanding
characteristic of Gothic
architecture. Beauvais is
considered the final
development of the style
established at Chartres and
Reims, a point beyond which
no one could go.

# Cologne Cathedral
## 1248–1322

Rayonnant forms quickly crossed the borders of France and found immediate welcome, most of all in the leading commercial cities, first among them Cologne. The first undertaking of reworking that city's old Ottonian basilica dates to the second decade of the 13th century, but only after the fire of 1248 did work truly begin on a completely new construction, based on an earlier design that was clearly inspired by French models. It seems quite probable that the patron, Archbishop Konrad von Hochstaden, a supporter of Louis IX's anti-Swabian policies, wanted the building to reflect the formal elegance of the structures going up in Paris at that time, such as Ste Chapelle. The work moved ahead very slowly. The cathedral was not yet finished when it was consecrated, in 1322; only in 1350 did work finally begin on the façade, and it was completed only between 1842 and 1880 on the basis of the original design.

The general design of the building repeats that of the cathedral of Amiens, but not without variations: the longitudinal body with projecting transept has a double-aisled nave, derived from Paris or Bourges; the choir has a double ambulatory and seven radiating chapels. The presence of a deep westwork, which shortens the nave and creates a feeling of centrality, is perhaps a holdover of local traditions. The proportions of the elevation present a significant upward movement, while the large windows let in a great deal of intense luminosity. The 'modern' aspects of Cologne are its abandonment of the engaged column derived from Chartres to adopt instead a clustered arcade pier, a group of shafts that rise straight up without interruption to the springers of the vaults, and its luminous glazed triforium, similar to an elegant work of filigree thanks to the elimination of the small arches from the pendentives. In the external view, the surfaces of the walls disappear more or less completely behind a refined play of piercing and narrow pinnacles that gives unity to the complex volumes of the building.

Cologne, like Strasbourg, which dates to the same period, became one of the principal centres for the elaboration of Rayonnant Gothic, so much so that unlike most of similar German buildings, it is difficult to recognize any holdovers of the Germanic tradition.

The exterior seems to repeat forms previously used at Amiens in the articulation of the buttresses and the extremely steep gables densely covered with blind tracery – their interiors decorated with the characteristic three-petal motif (*Dreistrahl*). From the side, the actual shape of the building disappears behind the elegant play of spires, and in fact the spires give the complex and highly articulated volume of the building a sense of unity.

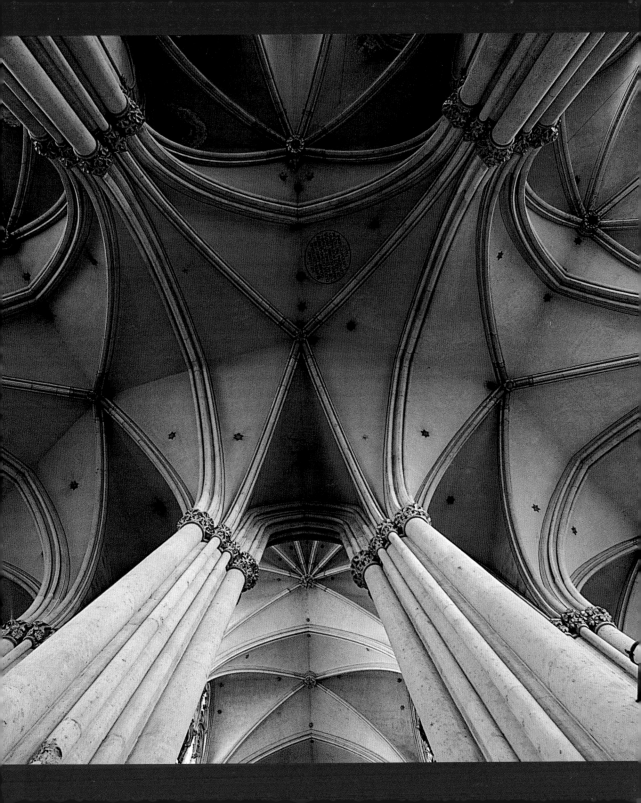

## Flamboyant Gothic
## End 14th–15th century

### Flamboyant architecture in France

The fundamental characteristic of Flamboyant Gothic is the embellishment of technical and decorative elements, for in fact it involved no important structural inventions. The decorative interweaving of ornate tracery forms – already identifiable in the upper part of the west façade of Rouen Cathedral, datable to 1370 – with patterns of double curving, undulating lines that imitate flames (Old French: *flambe*) give the style its name. Flamboyant Gothic architecture abandoned the visual highlighting of lines of force along frameworks – the principle that until then had regulated the main phases in Gothic architecture – in favour of new, completely particular formal criteria. Preference was now given to plant forms or similar shapes, along with similar naturalistic motifs drawn from the French art of the period. The Flamboyant language found its most successful expression in façades, on which it released with exuberant freedom curving and twisting lines, swirling curvilinear and pointed tracery, canopied niches, richly decorated splayed portals, steep gables, and crockets, all of them positioned freely in space, mirroring and overlapping others behind them to create an overall effect of dynamic movement in which the individual elements play roles that vary according to the viewer's point of view. The result of the whole is a scenically mobile vision, a dense multilayered language that lets pass no opportunity to present the richest and most imaginative decorative themes.

The same style saw the propensity in interiors to devise new and curious solutions for the attachments of ribs, vaults, and columns, whereas interest in devising innovative planar and typological-functional solutions diminished. The pronounced freedom of creativity and the surprising effects that it tended to achieve meant an approach to design that was adopted in different regions and was applied to different kinds of works, but it was most often employed in architecture promoted by the court or by members of the ecclesiastical hierarchy.

*Opposite*
**Hôtel de Cluny,
Paris, 1485–98**
The most important expressions of French late Gothic culture are found in religious architecture, but there were also important examples in the field of secular architecture, both private and public. The Hôtel de Cluny, residence of the abbots of the abbey of Cluny, is striking for the strong Flamboyant accentuation of the detail elements. The chapel is distinguished for the originality of its constructive and formal characteristics, which make it one of the most interesting expression of the Parisian Flamboyant.

**Palace of the Duc de Berry, Poitiers,** *c.* **1386**
The magnificent palace of the duke of Berry is an exceptional example of the Flamboyant style applied within the sphere of court patronage. This is most evident in the rear wall of the main salon. Designed by Guy de Dammartin as a stage, the impressive fireplace acts as backdrop, with a gallery for musicians. The large expanse of glass is broken down into mullioned windows and pointed gable located on different planes, creating a highly refined interplay of backgrounds of rare beauty.

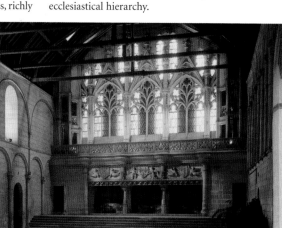

**St Maclou, Rouen,
from 1434, 1500–14**
Among the most important works of the late French Middle Ages, the church of St Maclou reached its highest expressive results in its western façade, built between 1500 and 1514 on a design by Ambroise Havel. The curved entrance porch culminates in a steep gable decorated with projecting crockets and internal curvilinear motifs that stand out freely against the wall of the building. Behind this, the angular buttresses of the main nave are rotated out 45 degrees from the plane of the façade, while a series of double rampant arches runs down the side of the façade. Thoroughly freed from their former support functions, the structural elements perform only a formal role, calling attention to their geometric qualities and evoking decorative suggestions completely similar to those of many other forms of religious art, from wooden sculpture to gold working.

# Cistercian architecture
## 12th–13th century

### The spread of the Gothic in Europe

The foundation in Burgundy of the monastery of Cîteaux in 1097 established the premise for the evolution of a type of building that was to have great fortune in the later centuries. With the approval of the rule of the order, which called for a return to origins, Bernard of Clairvaux became the promoter of an architecture that reflected the same ideals of simplicity and clarity. From the first foundations – La Ferté, Pontigny, Morimond, and Clairvaux – the building programme was dominated by that particular and strict religious spirit and thus was squarely opposed to the prolixity of the volumes and decorations of the architecture found not only at Cluny, but also at the St Denis of Suger. The arrangement of the monastic buildings around the cloister was based on the oldest Benedictine models, and because of ironclad rules concerning the distribution of buildings, which were always the same and made using the greatest economy of means, the order imposed the same bare and functional monumentality everywhere. The church of Fontenay may well be still perfectly Romanesque, but the order was precocious in its adoption of pointed barrel vaults in the annexed buildings, such as the chapter hall of Fontenay itself, datable to 1150; Pontigny was completely covered with pointed vaults around 1160. Since the adoption of the pointed vault did not result in the clear and rigorous division of space typical of Gothic cathedrals, 12th-century Cistercian architecture has been defined as 'reduced Gothic,' meaning reduced to the technical procedures and to the beginning of a new luminous spatial definition that borrows decorative forms from other nonmonastic buildings. Only after the building of the new apse of Pontigny in 1185 did Cistercian architecture begin to abandon its primitive simplicity to approach the sumptuous style of the great cathedrals, a layout with rectangular bays arranged transversally. With this, Cistercian architecture can be said to have adhered to the Gothic, even though it did so with forms and types that differed from those of the great 12th-century cathedrals of northern France. The Cistercians rejected complex typologies, adopting rectilinear apses and transepts often with 'orientated' chapels and, at least in the beginning, they did without crossing towers, harmonic façades, and bell towers, prohibited by the rule of their order. The order expanded at an astonishing rate; by the middle of the 12th century the Cistercians' simplified Gothic had been exported to distant regions where there was absolutely no inclination for the new architecture: the French Midi, Spain, Italy, England, the Holy Roman Empire. After 1200 the influence of the early Cistercian architecture arrived in Poland and Hungary, performing a formative role in those territories.

**Abbey, Salem, *c.* 1414**
The role of the Cistercian builders as bearers of the French Gothic and their flexibility in incorporating the most varied adaptations are clear in the finely worked mullion windows of Salem, in which decorative forms from the Flamboyant Gothic are associated with the completely local use of brick exploiting its pictorial resources.

**Abbey, S Galgano, begun 1224**
The Cistercian order contributed to the introduction of northern European forms to Italy. However, the construction techniques of their builders were not based on 'modern' Gothic systems but on the almost literal repetition of Burgundian models. The layout, cruciform pillars, and arcades of S Galgano, near Siena, are complete copies of those of Fontenay, although here they are given a greater sense of verticality.

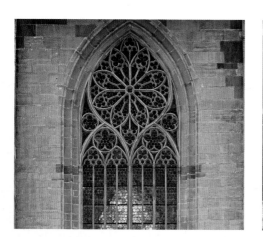

**...bey church,**
**...vaulx, 1132**

...he 1130s, and thus quite
...y, the Cistercians arrived
...ngland and erected a
...at number of conventual
...rches, today almost all in
...n. The church of Rievaulx
...lares its French matrix in
...elevation on three levels
...ded by horizontal
...nices and by its projecting
...nsept, all of which are
...ociated with the strong
...culation of the walls and
...richly profiled arcades of
...nted arches.

*...posite*

**...nastery, Poblet, 1151**

...he second half of the
...century, a great number
...Cistercian monasteries
...e created in Spain,
...eading to that territory
...first elements of
...thern Gothic, most of all
...pointed vault. However,
...pite the use of pointed
...hes and ribbed vaults, as
...he lavabo of Poblet, the
...out remained traditional
...l the general heaviness of
...volumes generates an
...ct closely tied to the
...ceding formulas.

# Early English Gothic

## c. 1200–90

### Early English

Some of the buildings made in England around the end of the 12th century reveal great originality in the interpretation of French models. In fact, one group of churches makes use of the elevation on three levels configured as longitudinal sections superimposed for the entire length of the nave without any vertical attachment, prefiguring the tendency to horizontality that was to be typical of England's Early Gothic style. After the loss of Anjou to France's Philip II in 1204, English builders further accentuated their autonomy from French models. Their highly original efforts put in shadow the rigorously logical structures of French architecture in favour of special decorative effects, such as the introduction of intertwined ribs or ribs along the top of the vault. But this was not all. The concept of space characterized by the perspective marking off of volumes, which reached its most convincing expression at Bourges, did not take hold on English soil. English cathedrals remain for the most part constructions with a longitudinal development thanks to the accentuated horizontality of the arcades and the galleries, while the verticality of the piers is attenuated or even eliminated. The continuity of wall surfaces prevails visually, even when the walls are broken by multiple openings. However, English builders did experiment with some of the 'peripheral' parts of cathedrals, coming up with some original creations. There is the sense of unbounded expansion, as in the Lady Chapel of Salisbury; there are also tracery decorations and mullion windows and the almost obsessive repetition on the exterior of the Rayonnant motif of the mullion window surmounted by an oculus. The interest in Rayonnant forms was limited to the treatment of surfaces, in particular the mullioned decoration of windows, which were given a new value without adopting the structural ramifications from France. At the same time the first screen façades made their appearance – similar to the late Romanesque versions in Lombardy or Aquitaine – wide façades that hide the longitudinal body of the church, making clear the rejection of the façade with two towers of French derivation in favour of a prevalent horizontality.

### Cathedral, Canterbury, choir, begun 1174

The reworking of the choir of Canterbury Cathedral reveals how quickly change in architectural language arrived in England. William of Sens reworked the theme of the *mur épais* in an original way, enlarging the traits of linearism through the use of little columns in dark marble that create a decorative effect substantially extraneous to the French experience and that would become a constant trait of the English Gothic. The new choir adopts – in a way completely exceptional to English architecture – the ambulatory, while the sinuous form of the walls makes it unique to medieval architecture.

### Cathedral, Lincoln, St Hugh's Choir, 1192–12..

In St Hugh's Choir, the heavy decoration typical of English Gothic architecture is accentuated. The lower wall area presents an extravagant wall treatment composed of a double series of false arcades, arranged one in front of the other. The rear arcade gives an illusionistic sense of depth and recalls typically English fondness for double walls and for heavy sculptural decoration.

**...hedral, Salisbury,
...ade, 1258–66**
...h its fame increased by
...paintings of John
...stable, the cathedral of
...sbury shows all its beauty
...he high crossing tower
...ped by a soaring spire.
...e most English Gothic
...edrals, it is developed
...narily in width, adopting
...reen façade juxtaposed to
...interior of the structure,
...ch is particularly rich in
...roscural effects thanks
...he articulation of
...erimposed registers of
...nted arcades creating
...es for sculptural
...oration. In comparison,
...doors seem to have been
...n little importance.

**Westminster Abbey,
London, 1245**
The reconstruction of
this abbey marked the
introduction of Rayonnant
forms to England. Its plan
shows the influence of
French inspiration in the
arrangement of the choir with
ambulatory and radiating
chapels, in the type of
windows, derived from Reims,
and in the creation of the
vaults without the use of thick
walls, but in other respects it
remains faithful to the English
building tradition. The
architect Henry of Reyns used
columns and pillars of dark
marble, steeply pointed and
profiled arches, and the setting
back of the upper windows,
which increases the horizontal
force of the triforium.

# Ornate English Gothic

## *c.* 1290–1330

### The Decorated or Curvilinear style

Between the end of the 13th and beginning of the 14th century, English builders remained faithful, for the most part, to earlier models, meaning the church typology with a very elongated layout, projecting transepts, and crossing towers, heights that were not excessive, and primarily horizontal developments, also in terms of the façades. They were conservative in terms of building techniques, using thick walls and making only limited use of flying buttresses. The result was that there was less focus on the definition of the bays in favour of the unitary effects of the treatment of the surfaces of the vaults, which were given complicated designs through the addition of supplementary ribbing. From the repertory of Rayonnant Gothic the English architects selected only the motif of the great rose window, but the application of this design had a drastic effect on the overall organization of English churches. Breaking the continuous wall changed the rhythm of the naves of English cathedrals, but since the English did not abandon the use of strong, thick walls, the windows set in them appeared 'sunken'. Around 1280–90 in constructions related to court patrons, geometric bar tracery was adopted to mullioned windows, a motif directly inspired by the most up-to-date French examples that was taken to the most daring results. This particular instance of the close observance of Rayonnant forms was centred at London and formed the basis for later creations in the Perpendicular Gothic. During the same years, however, further variations in the design of mullioned windows marked the beginning of a new phase, which within the field of Decorated Gothic came to be known as the Curvilinear style. The basic characteristic is the adoption of the curving line of the ogee arch. The impact of this form went beyond its importance in the enlargement of the ornamental vocabulary, for the sense of fluidity and movement was soon extended to three-dimensional structures, radically changing the entire concept of space and dissolving the former solidity of walls. The functional reasoning behind the construction of buildings was replaced by an order of values that saw the emergence of a new cultural climate more attentive to formal components.

**Cathedral, Ely, octagon, 1322–42**
English architects introduce new approaches to space, making use of multiple vis directions and new applications of perspective An outstanding example is crossing tower at Ely, rebui in the form of an octagon, design attributed to the sacristan Alan of Walsingh The fantastic visual effects achieves, with its dimensio expanded in width and he through the use of a specia technology, locate the octa lantern of Ely in the avant-garde of contemporary European architecture.

**...thedral, Wells, c. 1338**
...e problem of giving
...bility to the crossing
...wer of Wells Cathedral led
... the creation of a support
...stem without comparison
... the field of ecclesiastical
...chitecture, consisting of
...ainer arches inserted
...tween the walls of the
...ve. The crossing is thus
...vided from the rest of the
...ilding, although the
...wer senses its enormous
...esence both because of
...e size of the arches and
...cause of the increased
...rkness in the area behind
...em, a result of the other
...eas of the nave being more
...rmeable to light. For a
...ng time, the new formal
...ult obtained through the
...roduction of these curves
...aracterized much of
...glish late Gothic.

*...posite*
**...thedral, York,**
**...apter House, 1286**
...e interior treatment of
...e walls of the northern
...nsept, with windows set
...hin the depth of the
...lls, amplifies the effects
... spatial expansion; the
...ver area is composed of a
...ies of polygonal niches.
...e resulting surface, with
... light that filters through
... enormous windows,
...kes the limits of the
...ce indefinite.

# English Perpendicular Gothic
## c. 1330–1500

**The Perpendicular style**

During the reign of King Edward III (1327–77), English architecture took another decisive step in its experimentation with spatial qualities. English patrons showed a marked preference for elegant, flowing forms suitable to exalting their elite condition within an extremely dynamic setting. Given the increased wealth of certain social groups – the major landowners, but most of all the upper levels of the clergy and the court – it was in works undertaken for the church or the monarchy that opportunities arose for experimentation in architecture. The name given to the new and final style of English Gothic, Perpendicular, refers to the structural organization adopted in the exterior and interior walls, based on the creation of a system of vertical lines of tracery; the angularity of the contrasting lines gives the style its other name, Rectilinear. Other decorative elements, such as dense rows of half-columns almost forming balustrades, ogee arches, rose windows, foliate patterns, and quatrefoils, continued to take second place to the main design and served to further enrich the overall effect.

The configuration of vaults, the related support elements, and their overall interrelationships were an area of great experimentation, becoming the central theme of this new architectural style. During this period England was the setting for spectacular autonomous creations revealing truly unorthodox approaches and imaginative applications that can be seen as an explicit challenge to the designs based on the customary procedures of French derivation. Thus the propensity for walls of glass and elaborate tracery, for fan vaults, and decorative moulding that rises upward to cover ceilings from rows of cone-shaped corbels. While no completely new works were made in England during this period, a large number of existing buildings were completed or enlarged, presenting opportunities for this style of Gothic to achieve its most original and imaginative expressions. The Perpendicular style responded perfectly to the demands of ecclesiastical architecture, but it proved no less suitable in other fields, most especially universities, leading to an interesting and stimulating exchange of ideas among the various sectors of architectural activity.

**Cathedral, Canterbury, cloister, c. 1380**
The cloister of Canterbury, designed by Henry Yevele, presents some of the most innovative aspects of the English Perpendicular style. As in Gloucester Cathedral, the ceiling is covered by a dense series of cone-shaped fan vaults, further enriched by supplementary ribbing and relief decoration that transfigures the ogee vaults.

**...hedral, Gloucester, ...ster, 1337–60**
...liam Ramsey may have
...lied French moulding in
...design for the cloister of
...St Paul's (destroyed in
...6), but the earliest
...viving example of the
...v architectural style is in
...ucester Cathedral, where
...reates astonishing effects
...ransparency,
...naterializing the walls in
...fantastic, surreal design
...he Perpendicular grid
...ering the cloister. This is
...the earliest surviving
...mple of a new structure,
...fan vault, a system of
...that spring upward from
...rs to form a conical
...tern of tracery. Further
...orative elements of

moulding are inserted along
the conical fan vaults,
creating outlines similar to
those of the great mullioned
windows in an ideal return
to the decorative fantasy of
the Decorated style. The fan
vault represents a highly
important technical advance
since it places the
mechanical elements of a
structure on the same
conceptual plane as those
more properly decorative.

**Palace of Westminster,
London, Hall of Richard II,
1377–99**
This complex wooden
structure, which recalls the
techniques of shipbuilding,
can be seen as one of the
finest expressions of 14th-
century English architecture.
Despite the three-
dimensional organization
of the elements and the
articulation of the supports,
which intersect in a complex
system of beams, the result
does not succeed in
overcoming the conceptual
image of a duplicity of
spatial values. As complex as
it is, the decorative carpentry
seems to be autonomous
from the areas beneath it.

# German Gothic
## End 12th–15th century

**Germany, land of 'resistance'**
Only with difficulty did the structural and linguistic concepts of Gothic architecture make their way into the German-language regions. Builders in the heart of the empire still adhered to traditional models and rejected the extreme consequences of the use of the flying buttress. Essentially faithful to massive proportions and 'thick-wall' techniques, German builders cultivated a taste for abundant architectural exterior decoration, without the effects of the scansions of volumes made possible through the use of buttresses and rampant arches. The eclipse of imperial authority following the death of Henry VI, and the Italian policies of Frederick II, resulted in a form of artistic regionalism, by which the ideas worked out in the many French cathedrals were either given different forms or were rejected outright by more conservative forces.

However, around 1230 this resistance began to give way and disappear in favour of the spatial concepts of the French Gothic. The acceptance of the Gothic by the empire's architects shows up most clearly in their adoption of Gothic structural supports; in the diocese of Trier the influence of French architecture appeared in the use of the engaged column and the Reims-style tall windows.

Early in the 14th century, when the empire's leading worksites were Strasbourg and Cologne, certain undertakings revealed the level of maturity reached by the German Gothic in its precocious passage to late Gothic forms. In the northeastern regions, a very interesting school of building in brickwork came into being, with outstanding examples in the abbeys of Doberan, Pelpin (Poland), and Chorin, while the St Catherine Chapel in St Stephen at Vienna (completed in 1369) has a singular star vault with a pendent boss supported by flying buttresses. St Mary-on-the-Sands at Wroclaw (*c.* 1340), in large part destroyed during World War II, presents a vault system based on the outlines of three triangles divided by ribs. The result is an effect of tension well expressed in the term *Springewölbe* ('jumping vault'), attributed to this configuration, which is widespread in Silesia.

**Cathedral, Strasbourg, begun 1176**
The story of the building of Strasbourg's cathedral presents the progressive evolution of Gothic forms from their initial rejection. Rhine builders to their full acceptance. The adoption of the great windows of the Chartres type met with immediate success, and from then on Strasbourg became one of the leading centres of the diffusion and elaboration of Rayonnant Gothic.

**Church of the Franciscans, Salzburg, detail of the vault, begun 1408**

**ienkirche, Prenzlau, un 1325**

reliance on brickwork in northern regions of the ire led to a style that, n the compact nature of orms, seemed in open rast with the extreme tness that is the goal of hic architecture. German itects overcame this and eeded in expressing the language through the of brick architecture, ting a special style of hic, *Backsteingotik*. The cture of churches made his style, from Lübeck to orin to Prenzlau, clearly als the desire to simplify Gothic of the great

cathedrals. It is a simplicity dictated in part by the materials used, which led to the elevation of flat wall surfaces of great formal and pictorial qualities.

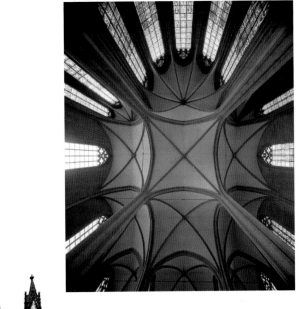

**Wiesenkirche, Soest, 1313–76**
The architect of the Wiesenkirche made a perfect *Hallenkirche* in the proportions between the aisles and the nave, based on the golden section. Late Gothic-style pillars, configured in such a way that the hierarchical structure of the elements that compose their profile cannot be made out, support a somewhat simple ribbed vault. The support elements are perfectly fused with those that are supported, the ribs continuing the columns without any visual interruption between the support part and the rib of the vault.

# The Parler family
## 14th century

### A dynasty of European architects

Over the course of the Middle Ages the term *parler* was used for the professional figure whose role was to translate an architect's design into stone. During the 14th century *parler* became a family name: from then on the Parlers went on to form one of the most important dynasties of architects of the 14th century, to whom is owed much of the process of renewal in central-eastern European architecture. The founder of the family was Heinrich, who trained in the work-site of the cathedral of Cologne and emigrated to Schwäbisch Gmünd to build the nave of the Cathedral of the Holy Cross, beginning an architectural typology destined to influence developments in later Austro-German architecture. Among his sons, Peter was a figure of primary importance in the field of the European late Gothic. He trained on his father's work-sites and worked at Strasbourg, Cologne, and Nuremberg before assuming direction of the work-site of the cathedral of Prague. Peter had two sons: Wenzel, named architect of the cathedral of Vienna in 1400–4, and Johann, author beside Jacob of the choir of Kutná Hora in Bohemia. Another member of the family, Heinrich III, is attested to in 1392, working on the cathedral of Milan.

Peter Parler was distinguished from the beginning of his design career – at Schwäbisch Gmünd and St Vitus at Prague – for the great freedom of solutions he applied in designing the ribbing of the vaults, all of it based on precise geometric rules in which prevailed the use of axes rotating 45 and 60 degrees with respect to the rectangular axes of the bays. The sources of Peter Parler's architecture are known: there is an awareness of English forms, even though it cannot be proved that he made a trip across the Channel, and also north German, specifically the worksites of Cologne and Strasbourg, in clear breaking with the thematics of the French Rayonnant architecture, of which he made an absolutely autonomous and original use. The influence of Peter Parler, and more in general of the family, extended to many centres in Bohemia and the German-Austrian region, as well as into the Tyrol and up to the Brabant and Flanders.

**St Barbara, Kutná Hora, begun 1388**
Commissioned in 1388 fr[om] Jacob Parler by the local guild of illuminators, the cathedral of St Barbara wa[s] completed in 1512 by the architect Benedikt Ried, w[ho] was an innovator working within the Parler traditio[n.] An admirable example of the German late Gothic, i[t] is a pluridimensional and pluridirectional space. At the centre of the nave the intersection of the variou[s] ribs forms floral tracery th[at] culminates in a kind of blossom at the centre of the vault.

**St Vitus, Prague, Golden Gate, 1367**
In the south porch of the cathedral of St Vitus is the portal called the Golden Gate, designed by Peter Parler. In the vestibule he used the thoroughly Engli[sh] solution of flying ribs, further complicated by the design of the ribbed vault.

*Opposite*
**Cathedral of the Holy Cross, Schwäbisch Gmünd, begun 1317**
The Cathedral of the Holy Cross marks the precociou[s] beginning of the late Goth[ic] in Germany and the definitive overcoming of Rayonnant forms. So different are the styles of ribbing used in the nave and choir – belonging to different cultural worlds – that they are attributed to different architects. The choir is known to be the work of Heinrich Parler; t[he] longitudinal body of the nave has been attributed t[o] his son Peter, who is also credited, whether directly or indirectly, with some of the principal and most significant examples of lat[e] Gothic architecture in central Europe.

# Prague

## Beginning 1344

### The creation of a new imperial capital

When Charles IV of Luxembourg became Holy Roman emperor in 1355, he put his residence at Prague, which on his insistence had been elevated to an archbishopric in 1344 by Pope Clement VI. Following his ascent to the throne, the city assumed a new role as imperial capital. Through the efforts of Charles, a venturesome and refined ruler, Prague became an important cultural and artistic centre, assuming the fascinating and thoroughly particular face that still distinguishes it. In 1348 the first university in central Europe was founded in Prague, complete with an important college, the Karolinum. Important architectural undertakings had already begun, the most important of which was the beginning of construction of the new cathedral of St Vitus in the part of the city within the walls of the castle (Hradčany). It was laid out by Mathias of Arras on the basis of a traditional arrangement and using traditional building methods, but it became the first clear example in Europe of a new way of seeing architecture when its direction passed into the hands of the twenty-three-year-old Peter Parler. The political and urbanistic policy that Charles IV applied when he reconfigured his capital city reworked the role played by the Vltava River, which until then had constituted – as was often the case in cities occupied by a court, in which the area of the court differed from that of the city's middle class – a dividing line between the two traditional urban areas. The new plan changed this relationship by creating a third urban centre, the small section known as Mala Strana ('Little Quarter') at the foot of the castle, making it a kind of hinge area between the area of the imperial residence, where work had started on construction of the cathedral, and the area inhabited by the influential middle class on the other side of the river. This turned Prague into a kind of triple city, making absolutely necessary the creation of a large stone bridge, the Charles Bridge, to replace the old and precarious wooden bridges.

**St Vitus, begun 1344**
Peter Parler quite casually changed the design by Mathias of Arras, altering the layout with the additions of the sacristy and the Wenceslas Chapel. The innovative system of the vaults – some stellar and triangular, others with the insertion of flying ribs, or with hanging arches and pendant bosses – creates an arrangement of English-origin styles. Equally innovative is the treatment of the walls, which completely changed the original scheme by giving strong accentuation to the geometric-rectangular components that frame the minor elements. The criteria of articulation becomes more complex through th[e] use of inclined surfaces th[at] produce the visual effect o[f] an undulating space, deep[...] in the area of the window which become the protagonists in the search for continuity that characterizes the whole.

**[Ch]arles Bridge, 1357**
[An] outstanding example of
[p]ublic work, the Charles
[Bri]dge – constructed in part
[un]der the direction of Peter
[Par]ler – presents a sinuous
[out]line based on sixteen
[pie]rs spaced by round
[arc]hes. A tower at each end
[con]trols access. The bridge's
[ge]ometric clarity makes it
[par]t of a technical-formal
[sty]le in widespread use in
[the] civilian architecture of
[the] period, but its outline
[and] the emphasis given to
[the] outlines of the arches
[giv]e it a special value. In
[kee]ping with the urban
[cus]toms and concepts of the
[tim]e, the bridge became one
[of] the city's main gathering
[spo]ts and thus also a symbol
[of] the city itself. In addition
[to] serving its principal
[fun]ctions as a city bridge,
[wit]h all the commercial,
[pol]itical, and legal aspects
[att]ached to those functions,
[it] was also a primary urban

axis, used in all the religious
and public celebrations
related to the activities and
functions of the imperial
court.

**Castle of Karlstein, 1348–57**
The impressive castle of
Karlstein, located a few
kilometres from Prague, may
well have been constructed
by Mathias of Arras and
Peter Parler. The favourite
residence of Charles IV, a
place of retirement for the
emperor, and a fortress
where the crown jewels were
stored, it stands atop a crag
as a recognizable symbol of
power. The original complex
was partially rebuilt during
the 19th century.

## Italian Gothic

### 13th–14th century

#### Civic pride

Enormous vitality and geographic variety had distinguished the architectural culture of Italy since the early 13th century, with some areas showing the effects of the French-Burgundian ideas brought to Italy by the Cistercians, and others holding true to the Romanesque and classical traditions. As a result, there were but few signs of Gothic forms and techniques in Italy. The absence of a strong central government prevented the adoption of a unitary style and made possible the persistence of local building traditions, which were often looked upon with civic pride. New constructions were relatively rare in many Italian cities, most of the building work involving instead the completion of works already started, and although these might include modern accents, no efforts were made to alter the original sense of space and, indeed, the goal was to maintain a characteristic compact and balanced atmosphere. The acceptance of the purely superficial value of the thin wall led Italy toward a design concept parallel to that of the French Gothic but alternative to it, with particular emphasis on the sense of perspective depth.

Over the course of the 14th century there was a large-scale resumption of building activity in Italy, both public and private, an expression of changes in urban spaces and buildings. With the exceptions of the cathedral of Milan and S Francesco in Bologna, the distinctive characteristic of the Gothic in Italy was the rejection of the external flying buttress. What prevailed instead, in both religious and secular structures, was the theme of the vaulted and ribbed covering over more or less square bays with naves and aisles of more or less the same height. Thickening the external wall where needed was all that was required to provide increased stability to the structure. Being compact and well defined, such architectural forms could be inserted amid the other elements of the urban landscape without any visual jarring. In all probability, the differences made to the French Gothic language when it was applied in Italy reflected the civic pride of the Italians as well as the particular urban realities of the cities.

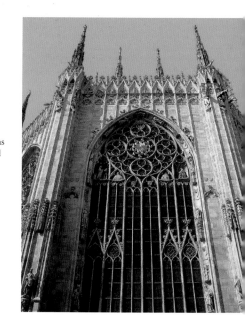

**Cathedral, Milan, apses, begun 1387**
Milan's cathedral reflects ideas drawn from the international world of late-14th-century Gothic, presenting in fact a summation, as well as a hybridization, of different currents and trends, with a preference given to those of the French Flamboyant style and the German. All of this was probably a result of the Visconti family's desire to see itself ranked among the major ruling families of Europe.

**S Maria del Fiore, Florenc[e], bell tower, 1334–60**
Compared to the original design by Giotto – an elegantly narrow parallelepiped marked off [by] stringcourses and topped b[y] a spire – the new architects Andrea Pisano and Francesco Talenti, while n[ot] going against the basic ide[a], doubled the scheme of the layout and the related decorative system in a hap[py] contamination between Cosmati-work columns an[d] classical notions already present in Florentine architecture. The decision to leave off the spire is indicative of the changes th[at] had taken place in Florenti[ne] taste during the period of work on the tower.

**Maria del Fiore, Florence,
[na]ve, begun 1366**
[Th]e design by Arnolfo di
[Ca]mbio had been based on
[th]e dialectical relationship
[be]tween the square plan of
[th]e eastern part and the
[lo]ngitudinal body; Francesco
[Ta]lenti imposed a new
[de]sign that was similar but
[in]volved greater sizes overall,
[re]sulting in an effect of airy
[sp]aciousness.

**[Ca]thedral, Orvieto,
[fa]çade, begun 1308**
[Lo]renzo Maitani designed
[th]e façade as an architectural
[el]ement completely
[un]related to the body of the
[ch]urch behind it. Based on
[th]e interrelation and
[in]tersection of geometric
[fig]ures, it is a masterpiece
[of] 'ornamental Gothic' and
[pl]ays an essential role in
[rel]ation to the urban space
[ar]ound it, affecting its
[pe]rception.

# The Venetian palace
## 14th–15th century

### The city on water

The acceptance of the Gothic architectural language in Venice, and its reworking into an autonomous style, took place by way of compromises, linguistic contaminations, and inevitable adjustments to the urban fabric. Gothic architecture arrived in Venice precisely when that city was going through major changes. It had become a great sea power, it was performing a key role as the only hinge between the West and the East, and the structure of its society and institutions was changing following the growth of its population, which on the threshold of the 14th century numbered 115,000. Elements of Gothic architecture had made their way into Venice in a perceptible way over the course of the 13th century, but their full acceptance had to wait until the middle of the 14th century. At that time the most important monastic buildings came into being, and work began on public and private buildings on a scale that came to involve the entire area of the basin of St Mark's, an undertaking of fundamental importance to the history of the urban structure and artistic culture of Venice. The desire of the dominant aristocratic class to strengthen the city's economy and to improve the city's image in general led to the development of a new type of city palace that would remain more or less unchanged over the coming centuries. Over the course of the 15th century this private patronage led to the adoption, in a more or less systematic way, of a C-shaped layout with three sides forming a closed court along the water of a canal. This arrangement offered the best interior illumination for the rooms, and the court took on the role as centre of domestic life, often emphasized by the level of artistry reached by the well heads located there and by the architectural importance given to the external stairs. The late Gothic Venetian palace repeats and reinforces the importance of the location of the palace's main salon on the second floor, the *piano nobile*, a fact that is translated on the façade in stately and noble mullioned windows, sometimes with several lights, and sometimes more than one window because of the use of two floors as the *piano nobile*, occupying the central part of the building and assuming the role of compositional and formal centre. In civil buildings,

Byzantine decorative motifs and learned citations of Islamic motifs were transformed into graphic embellishments used on the façades over water together with the perfect rhythm of the windows and the application of precious materials. The reiteration of decorative motifs – small towers, Flamboyant Gothic balconies, mullioned windows, thin stone columns, the characteristic trilobed arch – demonstrates an aesthetic that turns building fronts into dynamic organisms. Here, as in all of the city, the primary relationship is between the façade and the water, and the architectural design dissolves in the formal values of light, colour, and movement. Secular Venetian architecture thus moved toward new frontiers that would encounter echoes and new ideas in the thoroughly original Flamboyant architecture that would provide the background to the special qualities of Venetian humanism.

**Ca' d'Oro, 1421–40**
The Ca' d'Oro was commissioned by Mario Contarini, member of one of Venice's most prestigious families, and its creation led to the establishment of many of the basic stylistic elements of Venetian late Gothic architecture. It was conceived exclusively in terms of its face on the canal, and the design of the façade is based on the contrasts between the chiaroscuro of the mullioned windows and the flat surfaces, between the openings in the balconies and the areas of marble surfaces. Matteo Raverti, who had worked on the cathedral of Milan, repeated the construction idea of the open loggia on the *piano nobile*, making use of the basic lexicon of Flamboyant Gothic and updating the traditional ways of expression. All the surfaces are dressed in blocks of a rare marble that cancel all sense of the brickwork structure, transfiguring it in the symbolic values of light. For this reason the Ca' d'Oro is quite correctly included among the 'golden architecture' works of 15th-century Venice.

**ge's Palace, begun
40, modified 1422–24**

e completion of the façade
he Doge's Palace involved
orksite that had opened
rly eighty years earlier, in
ch the structural factors
olved in the creation of the
a del Maggior Consiglio
been transformed into
hitectural factors. The
rall image is based on the
trast between the two
er levels, an arcade and an
n loggia, and the upper
ck, with its long extension
decorative dressing. The
ividual architectural
ments lead back to the
me of the Flamboyant
thic as translated in the

exuberant version of Venetian
Gothic. The façade can be
taken as emblematic of the
Venetian figurative theory of
architecture, composed of
light and chromatic effects
that dematerialize surfaces.
The way the 15th-century
forms of the Doge's Palace
remain closely faithful to
models from the preceding
century – during a period
when Florence was already
opening the way to the
Renaissance – legitimizes the
validity and the courtly
function of the late Venetian
Gothic understood as a
reference to tradition and
a factor of stability and
grandeur.

**Ca' Foscari, begun 1452**

The Ca' Foscari – judged by
Ruskin to be the noblest
example of 15th-century
Gothic in Venice – is striking
for its compositional rigour
and for its obvious desire to
make itself a model of
Venetian late Gothic
architecture. Its canal façade
is notable for its balanced play
of empty and full spaces, light
and shadow, for the rhythm
of its series of mullioned
windows, and for the areas of
bare wall held within angular
cornices and small quoins
made of Istrian stone.

# Spanish Gothic
## 13th–15th century

**The influence of the Gothic on the Iberian peninsula**
The introduction of Gothic forms to the Iberian peninsula occurred during the ongoing process of the military and political reconquest of that region by the Christian kingdoms; it met resistance from the strong Romanesque tradition, which had become blended with elements from Islamic art to form a highly original synthesis. By the last years of the 12th century, however, Spain was coming into contact with architectural ideas from northern France by way of the pilgrimage routes leading over the Pyrenees. This contact did not lead to the adoption of the ribbed vault and was reflected instead in the iconographic programmes involving sculptural cycles and the adoption of the Burgundian ambulatory choir. By the year 1225, when the bishop of León promoted the construction of a cathedral, French ideas were receiving a different reception on Iberian soil, although the versions adopted were related to models of forty years earlier. León Cathedral repeats the layout of Reims and uses the Champagne-

region model of the *mur épais* gallery and the engaged column of Chartres. Not until the end of the 13th century, in Catalonia and the Balearic Islands, does the tendency to configure the interior of a building as a vast, unified space expanding in every direction appear in Spain (and at the same time that similar ideas were being employed in southern France). These new constructions did away with the succession of spaces and the individuation of the bays, dissolving the material solidity of wall surfaces and no longer revealing the supporting structure, whether real or illusory. The area along the Pyrenees continued to be a highly original landscape in the elaboration of innovative and high-quality spatial and constructive forms, leading to the great Majorcan churches. During the same period between the 13th and 14th century, the cloister came to constitute an integral part of the church, and the piercing that decorates the arcades of the porticoes displays unbridled imaginative fantasy, with clear reference to the forms of the Moorish tradition.

**Cathedral, Palma de Mallorca, 1420–1427**
The support structures arranged along the southe[r] side of the cathedral, base[d] on a system of buttresses a[nd] double rampant arches wi[th] the addition of masonry walls, followed a route already well known to Fre[nch] Gothic architecture. Here, however, the dense rows o[f] buttresses are transformed into a massive stone wall [cut] by the dark grooves of shadow, achieving strong visual effects. Palma reject[s] every aspect of the openin[g] of walls so typical of the French Rayonnant style, and the architectural mass looks much like a fortified structure overlooking the

## ...ulalia, Barcelona, ...gun 1298

...e desire for open,
...panding spaces, the hunger
...breathtaking scale, the
...sire to rework the ways of
...ning architectural volumes
... displayed in the radical
...utions of S Eulalia. A
...sterpiece of technical
...lls in the service of a
...ghly original spatial
...ncept, this cathedral
...ms to combine the effects
...the German hall church,
...'classical' French
...hedral, and the single-
...ve Catalan churches.

## Cathedral, Burgos, 1223/24–60

Burgos seems like a
simplification of the French
Gothic, perhaps a result of
financial limitations or
perhaps a reflection of the
fact that the giant scale of
the cathedrals of northern
Europe remained
substantially foreign to
environments still tied to
Romanesque traditions.
Standing on the northern
slope of a steep hill, the
cathedral is best known for
its 15th-century eastern
towers. The extraordinary
sculptural decoration on
the Portada del Sarmental
follows the model of
Gothic sculpture with its
strong charge of realism
and extraordinarily
vigorous modelling.

# S Maria da Vitória, Batalha

## Begun 1387

In Portugal, the passage from Romanesque elements to a more properly Gothic style of architecture took place late. In fact, throughout all of the 14th century the building activity in Portugal followed a somewhat slow rhythm, finally receiving a great impulse in patronage with the ascent to the throne, in 1385, of John I, establishing the house of Aviz and beginning a glorious period in Portuguese history known as the Juanino. The Dominican monastery of St Mary of the Victory, which the king had built to commemorate his victory (1385) over John I of Castile, thus assuring Portuguese independence, was designed by the architects Alfonso Domingues and Jaime Huguet. It is composed of a church and three magnificent cloisters, all displaying linguistic components of differing provenance. French elements appear in the elevated longitudinal body, and the exterior decorative details reveal themes typical of Flamboyant Gothic.

The outline of the vaults, with additional linear ribbing, and the organization of the prevalently horizontal façade repeat schemes from English Gothic, both Curvilinear and Perpendicular.

As a whole, the complex of S Maria da Vitória represents not only the most important work of Portuguese architecture but also a masterpiece of art of the 14th–15th century. Batalha is perhaps the monument that best incarnates the drive for the renewal of the artistic spirit during the Gothic period. It should not be forgotten, however, that the monastery is the result of a highly singular set of circumstances. It is the product of a king who wanted its architecture to affirm a principle of political legitimization and thus its message was directed for the most part outside the country in which it was made. For this reason its style is not a synthesis of the varieties of Portuguese architecture. Instead, it makes use of international components, most of all French and English, to express and to symbolize the ideas and the political policies of the sovereign and his relationship with the monarchies with more long-standing traditions.

A complex system of buttresses on the exterior counters the thrust of the vaults. The highly particular shape of these buttresses, which look like triangles pushed against the walls to form arches, produces an effect of extreme lightness but also brings into question their real effectiveness. Small oculus windows are opened in the walls between the buttresses, and large windows are located along the aisles, filling them with great luminosity.

# The architecture of the
## mendicant orders
### From *c.* 1250

## The urban convent

In the midst of the growth of cities in the medieval world, mendicant orders – Augustinians, Dominicans, Franciscans – drew attention to the less pleasant aspects of the new social system, promoting reforms to mitigate the inequalities in wealth and also highlighting the dissolute style of life generated by wealth. The urban convent, although in many senses indebted to Benedictine monasteries, developed an L-shaped layout in which the church and the monastic areas flanked a square, used for preaching. The single-nave church was chosen as the best type to meet these requirements since it combined simplicity, economy, rapid construction, and constructive severity. It was also large, big enough for crowds of the faithful to assemble in an area without divisions and without obstacles to acoustics. For their church model, the German mendicant orders turned to the severe forms of Cistercian architecture, further unifying the interior space by eliminating the transept and the ambulatory choir with chapels, and elaborating a new type of choir, the *Langchor*, separated from the nave by a screen. Equally original were the mendicant churches built in Italy. In the Po area these were based on the local Cistercian tradition, simplifying their construction requirements; in the central regions of the peninsula, where ideology rejected the superfluous, the preferred form was a single-nave church covered with a roof with high, bare walls pierced by large windows and a cross-vaulted choir with a square layout and minor chapels but no aisles. This was the Cistercian 'barn', simple and spare, but enormous and filled with dramatic light. From the outside such churches were simple, square structures, with few formal qualifications, but they were unmistakable within the urban fabric. The purely superficial value given to walls, dematerialized and without thickness, led to an effort parallel to the elaborations of the French Gothic, but with more focus on the visual effects of perspective. The theme of a unitary space, achieved by the great height of the aisles and pervaded by abundant light, more intense under the vaults, was developed most of all in Tuscany, with its purest expression in the Dominican church of S Maria Novella (1279) and the Franciscan church of Santa Croce (1294–95), both in Florence.

**Church of the Dominicans Colmar, 1283**
The eastern end of the churches of the German mendicant orders has a different quality from that of other churches, as is clear at Colmar, where a large bare space, geometrically defined but without a prevalent direction, is juxtaposed to the longitudinal extension of the choir, in which the viewer's gaze is lost in a sort of luminous box. The lightness of the structure and the simple, elongated supports go against the preference of German builders for solid, balanced forms.

**S Maria Gloriosa dei Frari, Venice, begun 1334**
The church of the Frari represents an architectural episode of great interest. Because of the danger of its support pilings sinking and causing damage, the church was given a system of internal reinforcements based, in keeping with centuries-old local tradition on wooden tie-beams in both longitudinal and transverse directions, both across the nave and between the arches of its arcades. The result is an interesting three-dimensional modulation of space, almost a cubic framework further emphasized by a diffuse and substantially homogeneous luminosity.

**Jacobin Church, Toulouse, begun 1260**
The most prestigious mendicant church in southern France was that of the Jacobins (Dominicans) of Toulouse, in which abundant light is concentrated on the ceiling vaults, highlighting their elegant graphic elements and the polychromy of their ribbing. The choir vault is supported by a column from which twenty-two ribs extend, and that column assumes the role of focal centre in the large, substantially unitary space. In fact, the cylindrical supports, thin, high, and widely spaced are located along the axis of the church and thus do not alter the overall effect of fluidity that fills the space.

**St Francis, Assisi, Upper Church, 1228–53**
The long, complicated history of the construction of St Francis involves the debate between those supporters who wished to remain completely faithful to the founder's ideals of absolute poverty and those who wanted to include the Franciscan movement in the contemporary world of the church. While the Lower Church adheres substantially to the language of the late Romanesque, the Upper is very much something new, clear and unitary, in which the abundance of Gothic solutions – from traceried windows to the clerestory gallery under the windows, the linearism of the supports, and the adoption of the 'skeleton' construction method – indicates a derivation directly from northern France. Such new forms make it clear that the patrons hoped to give this 'monument-symbol' of the order a modern and international image.

# The secular heart of the medieval city
## 13th–15th century

### Secular construction in the late Middle Ages

During the late Middle Ages, demographic growth, developments in manufacturing and commerce, along with the resulting wealth and importance of cities turned the more important urban centres into political centres of great power. Between imperial assemblies, church councils, and guild meetings, cities came to assume administrative roles while also serving emblematic roles on the international stage. Civil architecture soon moved well past its purely functional character and came into competition with ecclesiastic and feudal architecture, repeating symbols from noble palaces and then making them its own and responding to the influence that the great cathedrals had on architectural styles. The birth of a purely urban architecture was a sign of the transformation of the feudal agrarian society into a middle-class city. The city palace, a building typology designed for the new dominant class, was shaped like a large rectangular block to replace the older multistorey hall-houses. By the early 13th century the building of such palaces was altering the street layouts of cities and as a result was having an important effect on the urban image. At the same time, administrative autonomy, a development of medieval urban civilization, led to the expansion and evolution of other building typologies that slowly acquired greater importance.

The town hall became the most important building. Very often erected on the square facing the cathedral, it became a contender in the struggle between sacred and profane architecture. As a symbol of citizen self-government, this building developed different typologies, functions, and spatial uses according to whether it was in a flowering commercial city of northern Europe or a proud commune in the southern area.

*Below left*

**Cloth market, Bruges, middle 13th–end 15th century**

Cloth markets were among the most impressive civil buildings in the urban culture of the late Middle Ages, a reflection of the importance of the cloth trade. This is true most of all in the cities of Brabant and the Flemish areas. The cloth market of Bruges displays the successful fusion of urban, feudal, and religious architectural elements to form a unitary whole.

**azzo Vecchio,
rence, c. 1299**

taly, the proliferation of
aces for communal
ernment attests to the
portance of propriety and
urban image. Many such
lic palaces arose after 1250,
ifying to the flowering of
mmunal life, and they are
erally characterized by a
se of openness toward the
side achieved through the
of porticoes and windows
t mitigate their otherwise
itary appearance. This is
true of Florence's Palazzo
chio, the ponderous volume
which confers on the
lding a decidedly martial
earance; the asymmetrical
ation of the tower has a
r significance as the visual
hor of the urban space.

*posite*
**n hall, Stralsund,
h–15th century**

in many cities of the
nseatic League, the town
l of Stralsund is perfectly
rted within the urban
ric. Its brick façade is a
gnificent and impressive
mple of Gothic art. It is
ed on a network of
dows and openings that
ieve unusual pictorial
cts and includes the
gular insertion of
ychrome majolica tondos
h an oriental flavour.

**Town hall, Löwen, 1448–63**

By the end of the 13th
century, accelerated
developments in international
relations – commercial,
manufacturing, banking, and
also artistic-cultural – had
given a strong impulse to
urban life in the areas of
Flanders and the Brabant. This
led to further developments in
the sphere of public building.
The town hall – a typology
destined to appear in
increasingly splendid
examples over the course of
the centuries – here appears
in a magnificent example,
proudly displaying its Gothic
façade, which can be taken as
a translation in stone of the
ambitions of the city's
burgeoning middle class.

# Palaces and fortresses in Spain

## 14th–15th century

### Civil architecture in Catalonia and Aragon

The architectural culture of the Catalonia-Aragon area was only outwardly part of the overall European Gothic. In truth, the area was the site of works that differed from the standard Gothic, in some cases because they still adhered to themes anchored in the local Romanesque tradition, and in others because they reflected the blending of certain Gothic elements with local elements. Civil architecture and buildings for the middle class received special attention, and in these areas the development of new languages and spatial values made possible the creation of architectural works that are both singular to the region and of special interest. The prevalent aspect of Catalan architecture in this period is the striking clarity and simplicity of spaces, volumes, and details, a result of using a building system in which large-size spaces were given wooden roofs supported by diaphragm arches and in which preference was given to building techniques that avoided the use of the buttress. The prevailing tone in both the structural and the linguistic style was one of severity and sobriety and was related to the elegant combination of rectilinear geometrics, consequent to designs made *ad quadratum* – based on the geometry of the square – and to flowing lines with twists and curves.

**Castle Nuovo, Naples, 145...**
Guillem Sagrera is credited with the arrangement of th... façade towers and, more in general, with the entire ove... scheme of this fortified roy... residence, which reflects the application of new developments in military architecture. The lower are... of the massive towers are decorated with a diamond-point pattern and with cor... spiral grooves, perhaps me... to deter the use of scaling ladders; in applying this decoration, Sagrera gave a... agility and elegance to area... that are usually left unador...

**Castell del Bellver, Palma de Mallorca, 1309–14**
Although this work of mili... architecture was erected to overlook and protect the c... the way its structure stand... out against the landscape seems to anticipate the sin... kind of architectural think... applied to cathedrals. The circular main body of the castle is built around a courtyard with two levels of arcades that provide illumination and openness... the interior rooms. The lo... arcade has classical arches; the upper one seems to re... the desire to achieve great... decorative results, employi... system of double, interwea... arches of Islamic derivatio... The highly particular appearance of this Majorc... castle, a result of the use of elements drawn from different cultural models,... reflects the ongoing proce... cultural synthesis then tak... place in Spain.

**...acio del Infantado, ...adalajara, 1480**
...e two-storey courtyard of ...adalajara, one of the most ...oressive works in the ...ire Catalan-Aragon area, ...s designed by Juan Guas. ...heavy emphasis on ...oration should be ...npared with other, similar ...rks by the architect, such ...he complex of S Gregorio ...alladolid.

**Palau de la Generalitat, Barcelona, 1416–25**
One of the most representative works of civil architecture in the Catalan-Aragon area, the Palau de la Generalitat presents a sumptuous courtyard with stairs and upper patio surrounded by slender arcades with thin columns.

# The seats of feudal power
## 13th–14th century

### Fortified residences

Gothic architecture was not limited to religious buildings, and nor should such buildings be seen as emblematic of the Gothic style. An equal amount of activity was dedicated to the building of castles and fortified residences, structures desired by the courts or by the centres of feudal power as a result of the great political and social instability of the period. The contrast in functions between defensive buildings and buildings designed as residences, along with attempts to blend the two types into one, represents the special problem surrounding the construction of the medieval fortress. The desire for conquest, the affirmation and expansion of power, led to the continuous updating of the techniques for waging war and thus dictated the equally constant evolution of defensive systems; at the same time, prestige and high rank bring their own special requirements in terms of 'suitable' furnishings in a residence.

The territorial disputes between France and England, including the so-called War of Bastides involving the construction of fortified towns along the borders of disputed areas, had a forceful impact on the design of residences. Defensive and residential needs were blended in the donjon, to which elements were added over the course of the 13th century, such as external defensive rings, scarps, bastions, towers, embrasures, and battlements.

So high were the costs of such complex defensive systems that they were available only to kings or other royalty, the members of powerful noble houses, or orders of knights, and of course such figures were the principal patrons. During the 13th century in southern Italy, the political ambitions of Holy Roman Emperor Frederick II led to building activity designed to create a kind of residential military architecture that would affirm the sovereign's presence in his territory and also establish a network of defensive settlements. All of these structures were conceived as emblems of imperial power and magnificence. They were based on Eastern, Byzantine, or Arabic models, although their architectural language belongs to the Romanesque tradition. Beginning in the 1220s, however, because of the activity of the Cistercians, perhaps with contributions from the architecture used by the knightly orders, Gothic forms began showing up in the decorative details as well as in the construction methods, including capitals, windows, and vaults. A further reflection of Frederick's policies is the resort to classicism, as in the use of Roman wall techniques (*opus reticulatum*) and the collection and reuse of ancient materials. The use of the classical language assumes a clear political and instrumental meaning as an affirmation of imperial ideology.

**Castel del Monte, Puglia, 1240**
The extraordinary octagor layout of Castel del Monte a synthesis of the different cultural and artistic impul brought to bear by Frederi The structure has been variously interpreted as a military construction, a hunting lodge, or an astronomical observatory. is based on a regular octag reproduced on both levels, each of which has eight same-size rooms with octagonal towers at the points, thus translating the Cistercian Gothic in forms that are knightly, courtly, a classical. The structure makes clear the desire to pursue an ideal of perfecti and abstract beauty with t aim of transmitting a sens of imperial grandeur.

**Coucy-le-Château, Aisne, 1220**
The external walls of the castle of Coucy reflect the importance of such defensive structures in the early 13th century, but the castle once included a donjon (destroyed during World War I), one of the first examples on French territory of the effort to add comfort, courtly splendour, and artistic creativity to such structures.

**Harlech, Gwynedd, 1283**
The type of castle with a four-sided court with corner towers and a twin-towered gatehouse appeared over the course of the 13th century in many European regions and in particular in Wales in the castles built by Edward I during his campaign of conquest. Of those, Harlech castle is one of the best preserved.

# The Palace of the Popes at Avignon
## 1334–52

In certain 14th-century residential buildings, the defensive function of the structure gradually began to take second place to other concerns. The French masterpiece of this evolution is the Palais des Papes at Avignon, a construction that is exceptional because of its size and complexity, built on a rocky bank adjacent to the cathedral.

The first pontifical residence, the Old Palace, constructed under Pope Benedict XII and designed by Pierre Poisson, reflects the image of an austere palace-fortress with its towers and high walls. On one side are the papal apartments, on the other are the chapel, the court buildings, and the conclave, arranged around a cloister. The New Palace, begun by Pope Clement VI (reigned 1342–52), is juxtaposed to the old one and looks nothing at all like it. Designed by Jean de Louvres, it is striking for its splendid interior laid out like a luxurious court with salons, staircases, and entrance halls, all decorated with corbels, portals, and windows of the finest handiwork. It is composed of an apparently endless sequence of meeting rooms, chapels, and apartments arranged around the court of honour. The compositional novelty is the southern wing, composed of two huge and splendid rooms, the Salle de la Grande Audience and the Great (Clementine) Chapel, headquarters of the pontifical coronation and the liturgical offices. Of special interest are the solutions adopted for the rooms made to serve technical or service needs, most of all the great kitchen complex with the associated storerooms as well as the areas related to the hygienic and sanitation systems. Significant stylistic details, from the shape of the clustered pillars and the richness of the ribbing of the vaults, as well as the abundance of decoration and the refined capitals and bases, indicate the late Gothic training of the architect in contrast to the bareness and simplicity of the Cistercian constructions built under Pope Benedict.

With its impressive proportions, the palace was described in the chronicles of the time as 'the most beautiful and the best fortified home in the world.' The Palace of the Popes is the image itself of pomp and of the cultural influence of the papal court.

The Salle de la Grande Audience, made to house the Papal Rota, is the masterpiece by the papal architect Jean de Louvres. The enormous space – 52 metres long, 16.8 wide, and 11 high – is divided into two aisles by bundled columns from which extend the ribs of the pointed cross vaults. On the walls the ribs rise from splendid figural corbels with subjects drawn from an imaginative bestiary. Within the walls of the papal palace flourished the so-called Avignon school of painting, a result of the encounter between the refined realism and chromatism of the Sienese Matteo Giovanetti and the graphic elegance of French painters, an early sign of Italy's artistic expansion into France during the 14th century.

The ground plan and internal arrangement of the rooms make clear the desire to provide a more elevated quality of life – one of the aspects of the new social and behavioural realities of late Gothic culture – while on the exterior, the new architectural culture is indicated by the treatment of the walls, with high blind arcades with pointed arches and a flurry of towers topped by pinnacles, crested moulding, projecting elements, and crenellations. Taken all together, the palace, connected to the surrounding countryside and town by a bridge, presents itself as an architectural microcosm expanded to the scale of a true urban nucleus.

## A century of cathedrals

The enormous architectural production in Spain between the 15th and 16th centuries reflects the important events taking place there during that period, events that caused profound changes throughout the Mediterranean basin. The acceleration and completion of the centuries-long Christian reconquest of the Iberian peninsula; the union of the kingdoms of Castile and Aragon, leading to the creation of Spain as a powerful territorial power; the policy of enlarging trade routes by sponsoring exploration that led to the discovery of the New World – all these events, which reached their culmination in 1492, were related.

This climate was the background to intense architectural activity in which many important works were made, and even if these can be viewed in relationship to the European late Gothic, they are recognizable for the presence of typological, functional, and linguistic elements drawn from the local tradition. The numerous cathedrals made in Spain's cities throughout the 15th century and later are a primary expression of this. These buildings reveal the tendency to repeat the same themes and the same solutions following two principal trends. One trend is characterized by the lingering of Mudejar elements, suitably decontextualized; the other trend involves the elaboration of linguistic themes imported from French or English architecture. Both groups have

in common the same typological-functional characteristics, through the presence of a vast presbyterial area, separated from the rest of the interior space by railings or screens that visually and ritually break the spatial unity of the nave – and that cause a fragmentary reading of the internal spatial values. Located inside this closed-off area is the main altar, decorated with splendid *retablos*. A further trend in architectural style began appearing at the end of the 14th century. This style – called both the Isabelline, after the queen, and the Hispano-Flemish, for its blend of Netherlandish and Mudejar forms – is an extreme variant of the late Gothic, blending themes from Flamboyant architecture and expressing them through lexical elements from the Mudejar matrix and the Renaissance. It is a court production, expressed with a rich language, heavy with decorative components. The principal exponents of this style were Juan de Colonia and his son Simón, Juan Guas, Enrique Egas, and Gil de Siloé. This Spanish architecture was expressed through the use of many linguistic elements drawn from various cultures. Heraldry was an important theme and the source of much formal inspiration – the coat of arms of the Catholic Kings appeared as an emblem on their cultural and architectural creations – and elements of heraldry mixed with the repertory of the international late Gothic (especially Flamboyant) to make particularly evocative creations.

**New Cathedral, Salamanca, begun 1513**
The construction of the New Cathedral of Salamanca marked an important moment in the history of Spanish architecture. The Old Cathedral was no longer large enough and nor was it representative of the city; Juan Gil de Hontañón maintained the plan of the Old Cathedral and used it to create a work that is typical of the late Gothic but is also an important expression of the Hispano-Flemish style which tends to accentuate calligraphic elements.

**Casa de las Conchas, Salamanca, begun 1493**
Over the course of the 15th century the so-called plateresque style spread across Salamanca. This style – *plateresque* is from the Spanish *plata*, 'silver', and means 'silversmith' – blends elements from the late Gothic with classical motifs and those drawn from the natural world. The House of the Shells, with its highly original exterior decoration, ranks among the most successful examples. This trend in Spanish architectural decoration can be compared to the taste for 'naturalistic' decorations in Italy during the same period, such as rocks and artificial grottoes, decorations with incrustations of real shells, pebbles, or other elements of the natural world.

**Juan Guas, San Juan de los Reyes, Toledo,** *c.* **1479–80**
One of the outstanding works of the Isabelline style, the Franciscan church of San Juan de los Reyes commemorates the victory of the Catholic Kings at the battle of Toro and in 1476 was given the function of royal mausoleum. The great cloister that flanks the church is notable for its rich decoration of piers and buttresses, highlighted by tracery outlining and by the curves of the arches of the upper loggia.

**Cathedral, Burgos,** *cimborio,* **Capilla del Condestable, 1492–1532**
The Condestable Chapel is a true nobleman's chapel marked by the presence of a tower-lantern, the so-called *cimborio.* Decorative elements are the protagonists as well as the primary constituents of the logical framework of the entire architectural layout of the interior. These elements include friezes, floral embellishments, escutcheons, and crested helmets. This architectural style leads back to the Mudejar artistic tradition; the *cimborio* is the element that best combines the different linguistic-figurative styles, from geometric patterns to details from local styles, including most of all the Arabic, as in the theme of the crossed arches that form the stellar outline of the vault.

# Cathedral of Seville
## 1401–1519

Of the architectural works in Spain that make use of
elements from France and England, none is of greater
importance than the cathedral of Seville. Work on
the cathedral began in 1401, atop the ruins of the
city's main mosque, of which only the great tower of
the minaret survives, transformed into a bell tower
and known as the Giralda because of its bronze
weathervane (*giralda* in Spanish), a figure of Faith
made during the Renaissance. The construction
lasted more than a century and came to involve
contributions from numerous local and foreign
masters, among them the Netherlandish Ysambert
and the French Carlín, and many foreign artists made
the stained glass, the sculptures, and the architectural
and decorative elements. The cathedral is laid out
with doubled aisles, with chapels set between the
buttresses and a transept that projects so little it is
legible only in elevation. The entire ground plan can
be reduced more or less to a rectangle and is thus
perhaps based on older churches that once existed in
the city. The elevations are configured so as to present
a clear volumetric definition of the complex, which
was built to establish a harmonic decline in the height
of the elements, beginning with the highest elevation
of the roof of the nave. The interior is illuminated by
large windows based on French Rayonnant Gothic,
although with decorative schemes drawn from the
Flamboyant, with effects of continual spatial dilation.
The corners of the flying buttresses on the exterior of
the building contribute to the hierarchical sense of
the volumes, visually joining them one to the next,
while the various vertical elements related to the
support structures form a veritable forest along the
top of the building.

   The cathedral of Seville, a true political and
religious monument, reveals the desire to exceed
all previous constructions both in size and in the
abundance of its decorations. It was the patrons
themselves who had this desire, which had nothing to
do with impressing their fellow citizens. They saw the
cathedral as an opportunity to compare themselves to
the international architectural culture and thus also
to challenge it, much as the Visconti-Sforzas used the
cathedral of Milan.

In the area where the nave and transept intersect, meaning the area occupied by the chancel and the altar, the richly refined design of the ribbing of the vault, the work of Juan Gil de Hontañón, is further complicated and enriched by the fact that each element of the ribbing – already projecting with a lacy design – is further decorated with tracery and openings above keystones at the main intersections.

# Manueline architecture in Portugal
## 15th–16th century

### The expansion of the kingdom

Until well past the middle of the 15th century, Portuguese builders carried on a tradition essentially based on the techniques involved in the use of pointed arches and pointed cross vaults – with the occasional emergence of archaic forms – following the custom of the European late Gothic. A new period began at the end of the 15th century, with the ascent to the Portuguese throne of Manuel I, known as Manuel the Fortunate. His reign (1495–1521) was a period of great expansion and splendour, with the creation of the Portuguese commercial empire, including new settlements in the Far East and the New World. During this period a new style of Portuguese architecture, known as the Manueline, began to take form. This was a composite style that came to have influence on works made in other areas of Europe and even outside Europe, in Mexico and India. A primary aspect of this style, and one that makes it different from the styles developed in other areas of the Iberian peninsula, is the absence of any linguistic or morphological references to Mudejar styles. Between the 15th and 16th century, new decorative schemes and languages were elaborated, all of them increasingly influenced by naturalistic or organic forms or those drawn from the marine world, such as knots and twisted rope. These elements were emblematic of the Portuguese world and were thus both European and oceanic; they also allude to developments in the field of navigation and to the geographic discoveries of the Portuguese (it was under Manuel that Vasco da Gama made his epochal voyage and Cabral reached Brazil), and to the kingdom's economic expansion, of which navigation and discovery were both the cause and effect. The Manueline style is an eclectic style, and as such it has been interpreted as a passing phase in the movement toward the arrival in Portugal of the new Renaissance culture. At first, only a few isolated formal aspects of the Renaissance style were accepted and adopted in Portugal, and its eventual arrival was the result of a process of contamination and combination among innovative factors and traditional systems, the whole process characterized by a fascinating imaginative frenzy seeking to identify new themes and linguistic symbols.

**Hieronymite Monastery**
**Belém, 1502–72**
An emblematic expression of Manueline art, the great monastic complex was erected near Lisbon at the place where the Tagus River enters the ocean, near the spot where Vasco da Gama set sail for India. Its creation was promoted by Manuel and it was first entrusted to Diogo Boytac, then to João de Castilho followed by Diego de Torralba. The last two brought about a decisive change in the Portuguese architectural style of the 16th century with the introduction of Renaissance elements and themes that marked the turn toward the classicist culture by then widespread in the rest of Europe. The ground plan is in itself innovative, but even more important are the specific qualities of the various architectural elements, from the cornice and bas-relief decoration that recall the *platteresque* tradition to the many elements drawn from the organic world, with a wealth of naturalistic and marine motifs. The perfect square of the cloister, blunted at the corners by the insertion of arches arranged at 45-degree angles to attenuate the rigidity of the scheme and disguise the corner column, consists of two porticoed floors covered with highly original decorations.

**t Tower, Belém, 1510–20**
t directly on the water,
tower is composed of
portions, a lower body
a terrace and an upper
y – the true tower – both
hich combine several
itectural styles. Certain
cts of the tower reflect
 typical military
itecture of the period,
as projecting side
ers with openings for
nons and battlements
crenellations. The
orative themes include
nents drawn from the
European styles of the
century, such as the
ll domes and the use of
dic coats of arms, along
themes from the Iberian
ition.

osite bottom
vent of Christ, Tomar,
il, 1510–15
e of the Knights Templar
ved to Portugal after the
secution of their order
he French in 1312. The
vent they established was
dified in the early 16th
ury with the addition of
stern body containing
chapter house and above
e gallery of the knights,
ch leads to the church.
entrance portal, located
he south face, is
ibuted to João de
tilho, who in keeping
his style combined the
ts and rotations of the
Gothic with Renaissance
nents. The windows are
ly decorated, including
typical decorative theme
opes.

# The international late Gothic
## 15th–16th century

### The waning of the Middle Ages

In some areas of Europe, the architectural styles associated with the Middle Ages were not abandoned until the 15th century, while in others they endured well into the opening decades of the 16th century, by which time Renaissance culture had been solidly affirmed in Italy. In Britain, despite a background of profound economic crisis and serious instability, the architectural policies of Edward IV and Richard III were designed to present a refined and magnificent image of their reign. Thus in the middle of the 15th century English architecture increased its traditional interest in decorative components, which had undergone an autonomous development since the dawn of the Gothic, resulting in innovative creations designed to serve specific formal and functional roles within the renewed interest in various types of ritual. In fact, the building programme promoted by the royal members of the house of York was notable both for its splendour and for the systematic introduction of heraldic themes. The principal aspect of the English Late Gothic was the use of the fan vault, which had been used early in English architecture but was now further refined and developed in its use with other elements of the pendant vault, its spatial effects creating a sort of gallery of branches in a forest or stalactites in a cave.

The most interesting architectural theme in Germany, related to the taste for the so-called Rectilinear style, was that of honeycomb vaults in stucco consisting of tracery in sharply angular designs that transformed the surfaces of vault cells into deeply worked elements and that was to become widespread in northern areas and in Bohemia. In this area, a new chapter in the late Gothic architecture of imperial Germany began with Benedikt Ried, the architect who did more than anyone else to bring to light the spatial and decorative potentials implicit in the poetics of the Parlers.

In Italy, the search for identity was beginning to take on a unitary form with an historical field of reference applied in the rethinking of the ideas and the forms of the ancient world. This movement would culminate in the Renaissance with a precise ideological point of view that would in fact eventually look upon the Gothic in a negative light.

**Benedikt Ried, Vladislav Hall, Hradčany, Prague, c. 1483–90**
This was the largest space Europe vaulted in a single span. It is covered by a vau that extends from wall to wall without intermediate supports: a spatial and structural figure complica by the presence of flowing interweaving ribs. The sinuous lines disguise the precise geometric construction of the surfac making it impossible to determine the role, wheth structural or graphic-decorative, that they are called on to play within th architectural context.

# King's College Chapel, Cambridge

## 1446–1515

The great developments that took place in ecclesiastic architecture between the 15th and 16th centuries were matched by events in the field of civil architecture, for which those same years were a period no less spectacular. The interest of the English crown in the cities of Cambridge and Oxford, where the principal university institutions had been established, meant that special attention was given to the construction of the university infrastructures and the related colleges.

A difficult and majestic undertaking, King's College Chapel of Cambridge was begun in 1446 by Reginald Ely to be completed by John Wastell only between 1508 and 1515. It can be considered the essence of the Perpendicular style. Its layout is related to similar technical and formal experiences already applied to religious buildings. The very high walls are filled with broad surfaces of glass mixed with elaborate and airy relief sculptures and heraldic decorations. The verticality of the structure is accentuated by thin columns that lead the eye upward to the vault. The vault, built early in the 16th century, is a masterpiece of vaulting and makes wonderful use of the thoroughly English fan vault. This typology, already introduced in the 1370s in the cloister of Gloucester and until then used only in smaller-size spaces, finds here the culmination of its technical-formal expressivity in a subtly but clearly articulated pattern. And thus, in a setting that has no equal in Europe, the mullions of the windows are applied to the surfaces of the walls. It is a masterpiece for its exquisite formal qualities and is also a marvel from the technical point of view: the fan vault of Cambridge was not constructed in the traditional way with separate ribs and cells, but was made of strips of carved stone, with a considerable weight.

The exterior of King's College Chapel has a simple rectangular shape and is composed of clear volumetric masses. It is an elongated parallelepiped that uses a castle typology that goes beyond the functional necessities of the building. The two angular corner towers, similar to those of English castles, frame an impressive façade taken up, as was then the custom, by an enormous window. The large windows are made possible by the dense series of buttresses that runs along the side of the building.

### Florence

As used by intellectuals during the 15th and 16th centuries, the term *rebirth* – renascence – implies the idea of a long period of decline having passed, a period that began at the close of the ancient world; it also implies awareness of living through a period of extraordinary creativity, the unquestioned leader of which was the city of Florence. The artistic flowering at the beginning of the 15th century seems closely related to the political ideals of that city and found its premise in the desire to revive the classical world and to match its grandeur. Therefore study of the ancient was not a matter of mere erudition but was a moral requirement: antiquity was not taken as a model to imitate but as a stimulus toward emulation of the *virtu* of the ancients, the spur for a plan to be carried out in the historical reality of the present day, in which the artist was aware of being an artificer, an instrument for the open-minded investigation of reality that includes a strictly 'secular' interpretation of all things sacred. The study of Vitruvius and his *De architectura* was behind the creation of several architectural works, and the special connection between the literary world and the artistic world reveals the will to free the arts from their 'mechanical' nature and to elevate them to the realm of the 'liberal' arts. The rebirth of the classical, whether used as a guideline for the creation of works with monumental harmony and proportion or treated as a repertory of details from antiquity to be reapplied today, was the key factor in the path taken by the new architecture. Knowledge of antiquity was not on its own enough to delineate the new course to be taken by architecture; there was also the codification of linear perspective, which was understood as a mathematical tool for the representation of space. It was the means for the direct appropriation of reality and was given normative value by Leon Battista Alberti in his *De pictura* ('On Painting') of 1436, which states that correct perspective construction is the fundamental basis, in both scientific and theoretical terms, for any work of art.

**Filippo Brunelleschi, Pazzi Chapel, Santa Croce, Florence, c. 1430–44**
A luminous and pleasing meditation on the central-plan type of building, the Pazzi Chapel is a cubic room covered by a dome expanded sideways by two barrel-vaulted wings. The geometric values of the space are emphasized by the cornices, the horizontal frieze, and the pilasters in *pietra serena* (sandstone) that stand out against the background of pale plaste[r] and follow the intersectio[n] of the planes and the perspective projections of the regular geometric soli[ds] that compose the space.

**[Gi]uliano da Sangallo, Villa [M]edici, Poggio a Caiano, [af]ter 1480**

[Th]e revival of the classical ideal [of] the relationship between [hu]mans and nature changed [th]e way the learned aristocracy [liv]ed in the country, no longer [en]closed within castle walls but [in] buildings that established a [di]rect relationship with the [sp]ace around them. At Poggio [a] Caiano, Giuliano da [Sa]ngallo created the model [for] the Renaissance villa. In [hi]s systematic use of elements [fr]om ancient architecture as [we]ll as in his arrangement of [th]e building he anticipated [th]e 16th-century [de]velopments of the villa; in [pa]rticular, his adaptation of [th]e façade of a classical [te]mple to a civil building [pr]edates the works of Palladio [by] nearly seventy years.

**Michelozzo, library of the monastery of S Marco, Florence, 1442–44**

In the construction of the Dominican monastery of S Marco at Florence, Michelozzo used elements from contemporary Florentine humanism to give new dignity to the traditional forms of monastic architecture. In the library, which served as the model for many others to come, he achieved a perfect balance through harmonious proportions and a composition based on simple architectural structures. Its simplicity is heightened by the bare plaster walls and ennobled by the classical citations made without ostentation and by the decorative elements.

# Filippo Brunelleschi,
## dome of S Maria del Fiore, Florence
### 1418–38

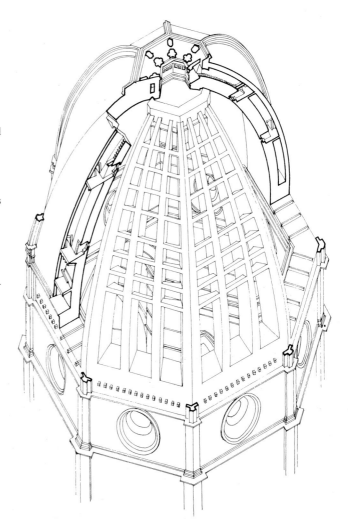

In 1436, Leon Battista Alberti dedicated the Italian-language edition of his *De pictura* to 'Pippo the architect' (Filippo Brunelleschi), and wrote about 'such a large structure, rising above the skies ample to cover with its shadow all the Tuscan people.'

The passage from Alberti is the first enthusiastic reference to the dome of S Maria del Fiore, designed by Brunelleschi to complete the cathedral, work on which had begun more than a century earlier. The dome, which was made to stand on the octagonal drum built in the 14th century by Arnolfo di Cambio, is an outstanding example of Brunelleschi's technical ingenuity. The great population and economic crises of the 14th century had led to the dispersion of skilled workers, and the carpenters necessary to make the wooden framework that would be needed to construct such a large dome were no longer available. However, Brunelleschi's in-depth study of the dome of the Pantheon at Rome, similar in size, suggested to him the possibility of raising the dome in Florence without the use of elaborate centring. Thus, instead of making use of a technique from the medieval tradition, Brunelleschi came up with a solution drawn from his study of antiquity: the dome would be built using a mobile framework. He also used a special technique for the arrangement of the bricks, which were laid in a herringbone pattern to give solidity to the curtain wall without increasing its weight, making it possible to balance the thrust without the need of further supports. The same quest for self-support also explains the use of a double-walled dome, the purpose being to halve the enormous downward thrust of the dome. All the stresses, all the problems of the distribution of weight and thrusts of the enormous structure, were thus resolved within the body of the building exactly as in ancient buildings, first among them the Pantheon. By no means was this a slavish imitation of ancient forms, nor was there homage to Arnolfi in the adoption of Gothic forms in the pointed arches of the ribs.

The dome Brunelleschi invented not only brought to a conclusion a building conceived in another epoch but profoundly altered its spatial values, with pale marble ribs that converge at the top to enclose red-brick sections that seem suspended in the air. The dome does not appear to weigh down on the walls beneath it and becomes an element that coordinates the volumes of the building and the urban space, a symbol of civic pride but also of the new concept of Florence as capital of a far larger territory. The hinge of the entire system of volumes and proportional relationships is the splendid lantern, conceived as an octagonal temple that draws light into the building, gathers and absorbs the force of the ribs, and becomes the vanishing point for all the perspective lines of the building and of the city itself

# Filippo Brunelleschi
## 1377–1446

### Architecture as an intellectual practice

Brunelleschi's interest in architecture dates to some-
time after 1401 (the year in which he lost the competition to design the bronze doors of the Florence baptistery), but he immediately threw himself into lively
experimentation – fed by his passionate research into
the forms and technical solutions adopted by ancient
architecture, studied during a visit to Rome, and by his
profound reflection on the medieval Tuscan tradition
– along with theoretical research into the perfection of
methods of perspective. From his earliest architectural works, Brunelleschi revealed himself as a new
kind of architect, presenting designs for all the definitive elements of a building and radically transforming the complex organization of the medieval worksite. A new concept of architecture was born with
him, architecture conceived as a work of intellectual
creativity, with architectural design understood as an
original and personal expression. His activity is most
clearly expressed in the creation of architectural forms
with harmonic proportions, both in the individual
elements that compose them and in the relationship
established with humans and with the urban space.
The application of ideas from antiquity to contemporary architecture, both to achieve harmony and
proportion and for use in antiquarian-style details, is
well represented by the two Florentine basilicas of S
Lorenzo and Santo Spirito, in which Brunelleschi took
on the Vitruvian subject of the column-architrave
construction. In the same way, in the design of his capitals he cited the most prestigious Roman remains, perhaps meticulously sketched during his visit to Rome,
and he preferred marble decorations, already an aspect
of the Tuscan Romanesque. He also made use of the
central-plan layout, as in the Old Sacristy of S Lorenzo,
the Pazzi Chapel in Santa Croce, and his unfinished
design for S Maria degli Angeli (1434–36).

**S Lorenzo, Florence,
1419–60**
Brunelleschi organized the
clear, unitary space of the
basilica of S Lorenzo
through the application
of geometric laws, in which
a calculated play of
proportions relates all the
architectural elements,
from the rhythmic
succession of the arcades to
the gradation of the light.
The diminishing sequence
of the arcades, accompanied
by the diminishing size of
the spaces, is organized in
accordance with Alberti's
perspective principle of the
'visual pyramid'.

**Santo Spirito,
Florence, 1436**
Compared to S Lorenzo,
Santo Spirito sensibly
accentuates the plastic
values, articulating the
space by means of a far
more stringent relationship
between the colonnades and
the semicircular-layout
chapels, following a
curvilinear progress that
brings the viewer's gaze
back to the central axis of
the nave. The light assists
in this by accentuating the
luminous values of the
area beneath the dome and
emphasizing its central
role in comparison to the
other areas of the church,
although it does so within a
harmonic and unitary space.

*Opposite bottom*
**Ospedale degli Innocenti,
Florence, loggia, 1419–39**
In the loggia of the
Ospedale degli Innocenti
Brunelleschi resolved the
relationship between
building and urban space
with exemplary clarity,
conceived as a connecting
element between the
building and the square.
The ancient tradition of
porticoed squares and the
medieval tradition of loggias
is here reworked in the
sequence of nine airy arches
cut out with geometric
clarity against the surface
of the façade, which leads
to the same number of
perfectly cubic bays, covered
by domed vaults.

# Leon Battista Alberti
## 1406–72

**A humanist passionate about the 'ancient'**

Born and educated in northern Italy, Leon Battista Alberti had an early education radically different from that of Brunelleschi. Only around 1428 did he arrive in Florence, preceded by his fame as a humanist, and he made friends with Brunelleschi, Donatello, and Masaccio. From the beginning, the reading of Vitruvius's treatise on architecture and his personal study of the ruins of ancient Rome stimulated his interest in architecture, an interest that was theoretical well before seeing an actual application. In 1450 Alberti began writing his *De re aedificatoria*, a work dedicated entirely to architecture and modelled on Vitruvius's text, of which it represents a modern interpretation. In this work Alberti affirms in an unequivocal and definitive way the new dignity of architecture, elevated so as to rank among the liberal arts; his work also marks the beginning of theoretical and historical thinking about art. All the buildings he made from then on responded to the reconciliation of the classical principles of art with lessons drawn from the direct study of Roman ruins, which often did not coincide with those principles, and he used this synthesis to give completely innovative forms to Renaissance architecture. The most important idea that Alberti drew from Vitruvius was that of the theory of proportion; the composition of a work of architecture must be based on symmetry and must be measurable thanks to the immediate perception of the existence of a basic unit of measurement – a module – following which the separate parts are formed in close concordance with the overall image.

**Palazzo Rucellai, Florence, façade, 1446–51**
The elaboration in Florence of a new type of noble residence, following the prototype designed by Michelozzo in Palazzo Medici (1444–59), reached pleasing results in Palazzo Rucellai, in which Alberti translated in stone the theoretical principles that he was expounding in his treatise on architecture in those same years. The palace represents a systematic declaration of classicism and geometric rigour in the superimposition of the orders of ancient architecture, in the splendid trabeated openings, and in the citations of *opus reticulatum* in the strip above the socle.

**S Andrea, Mantua, façade, c. 1470**
Understood as an exercise in the adaptation of a classical tympanum to the requirements of a traditional Christian church, the façade of S Andrea combines this element with the typology of the triumphal arch. One sees here the opening toward new concepts of architecture from the vision of antiquity as a source of rules and authority to a concept of it as an inexhaustible trove of ideas to be freely and autonomously adapted.

**Tempietto of Santo Sepolcro in S Pancrazio, Florence, 1467**
A highly original version of a funeral monument, S Pancrazio blends accurate and systematic classical citations – the fluted pilaster strips that frame the marble panels and the architrave with an inscription in capital letters with which Alberti defines the volumes – with the free invention of the inlaid tondos and the motif of the Florentine lily, transformed into a 'Flamboyant' crowning piece inspired by those on Venetian palaces and serving the function of medium between the compact volume of the sacellum and the area of the chapel.

**Tempio Malatestiano, Rimini, *c.* 1450**
In the ingenious reconstruction of the sepulchral church of the Malatesta family, Alberti incorporated the original building within a sumptuous marble classical temple; the façade repeats the fluted columns from the nearby Arch of Augustus, and the series of arcades on the sides is reminiscent of Roman aqueducts. A medallion made by Matteo de' Pasti reveals that the original design called for a large hemispherical dome not unlike that on the Pantheon, which was probably meant to accentuate the building's monumental appearance.

# The Renaissance city

## 1454–92

### The polycentric reality of Italy

The complex and articulated Renaissance concept of history and of the individual, intended to reveal the elements of continuity between classical culture and Christian truth, led to the development of a new ideal of the city. Patristic themes, such as the Augustinian City of God, and classical ideas, such as the Vitruvian city, flowed together in the definition of an orderly and functional city, a reflection of harmonious community life. While nothing could have been farther from reality, the theoretical ideal proved irresistible and rapidly conquered the figurative culture, increasingly eager to see its ideas brought to life in architectural and urban contexts. The peninsula's powerful polycentric reality and the enduring vitality of local traditions made 15th-century Italy such an extremely varied landscape that one must speak of as many 'renaissances' as there were cities in which they were elaborated. Without question, the new models originated in Florence, but every city and every court interpreted them and adapted them to their particular requirements. The planning of the Renaissance city was based on its new role as the capital of a far larger area than in the past and implied perfect congruence between political programmes and their application in reality. The rationalization of urban planning began with Alberti's treatise on architecture and with the ideas of such Renaissance theorists as Filarete and Francesco di Giorgio Martini, who took on the theme of the 'ideal city', meaning a city designed *ex novo* following the principles of rationality, proportion, and symmetry. The city changed face as new building typologies were inserted on medieval streets and between medieval buildings. Most of the new typologies were related to private patronage, such as the noble palace, but at the same time new open spaces were created – streets, squares – for the public display of princely power.

**Bernardo Rossellino, plan for the square and cathedr Pienza, 1459–62**
In reworking the ancient square of Pienza, Rossellin applied criteria based on st perspective rules. The trapezoidal shape, an application of Alberti's 'vis pyramid' to a ground plan, visually confers greater breadth, emphasizing the r of the cathedral's façade as scenographic backdrop, as well as views toward the landscape. The plan for Pienza should not be seen as only an attempt to give scenographic monumental to the symbolic centre of th square but as a true work c urban planning.

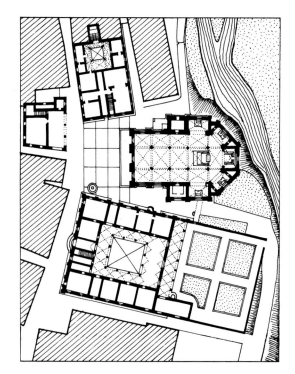

ciano Laurana, Ducal
lace, Urbino, begun 1460
e painted panel known as
e Ideal City, variously
ributed to Laurana and
other artists, including
ancesco di Giorgio Martini,
th its abstract mathematical
dering of a city square,
table classical references,
d perfectly geometric
nple, is a work from Urbino
d recalls Alberti's theories,
t as it recalls the pictorial
rld, so clear and limpid, of
ero della Francesca. It was
ong similar intellectual
siderations that the
hitectural development
the city's ducal palace,
idence of Federico da
ontefeltro, took shape.
urana designed an
pressive building arranged
und a courtyard of honour,
egular, symmetrical nucleus
at in reality expanded to
ery side in an extension of
omalous episodes,
ceptions, and asymmetries,
an original concept unique

on the panorama of 15th-
century architecture.

**Filarete, Sforzinda, 1460–64**
The artists summoned to
Milan by Francesco Sforza
contributed to the arrival of
Renaissance art in Lombardy.
The design of the Ospedale
Maggiore, a complex with a
rectangular layout and central
chapel around which the other
buildings were symmetrically
arranged, is based on ideas
that Filarete expressed in his
treatise on architecture, in
which he took on the theme
of the ideal city – called
Sforzinda in homage to the
duke – designed with a star-
shaped layout and radial
streets. The buildings Filarete
imagined were based on a
modern structure, using the
repetition of simple geometric
forms, with an exuberant
decoration that overcomes the
structural elements and
cancels the play of volumes.

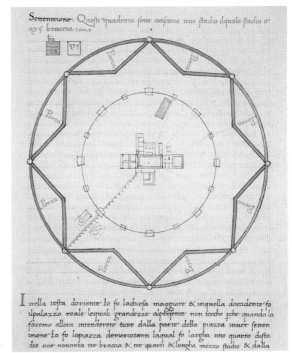

# Donato Bramante
## 1444–1514

## Architecture and experimentation

At the end of the 15th century, two schools of Renaissance thought, one from Florence, the other from Urbino, found themselves in the same spot when the Florentine Leonardo da Vinci and the Urbinate Donato Bramante arrived in Milan to serve that city's ruler, Ludovico Sforza. In Lombardy, Bramante applied his ideas to a series of works that can be seen as a series of experiments based on certain fundamental themes, such as the relationship between figures and space and the central-plan layout. Each of these experiments marks a step along the route toward the creation of a unitary space and the overcoming of the Florentine concept of perspective. In S Satiro, the first instance of the application to a building of the expressive means of perspective illusionism, the concept of centralized space led Bramante to make a sort of equivalence between real space and illusory space, with the use of perspective to invent space that is not there. When, in 1499, France's Louis XII invaded Italy and expelled Ludovico from Milan, Bramante went to Rome; his encounter with Pope Julius II in 1503 marks the beginning of the period of great building projects in that city, which began with the arrangement of the valley between the complex of the Vatican Palaces and the summer residence of Innocent VIII on the hill of the Belvedere. The decision to articulate the space on three levels joined by stairs and ending scenographically with a monumental semicircular square, inspired by the parks and villas of imperial Rome, represented an act of ingenuity, grandiose and innovative and thus a paradigm to be followed by future architects. At the same time Bramante was called on to reconstruct the basilica of St Peter's; the 'infinite designs' he famously made concentrated on the papal idea of a grand, central-plan building dominated by a hemispherical dome. From 1505 until his death, in all the works to which he dedicated himself, Bramante kept St Peter's in mind as his final objective, working to resolve the problem of the relationship of the building to the space around it and also thinking of the design of those urban spaces.

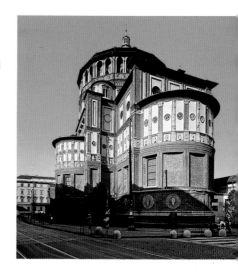

**Tribune of S Maria delle Grazie, Milan, begun 1492**
The final achievement in Milan of Bramante's experimentation with the central plan, the apsidal tribune of S Maria delle Grazie is notable for its ample breadth and monumental conception. On the exterior, the connections between the volumes and their subordinate relationship to the great dome hidden by the lantern are presented with great clarity. Bramante here repeats early Christian and medieval forms from the Po area, from S Lorenzo in Milan to the cathedral of Parma, blended with the study of the 15th-century forms of the Old Sacristy in Florence and the Portinari Chapel in Milan.

**Tempietto of S Pietro in Montorio, Rome, begun 1502**

The close association of ancient models and the desire for monumentality are clearly present in the little temple of S Pietro in Montorio, built for the king of Spain as a commemorative chapel on the site where St Peter was believed to have been crucified. Although the courtyard around it was not restructured into a circular cloister, as originally planned, the little temple has a powerful charge of communicative force and acts as the centre of the space; the rigour with which Bramante applied the recurrent geometric elements of the circle and the cylinder reveals his desire to create an independent type, valid as a model in terms of methods for using the column as a module with which to generate architecture and as a model in his proposed historical synthesis between Christian Renaissance Rome and the Rome of antiquity.

*opposite*

**Cloister of S Maria della Pace, Rome, 1500–4**

Of fundamental importance in Bramante's career, the cloister of S Maria della Pace makes clear reference to the cloisters of Lombardy. At the same time, however, the tight structure of the space and the apparent simplicity of the geometric relationships and those between light and shadow indicate a more direct relationship to ancient models, including the explicit desire to give the work a sense of monumentality despite its small size.

**The late Renaissance in the city of the popes**

The years of the supremacy of Rome were marked by two extraordinary papal art patrons, Julius II (reigned 1503–13) and Leo X (reigned 1513–21). The cultural primacy of Rome and the exceptional quality of the artistic creations during this period were the result of a particular historical moment: papal Rome before its sack in 1527 offered hospitality to the diaspora of artists following the fall of the principal centres on the Italian peninsula, and the works sponsored were part of the general attempt to get past the many local variants of 15th-century art to achieve a unitary language. The creation of an 'Italian' art signified the accomplishment of what could not be done on the political plane, confirming the pre-eminent position of the visual arts in Renaissance culture. Julius II's ambitious goals sought the reconstruction of the greatness of the papal state, with the role of the pope understood as *imperator* ('emperor') in the classical sense. This resulted in the visible signs of the restoration of the city through the activity of the leading talents of the period: Bramante, Michelangelo, Raphael, the Sangallos, and Peruzzi.

Julius's successor, Leo X, began a different policy in the promotion of the arts, one profoundly marked by his personal interests and those of his cultural circle. His favourite artist, and thus the leading artist of his papacy, was Raphael, whose architectural ideas point toward a more attentive affirmation of the ancient world, stimulated by the most recent archaeological discoveries. By way of large-scale archaeological undertakings as well as the creation of buildings – both enterprises carried on with the most modern means – Raphael undertook to reaffirm the historical status of the city as the *caput mundi* of Christianity.

The architecture of Renaissance Rome led to two different artistic epilogues. On the one hand there was the pictorial and naturalistic concept of architecture promoted by Raphael and by antiquarian interests and splendidly interpreted by Pirro Ligorio; on the other was the increasing involvement of Michelangelo in papal undertakings, and he developed his own, increasingly subjective interpretation of classical structures and orders, transforming them into dynamic forms.

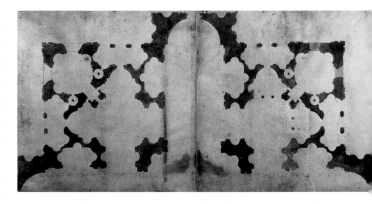

**...mante, plan for the ...lica of St Peter's, 1505–6**
...other building is so closely ...ciated with the centrality ...universality of the ...holic Church. Bramante ...v ideas from ancient ...dings and applied what he ...learned from experiments ...the spatial values of ...lar geometric bodies, and ...nese he added a symbolic ...liturgical programme that ...be taken as proof that ...aissance artists did not use ...central-plan layout simply ...nesthetic preferences but as ...result of theoretical and ...nal reflection.

**...o Ligorio, casino ...ius IV, 1558–62**
...le for Pope Pius IV as a ...to rest in the Vatican ...lens, the casino is based on ...humanistic ideal of the ...ceful relationship between ...nans and nature. The ...cture follows the slope of a ...alternating stairs, grottoes, ...rtyards, and vestibules. The ...berant plastic decoration ...ne views creates ...nterrupted chromatic ...ations along the surfaces.

*...t*

**...onio da Sangallo the ...nger, Palazzo Farnese, ...ibule, begun 1517**
...palace is the outstanding ...tion of the Farnese family ...ome and is also the ...rest expression of the ...ily's power and thus also ...ghly successful ...erstanding of the desire ...ne patron. The maturity ...ntonio da Sangallo is ...aled in the originality ...n which he reworks the ...entine concept of the ...ce as a solid, ...nogeneous block.

**Cosmic symbolism expressed in solid reality**

Theoretical speculations concerning the ideal form of the central-plan church show up throughout all of Italian Renaissance art. Based on the harmonious integration of two simple geometric solids, the sphere and the cube, this structure represented the apex of spatial synthesis and was also the most visible translation in rational forms of the cosmic symbolism of the celestial vault and the worlds revolving around the earth, meaning around mankind, since man was the ideal centre of the universe. Since this cosmic image had been adapted from that of the ancient world, Renaissance architects were able to achieve a symbolic encounter between the classical and the Christian.

Experimentations with the central-plan layout began in the middle of the 15th century with Brunelleschi and continued with the tribune of SS Annunziata by Michelozzo. Alberti theorized about the central plan in his treatise on architecture, and with him it became the ideal model of the temple-church. During the second half of the century, not a single architect failed to take on the theme. Filarete and Francesco di Giorgio Martini did so in their treatises, Giuliano da Sangallo in his many studies of ancient buildings and in his plans, and Leonardo in his discussion of the spherical space. The same was true of painters. The many examples include Perugino's backgrounds in his *Consignment of the Keys to Peter* and *Marriage of the Virgin* or, even better, in the affirmation of the central space by Raphael in the *Marriage of the Virgin* in the Brera. But the works that the 16th century considered the fundamental models for this layout were the structures Bramante made in Rome, based on his knowledge of antiquity. The century began with a true exaltation of the central plan, from the many versions in Lombardy to the more classicist interpretations in central Italy, outstanding examples of which are S Biagio at Montepulciano and S Maria della Consolazione at Todi.

**Antonio da Sangallo the Elder, S Biagio, Montepulciano, 1518–45**
In this work Antonio da Sangallo translated the rationalism of 15th-centu[..] military architecture with[..] forms from Bramante. Th[..] close connection to St Pe[..] is clear in the introductio[..] of the bell towers that fla[..] the dome and in the Gree[..] cross layout.

**S Maria della Consolazio[..] Todi, begun 1504**
Harmonious and cohere[..] monumentality, clarity of volumetric layout, and th[..] perfect angle of the dome hidden behind the four-coned design of S Maria della Consolazione is a symbolic programme evoking Pentecost. The continuity of the modulations that wrap the outer body was a novelty; it reveals the gre[..] breadth of the internal space, which is centralize[..] but also expanded outwa[..] by the tribunes.

*Opposite*
**Giuliano da Sangallo, S Maria delle Carceri, Prato, begun 1485**
Giuliano da Sangallo's involvement in the most innovative architecture is measurable in the contribution he offered i[..] the extremely elegant and harmonious building wit[..] its Greek-cross layout bas[..] on the Constantinian mo[..] The moulding of the imposts, the dome, and t[..] vaults, indebted to Albert[..] prototypes, are modelled with the intention to transcribe notions drawn from late antiquity in modern terms.

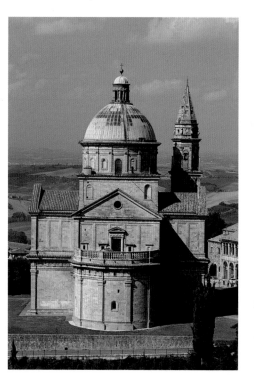

# Raphael and his school
## *c.* 1514–50

## The Roman villa

During the years of the pontificate of Leo X, with the death of Bramante (1513) and the departure of Michelangelo for Florence (1514), Raphael became the most sensitive interpreter of the Roman artistic climate. His association with such figures as Baldassar Castiglione and Cardinal Bibbiena increased his interest in antiquity, which was further stimulated by recent archaeological discoveries. The wall decorations found on Roman buildings and the excavation of the ruins of Nero's *Domus Aurea* ('Golden House') inspired his use of decorative motifs applied in stucco or fresco and conceived in a close relationship with architecture. His career began with the 15th-century Tuscan tradition: the forms of S Eligio degli Orefici (*c.* 1513) reflect Bramante, but the extreme clarity and simplicity of the Greek-cross layout and the refinement of the details and the diffuse and airy luminosity of the interior are purely creations of Raphael. The Chigi Chapel in S Maria del Popolo (*c.* 1515) marked a further step in the new and stringent harmony between architectural structure and decoration applied in a way that did not diminish the clarity and force of the layout. From there to the Villa Madama and the Vatican Loggias, Raphael, in his architecture as in his paintings, abandoned airy clarity to become monumental and magniloquent.

*Above*
**Baldassare Peruzzi, Villa Chigi, known as La Farnesina, Rome, 1509–11**
Peruzzi here combined the 15th-century typology of the urban palace with an innovation that expressed the new relationship with nature: the garden façade, which

creates a relationship between the interior and exterior by way of the ground-floor loggia. The architectural language blends the sharp linearism of Sienese extraction with the new taste for scenographic effects and with the skilful integration of architecture and painted decoration.

*Opposite*
**Raphael, Villa Madama, Rome, begun 1517**
Not unaware of the results obtained by Peruzzi in La Farnesina, Raphael set abou[t] a similar revival of the Rom[an] villa, but with greater philological strictness, in th[e] grandiose undertaking of t[he] Villa Madama, in which he ably achieves the harmonic integration between architecture and classical-s[tyle] decoration, between buildi[ng] and nature.

**Jacopo Vignola, Villa Giuli[a] Rome, 1550–55**
Around the middle of the 16th century, Vignola beca[me] the leading interpreter of t[he] cultural climate in Rome a[nd] the policies of the Farnese family. Rejecting both the antidogmatism of Michelangelo and the archaeological classicism o[f] Pirro Ligorio, he set in motion an operation of linguistic synthesis that wa[s] related to Bramante and, even more, to Alberti.

# Toward mannerism

## *c.* 1520–1600

### The dispersal of Raphael's students

Raphael died in 1520, and in 1527 the city of Rome was sacked. Violence, famine, and plague cast the decade in bleak tones. The circle of artists that had grown up in the shadow of the great master, from Giulio Romano to Baldassare Peruzzi, departed Rome, spreading the 'modern manner' they had learned from him throughout Italy, where it was variously interpreted and, in certain senses, contradicted. As a variant trend within the sphere of Renaissance culture, mannerism confronted the dialectic between subject and object and the relationship between individual and reality. The outstanding element of manneristic architecture was the ongoing tension between classicism and anticlassicism, rationalism and irrationalism, tradition and nonconformity, naturalism and exaggerated intellectualism. Deformation of the rules of proportion, striking individualism, tendencies to emotional or highly sophisticated artistic forms, artificial settings: all these were to have great fortune in the Netherlandish and Germanic areas during the Reformation, where Vitruvian academicism was contested by a spasmodic search for variety, for something different, as though trying to mix the antiquarian repertory with stimuli from the final expressions of the Gothic.

**Giulio Romano, Palazzo del Te, Mantua, 1527–34**
In Palazzo del Te – fascinating and significant theatre of the new cultural atmosphere and site of the amusements and amorous delights of Federico Gonzaga – Giulio Romano created a scenographic organism that delights with its astonishing dialectical composition between irrationality and nature, rationality and man as the artificer. The continuous allusions to an instable structure and the variety of interpretations presented by the images announce freedom from classical rules, which, however, were still possessed of such vitality that they could be continuously reinvented.

**Baldassare Peruzzi, Palazzo Massimo alle Colonne, Rome, 1532–36**
In the façade, which curves slightly to follow the route of the street, Peruzzi demonstrated a special sensitivity for the relationship between architecture and external space. The liberty with which he drew on models from ancient and modern traditions is revealed in the successful blending of the severe classical-style entry portico with themes from Bramante. His consummate scenographic skill shows in the skilled use of oblique light, which identifies the six Doric columns emerging from the portico, reveals the smooth rustication of the stones, and makes the window pediments stand out.

**Giorgio Vasari, Palazzo degl Uffizi, Florence, begun 1560**
Within the sphere of the urban-reconstruction projec that redesigned the monumental face of Florenc in the 16th century, Vasari made this complex urban structure, designed to create a scenographic connection between Palazzo Vecchio and Palazzo Pitti. The two elegan parallel wings of the Uffizi form a long, narrow square, one end of which ends with linking wing with a luminou Serlian motif facing the Arn and the other with a scenographic view that has Piazza della Signoria as its backdrop.

# Michelangelo Buonarroti
## 1475–1564

### From neo-Platonism to moral tension

Growing up at the court of Lorenzo de' Medici, Michelangelo was profoundly affected by neo-Platonic culture, and from the very beginning of his career he presented himself as the heir and continuator of 15th-century Tuscan tradition. He fled Florence on the death of Lorenzo, returning with the restoration of the Medici in 1515. The intense activity of his Florentine years (1515–34) is of particular importance since it involved him in the dialectic between the 'classicist' and 'manneristic' schools. These years were of importance to Michelangelo's career since they saw his first completed, and also highly important, creations in the field of architecture, such as the Laurentian Library and the New Sacristy of S Lorenzo (begun 1520). These are important works not so much because they represent a prototype or new model but because they make clear the deliberate attempt to alter the classical order. They mark the beginning of a new concept of space, no longer taken as a closed, defined entity, but rendered dynamic and plastic so as to emotionally involve the spectator. When he returned to Rome in 1534, Michelangelo became deeply involved in the difficult climate of the 'Catholic Reformation'. He joined the circle of intellectuals around Vittoria Colonna, sharing the humanistic basis of their hopes, later disappointed, to keep open a dialogue between Protestants and Catholics. For Michelangelo, the Counter-Reformation marked the beginning of a period of profound anxiety that he transformed into an increasingly dramatic and solitary approach to his art. These are the years of his *Last Judgment*, but also those in which his architectural activity became predominant, part of the reworking of the city promoted by Pope Paul III (reigned 1534–49) in his desire to reaffirm Rome as the political and moral capital of Christianity. Michelangelo was responsible for some of the most symbolic works in the city, including the reworking of the Piazza del Campidoglio (begun 1537) and St Peter's (begun 1546).

**Piazza del Campidoglio, Rome, begun 1537**
The monumental rearrangement of the area of the Campidoglio, symbolic site and headquarters since antiquity of the civil administration, marked a radical change in 16th-century urban planning. In the design by Michelangelo the dynamic expansion of the space, created by distancing the two side palaces at the point where the square is connected to the city – by way of a majestic stairway ramp and the scenographic framing of the Palazzo Senatorio – is emphasized by the star-shaped design of the pavement, enclosed within an oval at the centre of which is located, the ideal centre of the space, the equestrian monument to Marcus Aurelius.

**...me of St Peter's,**
**...tican, begun 1546**
...chelangelo brought the
...ilding of St Peter's back to
...amante's original idea of the
...ntral plan, concentrating his
...ention on the dome,
...derstood as the concluding
...ment of the building and
... its coordinator. The high
...um serves the function of
...nnecting to the volumes
...derneath and its windows
...ovide the light that defines
... enormous space. The
...me rises from the drum,
...force concentrated in
... lantern. The clear
...unelleschian geometries –
...ich Michelangelo was well
...are of and reworked in the
...option of the double-walled
...me – are transformed in a
...stic and dynamic tension
...t involves all the
...npositional elements.

**Anteroom of the Laurentian**
**Library, Florence, begun 1523**
In the anteroom of the
Laurentian Library,
Michelangelo undermined the
conventional principles of
architecture of his time,
inverting the relationship
between supporting elements
and those supported. The
diminution of the functional
elements and the enlargement
of the decorative elements
creates a dynamic tension in
the small space that finds
release in the triple staircase;
the curving steps seem to flow
downward like a waterfall,
only barely held in place by
the side balustrades, which in
fact open outward at the
second section to permit the
release of two side ramps
without balusters.

# Jacopo Vignola

## Palazzo Farnese, Caprarola

### 1550–59

The most up-to-date artworks in late-16th-century Rome were part of the cultural climate created by the Farnese family. In that climate, both the new antimannerist orientation of Counter-Reformation art and the final virtuosic and erudite manifestations of mannerism coexisted.

Rulers of both Parma and Piacenza, the powerful noble family left its indelible feudal mark on the territory of Latium when it entrusted the organization of its vast holdings first to Antonio da Sangallo and then to Vignola. The presence of this power is still perfectly legible today at Caprarola, not so much in the imposing shape of the aristocratic residence but in the way the building dominates the surrounding medieval town. In fact, the ancient town is divided in two by a straight street axis that aligns the houses along a 'telescopic perspective view', at the end of which a series of scenic terraces and ramps leads to where the villa-castle stands. The position and pentagonal layout of the building date to the plans made in the first half of the 16th century by Antonio da Sangallo and Baldassare Peruzzi. But it was under Vignola and the patron Alessandro Farnese (Pope Paul III) that the medieval town was reconstructed and the building was conceived as the summer residence of the Farnese court. The Caprarola palace is a manifest symbol of this aristocracy, both in the relationship of the building to the external spaces – the town at its feet, behind the refined symmetries of the Italian garden with its fountains and pavilions – and in the complicated heraldic, mythological, and celebrative world of the building's pictorial decorations, created under the direction of the Zuccari brothers, which exalts the glories of the noble family.

Vignola's meditation on Bramante's model of the courtyard appears here in the helicoidal stairway, the fluid route of which terminates in the ingenious solution of an airy space covered by a dome. Inventive originality, technical ability, and virtuosic talent indicate the maturity of the architect's vocabulary as well as the sources of his creativity and their perfect assimilation. As for the palace itself, the existing pentagonal foundations of a fortress inspired Vignola to the invention of an austere and solemn exterior, marked off by angular rustications, pilasters, and clear horizon lines. The interior is arranged around the perfect centrality of a circular courtyard enlivened by festive grotesque decoration.

# Renaissance architecture
## in the Veneto region and Venice
## 16th century

**The Bramante–Raphael culture in luministic light**

The artists most responsible for the spread of Roman mannerism to the Veneto region of northern Italy included Giovanni Maria Falconetto, Michele Sanmicheli, Jacopo Sansovino, and Sebastiano Serlio; all were from Rome, and all had trained in the architectural climate dominated by the figure of Raphael. In 1524, Falconetto was in Padua, working in the service of Alvise Cornaro – a learned patrician scholar of Vitruvius and Alberti – and he designed a loggia and the so-called Odeo, which blend elements of the Bramante–Raphael tradition with the pictorial style of the Veneto. In Verona, Sanmicheli divided his activity between works of military architecture and city planning, with refined and original formal experiments expressed in a series of aristocratic palaces in which Bramante's proportional relationships are altered, bringing to the surface every individual element to show off its particular chromatic and luminous quality.

The architecture of Venice was dominated by the artistic personalities of Serlio and Sansovino. The first, a student of Peruzzi, was famous less for his works than for his famous treatise on architecture, the first such work to use images more than text to communicate and inform. The vast range of architectural typologies it illustrates, from the single element to the urban scene, furnished an inexhaustible repertory based on the concepts of research, experimentation, and variation that are at the base of mannerist culture. Sansovino began his fortunate Venetian activity with a series of works destined to have an indelible effect on the layout of the city: the urban arrangement of the St Mark's area, in which he revealed all the maturity of his personal interpretation of Roman classicism and Veneto pictorialness, and the Palazzo Corner (begun 1537), which represents one of the most successful interpretations of the inheritance of Bramante, Raphael, and Peruzzi, onto which he grafted suggestions from Michelangelo for a more vigorous plasticism and the accentuation of the chiaroscural values.

**Mauro Codussi, S Zaccaria, Venice, 1483**
It took an ingenious architect, full of knowledge of Tuscan architecture, and primarily that of Alberti, to impose on Venice, still ensconced in its late Gothic tradition, the models of 15th-century Renaissance architecture. In S Zaccaria, Codussi designed a linear façade crowned at its uppermost level by a semicircular tympanum with curvilinear connections on its sides. This scheme represents a solution to the problem presented by Alberti in the Tempio Malatestiano, which it interprets here in a monumental style.

**ichele Sanmicheli, Porta lio, Verona, 1533–40**

the gates he made for the w city walls of Verona, nmicheli brought to bear tions from his two areas expertise, blending the nctional aspects of military chitecture he had learned as litary engineer to the netian Republic with the ore stately language of chitecture he applied in e creation of city palaces, hieving results of dignified onumentality in a ssicism highlighted by a ofound play of light and najestic sense of form.

**Jacopo Sansovino, Marcian Library, Venice, begun 1537**

The space of Venice, that fluid medium full of luminous vibrations, reflections, and transparencies that eliminate the borders between buildings and the surrounding atmosphere, found a sublime interpretation in Sansovino. In the Marcian Library, official headquarters of Venetian culture, he used a plastic system of supports of Roman and Bramante origin with decorative motifs drawn from antiquity, all of it resolved in the pictorial values of the contrast between the supporting elements in full light and the openings in shadow. The monumental, symbolic aspects of this building are related to its admirable creativity but also to its relation to the buildings that compose the surrounding space, which is the political and religious centre of the city, thus monumental and symbolic in itself.

# Andrea Palladio
## 1508–80

### Ancient architecture used as model

The pseudonym Palladio, assumed by Andrea di Pietro della Gondola around 1540, clearly indicates the 'classicist' vocation that was the distinctive feature of his work from the beginning. His association with such humanists as Trissino, the Barbaro family, and the Cornaros provided him with an education full of universalistic ideals, the point of departure being knowledge of Vitruvius. Palladio went beyond the rhetoric of the academic approach to the antique, justifying the forms of his architecture, which were often anticlassical, on the basis of their validity. His *Four Books of Architecture* (1570) present his beliefs in Vitruvius and in the use of ancient architecture as a reference point. Because of his many works there – Palazzo della Ragione, Loggia del Capitanato (1571), Palazzo Chiericati (begun 1550), and the theatre for the Accademia Olimpica – Palladio gave Vicenza most of its monumental face, and the villas he created had an equal impact on the Veneto landscape, but his works in Venice have a special kind of importance. Palladio was a 'civil' architect by calling, and in Venice he found himself facing religious buildings for the first time. In the fourth book of his treatise he presents his thoroughly Renaissance preference for the central plan as the demonstration of the 'unity' and the 'Infinite Essence' of God, and S Giorgio Maggiore (1566) and Il Redentore are meditations on the combinations of a longitudinal nave and a central layout, dominated by a dome that has its own impact on the urban landscape.

**Teatro Olimpico, Vicenza, begun 1580**
In the last example of his architectural style, the theatre designed for the Accademia Olimpica, the first resident theatre company in Italy, Palladio reflected on ancient theatre, on perspective space, and on scenographic and illusionistic architecture. His ingenious creation of a proscenium with a fixed classical scenic background created a model that became standard in later theatrical architecture.

**Villa Barbaro, Maser, *c.* 1555**
The Palladian villas scattered across the Venetian mainland present a type of architecture that serves two functions, and does so perfectly: they are both farms and country houses. Thus they blend functionality with aesthetic appeal. The fact that the villas are functioning farms is clearly indicated by the lower-roofed porticoes that flank the central body, which are in fact utility wings for storage and services.

*Opposite top*
**Plan for the Palazzo della Ragione, Vicenza, 1549**
In his plan for rebuilding Vicenza's medieval town hall, the Palazzo della Ragione, also known as the Basilica, Palladio delineated a new idea of space in which the outline and rhythm of the whole are augmented by the plasticity of the framework and its chiaroscural values. The centrepiece of the city's aristocratic image, the palace is surrounded by a stately classical-style loggia. The monumental sense of its form fully exploits the irregular shape of the square.

*Opposite*
**Il Redentore, Venice, begun 1576**
Palladio achieved a complex and organic organism through the coordination of distinct spatial cells that correspond to symbolic and functional needs and by creating a new scenic background for Venice's architecture. The façade is dominated by the dome – as if this were a church with a central plan – and by the perspectively flattened pronaos.

# Andrea Palladio

## Villa La Rotonda, Vicenza

### Begun 1567

The theme of the villa, so dear to humanistic culture, was of central importance to much of Palladio's fecund career, and he demonstrated great freedom of creativity in this field even while making precise references to the classical world and the Vitruvian model.

The famous Almerico-Capri villa, known as La Rotonda, is considered emblematic of Palladian architecture. The name Rotonda expresses its essence: in fact, it is designed to be admired from all four sides, and its unusual symmetrical layout, dominated by a central dome with four fronts, each with a pronaos, is justified by its physical location at the top of a hill. It is thus a suburban palace, and Palladio himself called it a 'belvedere', so the site generated the architectural form. But this is not all: the Rotonda is not a country house-farm but was conceived as a temple dedicated to humanistic leisure pursuits, an expression of the cultural interests and ambitions of the patron, the canon Paolo Almerico. The building is an expression of archaeological discoveries, primarily ancient pagan sanctuaries. Palladio drew on such sources for its central plan and also made use of symbolic elements from sacred architecture, in particular the pronaos and the dome. Applied here to a secular building, they exalt the rank of those who inhabit it. The central hall beneath the dome is an expression of the Renaissance ideal of man as the centre of the universe and measure of all things, while the orientation of the villa, with its four doors facing the four cardinal directions, is probably related to the kind of cosmic symbolism that permeated the learned society of the time. In that regard, it is worth recalling that the original design called for an opening at the very top of the dome for rain water, which was then collected through a hole in a sort of impluvium located at the centre of the floor. The internal decoration in stuccoes and frescoes follows such a unitary design that it seems probable that Palladio himself took part in its planning.

No autograph design of the villa has survived, only a woodcut published in 1570 in the *Four Books of Architecture*. The fact that it appears in the chapter on palaces indicates that Palladio did not think of it as a vacation home but as an urban palace in every sense. The plan makes clear the building's simple layout as a cubic prism with a circular central hall and four halls that lead like the arms of a Greek cross to the hexastyle Ionic pronaos at the top of high stairs. Study of the elevation reveals that certain details of the building differ from what was originally planned, most of all in the area of the dome, which was designed to be round but was instead flattened and covered by a stepped roof (perhaps the work of Scamozzi).

MARIVS CAPRA
GABRIELIS F.

# The Catholic Counter-Reformation
## Begun 1545

### Architecture and Jesuits

The instrument with which the church of Rome enacted the overall revision and redefinition of its doctrinal principles was the Council of Trent, which assembled several times between 1545 and 1563, convoked to meet the crisis caused by the Protestant Reformation. The church was profoundly aware of the extraordinary communicative power of the arts as a means of religious propaganda, and among the council's many decisions were measures to control artistic expression. Beginning around 1560, Rome became the theatre of a large-scale effort to rebuild, restore, and embellish the church's artistic patrimony, all of it designed to return the church to the early ideals of simplicity. The city of Rome thus became the site where all the models of Counter-Reformation culture were established, designed to make the sites and leading figures of the Catholic faith recognizable and intelligible.

At the same time, the creation of new religious orders, understood as the militias of the new reformed church, conferred vital energy on the structure of the church. The Company of Jesus, founded in 1540 by Ignatius of Loyola and approved by Pope Paul III, became a formidable instrument in the spread of the faith, so much so that the Jesuits underwent rapid expansion, eventually coming to play key roles in the ecclesiastic hierarchy. The Jesuit order, despite its powerful structure, was responsible for the creation of completely new architectural works and figurative models, works that in many ways foretold baroque art. In designing the Church of the Gesù in Rome, Vignola created a typology that was to be replicated many times in the foundations of Jesuit missions throughout the world. It fixed the concept of the sacred structure as a space for preaching in which the distinction was clearly made between the clergy and the faithful, between liturgical acts and worship.

**Church of the Jesuit convent, Tepotzotlán (Mexico), 1760–62**
In the Americas, the missionary spirit of the members of the Society of Jesus was translated in architectural forms, and far from denying the existence of popular sentiments and traditions, these tended to give in to local customs in art and architecture. With its baroque exuberance, the façade of Tepotzotlán demonstrates how the approach to art taken by the Jesuits had changed over the centuries and also how the order had learned that success comes only through versatility, adaptability, and the compromise of forms.

**...opo Vignola, Church of ...Gesù, Rome, 1568–71**

...model of the post-
...dentine church, the
...urch of the Gesù gives
...ysical shape to the new
...ctional demands and new
...votional orientations. The
...tely rhythms of the great
...rel-vaulted nave grow in a
...scendo as one approaches
... vast and luminous dome,
...fully preceded by the
...atrical expedient of a less
...ghtly illuminated bay.
...nola synthesizes ideas
...erti used in S Andrea,
...as drawn from ancient
...hitecture, along with the
...naissance reflection on the
...minant and centralizing
...wer of the dome, no longer
...derstood in the humanist
...se as a symbol of cosmic
...der, but as a symbol of the
...ocess of the soul's ascent
...ward God.

**...drés Garcia de Quiñones,
...urtyard of the Collegio
...al de la Compañía de
...us, Salamanca, c. 1760**

...thplace of Ignatius of
...yola, Spain is rich in Jesuit
...ablishments that testify to
... order's extraordinary
...wth. The complex of La
...recía, which includes the
...urch, seminary, and
...nvent, displays the changes
...t took place in the art of
... Jesuits over the course of
... century and half of its
...nstruction. The church,
...signed by Juan de Gómez
... Mora and begun in 1617,
...esents a conceptual scheme
...sed on that of the Gesù in
...me, but the monumental
...ister of the seminary unites
...Roman' monumentality
...h a thoroughly Spanish
...atment of the decorated
...rfaces.

# The Italian garden
## and the mannerist garden
### 15th–16th century

**From harmonious geometries to natural scenography**
The 'Italian' garden took form and reached maturity in
the pleasure villas of the 15th and 16th centuries. This
was a garden constructed in accordance with harmonious geometries, and over the course of the 16th century it expanded to include increasingly open and natural spaces and was embellished by waterworks displays,
fountains, sculpture, and grottoes. The evolution of these
enthralling spaces involved the refashioning of natural
material in a style that gave primacy to artifice. The idea
of the garden came into being from the contrast between
the serene harmonies of the bucolic world and the dis-
cordances of urban life. The garden was originally presented as a simple layout attached to a villa, with pergo-
las, hedges, and fountains distributed in accordance with
specific formal orientations. Any compositional-topi-
ary ingredients as well as those sculptural and architectural were applied in a parsimonious fashion and were
arranged with utter simplicity. It was not long, however, before a break with this occurred. Alberti himself
had introduced the notion of inserting 'tricks' in the
purity of a natural composition, and Bernardo Rucellai
shaped plant material into astonishing shapes using topiary art. This evolution, inseparable from the shattering
of the notion of *imitatio naturae*, moved along at an
equal pace with developments in ideas concerning the
scenographic and the spectacular. No longer the setting
for learned humanist conversations, the garden became
a theatrical backdrop for magnificent celebrations.

**Park of the Villa Orsini,
Bomarzo, the Leaning
House, begun 1550**
In the 'sacred wood' of
Bomarzo, Vicino Orsini gave
free rein to his literary
passions, arranging a
fantastic collection of rock
sculptures alternating with
mythological figures and
small classical temples. In this
pagan woodland, the
irrational and apparently
random nature of a park
animated by 'wonders' is set
in opposition to the
geometric layouts of
contemporary 'Italian'

gardens. Orsini's restless
mind presents a style that
contrasts sharply with the
usual serene meditation on
the difference between the
natural and the artificial.

**Bernardo Buontalenti,
grotto in the Boboli
Gardens, Florence, 1583–88**
In the midst of the Boboli
Gardens – one of the
prototypes of the 'Italian'
garden that enjoyed such
great fortune in Europe –
Buontalenti inserts a large,
bizarre grotto of typically
mannerist taste. A Serlian-

motif façade adorned with
relief statues leads to three
internal rooms, covered in
false rocky concretions,
stalactites, shells, stuccowor
and frescoes, with a beautif
fountain by Giambologna. I
placing the unfinished *Slave*
by Michelangelo (today
replaced by copies), carved
for the tomb of Julius II, in
the four corners of the spac
Buontalenti makes clear his
intention to completely
overturn the meaning of th
works, which are used here
mere decorations against th
artificial setting of the grott

opo Vignola, Villa
nte, Bagnaia, Water
ain, begun 1566
th the complex of the
la Lante estate – with its
o small twin palaces and
ian garden with
ntains, waterworks,
races, and adjacent large
k – Vignola created a
del for the design of
ian and French gardens
he end of the 16th
tury and into the next
tury. The Water Chain,
ort of waterfall in which
ter swirls down along
ne meanders, some
ved in the form of crab
ws, the coat of arms of

Cardinal Gambara,
represents the ingenuity of
Vignola in combining water
and stone to form a kind of
ceremonial path.

**Pirro Ligorio, Villa
d'Este, Tivoli, Avenue
of One Hundred
Fountains, begun 1550**
The thoroughly mannerist
delight in contrasting
architecture and nature is
clear in the picturesque
inventions of fountains, fish
ponds, a water organ (played
by the action of water),
ecstatic plastic decorations,
and even more in the
scenographic terraces that

regulate the relationship
between the architecture and
the surrounding natural
landscape. Hadrian's nearby
villa stimulated Ligorio's
antiquarian erudition, which
he translated in a new,
unconventional classicism,
full of happy inventions,
such as the adoption of the
oval layout arranged on its
shorter axis or the use of the
dynamic qualities of water,
which are made to perform
the leading role.

# International mannerism
## in France
## 16th century

### Royal residences

For France, the end of the Hundred Years' War coincided with a period of architectural modernization. First to be updated were two typologies still tied to medieval forms, the urban habitation – the *hôtel* – and the castle, which lost most of its grimmer features to evolve into a comfortable residence, a *château*. Italian models were applied to these two basic structures by the Italian artists and architects summoned to France by aristocratic families as well as by the French court. Many of these artists settled permanently in the Loire valley. Blois, Chenonceaux, and the monumental Chambord are among the outstanding creations of this international laboratory of the 'modern manner', which united architecture, decoration, and garden design. King Francis I saw the importation of Italian culture as an opportunity to deck-out his reign's celebratory needs in suitably classical forms, and after 1528 he moved the court in a decidedly modern direction. Thus Renaissance forms as well as those of early mannerism were applied in the full maturity of their ideological and formal expressions. The restructuring of the château of Fontainebleau became the centre for the elaboration and spread of modern taste, and the arrival of Leonardo da Vinci, soon followed by Rosso Fiorentino, Vignola, Primaticcio, and Serlio – the last-named being an active spreader of the infinite possibilities of Renaissance architecture – inevitably led to a mannerist imprint that was highly suitable to the eclectic and naturalistic taste of the French world. The concentration of these artists at Fontainebleau created an exemplary situation for the process of the acceptance, adaptation, reaction, and elaboration of new forms of mannerist models. Casually adopting mannerist elements, such as the giant order on rigid symmetrical layouts, and matching Bramatesque porticoes to steeply pitched roofs, French architecture arrived at a synthesis that led to a thoroughly national, while also somewhat unorthodox, interpretation of the classical style.

**Thomas Bohier, Château of Chenonceaux, 1515–23**
The unusual and strikingly picturesque site of Chenonceaux, set directly over the Cher River, and the survival of certain castle elements, such as the corner towers and the pitched roofs, gives the château the enchanted appearance of a Gothic castle. Even so, it has open courtyards, windows without defensive elements, and an Italian-style staircase.

**Château of Anet, 1545–55**
French architecture acquired
full independence with
Philibert de L'Orme,
although his apprenticeship
took place in Italy. Although
fragmentary, the château of
Anet presents an
architectural concept alien
to both the compromises of
Serlio and the decorative
casualness of Lescot, as in
the Louvre, a work
contemporary to this one.
The chapel achieves a sense
of great balance in the highly
elegant portico with its
twinned columns, in the
complex shape of the domes,
inspired by the Tepidarium
of the Baths of Diocletian,
and in the lantern, which
repeats Lombard forms.

**Château of Blois,
rs, 1515–24**
hough Château Blois
sents typically Italian
nents – porticoes,
umns, niches – it is still
a hybrid construction with
Gothic holdovers. The
famous open polygonal
staircase turret, a stylistically
unorthodox element that
recurs in many 16th-century
French châteaux, was
probably inspired by
sketches that Leonardo da
Vinci had made thirty years
earlier in Milan.

**Château of Chambord,
begun 1519**
Begun as a hunting lodge for
Francis I, this soon became
the most striking example
of the mixture of French
tradition and Italianate
architecture. Its pronounced
geometry reflects the
influence of Renaissance
ideas, and its powerful
cylindrical towers, an
inheritance from ancient
medieval castles, are
mellowed by elegant Italian-
style decoration. The
fairytale nature of the roof,
with its forest of towers,
chimneys, and crowning
pieces, is a reinterpretation
of Gothic spires in
Renaissance terms.

# The Château of Fontainebleau
## Begun 1528

In 1528 Francis I asked the architect Gilles Le Breton to begin transforming the hunting lodge of Fontainebleau into his ceremonial residence. Le Breton was responsible for the construction of the Porte Dorée and the long gallery that connects the old medieval tower with the new buildings arranged at the end of the Cour du Cheval Blanc, a gallery that makes reference to Bramante's design for the Belvedere, which had already been adopted a year earlier in England at Hampton Court. Although Le Breton's style makes use of a predictable mixture of traditional forms and 'modern' elements, his use of what might be called mannerist elements seems coincidental. Only with the arrival on the scene of Rosso Fiorentino and Primaticcio was there a radical change in the criteria informing the French decorative arts. From then on, the ongoing worksite at Fontainebleau, in which architecture, decoration, and furnishings were closely integrated, became one of the most creative and interesting centres of international mannerism. The first phase of the 'Fontainebleau school' was really a period of Italian history transplanted to French soil: Rosso and Primaticcio, creators of the superb decoration of the Galerie François I, enriched and renewed the formal repertory of the Roman school to create an entirely new harmony, with the perfect fusion of figural and decorative elements. When, in 1541, Sebastiano Serlio, author of a famous treatise on art, was nominated *architecte ordinaire*, it marked a break with the rhythmic regularity and symmetry of the plans for the palace until then. The most purely classical citation in the château, the Porte Dorée, presents superimposed loggias inserted amid wide pilasters, with a clear sign of mannerism in the continuous sequence of the windows. In the 1560s, the Aile de la Belle Cheminée was completed, making use of a language that was by then totally French.

e 'modern manner' ched one of its heights he creations of Rosso rentino and Primaticcio, n the Galerie François I, ere they employed ccoes and painting to ul every sense of the hitectural structure. Their k marks the first time t stucco framing had been en so much projection, so ch in fact that it seems to ach itself from the wall, s assuming so much portance that it becomes e of the major elements in decoration. There is no ubt that the precedents for s were all Italian – from Sala di Constantino in Vatican to the Sala degli cchi in Palazzo del Te at ntua, both works by

Giulio Romano – and it may well be related to the decorations of the enormous fireplaces, which beginning in 1515 constituted a recurrent element in the new French châteaux. The result achieved at Fontainebleau is admirable: the elegantly slender nude figures, the spiralling forms of the frames, and the strapwork represent the height of the inventiveness and the complexity of Italian mannerist art, inserted directly in the figurative culture of France.

# Spain

## 16th century

**International mannerism with the *plateresque* and ideas from Italy**

Spain was still primarily Gothic during the late 15th century, and the introduction of the ideas and forms of the Italian Renaissance was hindered by the late adoption of the *plateresque* style. Renaissance motifs were interpreted in purely decorative terms – much as Islamic and Gothic ornamentations were treated as purely formal elements – and were applied to structures that were still medieval, such as the façade of the Hospital de Santa Cruz at Toledo, begun by Enrique Egas, or the façade of the university of Salamanca. Only the patrons from the court of Charles V and Philip II, who were in close contact with Italy because of Spain's possession of the Kingdom of Naples, were aware of the new classical architecture.

Some buildings from the early 16th century seem to reflect an awareness of Italian Renaissance art on the part of the architects, such as Lorenzo Vázquez, Enrique Egas, Diego de Siloe, Alonso Covarrubias, and Rodrigo Gil de Hontañón. For example, motifs from Bramante are perhaps recognizable in the courtyard of the royal hospice of Santiago de Compostela (1501). It was the Escorial, the monastery-palace-mausoleum built by Philip II, that marked the turn toward a stately classicism more in keeping with the strictness of the Spanish religious reform. The reign of Philip II marked the beginning of a period of decline, or at least retreat, a closing-in caused by Spain's declining political and military fortunes, all of which, paradoxically, set the scene for the beginning of the Golden Age of Iberian culture.

**Pedro Machuca, Alhambra Granada, circular courtyard colonnade of Charles V, 1526–68**
The adoption of a style related to the precepts of Roman classicism, expressed by uniform geometric decoration, is clear in the unfinished palace built for Charles V in the courtyard of the Alhambra. Machuca had trained in Italy on the works of Bramante and Raphael, and his design called for an architectural creation of great breadth in the two-floored portico with columns that make use of the orthodox Doric and Ionic orders, perhaps inspired by Bramante's courtyard in Palazzo Massimo. The classicism of the courtyard of Charles V had a spectacular effect on the traditional Spanish architecture of the period.

**azar, Toledo, begun 1537**

nso Covarrubias
gned the overall
plex of the Alcazar, but
façade was the work of
rigo Gil de Hontañón.
esents Italian forms –
ied with purely
orative intent on a large-
block that is only barely
culated – used to achieve
ckward-looking theme.
style of the courtyard
ers from that of the
de and presents notable
mblances with the
rtyard of the Palazzo
a Cancelleria in Rome.
ay be the work of
ncisco de Villalpando,
succeeded Covarrubias
was a promoter of a
re severely classical style.

**Lorenzo Vázquez, Palacio Medinaceli, Cogolludo, 1492–95**
The first example of incontestably Italian taste in Spain, Palacio Medinaceli, built by Lorenzo Vázquez between 1492 and 1495 for Duke Medinaceli, is directly related to 15th-century Italian prototypes in its compact form and in the rustication of its stonework, suggesting the possibility that Vázquez got his training in Italy.

# Juan B. de Toledo, Juan de Herrera

## El Escorial

## 1559–84

The image of Philip II of Spain is tied to the architectural undertaking of the Escorial, the colossal palace built in grey granite outside Madrid. Conceived as a sanctuary, monastery, residence, and fortress, the complex was begun by Juan Bautista de Toledo and was completed by his assistant Juan de Herrera.

Herrera's work shows clear signs of the influence of both Vignola and Serlio, but in fact the king himself played an important role during the design stage of the building, and the many changes he made to the original design reflect his Italian-leaning taste as well as his strict religious devotion. The layout of the complex reflects the importance of the church, even though the church itself was not designed until later; it is surrounded by a series of courtyards enclosed in an impressive block that is 204 metres by 161. It echoes the colossal late-imperial (AD 295–305) constructions of Diocletian's palace at Split in the reconstruction given by Palladio and the gridwork structures designed by Filarete for Milan's Ospedale Maggiore. The layout of the Escorial is also meant to mirror the shape of the gridiron on which St Laurence was martyred, for the building was made to celebrate the Spanish victory over the French at St Quentin, on 10 August 1557, the feast day of St Laurence. In the Escorial the unitary sense of the overall concept and the decoration reduced to the minimum follow the precepts of the Italian school but do so in accordance with the rigour of Spanish religious reform. The construction of the Escorial began a new period in Spanish architecture, one that was marked by the rejection of the late Gothic and the *plateresque* in favour of a 'Roman' architecture in keeping with the rules of Vitruvius. It also signalled the beginning of absolutism on Iberian soil. Philip II's decision to group the royal palace together with the tombs of the Habsburgs and the convent is a demonstration of the identification of temporal power with the spiritual. It is significant that the building stands between the end of the Renaissance and the onset of Spain's Golden Age.

The church is clearly based on Italian examples, most especially St Peter's. The columns and the vestibule are related to the design handed down in an engraving by Sangallo. There are also suggestions from Galeazzo Alessi in the exterior front, similar to that of S Maria di Carignano in Genoa, and from Pellegrino Tibaldi in the unusual solution of the external gallery reserved for the clergy, as already done at S Fedele in Milan.

### Renaissance models in hybrid forms

Spreading northward across the Alps, Italian Renaissance ideas were not always welcomed straight away. The tradition of Gothic architecture hindered their adoption in German-language areas. Far from being embraced, Italian models were used only in the fashioning of unusual hybrids. Changes taking place in the private residences of the aristocracy – becoming more comfortable, less military – made possible the first adoption of new forms, for the work was entrusted to Italian artists or at least to artists trained in Italy. Giulio Romano was among the 'Italian corps' that worked on the home of Ludwig of Bavaria (Landshut, 1536–40), and the Fugger Chapel at Augsburg (1509–18), despite the presence of a Gothic vault, shows explicit references to ideas from Venetian architecture and was used as a model of the classical in the apprenticeship of German artists.

The achievement of a national Renaissance style in Germany took place in the second half of the 16th century and had little to do with Italian models, revealing instead the more direct influence of Flemish architecture. That same period also saw the publication of the first German treatises on architecture, from that of Hans Blum on the five orders (1550) to the fantasies of Wendel Dietterlin (1593), whose book included 203 engravings that were far from classical rigour and that served as a source for strapwork.

**Schloss Ambras, Innsbruck, Spanischer Saal, end 16th century**
In keeping with the style of the international manner, the Spanischer Saal in the palace of Ambras has the appearance of a late Renaissance aristocratic residence.

**Residenz, Munich, Antiquarium, 1569–71**
With its solid Catholic tradition, Munich was the site of many works reflecting the spirit of the Roman Catholic Counter-Reformation. The large barrel vault, decorated with grotesques, is an exquisitely classical architectural typology.

*Opposite*
**Schloss Heidelberg, 1556–**
Elector Otto Henry did his best to introduce to Germany the study and culture of humanism as well as antique forms of architecture, probably based on Serlio's treatise. Over the course of the 16th century a 'modern' wing was added to the medieval palace of Heidelberg. Known as the *Ottheinrichsbau*, it has three floors with large double windows decorated with a variety of pediment types.

**Between Gothic and Renaissance**

The Low Countries came in contact with the mature, magisterial style of the Renaissance by way of Raphael, who made cartoons for the Vatican tapestries manufactured at Brussels under the supervision of Tommaso Vincidor. Thus the court and upper classes began to seek inspiration from Italian models. When Margaret of Austria set about work on the reconstruction of the palace of Mechelen, she turned, around 1530, to Vincidor himself, and although he proved unable to reproduce a fully Roman style, he did create one of the most classical buildings of that time in that setting. In the same way, the great wealth of the Flemish cities, which had become leading centres of the European economy, permitted many public patrons to turn to the forms of Roman classicism. It must be pointed out

that the imitation of those forms was not always accompanied by an understanding of the principles behind them. Hence the ease with which some of the most superficial aspects of classical works – and only those parts – were assimilated, resulting in a superabundance of decoration. Northern European architects made an easy transition from an exuberant late Gothic to an equally flamboyant pseudoclassicalism without an intermediate, truly classical, stage. Some of the blame for this goes to the rapid diffusion of Serlio's treatise on architecture, which reduced Renaissance architectural forms to simple diagrams, making them easy to understand and thus simple to replicate, even by artisans. Little time was involved in the sudden appearance of the monstrous strapwork that came to characterize Flemish and German mannerism.

**Cornelis Floris, Stadhuis, Antwerp, 1561–65**
The rise in economic activity and the conseque[n]t wealth favoured importan[t] public works. Antwerp's town hall is typical of the buildings of early Flemis[h] classicism. The façade, similar to Gothic precedents, is based on classical orders probably drawn from Serlio. The u[se] of a limited number of decorative elements and t[he] adoption of rusticated sto[ne] gives the building a sense [of] simple harmony.

**De Zalm, Mechelen, 1530–34**
'The Salmon', one of the earliest houses in northern Europe to use Renaissance decoration, was inspired by the palace designed by Vincidor. Its design also includes local elements, most of all the steep sloping roof, a characteristic of the northern area.

**Lieven de Key, Vleeshal, Haarlem, 1602–3**
Near the end of the 16th century, Dutch architecture took off on an independent route in which town halls, municipal weigh-houses, and general markets were often given a classical style. In its elegant chromatic divisions, which seem related to earlier brick buildings of the Baltic region, and in the particular shape of its stepped gables, Haarlem's Butcher's Hall almost seems to prefigure baroque forms.

# England

## 16th century

### The Tudor dynasty

The fertile season of the English late Gothic ended around the beginning of the 16th century. By way of the leading expressions of Italian and French late Renaissance architecture, aspects of classicism had begun filtering into England, used in combination with the English tradition or as an alternative to it. England remained substantially extraneous to Renaissance trends, and 'Italianate' works were banned during Henry VIII's struggle with Rome in the 1530s. The works of reference in architecture became those of the Flemish or French Renaissance, the motifs of which were grafted onto the Perpendicular Gothic, leading to the Elizabethan and later Jacobean styles. The political stability under the Tudors made it possible to put more emphasis on the comfort of buildings than on their defensive nature. The policies of the dynasty and the sequestering of church goods favoured the growth of a new aristocracy that dedicated its resources to new and quite splendid residences. In architectural terms, this period saw the beginning of a national style not extraneous to the intellectual postulates of classical architecture, although it drew its inspiration from second-hand sources, such as those of De Vries or Dietterlin, despite the popularity of the Italian Serlio. Italian influence was first felt in the adoption, often the blind imitation, of decorative forms, often many years before any understanding of the inner structural principles.

**Robert Smythson, Longleat House, 1568**
One of the finest examples of Elizabethan architecture in Britain is Longleat House in Wiltshire, built by Sir John Thynne and designed by Robert Smythson, the leading exponent of English architecture during Elizabeth's reign. What is surprising here is the measured sobriety of the masses, the luminosity, and the refined use of details, such as the proportions between empty and full areas, which radically distance it from the feudal fortified home. The typically English use of bow windows becomes the expedient for counterbalancing with vertical scansions the horizontal rhythm of the trabeations, resulting in surfaces with a reticulate articulation.

**Palace of Hampton Court, 1539–40**
The palace of Hampton Court was originally the residence of the splendid court of Cardinal Thomas Wolsey, but with his downfall it passed into the hands of King Henry VIII who decided on a series of enlargements. The buildings general layout is based on series of internal courtyard surrounded on all four sides by bodies, based on the analogous traditional English scheme that presides over the colleges of Oxford and Cambridge.

**Sutton Place, Surrey, begun c. 1523**

Built by Sir Richard Weston, connoisseur of French architecture, Sutton Place is laid out around a central courtyard and has a large gate-house. Despite its substantially traditional layout, it has two absolutely innovative elements: the large main entrance at the centre of the front, which meets the need for symmetry, and the long 'gallery', a typology derived from Hampton Court and later used at Fontainebleau.

# The triumph of the baroque
## 17th–18th century

### Royal and papal splendours

Toward the close of the 16th century a style came into being that expressed a new concept of nature and the world, of the relationships among people, and of the function of art itself in the realms of both secular and religious power and in the private realm dedicated to the enjoyment of beauty.

This style was the baroque, and the capital of baroque architecture was papal Rome, with Gian Lorenzo Bernini and Francesco Borromini its leading exponents. Baroque architecture is the expression of a civilization of awe-inspiring, splendid, magniloquent images exploited by the powerful to disguise a far different reality, dramatic and full of strife: it is a tool for persuasion and propaganda. In its effort to triumph over the Protestant heresy, the Roman church used artistic representations to spread the ideas of the Catholic religion; in the same way, Europe's great monarchs called upon artists to use it to exalt their power and prestige. This architectural language used 'rhetorical figures' – the alteration of classical proportions, the effects of gigantism, the expansion of spaces, and the dynamism of forms – in the constant search for surprising and paradoxical effects. At the same

time, the interaction between the arts was put to the service of a display that preferred theatrical and illusionistic effects because of their ability to turn the public into both spectator and participant at once.

The Galilean vision of the universe had given the arts a yearning for the infinite, expressed and at the same time manipulated in the marvellous optical tricks and effects of the period, in the exploration of the uncertain borders between truth and verisimilitude. Artists mimicked the creative processes of nature and transposed natural reality into something artificial, even using light, water, and fire in their artistic creations. The palace and its façade, conceived as a theatrical backdrop, assumed a fundamental value, while the royal palaces in the countryside, from Versailles to Caserta, became emblematic expressions of 17th-century absolutism. The church reproposed the basilican scheme, often using the ellipse as the geometric model of reference in increasingly audacious combination effects that made the dome the visual centre of urban space. At the same time the cities of Europe were being redefined with the creation of new, more easily travelled street systems, usually with right-angled or radial arrangements and vast squares.

**Baldassare Longhena, S Maria della Salute, Venice, 1631–87**
This is one of the best examples of the dome understood as the outstanding visual centre of an urban space. Longhena arranged the external volume of the church following a new scenographic model.

**Francesco Borromini, Oratory of S Philip Neri, Rome, façade, 1637–50**
A meditation between interior and exterior and protagonist of the urban scene, the baroque façade is the crux of the overall design. Borromini designed simple and austere forms thanks to the fine texture of the brickwork, which changes according to the light and emphasizes the play between concavities and convexities.

**an Lorenzo Bernini,
ldacchino of the basilica
St Peter's, Vatican, 1624**

working out the
angement of the area of the
in altar, Bernini blended
idea of the original
angement with the idea of
king the 12-columned
*gula* that had stood at the
d of the nave in the Old
silica built under
nstantine. The size of the
dacchino is related to the
ce beneath the dome by
chelangelo, which thus
kes this dynamic and
nsparent structure the
nbolic centre of the
lding. The chromatic play
black and gold against the
ite of the pilasters and the
ion of the architecture with
sculpture are emblematic
how the boundaries among
various arts are eliminated
this work, in which the
sire for the spectacular
nds natural, fantastic, and
hitectural forms.

*posite*

**useppe Gricci, porcelain
oinet from the royal palace
Portici (Capodimonte,
ples), 1757–59**

er the course of the 18th
atury the aristocracy no
ger felt obliged to justify
power through celebratory
rks and sought instead to
lt the private aspects of its
gant and sophisticated life.
e interiors of palaces were
corated in a free and
aginative way making use
an abundant repertory. The
mmetries of the rococo
nd complicity in Chinese
corations, which experienced
eir apogee in Europe during
e 18th century; entire
hinese' settings were created
d decked out with porcelain
local manufacture.

### A capital of European importance

The end of the 16th century found Rome capital of the only Italian state of European importance. Awareness of its role led to an ambitious plan of urban restructuring, promoted by Pope Sixtus V and entrusted to Domenico Fontana. This plan gave the city the visual points of reference for which the modern city is famous.

The Jubilee Year 1600 celebrated *Roma triumphans*; the spirit of the Catholic Counter-Reformation provided the reason for enlarging the city following a new concept of urban space based on the flowing monumental and scenographic continuity of the streets and squares, with churches, palaces, fountains, and monuments located at points of convergence and turned into elements of such formal impact that they would inspire an emotional and also edifying response. They were meant as expressions of universal values. The city's most important monument in terms of concentrated symbolic value was still St Peter's; but the palaces of the aristocratic families and their façades assumed a primary value within the urban fabric. An outstanding example is Palazzo Montecitorio, commissioned from Bernini by the Pamphili family (1650–55); through the mediation of Johann Fischer von Erlach it became a model that spread during the late baroque to Austria and central European architecture. The same applies to Rome's churches. The façade of S Susanna, designed by Carlo Maderno (1595–1603), was arranged to serve the role of urban centrepiece. The 'trident' shape of the streets leading out of Piazza del Popolo represents the prototype for a basic motif of the new baroque city, a series of streets converging on a square or other open space in the urban fabric, its importance further emphasized by an obelisk or other notable work. Carlo Rainaldi's construction (1662) of two twin churches is an example of buildings made to serve a function within the urban layout, forming part of a monumental entrance to the city. The open and more trafficked spaces of baroque Rome were enlivened with fountains that made a connection between the architectural setting and nature. Bernini created absolutely innovative models in this regard. He translated the love of water – its movement, transparencies, and sounds, but most of all its symbolism in the relationship between water and life – into some of the most exciting inventions of baroque art.

**Pietro da Cortona, S Maria della Pace, 1656–57**
In this case the façade is an autonomous organism related to the urban space. The church has a projecting, semioval portico exalted by the exedra, while the movement suggested by the convexity of the upper walls is transmitted in a dynamic way to the wings, which are arranged to form a small, fan-shaped square. S Maria della Pace represents the modalities with which 17th-century architects moulded and modified urban spaces through the skilled use of volume and light.

**zza Navona**
rimary example of the
oque concept of urban
ce, Piazza Navona resulted
n Pope Innocent X's
ire to give dignity and
anicity to the area
upied by his family's
ace. Bernini's Four Rivers
untain (1648–51), located
he centre of the piazza's
ptical shape, represents an
raordinary example of the
thesis between nature and
fice as well as the
vation of ephemeral,
ive displays to a
numental level. The

square was given
compositional balance
through the location of
another two fountains at
the far ends of the space;
Borromini gave further
support to this in the concave
and convex façade of S
Agnese in Agone (1653–57),
and the church's high drum
and pair of bell towers act
against the horizontal
extension of the square.

**Carlo Maderno, Palazzo
Barberini, begun 1625**
Designed by Maderno
during the years of the
pontificate of Urban VIII,
the palace was completed by
Bernini in collaboration with
Borromini. The H-shaped
layout declares its inspiration
from the typology of the

villa. The wings that project
from the central body,
pierced by the luminous
crescendo of the portico
and the loggia, manifest the
desire to connect the
building to its urban space,
while the garden behind it is
understood as the means to
relate the palace to nature.

# Gian Lorenzo Bernini
## 1598–1680

### Architect to the popes

Pope Urban VIII and Bernini: their names often appear paired because of the exceptional duration of their relationship and the importance of the undertakings they shared. What they did represents the best that baroque Rome can offer in terms of the translation into stone of the desire to celebrate the Catholic Church and the triumph of the pope's family, the Barberini. In his first official commission – the baldacchino in St Peter's – Bernini did not disappoint, turning the space of the church into a highly theatrical site and performing an act of artistic syncretism that astonishes and also emotionally involves the spectator. In this work Bernini already reveals his exceptional artistic qualities: the facility in creation, his technical mastery of a wide variety of materials, his tireless imagination and deep knowledge of historical sources, geometry, and perspective.

Urban VIII died in 1644, the pontifical throne was taken by Innocent X, and the direction of the church's cultural policies changed. Bernini found himself distanced from papal worksites, with preference given to the moral tension in the works by his rival, Borromini. This temporary exclusion from the major papal commissions did not mean a pause in his activity, and indeed these years were marked by some of his most important works: the Cornaro Chapel and the Palazzo Montecitorio, which was based on the model of Palazzo Farnese but overcame its conception as a solid geometric block with new effects of side dilation that became characteristic of Bernini's future architecture. The return of papal patronage under Pope Alexander VIII marked the return of Bernini to St Peter's, where he worked on the splendid arrangement of the square. He also worked on three churches during these years, taking on the theme of the central-plan layout and displaying his maturity as an architect: S Tommaso di Villanova at Castelgandolfo (1658–61), the church of the Assunta at Ariccia, and S Andrea al Quirinale in Rome. As an indication of his fame, by then international, in 1661 he was summoned by France's Louis XIV to participate in the competition for the enlargement of the Louvre.

The grand project he submitted was never made. Perhaps Roman lavishness did not meet with approval from the cautious financial administration under Colbert or with the practical needs of a building that was supposed to be celebratory, yes, but also functional.

**Cornaro Chapel, S Maria della Vittoria, Rome, 1647–52**

In the Cornaro Chapel, Bernini made full use of hi experiments in the use of light in artistic creations a also affirmed, with striking sureness, the unification of architecture, sculpture, and painting. The spectacular sculptural group of *The Ecstasy of St Theresa* canno be extracted from the chap – of which it is the centrepiece – for the chape tests the processes of the Borromini-style elastic deformation of a framewor The supernatural event tha takes place on the altar is witnessed by members of t Cornaro family, located in what seem to be theatre bo on the sides of the chapel.

**Scala Regia, Vatican Palace Vatican, 1663–66**

In the Scala Regia Bernini resolved the problem of an irregular space, dividing th stairs into two flights and accentuating the detachme with the arrangement of th light sources: effects of perspective diminution disguise the actual size of t space, the walls narrow and the columns get smaller as one climbs the stairs. The effect is ingenious, most of in the arrangement of the columns, which gives the space a sense of grandeur a solemnity, although there a clear references to the false perspective colonnade in Palazzo Spada by Borromir

**...urch of the Assunta, ...ccia, 1662–64**

...e square and church in
...ccia present one of
...oque Europe's most
...tanding examples of an
...anistic-architectural
...mplex. The church has a
...ular plan preceded by a
...le-arched portico; that
...out is echoed by an
...erior cylindrical wall that
...ps around it and ends in
...ir of porticoed wings.
...nini here makes a clear
...rence to the Pantheon
...l the project, from around
...0, to restore it and rework
... surrounding square.

**...ndrea al Quirinale, ...ne, façade, 1658–61**

...the façade of S Andrea
...Quirinale Bernini repeats
...tro da Cortona's façade
...S Maria della Pace and
...ablishes the interplay
...ween the building and
...urban setting through
...use of an exedra and a
...nvex pronaos that invite
...passer-by to enter. These
...npositional elements are
...eated inside in the
...tinction between the
...ptic room and the area
...he main altar, in which
...rnini achieved astonishing
...cts of expansion thanks
...the skilled use of colour
...l light.

# The basilica and square of St Peter's

## Vatican

## 1504–1657

The history of the construction of St Peter's revolves around the debate between a central-plan layout and a basilican layout and the attempt to achieve a synthesis of the two. Early in the 16th century, when Pope Julius II decided to rebuild the basilica, the central plan devised by Bramante was the prevailing model, and his Greek cross was destined to become the model for all later plans. In 1514, by which time Bramante's cross had been partially constructed, his successor, Raphael, applied a longitudinal layout to it, and this was continued after Raphael's death (1520) by Antonio da Sangallo the Younger. The forced application of the longitudinal extension to the central-plan layout reveals how even at this date the question of the appearance of St Peter's was still strongly animated by conservative tendencies tied to models of the Latin cross. This quarrel was apparently resolved in 1547 when Michelangelo reaffirmed the validity of the central plan, holding that to move away from the original plan by Bramante was the same as moving away from the 'truth'. His design returned to the Greek cross, which he amplified in terms of its spatial unity and plastic values by making all its parts dynamically converge and conclude in the vertical tension of the dome – made after Michelangelo's death by Giacomo della Porta – thus bringing the 16th-century debate to a conclusion. Over the course of the 17th century a new and final phase began in the history of the basilica, with Domenico Fontana and Carlo Maderno working on the church and Bernini reworking the square in front of it. Maderno's efforts to tone down the difference between the Michelangeloesque concept of a 'monument' and the Counter-Reformation idea of the church as a place of worship open to the faithful and to the city led him to devise the horizontal profile of the façade as the best means to call attention to the dome. The giant colonnade that was adopted strives to achieve an orderly rhythm and to graduate the plasticism, but it does not succeed in giving life back to a structure that was meant to be developed in depth but that is now translated across a single flat plane.

# Francesco Borromini
## 1599–1667

### An artisan genius

The serene and brilliant Bernini grew up in Rome during the fervid years at the opening of the century and developed a keen awareness of the city's points of reference; the introverted and intransigent Borromini arrived in Rome around 1619, following artisan training as a mason's apprentice in the workshop of the cathedral of Milan, and had a difficult relationship with culture and tradition. Borromini worked in the shadow of Maderno and Bernini – in fierce competition with the latter – while at the same time being fascinated by the works of Michelangelo, who was considered an insuperable model for his spiritual tension even more than for his formal creativity. Borromini's full affirmation as an architect took place outside the pontifical sphere. In 1634 the Trinitarian order commissioned him to make the complex of S Carlo alle Quattro Fontane, and all the revolutionary power of his work exploded, forcing a new world of forms onto architecture. Borromini designed his architecture by working out geometric units or modules, the elasticity and complexity of which were derived from the concept of the building as an organic whole, characterized by the play of compression and dilation of the forces redirected to form spatial unities. He made much use of the humblest materials, ennobling them and rendering them precious through his technical skills and the morality of his concept of his craft: white plaster smoothed and smoothed again a thousand times, stucco worked with wondrous skill, finely woven brickwork. His novelties were disconcerting to Rome but awakened great interest all the same: the Falconieri and Spada palaces, the Oratory of S Philip Neri, the churches of S Agnese in Agone, S Ivo alla Sapienza, and S Andrea delle Fratte, the Collegio di Propaganda Fide, and the restoration of St John Lateran present examples of how Borromini made free and extraordinary use of the traditional repertory, from late antiquity to Michelangelo, from notions from the Oriental world to those from the natural world, melding all the components of his artistic training in the search for new architectural forms and doing so with single-minded, total dedication.

**Stairway in Palazzo Barberini, Rome, 1632**
In Palazzo Barberini Borromini introduced various innovations intended to solve problems left by Maderno and Bernini. He was responsible for the axial alignment of the various parts of the building and most of all the connection of the great vestibule with the stairs and the fusion of the vestibule itself with the adjacent oval hall.

**Perspective colonnade, Palazzo Spada, Rome, 1635**
Borromini applied the principle of perspective diminution in the singular invention of the gallery in Palazzo Spada, in which the decreasing height of the columns and decreasing width of the lacunar barrel vaults make the actual length of 8.6 metres look like it extends to 37. It seems quite likely that Borromini got the idea for this perspective illusion from Bramante's choir in S Maria presso S Satiro in Milan.

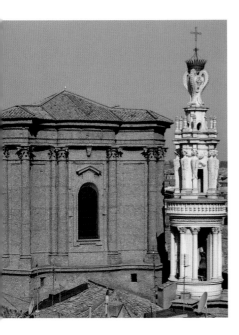

**S Andrea delle Fratte, Rome, dome cladding and bell tower, 1653–65**
The unfinished dome of S Andrea delle Fratte relates to the Borrominian idea of internal forces that tend to expand and external forces that compress and contract. The dome transforms the traditional typology of the dome, static and closed, into a dynamic and radiant organism. Borromini's ingenious and revolutionary solutions were a bold transgression of the ordinary and tranquillizing forms of Roman domes. The bell tower creates an urban focal point that changes appearance according to the position of the spectator.

**S Carlo alle Quattro Fontane, Rome, cloister, begun 1634**
This minuscule cloister's compact spatial unity, full of internal tension, is the fruit of an extreme liberty in the treatment of the concept of architectural 'order'. The traditional elements, such as the Serlian motif, the column-pilaster strip relationship, and the quadrangular layout of the Renaissance courtyard are applied following a syntax that reworks the concept of space understood as uninterrupted and dynamic continuity. Ninety-degree angles are replaced by convex curves, giving an unusual rhythm to the sequence.

# Francesco Borromini

## S Ivo alla Sapienza, Rome

### 1642–62

Borromini was named architect of the Sapienza in 1632 to complete the works begun by Pirro Ligorio and Giacomo della Porta, but he was not able to work independently on the church until 1642. The masonry areas were more or less finished by 1650, but the church was not completed until 1662.

As in S Carlo alle Quattro Fontane, Borromini departed from the concept of the central plan, taking on instead a geometric scheme – unusual in the Italian architectural tradition and probably inspired by the architecture of late antiquity – based on the superimposition of two equilateral triangles to form a hexagonal star-shaped space with a contoured profile. The presence of concave terminations in place of the points of one triangle and convex terminations in the place of the other, forms a complex and dynamic play of elements that alternate and contrast with one another across the space of the church. The space is made homogeneous and unitary thanks to the use of large pilaster strips that call attention to the dramatic outline, which is repeated in the powerful cornice that supports the dome, although the latter covers the body of the church without any transitional structural elements. Here the stellar motif is again repeated and driven vertiginously upward to conclude in the geometric purity of the circle on which the narrow lantern stands.

On the exterior, Borromini concentrated on the dome, masked by a high drum that contrasts its convexity with the concavity of the hemicycle that terminates the 16th-century porticoed courtyard, used as the façade of the church and involved in its dynamic conception. S Ivo is considered Borromini's masterpiece, the place where his style reached its highest point with the total and fully aware application of all the formal and technical means at his disposal. The church's symbolic structure – based on the shape of a bee, heraldic symbol of the Barberini family – is imposed on the surrounding space in a vertical play of dynamic expansion and contraction that seems to have more than a few affinities with Gothic structures. In point of fact, S Ivo demonstrates how Borromini drew inspiration more from the medieval tradition of northern Europe than from the tradition of contemporary Rome.

In S Ivo Borromini created a unified architectural system based on the contoured outline of the base of the dome, which mirrors the shape of the ground plan, which seems to transform itself into a perfect circle while the decorative motifs give the structure a continuous upward surge. The prominent areas in this extraordinary invention are flooded with light, which exalts the white of the plaster and stucco decorations. The uppermost area of the dome is dressed in a stepped motif marked off by buttresses that support the vertical rush of the lantern and the dramatic spiral of the crown. Along the spiral and upward along the metallic frame the energies of the building reach freedom in the sky, in an effect that must have been disconcerting on the panorama of a city full of big, round domes.

# Turin

## Late 16th–17th century

### A new capital between Paris and Rome

The growth of Turin over the course of the 17th century represents a more or less unique case on the panorama of Italian baroque architecture, and the scale of Turin's building programme, the quality of the creations, and the prestige of the architects involved laid the basis for that city's 18th-century importance. The Savoy monarchy promoted the enlargement and restructuring of the city in the hope of giving Turin the appearance of a modern capital and also making it the site for the encounter and synthesis of the two major areas of cultural developments in the late 17th century, Paris and Rome.

Ascanio Vitozzi designed Piazza Castello and directed the opening of Via Nuova (1584), designed to give regularity to the urban space by means of a series of uniform façades, following a principle developed in France. In 1620, Carlo di Castellamonte made a new plan for urban expansion that followed the chessboard pattern of the ancient centre, and he designed the broad rectangular space of Piazza Reale; his son Amedeo repeated his rectangular layout in a further enlargement in 1673. The rationality of the designs and the primary role given to the square indicate ties to models from northern Europe, a relationship further bolstered by the desire of the Savoy rulers to draw inspiration from the political model of the French monarchy. The chief characteristic of the buildings made in Turin during this period are regularity, symmetry, and decorum, with an emphasis on symbolic and celebrative values. Outstanding within this context are the domes designed by Guarino Guarini – in which the scientist-architect evokes the infinity of space, arranging geometric elements in multiple combinations on a rational base – and two undertakings designed to increase the city's prestige: the triumphant gate of Porta Po (1676; destroyed) and Guarini's Palazzo Carignano. Many aspects of Guarini's work reveal knowledge of Borromini, even if he tends to break the spatial unity, composing his structures from the aggregation of independent spatial cells (*ars combinatoria*), which he uses to create surprising effects, reaching almost disorientation. A maniacal sense of geometry, continuous symbolic allusions, references to architectural types not usually found in the Italian tradition – from the Arabic-Moresque to the Gothic – are blended with mathematical precision, structural rigour, and the solid competence of an engineer.

**Guarino Guarini, Palazzo Carignano, 1679–85**
Guarini altered the traditional palace layout with the insertion of a large elliptical space along the longitudinal axis. The façade is enlivened by the flowing alternation of concave and convex volumes and present a splendid dressing in brick worked with outstanding artisan mastery in every decorative detail.

**Guarino Guarini, Cathedral, Chapel of the Holy Shroud, 1657–90**

Conceived by Amedeo di Castellamonte to hold the most sacred relic of Christianity, the chapel was designed by Guarini, who changed the original circular layout into a triangular scheme on which the drum of the dome is supported by means of pendentives. Beyond this begins the wonderful fantasy of a cone-spire whose dynamic forms swirl around a central axis, spiralling upward.

**Guarino Guarini, dome of S Lorenzo, 1678–79**

S Lorenzo has a complex octagonal scheme, notable for the series of columns – audaciously isolated – that supports a dome composed of ribs that interweave to form a star and end in a smaller dome. Guarini replaced the spherical dome with a transparent dome, based on the style of the Gothic and pierced by light and evocative of an infinite space.

## The creation of a national style

In baroque France, urban planning and architecture became the metaphor for absolute power. Place des Vosges, Les Invalides, the completion of the Louvre, and the enlargement of the royal palace of Versailles are only a few of the more spectacular creations of the period. Over the span of a few decades, the coherence of these works, the financial and organizational efforts behind them, and their artistic qualities put France in a leading position in terms of European architecture. In accordance with the centralizing structure of the state, Paris and the court became promoters of the extraordinary building of this period in which even private palaces were based on the royal model. Thus architecture became the expression of a strongly hierarchical society, and it did so using two basic styles, on the one hand classicism, held as the most suitable model for celebratory buildings, and on the other the rococo, which was reserved for purely decorative uses.

Under Louis XIV, attention was directed to the exaltation of the image of the city, which was imbued with ideological and symbolic elements. The Académie de l'Architecture, founded in 1671, became a driving force behind this art, as well as the theoretical and directive instrument behind the building policies of the age. The leading architects of this period were Salomon de Brosse, François Mansart, and Louis Le Vau. All three developed new models for the country residence, but the many details, ground plans, and volumes of these were always controlled by a compositional precision that negated the tensions explicit in so much of contemporary baroque architecture. The rejection of the baroque, a rejection that was more cultural than formal, is clear in the abandonment of the project that Louis XIV commissioned from Bernini in 1665 for the completion of the Louvre; instead of the dynamic perspectives that Bernini proposed, preference was given a severe classical-style portico designed by Louis Le Vau and Claude Perrault.

The field of ecclesiastic architecture did not experience the kind of innovative drive applied in the secular field. In seeking representative forms with urbanistic efficacy, the French architects limited themselves to traditional models. Only very slowly did a true French baroque church come into being, and it found its expression in the strong and dominant spatiality of the dome.

**Jules Hardouin Mansart, Dôme des Invalides, Paris, 1675–1706**
Commissioned by Louis XIV, the church presents the perfect synthesis between monumentality and elegance and between classical and baroque elements that is typical of official French art.

The impressive dome, inspired by Michelangelo's atop St Peter's, is composed of a double layer, with windows opened in the attic, invisible from the interior, that add light, creating dramatic spatial effects. The strong dynamism culminates in a lantern topped by a

pinnacle, an original syncretism between classic spatiality and Gothic verticality. Mansart's original design also include the creation of two wings forming a quarter of a circle, based on Bernini's design for St Peter's Square and never made.

**uis Le Vau, château of
aux-le-Vicomte, 1656–61**
rrounded by an old-style
oat with water, Vaux-le-
comte overlooks
mptuous gardens designed
André Le Nôtre, who here
augurated the relationship
tween architecture and
ndscape that would become
pical of the French garden.
deed, the château's
raordinary novelty – the
ntral nucleus is a replica
the layout of Palazzo
rberini – is its placement
tween court and garden'
d its tie to the landscape.
e arrangement of the
rious parts of the château –
m the service buildings to
e court of honour to the
ge central salon that
erlooks the garden – was
stined to become a constant
ment in the design of
most any celebratory
ilding in France.

**Salomon de Brosse, Palais
du Luxembourg, Paris,
1615–24, view of the garden
façade and the wing given a
'period' reconstruction in
the 19th century**
In the Palais du Luxembourg
De Brosse revolutionized the
traditional architectural
typology of the mansion,
designing a *corps-de-logis*
with angular pavilions, side
bodies, and a lower entry
wing topped at the centre
by a dome. The individual
elements are strongly and
clearly articulated, and the
treatment of the roofs, as
is traditional in France,
emphasizes this articulation
while also uniting the various
volumes. The interiors were
also innovative: the pavilions
house apartments that
anticipate the future division
of spaces in order to obtain
increased comfort and
functionality.

### New urban planning in Paris

France eventually overcame the stagnation in new construction caused by the Wars of Religion, and the return of the royal court to Paris led to the revival of building activity there. In the city, under the close scrutiny of the authorities and driven by powerful speculative interests, the urban grid was transformed by way of large-scale undertakings that presented singular elements of novelty. King Henry IV's undertakings in Paris led to the golden period of French architecture, which at the outset followed the models adopted in the Rome of Pope Sixtus V. The French king concentrated on the organization of a new and modern city that would reflect the power of its sovereign. Even so, Paris did not come into being on the basis of an overall urban plan like that of Sixtus's for Rome and instead resulted from a series of monumental undertakings that gradually converged to form a coherent and systematic structure.

The redefinition of Paris was based on two thoroughly original formations: Place Royale (today's Place des Vosges) – located in the heart of the residential quarter of the capital, the Marais – and Place Dauphine, located on the tip of the Ile de la Cité. The strictly geometric arrangement of Place Royale became the prototype for similar urban structures. The new residential constructions in stone and brick defined the style of middle-class apartments in the city. The most important new element was the uniform design of the building fronts, imposed by decree. The buildings thus frame a large public space articulated on the basis of a rational functional organization: pedestrian circulation, commercial circulation, and gardens. The autonomous composition of building fronts was thus replaced by the baroque taste for the unitary definition of space, with a statue of the ruler as the visual heart of the space. This was a concept of perspective focus borrowed from Rome's Piazza del Campidoglio, where a statue of Marcus Aurelius is located at the centre of a space taken to symbolize the centre of the world. This scheme was to be replicated in the Place des Victoires (1682–87) and in the Place Vendôme, becoming commonplace not only in France but in the rest of Europe. Around 1610 Place de France also represented the first stellar composition in baroque urban planning, in this case eight radial streets meeting at a gate.

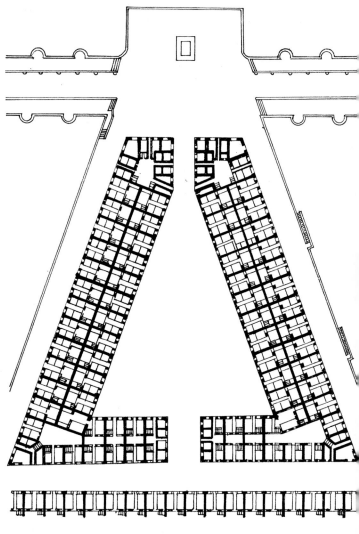

**Place Dauphine, Paris, plan, 1607**
Place Dauphine, on the Ile de la Cité, demonstrates the results of further reflection on both practical and theoretical needs. The triangular shape of the square, located at a strategic point in the city, makes it the point of departure for an axial system that was to run across the entire city, and at the same time the square presents the role of the Seine as backbone of the expanding city. Where the transverse axis of Pont Neuf crosses the trident created by the sides of the square and the two rows of converging buildings is located the statue of Henry IV, focal point of the entire city.

**ce Vendôme, Paris, 1689**
one had a greater impact
the appearance of French
itecture during the late
n century than the official
rt architect Jules Hardouin
nsart. In keeping with the
dition established by the
e Royale, he created two
focal points in Paris: the
ular Place des Victoires
32–87) and Place
dôme, originally the
ation of royal institutions.

**ce des Vosges,
is, 1604–12**
d out on a piece of royal
perty in Paris, Place des
ges has a square shape that
eightened by the elegance
he almost continuous
tain of walls – it is broken
y by the two streets giving
ess to the square – that

surrounds the square. The
space is given further
structure by the rhythmic
application of materials: white
stone highlights the outlines
of the architecture, the bodies
of the buildings are in
brickwork, the roofs are in
slate. The articulation of the
building façades reflects and
reveals the different functions
of the floors: shops on the
ground floor, apartments on
the *piano nobile*, servants'
quarters in the attics. The
square was given a precise
symmetry by the location of
the Pavillon du Roi and the
Pavillon de la Reine facing
each other on the north and
south sides of the square. At
the centre stood the
equestrian statue of Louis
XIII (1639), ordered by
Cardinal de Richelieu.

# The hôtel particulier
## 17th–18th century

### Residential typologies in France

With the *hôtel particulier* ('town house'), the Parisian residential typology developed new models of homes for the aristocracy. The Parisian nobility and upper middle class competed in the construction of residences, and although they were private homes, these buildings took on increasingly public traits. Unlike the Italian palace, which is positioned on the closed perimeter of a block, the private mansion is connected to the city around it by means of a partially opened courtyard surrounded by the two low wings of the service areas. This so-called *cour d'honneur* sets the main residential body back from the street, to which it runs parallel. Based in part on the châteaux of the countryside, with further influence from the such buildings as the Hôtel de Cluny and the Grande Ferrare (the residence of the cardinal of Ferrara, designed by Serlio in 1546, set the model for a city mansion for more than a century), the private mansion proved highly flexible – easily adapted to the irregularity of building lots – permitting architects like Mansart, Le Vau, and Le Pautre to experiment with layouts that tend to eliminate halls and galleries, altering the basic sequence of rooms in order to achieve the more scenographic enfilade arrangement. Elimination of the central axis between the side of the courtyard and the garden became normal, often compensated by doubling of the interior court. The vestibule and the area of the main staircase were the primary areas for celebratory functions, in large part because they were designed to prefigure the rest of the house.

Over the course of the 17th century, with improvements in the standard of living in French homes, and most especially in private mansions, more and more interest was shown to the decoration of rooms designed to serve specialized functions.

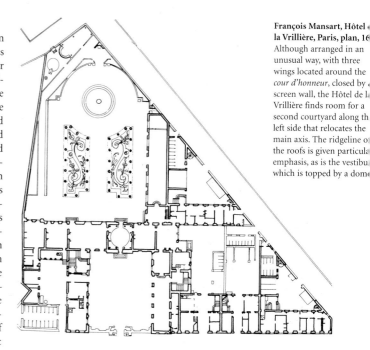

**François Mansart, Hôtel la Vrillière, Paris, plan, 16**
Although arranged in an unusual way, with three wings located around the *cour d'honneur*, closed by screen wall, the Hôtel de l Vrillière finds room for a second courtyard along th left side that relocates the main axis. The ridgeline o the roofs is given particula emphasis, as is the vestibu which is topped by a dome.

**Antoine Le Pautre, Hôtel de Beauvais, Paris, 1652–55**
Le Pautre here demonstrated great skill in exploiting an irregularly shaped building lot. He emphasized the passage from the entrance to the courtyard with side walls articulated with giant columns terminating in an aedicule. At the same time the space of the irregular shape of the building front is circumscribed by a powerfully projecting cornice with great sculptural qualities.

*opposite*
**Louis Le Vau, Hôtel Lambert, Paris, 1640–44**
Made on the Ile de la Cité for Nicolas Lambert, this mansion skilfully adapts the usual scheme to a building lot that did not offer a great deal of depth. In the courtyard, a Doric trabeation wraps the entire space, giving it a sense of continuity that is reinforced by the rounded corners at the end of the façade. Here Le Vau conceived a highly innovative arrangement to make up for the lack of depth of the lot, placing the garden to the side of the *cour d'honneur* instead of on the entrance-courtyard-house axis. The decoration of the façade unites French elegance with Roman monumentality; the dominant motif is the colossal pilaster, with the stairway and Doric columns isolated on the ground floor. The garden façade presents one of Le Vau's most marvellous inventions: floor-to-ceiling windows that act as doors – French windows – destined to become a constant element of the French château.

# Louis Le Vau and Jules H. Mansart
## The Royal Palace of Versailles
### 1661–98

Expression of 17th-century absolutism and inevitable model for all European courts until the end of the 18th century, the palace of Versailles began in 1661 around a hunting lodge built for Louis XIII and came to represent the desire for self-celebration and the taste of the period of Louis XIV. It constitutes the apogee of European architecture of the royal palace not only because of its size and splendour and the modernity of its construction, but also for its perfect presentation of absolute power. Direction of the undertaking was entrusted to Le Vau, and he was responsible for the central nucleus of the palace, the two wings of the courtyard, the *cour d'honneur*, where the roads from Paris converge, the garden façade, and the unusual adoption of the flat 'Italian-style' roof, perhaps derived from Bernini's proposed plan for the Louvre. The selection of Le Vau, who had already made the revolutionary château of Vaux-le-Vicomte, reveals the desire for a structure with close ties to the surrounding nature as in the concept of 'between court and garden', exemplified by the planning of an axial system and the arrangement of the park.

The transfer of the court and the entire governmental apparatus to the palace in 1667 put in motion a giant project of reworking that was entrusted to Mansart, who enlarged the entire complex by connecting the large entry courtyard and the two wings ending to the north and south of the central body. Mansart also closed off the garden façade with the creation on the first floor of the famous Galerie des Glaces ('Hall of Mirrors'), which, although derived from Fontainebleau and from similar English creations, outdid all that had been made until then, at least from the monumental point of view. The gigantic scale of Versailles repeats the architectural theme of 'creation by division' – a series of simple repetitions rhythmically marked off by the repetition of the large windows – which expresses the fundamental values of the baroque age and in which the focal point of the interior, as well as of the entire building, is the king's bed.

The royal palace's close relationship to its park was of fundamental importance, for the park, exactly like the palace itself, was made to serve the ceremonial and celebratory requirements of the king. Designed for the amusements of the court, the park constitutes the natural and ideal backdrop for endless festivities based on the close relationship typical of baroque art between celebration and architecture, between the ephemeral and the permanent. From the original concept, the palace was seen as the centre of an urbanistic system and a reworking of the landscape.

Such was the goal of André Le Nôtre, inventor of the 'French' garden, who began work at Versailles in 1662. Although it maintains the symmetry of Italian tradition, the park of Versailles has a network of axial pathways leading off to the horizon. These paths are cadenced by *rond-points*, pavilions, arboreal architecture, wider areas that suddenly appear ahead, stairways, terraces, ponds, and monumental fountains that expand the visual perception of space and add a sense of wonder. The apparently endless Galerie des Glaces, designed by Mansart between 1678

and 1684, received abundant light from large French windows on one side, matched one by one on the opposite wall by mirrors. The use of mirrors in the place usually occupied by painted decoration serves a function of primary importance, that of reflecting and multiplying light. The ornamentations – the canvases along the ceiling that celebrate the apotheosis of the king, the polychrome marbles, the gilt bronzes – were organized by Charles Le Brun, and in this undertaking he can be said to have reached the peak of the expressive possibilities of French baroque art.

# English classicism

## 17th century

### Inigo Jones and Christopher Wren

By around 1620, an explicitly classical architectural language had taken root in England. Inigo Jones, who had travelled in Italy and studied Roman and Renaissance architecture, prepared building designs notable for their symmetry and simplicity, traits typical of an ideal classical vision well-suited to the complex, pluralistic character of English society. Working for the royal court, he made buildings in which Palladian themes, filtered through French classicism, are reinterpreted to create a 'neutral' architecture using ancient orders and their spatial connections in favour of a language with perennial application.

The Civil War and Great Fire of London (1666) marked important steps in the break with 17th-century architecture. Christopher Wren worked out a plan for the reconstruction of the city based on perspective axes with squares as focal points. The reconstruction of fifty-one city churches beginning in 1670 – designed on the basis of a reduction of the traditional basilican schemes, with special attention given to bell towers, understood as vantage points – was an important step in the history of modern English architecture. The undertaking gave Wren the opportunity to apply the sources of his architecture, from the classical to the Gothic to the baroque, with great versatility and freedom, up to the limits of eclecticism. The ideas he worked out found their culmination in St Paul's.

**Inigo Jones, Banqueting House, Whitehall, London, 1619–22**
Jones used the theme of the Roman basilica in a monumental manner in the Banqueting House, which has a bi-axial rectangular hall on two floors articulated by superimposed rows of columns. The orders on the interior correspond to the exterior in a refined play of correspondences. Coupled pilasters mark the corners, and the three central bays are emphasized by engaged columns. This harmonious articulation rests on a rusticated base with a mannerist flavour that has lost, however, its function as contrast.

**Christopher Wren, Greenwich Hospital, London, begun 1695**
Greenwich Hospital stands out from among the public buildings Wren designed because of the great synthesis between baroque scenography and classical composure. The long perspective view created by the avenue between the colonnades and by the garden on the Thames concludes at Queen's House by Inigo Jones.

**ristopher Wren,
Stephen, Walbrook,
ndon, 1672–87**
Stephen has a combined
n in which a flattened
ne is placed atop an
agonal plan, defined by
umns, inserted in a
tangular body. The result
simple but ingenious
thesis of longitudinal,
tral, and cross plans
t Murray called 'the
hitectural equivalent of
Anglican compromise
ween Calvinist austerity
l the splendour of the
man baroque'.

**Inigo Jones, Queen's House,
Greenwich, 1615–35**
The first qualitatively
interesting work by Jones,
the Queen's House presents a
compact cubic block that
makes clear reference to the
classical Italian tradition,
most of all the first floor in
rusticated stone, the use of
Ionic columns in the garden
loggia, and the flat roof.
Even so, the high windows
and elongated proportions
have a northern flavour
and create an attenuated
play of tensions, including
a certain emphasis on the
principal axis.

# Christopher Wren

## St Paul's Cathedral, London

### 1675–1710

A unique fragment of the plan for the reconstruction of London that Wren worked out after the 1666 fire, St Paul's Cathedral is a synthesis of baroque elements – towers on the façades, niches, perspective illusions – inserted in a classical context dominated by the great dome. In keeping with the experiments he had tried out in 1672 in St Stephen Walbrook, Wren's original design, dated 1673 – and magnificently illustrated by the wooden model preserved in the cathedral itself – aimed at a monumental synthesis of a central space – clearly derived form Michelangelo's plan for the basilica of St Peter's in Rome – flanked by minor domed spaces located along the diagonals in perfect conformity with the baroque demand for an integrated space. But while Michelangelo's plan was closed and centripetal, Wren's established an active relationship between the spatial complex and the external area by means of concave walls and introduced a longitudinal axis by way of the domed vestibule and the classical portico.

This first plan, however, was rejected by the London clergy. The final version, presented in 1675, combines a longitudinal cruciform plan and a dome-covered centre set atop a colonnaded drum, much like St Stephen.

The monumentality of the cathedral, both inside and outside, represents one of the greatest creations of English baroque architecture, which in the evident will to rival St Peter's introduces important innovations. Wren's ingenious structure resolves all the formal and structural elements – from the overall appearance to the smallest detail – in a fluid and harmonious design that bursts onto the panorama of the London skyline.

The western front has a two-storied portico with coupled columns topped by a classical triangular tympanum. The two side towers are brought into harmony with this by way of pairs of pilaster strips. The Borromini-style structures atop the bell towers seem out of place. The extraordinary classical dome, clearly derived from Palladio, represents the ideas of English architecture of the period; the colonnade around the drum, with its strongly chiaroscuro values, is intimately baroque. At the crossing of the cathedral the extraordinary width of the central nave and of the two side aisles is resolved thanks to the skilful use of light, which pours in from windows along the drum to highlight the spaces.

# Sicily
## The far border of the European baroque
### 1693–c. 1800

### The earthquake of 1693

The terrible earthquake that destroyed much of south-eastern Sicily towards the end of the 17th century struck the heart of a region already tried by serious economic problems and by the deterioration of the political situation, a result of the increasingly clear crisis in the Spanish government. As part of their efforts to maintain control of the island, the Sicilian aristocracy and the Spanish government performed primary roles in the reconstruction efforts, which became part of the process of urbanization that had started during the second half of the 16th century and was at that very moment reaching its height. The plans for the new cities generally involved open, flexible schemes, although they always included a central square with the major buildings, meaning the church and the baronial palace. The rebuilding of the Sicilian cities following the 1693 earthquake, from Catania to Ragusa, Noto to Modica, presented the historical opportunity for the development of autonomous architectural forms that were unique on the panorama of the European baroque. The importance of this 'provincial' phenomenon resided not only in the extraordinary quality of the individual creations, but also in the homogeneity of the undertakings, in the diffusion of the motifs, and in the compactness of the whole, as well as their high environmental value. For models, the architects turned to works of Roman derivation, from the fanciful inventions of Borromini to the academic language of Domenico Fontana, but these were applied loosely, haphazardly, as a repertory from which to draw individual motifs and ideas that then could be reassembled at will. A distinctive characteristic of these is their scenographic interest – which is expressed in the emphasis on façades, locations on squares, stairs, and courtyards – and their decorative flair, often exuberant, both in exteriors full of sculptures and in interiors dressed in frescoes and stuccoes.

**Rosario Gagliardi, S Giorgio, Modica, 1738** Standing at the top of a spectacular stairway, the church of S Giorgio represents one of the heights of the Sicilian baroque, its splendid façade standing out from the surrounding urban context. Gagliardi uses here ideas very similar to those he later applied at Ragusa, but the effect seems far less powerful and almost decadent.

**Rosario Gagliardi, S Giorgio, Ragusa Ibla, 1746–66** Gagliardi was a leading exponent of the Sicilian baroque, and the cathedral of S Giorgio is one of his most important works because of the harmonic synthesis between the convexity of the façade and the decorative elements that compose it. The sense of verticality is accentuated by the groups of superimposed columns, which create a dynamic movement toward the centre that culminates in the plane of the bell tower. The result is a kind of tower-façade borrowed from northern European architecture and thus unusual in Italy but with a long tradition in Sicily.

*From the end of the 16th century to the early 17th, Lecce was enriched by numerous buildings, both religious and secular. What the architecture of these buildings has in common, and what makes the structures recognizable, is decorative exuberance and the reinterpretation of local traditions. This did not involve substantial transformations of architectural structures but only a way of reworking surfaces, covering them with a dense accumulation of plastic elements and traditional forms. The church of Santa Croce is the highest expression of this style, which was reminiscent of ancient and medieval architecture variously influenced by 17th-century ideas from cities in contact with Puglia for commercial reasons, cities that from a distance reflected the most independent and capricious developments of baroque Spain.*

**...hedral, Noto, begun 1693**

...construction of the ...city of Noto, eight ...metres from the original ...was primarily the work ...Rosario Gagliardi and ...cenzo Sinatra. It is ...able for the freedom ...s creations and for its ...ed adaptation to the ...ural site, factors that ...te a series of striking ...nographic effects, ...ough they also highlight ...divisions of the social ...rarchy. In the lower part ...he city, site of the places ...ower and institutions, ...most important ...dings are set in ...nographic locations, ...h as the magnificent ...hedral, at the top of ...ramatic flight of stairs.

### Architecture and decorative exuberance

The rigid classicism of the Escorial, the spirituality of the Counter-Reformation, and the centralization of the state provided the themes for Spanish architecture throughout the 17th century. So it was that classical harmony gradually gave way to a more accentuated hierarchy of individual elements thanks to the sculptural elaboration of walls, the use of a variety of contrasting materials, and the increased ornamentation of façades. Even so, at various places far from court, buildings were made that testify to the beginning of baroque architecture in Spain. At Granada in the 18th century the canons of classical architecture began taking on decorative elements that were freely interpreted thanks to the use of stucco. The leading architect was Francisco Hurtado Izquierdo, whose decorative forms, based on classical elements that he fragmented and multiplied in a prismatic manner, represent one of the most original contributions of Spanish architecture. Around 1720 the mixed nature of the architecture in Spain's cities gave way to the court art of the Bourbons, primarily inspired by Italian and French classicism and initially led by a group of Italian architects, from Giovanni Battista Sacchetti to Filippo Juvarra. Soon enough, however, a local style came into being based on an extreme version of the baroque and characterized by the sumptuous and exuberant sculptural decoration of walls. This style came to be called Churrigueresque from José Benito de Churriguera and his brothers.

**José Benito de Churrigue[ra],
cathedral of Santiago de
Compostela, 1738–49**
The spectacular nature of
the external decoration of
Spanish baroque architect[ure]
and the particular focus o[n]
the communicative force
of sacred art in its
most popular aspects reac[h]
astonishing heights in the
exuberant decoration on
the façade of the ancient
cathedral of Santiago de
Compostela.

**Santiago Bonavia and
Francisco Sabatini, Aranj[uez]
Palace, 1748 and 1771**
The 18th-century
reconstruction was placed
over the original design by
Juan de Herrera, creating a[ ]
building with four wings a[nd]
a western façade accentua[ted]
by corner towers. This retu[rn]
in the middle of the 18th
century, to the architecture
of the preceding century w[as]
part of the policy adopted
the Bourbon rulers, who
unlike the preceding
generation sought legitima[cy]
in the forceful repetition o[f]
Spanish tradition.

**Francisco Hurtado Izquierdo, sacristy of the Cartuja, Granada, 1732–45**
Strongly considered the quintessence of Spanish decadence, the narrow space of the sacristy of the Carthusian monastery is striking for the superabundance of plastic and stucco decoration on the structural elements, which nonetheless remain clearly visible. The various decorative motifs inspired by classical models – parts of capitals, cornices, volutes, candelabra, and the so-called pig ears – cover the wall supports with the clear intention of creating a surreal play of light and decoration in which the rhetorical language of the baroque is transformed into a dialectic among fleeting, ephemeral elements similar to rococo art.

**Narciso de Tomé, cathedral, Toledo, El Transparente, 1721–32**
With El Transparente, Tomé created what may well be the most spectacular construction of the Spanish baroque, a perfect, total work of art that transforms the traditional typology of the *camarín* – the space in which the tabernacle is stored – into a plastic-architectural structure, a sort of *retablo* in which architecture, sculpture, and painting, exalted by the light that pours down from above, reach a perfect fusion with great theatrical force.

# Portugal

## 1640–1755

### From a minimalist aesthetic to the pharaonic delirium of John V

In 1530 Portugal began a radical rejection of the decorative wealth of the Manueline style, turning instead to a minimalist aesthetic with roots in military architecture, which for quite some time had become a status symbol in Portugal, one of Europe's leading colonial powers.

So it was that by the time Philip II of Spain assumed the Portuguese crown (1580), Portugal had had time to develop its own, thoroughly original version of mannerist architecture, a style so austere it was called *arquitectura chcā* ('sober architecture'). The spread of the architectural treatises by De Vries and Dietterlin at the beginning of the 17th century resulted in a solid turn toward the forms of the Flemish baroque. With the restoration of the Portuguese monarchy in 1640, the court and nobility showed off their regained power in iconographic and scenographic projects perfectly in keeping with the celebrative nature of the baroque, such as the splendid Fronteira Palace at Benfica (begun 1667) in which the application of the *azulejo* tradition reached rare levels of quality.

Early in the 18th century, during the reign of John V, Rome became the model against which all Portuguese architecture was measured, up to the point of grotesque levels in the drive to create a second Rome on the banks of the Tagus. An outstanding example of the king's outlandish programme of self-celebratory building – a programme that led the country toward bankruptcy – is the monastery of Mafra (begun 1717). This pharaonic plan, designed by the German architect Johann Friedrich Ludwig, was never inhabited. The death of John V and the disastrous earthquake of 1755, which razed to the ground nearly two-thirds of the city of Lisbon, led to a sudden change in Portugal's building policies. The demands made by the reconstruction work presented the opportunity for a complete change and for the undertaking of projects that in some senses anticipate the urban-planning schemes of the 19th century.

**al Palace, Queluz,**
**un 1747**

eus Vicente made this
l of Portuguese rococo
itecture, an elegant building
three wings that surround
ge court of honour, and
shed its interiors following
French model with a rich
ille decoration, tapestries
paintings. The gardens,
designed by Jean-Baptiste
illon beginning in 1758 and
d on designs by Le Nôtre,
al the refined taste of the
en régime.

**n Jesus do Monte,**
**ga, 1784–1811**

side Lisbon, certain areas
ortugal developed
onomous architectural
ols, among them Braga,
mportant centre of the
uguese late baroque thanks
he archbishop D. Rodrigo de
ura Teles, who not only
rged his private palace but
fountains, squares, and
nasteries built. Constructed
a hill, Bom Jesus is a Sacre
nte; its layout represents the
ions of the Cross, with a
way that zigzags its way up
hill past a series of garden
aces, with fountains and
els, ending at the church,
n all an extraordinary
ture of Christian, ancient,
pagan motifs.

*t*

**ola Nasoni, André Soares,**
**ctuary of Nossa Senhora**
**Remédios, Lamego,**
**0–61**

he north of the country,
Sienese painter Nicola
soni founded a school with
ng pictorial traits, whose
orations are similar to those
de for state ceremonies or
atrical use. It is a style
ring traces of the Italian
oco.

207

# Colonial baroque

## 18th century

### The encounter of different cultures

Around 1650, baroque forms began to appear in Latin America, where they were applied atop the stylistic stratifications deposited by Spanish domination dating back to the early 16th century. There were also contributions from local traditions and hybrid forms that resulted from crosses. Despite the reception of the treatises by Vignola and Serlio over the course of the 16th century and the uniformity of typologies established by the various religious orders, with the adoption of an apparently homogeneous language, resemblances between colonial architecture and the architecture of the mother countries Spain and Portugal are often only superficial. New World architects often demonstrated uncommon inventiveness in adapting European building techniques to geographical needs, while the completely different climatic conditions demanded different spatial concepts, and the constant danger of earthquakes required different calculations in terms of construction techniques. Encounters between different cultures sometimes resulted in especially innovative forms: the Mexican *atrien* repeat a traditional typology adapted to the needs of evangelization. The *capillas posas* ('open chapels') are as stunning as they are functional: a pragmatic concession to the type of life of the indigenous peoples, indissolubly tied to nature. The rich stucco decorations of Mexico repeat the exuberance of the Spanish Churrigueresque, fully exploiting the artisanal implications of the baroque language. In the more primitive regions – the Caribbean and Central America – the architecture of the colonies made fewer compromises, and forms strongly related to the mother countries were directly transplanted to the New World. In its drive to astonish and convert the indigenous peoples, the Catholic Church became the true motive force in the conquest, with architecture and the rhetoric related to it primary means to achieve that goal. In this way cathedrals, parish churches, the churches of the religious orders, and sanctuaries became visible signs of the functioning of the colonial system, which drove secular architecture into roles of a secondary importance.

**Mexico, S Domingo at San Cristóbal de las Casas, *c.* 1700**
Mexican churches often present a variant of the canons of Spanish baroque. The façade is transformed into a wall for the exhibition of a rich figurative and ornamental repertory structurally similar to a *retablo* (unlike the churches of Central America, which had more accentuated plastic decorations), with an architectural vocabulary based on mannerist treatises but not without local plant and animal motifs.

atemala, church of the
vent of La Merced,
tigua, 1552
umes and colours
duce a lively and dynamic
mony. The façade of the
rch of the convent of La
ced unites an exuberant
amental composition
a highly vital and
nmunicative efficacy: the
*fronte*, or main façade,
e support for an
orate decoration in
ch classical-style themes
ear across the surface
thoroughly baroque
ndance.

*posite bottom*
**zil, sanctuary of Bom
us de Matozinhos,
gonhas do Campo,
7–early 19th century**
Portuguese colonization
3razil was limited to the
stal strip of the country,
ere Portuguese models
imported without
stantial concessions to
l traditions. An example
e façade with two bell
ers of the sanctuary of
n Jesus, which presents
duced version of the
rch of the same name
3raga.

# Filippo Juvarra

## 1678–1736

### A Sicilian architect at the Savoy court

In Italy, the evolution toward the late baroque-rococo clearly revealed its roots in Borromini, expressed through the forms of soft and graceful modelling, but without decorative excesses. The great architect of this period was Filippo Juvarra, who went from his birthplace of Sicily to work in Turin at the Savoy court, passing through Rome on the way and the school of Carlo Fontana.

The force of Juvarra's personality is measurable in the fact that he was able to break free of the confines of the city-fortress of Turin and project that city's character onto the surrounding countryside. He did this in the creation of two symbolic sites of power, one religious, the church on the hill of Superga, its exterior similar to the Pantheon, and the other secular, the hunting palace of Stupinigi. Juvarra's urbanistic undertakings were always attentive to the quality of the historical space of Turin; the creations he made outside the city are an affirmation of open space. The difference between the two reveals Juvarra's great flexibility and the wealth of his architectural language. Ranging from the Renaissance tradition to models of antiquity, from outstanding works of the 17th century to contemporary creations, such as the abbeys in the German area, he always found the most suitable language for each site. Throughout all of his career as an architect, Juvarra constantly demonstrated a lively interest in developments taking place in the architecture of northern Europe. His European travels testify to his position as one of the unquestioned leaders in the international architectural world of the first half of the 18th century.

**Galleria di Diana, Venaria Reale, 1714–29**
The diaphanous, elongated space of the gallery, exalted by the pale tones of the wall coverings, fully reveals Juvarra's skill in the use of light, which here penetrate the space in an elegant play that accentuates the scenographic effects.

**Hunting Palace, Stupinigi, begun 1729**
Just outside the city, dramatically located at the end of an avenue, the hunt palace of Stupinigi seems to spread across the surrounding landscape, its body spread open in wings that extend scenographic sensibilities a pleasing liveliness outward infinity. Some of the characteristics of Juvarra's s can be identified at Stupin the enclosed but enlivened space and the scenographi effects of perspective views that join the architecture to the surrounding nature.

*Opposite*
**Church at Superga, begun 1715**
Superga presents the thematic nuclei of Juvarra's architectural style: the cent plan, the prevalent vertical of the central structure and of the dome, the relationsh between the body of the church and the classical-st portico, the façade, with its two side towers that frame dome, with its memories of Michelangelo. The new tas represented not so much b new compositional elemen as by the loose rhythm of spaces and the coordination of the individual parts, giv the architectural structures the sense of a dynamic forward movement.

# The Austrian late baroque
## 18th century

### The creation of a 'state art'

The great season of the Austrian late baroque began only after 1683, the year in which the Turks were defeated, leading to the full affirmation of Habsburg power. As part of its campaign to consolidate its position as a European power, Austria undertook the creation of a 'state art' ideologically similar to the state art of France under Louis XIV. Emblematic of this rhetoric of persuasion was the planning of a Viennese Versailles, the palace of Schönbrunn, for which Johann Fischer von Erlach made a design around 1695. This monumental residence was another expression of the divine right of kings. Not only does the proposed design encompass the infinite variations of Fischer von Erlach's art, with his idea of 'historical architecture,' it also laid the basis for a thoroughly German middle course between the extremes of Italian baroque and French classicism. The fact that the palace was not

constructed following these forms reveals the inability of Habsburg architecture to translate its ideals into reality, and the restructuring carried out by Nikolaus Pacassi between 1744 and 1749 marked the loss of persuasive force in the tendency to tone down baroque rhetoric and dynamism into elementary, purely geometric relationships. The rhetorical grandiosity persisted only in religious architecture. The idea of the architectural definition of a 'sacred place' meant that religious architecture went through a splendid flowering in this period, most particularly in the major abbeys, which were seen as focal points for the territory around them.

At the same time the city of Vienna was enlarged, with numerous new palaces and gardens located in a ring around the city, thus without making any dents in the original layout of the old city, the focal point of which was still the medieval cathedral of St Stephen.

ce of Schönbrunn,
iette, completed 1775

Gloriette, an airy
cture erected in honour
e victory over Frederick
reat at Kolin (1756),
ds on a hill overlooking
alace and looks
thing like a transparent
in. The pavilion, located
e end of the central axis
crosses the garden, is
rofoundly baroque in
ntral body, with large
h windows, and in
air of porticoed wings,
h are reached by way
enographic stairways.

nn Michael Prunner,
ty Church, Stadl-Paura
Lambach, 1717–24

unusual central plan –
ngle with curving sides
ich the three corner
rs were applied – is
posed of spatial cells
nt to symbolize the
ty. An elegant cornice
around the body of
hurch, giving it
mism and at the same
creating a relationship
een the towers and the
ral body.

# Johann Bernhard Fischer von Erlach
## 1656–1723

### The celebration of Austrian power

Johann Bernhard Fischer von Erlach, having brought to completion all the moral and formal movements of 17th-century art, set himself squarely on the path leading to the novelties of the next century. With him, thanks to the synthesis expressed in the *Entwurff einer historichen Architektur*, the first monumental illustrated history of architecture, Austria assumed the leadership of the German high baroque. Historical awareness gave his works a vast breadth and a variety of themes, the common denominator of which was 'Roman' monumentality, a result of his training in Rome in the circle of Bernini. The fundamental, recurrent theme of his architecture – the oval topped by a dome – is also the baroque motif par excellence because of its clear synthesis of centralization and extension. War with France led him to conceive the idea of using architecture to express the greatness of the empire and to celebrate Austria as a power. He wanted to create a 'historical architecture' that would blend all preceding ideas to form a new and original unity. It was within this climate that the great design for the palace of Schönbrunn took form, a demonstration of how the overriding mission of the high baroque in central Europe had become the construction of a royal palace, a work that Fischer von Erlach had already hinted at in designs for palaces, villas, and hunting lodges. The architecture of Fischer von Erlach here proves itself unequalled in the sensibility of the articulation of the façades through subtle gradations of rhythm, the plastic dynamism of doors and windows, even the achievement of maximum spatial effect in the narrow spaces of interior staircases.

Fischer von Erlach also created several extraordinary works in the field of church architecture – the Church of the Trinity and the University Church in Salzburg and the Karlskirche in Vienna – that are of particular significance for their rejection of the longitudinal layout in favour of simple, enclosed spatial forms based on an oval crossed by the arms of a cross in atmospheres that achieve outcomes of impressive clarity.

**Palace of Prince Eugene, Vienna, stairs, begun 1696**
The city palace of Prince Eugene was built as part of the overall urban renewal of Vienna. Its entrance area reveals the influence of the grandiose and solemn style of the late baroque. This homage to gigantism gives way to a purposefully sober language in the monumental stairway, which uses splendid plastic and spatial creativity to express – along with m allusions to the patron of work – the idea of the asc from the realm of Hercu to that of Helios-Apollo.

**Karlskirche, Vienna,**
**[inter]ior, 1715–37**

[The] Karlskirche was
[com]missioned by Charles VI
[to f]ulfil a vow made during
[the] plague of 1713. Its
[unu]sual stateliness results
[fro]m the triad of columned
[por]tico, dome, and
[triu]mphal columns, all of
[the]m indebted to the
[clas]sical Roman tradition.
[Th]e oval nucleus of the
[com]position generates the
[enti]re structure. The
[dyn]amic torsion of the
[inte]rior spaces is difficult
[to i]magine on the basis
[of t]he linear façade. The
[chu]rch surpasses the
[lim]itations of local
[trad]itions in its drive to
[sym]bolize the political
[am]bitions of the house
[of H]absburg.

**University Church,**
**Salzburg, begun 1696,**
**consecrated 1707**

The archbishop of Salzburg
gave Fischer von Erlach
responsibility for improving
the appearance of Salzburg,
promoted as the 'Rome of
the North'. The architect
focused his energies on the
harmonious relationship –
both aesthetic and functional
– between the new buildings
and the city, with particular
emphasis on achieving
scenographic effects through
the insertion of building
fronts in the urban context.
In the University Church
he put the façade in sharp
contrast with the side towers,
creating a convex form and
extending the façade beyond
the perimeter line of the
front of the church. The
successful relationship
established between the
powerful façade and the
small square creates one of
the most monumental spaces
of the epoch.

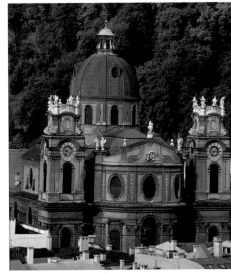

# Johann Lukas von Hildebrandt

## Upper Belvedere, Vienna

### 1721–22

While Fischer von Erlach gave form to the 'imperial' aspects of the Austrian state, Johann Lukas von Hildebrandt – although embracing his rival's principle of the historical synthesis of architecture – was already revealing in his creations the refinements and sensibilities of the rococo, and he was responsible for the very best of the palaces with gardens of the Austrian high baroque.

The highpoint of his career as palace builder was his design for the Belvedere, the summer residence made for Prince Eugene of Savoy. The complex is composed of two separate buildings, the Lower Belvedere (1714–16) and the larger Upper Belvedere (1721–22), the two of them connected by a terraced garden already designed in the French style around 1700.

The Upper Belvedere is a highly original structure in which the boundless vistas of the baroque garden have been reduced to the area of an enclosed space, although it is furnished with parterres and woods; at the same time, because of its elevated position, the palace dominates the surrounding space.

What is most striking about the building – both unusual and also unexpected – is that it is composed of a series of component parts of different height, a feature unique on the panorama of 18th-century architecture. The central pavilion, which houses the Marble Hall, is raised; in front of it are a staircase and an animated segmented cornice. Each of the two wings ends in a domed octagonal pavilion that continues and then concludes the rhythm derived from the varying heights of the structures. In doing this, Hildebrandt applied a new and unusual concept: the wings decrease in height toward the pavilions, and behind the body of the central body the salon rises to crown the entire building. The ascending and descending progress of the roofs, as well as the advance and retreat of the bodies, is made dynamic and given unity by the decorative system, the heart of which is the entire lower floor, emphasized by a plastic cornice that also embraces the side pavilions.

The Upper Belvedere is considered one of the most successful works of secular architecture of the late baroque. In it Hildebrandt united all the leading trends of the period in a highly original synthesis: the volumetric integration and the external walls create a vibrant surface in which forms appear, disappear, and are transformed.

No other work by Hildebrandt presents his sense of spatiality and the articulation of space with clarity equal to the façade the Upper Belvedere. Even so, the artifice employed leads to two ways of perceiving this great work of integration between architecture and nature. T[]e first way is from the distan[] but the true complexity of the volumes of which the Belvedere is composed can[] be perceived only from nea[] the entrance, for the build[] can be reached only from [] side due to the large body of water in front of it.

debrandt used precise
proportional measurements
his creation of the stair-
e hall and the contiguous
ms, creating a 'winding'
uence of spaces between
ground-floor room, the
ryway, and the Marble
ll. The ground-floor room
lecorated by powerful
antids designed by
renzo Mattielli that
pport the roof vaults.

# Jacob Prandtauer

## Abbey of Melk

### 1702–38

The Benedictine monastery of Melk, built high above the Danube River between 1702 and 1738 in a grand late baroque style that is lightweight and integrated with the surrounding natural environment, is without doubt one of the most monumental and spectacular complexes in Austria. Elegant apartments, splendid stairways, and sumptuous halls were not exclusive to royal palaces and could also be found in the most important abbeys, and indeed with these constructions the prince abbots – who also possessed large holdings of land as well as political power – competed with the imperial court at Vienna.

The creator of this masterpiece, in which echoes of Borromini and Guarini are readily heard, was Jacob Prandtauer. Prandtauer laid out the entire complex along an east-west axis that runs from the entrance through the atrium then into the prelates' court; from there it continues through the choir and the central nave of the church to end in the courtyard high above the Danube. The curve of the end portion, which perfectly matches the shape of the rocky base beneath it, reveals a profound interrelationship between architecture and nature, a concordance purposefully created by the architect between natural movement and architectural movement, a true inaccessible *civitas Dei*.

The dynamic progress of the entire building toward the river is perfectly demonstrated by the incredible length of the southern wing in a play of architecture and landscape that can be viewed from several perspectives.

Because of its extraordinary position and exceptional size, the abbey of Melk offered Prandtauer opportunities to experiment with the plastic and dynamic aspects of architecture; it also involved him in the design of a highly complicated structure composed of a variety of different buildings that had to form a homogeneous whole and that were limited by the topographical shape of the site.

The dramatic appearance of the exterior is also true for the interior of the church, in which the structure of the supporting architectural elements (pilasters, fluted pillars, decorated archivolts), similar to a filigree, and the stucco decoration stand out plastically thanks to the light that floods in from the large windows in the nave and the drum of the dome.

Approaching the monastery from the river one encounters the most important component parts of the complex, the magnificent semicircular panoramic gallery and the roof terrace, so vaguely reminiscent of Palladio, the two pavilion wings, one housing the marble hall, the other the library, the superb façade of the church framed by its two

bell towers, the high dome, and the incredible longitudinal extensions of the conventual rooms. The close integration of the various volumes becomes clear, with the symbolic centrality of the church, along with the astonishing chiaroscuro effects given by the yellow-white colour, which are reflected in the water of the Danube.

# The German late baroque

## 18th century

**The perfect fusion of constructed architecture and painted architecture**

The Thirty Years' War (1618–48) halted Germany's advances towards the new Italian and French architecture, and forms influenced by the baroque did not appear there until the early 18th century. Only then did the patrons, both secular and ecclesiastical, have sufficient funds to promote building activity, whether in the service of absolute power or in support of the Counter-Reformation. The particular political situation in 18th-century Germany, with power dispersed among numerous small or large states, created an architectural landscape that was anything but homogeneous, dominated instead by regional schools that multiplied princely residences, usually characterized by opulent rococo taste, each one a physical expression of some local lord. Swabia, Bavaria, Franconia, Dresden, and Potsdam can be considered of equal rank as centres of late baroque art.

A peculiar aspect of the German late baroque is the perfect fusion of constructed architecture and painted architecture, leading to fascinating imaginary and illusionistic architecture that becomes an extension of real architecture. This special style appears not only in the vaults of churches but also in the wonderful ceiling frescoes in the heart of the lord's palace: the vestibule or the stairway of honour. This same period also saw a widespread sense of dynamism – most of all in sacred buildings – a use of undulating columns and pilasters surging upward. The combination of these manifold architectural structures with complex, 'syncopated' layouts resulted in what is perhaps the most original expression of the German rococo. An excellent example is the small but glowing church of St Johann Nepomuk in Munich (1733–46), with its dynamic galleries and twisting columns, where the Asam brothers imported Roman baroque models and exalted them through the virtuoso application of illumination and decoration. This is an architecture of true grandeur thanks to the perfect balance of architecture, painting, and sculpture in a thoroughly theatrical staging.

**Matthäus Daniel Pöppelmann and Balthasar Permoser, Zwinger Pavilion Dresden, 1709–32**
Built at the request of Augustus II, king of Saxony, as a site for celebrations, the Zwinger – a structure emblematic of the architectural development of Dresden – presents a completely particular architecture articulated in pavilions, porticoed wings, and scenographic stairways. As designed by Pöppelmann the Zwinger has a structure that is both dynamic and structurally complex, played on the chiaroscuro of the full and empty spaces in which sculpture and architecture work together to create an indivisible whole designed to celebrate power.

**Johann Michael Fischer, Abbey Church, Ottobeuren, 1748–66**
The church of the Benedictine abbey of Ottobeuren is a true masterpiece of the Swabian rococo, its interior presenting an astonishing fusion of architectural structure and decoration that alters the perception of its space. The exterior, however, is far more sober, with dynamically varying profiles. This difference between interior and exterior spaces is in fact a characteristic trait of Bavarian architecture.

**Dominikus Zimmerman,**
**pilgrimage church, Die**
**Wies, 1744–54**
Zimmerman chose to enclose
the oval plan of the church
with paired pillars of an
unusual quadrangular shape
and inserted a long choir to
increase the effect of
perspective space and with it
the sense of holiness. The rich
rocaille stucco decoration
dematerializes the
architectural structure,
reducing it to light and colour.

# Balthasar Neumann
## 1687–1753

### A continuous variety of spatial combinations

Balthasar Neumann was quite probably the most talented architect of the entire European rococo, and he was active in both secular and religious buildings. His strong personality left its mark in the special style of late baroque German architecture, most especially that of Franconia. The fortunate encounter between the still young architect and the Schönborn dynasty of prince-bishops led to a fecund period characterized by the construction of splendid buildings and a brilliant artistic life. The great turning point in his career was the commission to rework the urban layout of the city and the creation of the residence of Würzburg, for these undertakings put him alongside such leading architects as Johann Dientzenhofer and Johann Lukas von Hildebrandt; the result was a further evolution in Neumann's architectural style, which was based on the powerful synthesis of traditional Viennese architecture and the new stimuli of French classicism. A fundamental aspect of his architectural style is the rejection of fantasy used for its own sake; Neumann's buildings are always based on an ideal combination of organizational force and sensibility for the plastic and the spatial, always within the continuous variety of the figural and structural forms, for which he drew on the most diverse traditions.

He turned to the field of sacred architecture most of all in his later career, and in these works he ingeniously combined the basilican plan and the concept of a central space. At Vierzehnheiligen, his masterpiece, within a luminous and apparently infinite space he composed a bi-axial system with a traditional Latin cross achieving a singular synthesis of all the fundamental concepts of baroque ecclesiastical architecture. At the same time he concentrated his work on the double expression of internal space by way of which the structural framework is clearly visible against the exterior wall, which is treated as a neutral surface.

**Church of Neresheim, 1745–92**
In the church at Neresheim Abbey, Neumann applied his concept of the interpenetration of longitudinal and centric spaces, achieving an ideal union of the late baroque and early classicism. The layout is composed of a series of transversal oval spaces covered by domes that are connected in a dynamic way to a 'circular temple' supported by four pairs of free-standing columns. The separate from the side areas and dissolve the parts, transforming the church in a large room.

**nctuary of
erzehnheiligen, 1743–73**
umann achieved here a
rfect synthesis of rococo
hitecture, combining a
mplex series of ovals, both
the vaults and in the plan,
th astonishing decoration
d annulling the borders of
e traditional iconology of
e sacred space by dissolving
e crossing to create a
minous domed space.

**sidenz, Würzburg,
irway, 1737**
the prince-bishop's palace
Würzburg Neumann
ade his 'theatre of light',
heatrical stairway with
ree flights freely extended
rough space, dominated by
e superb vault frescoed by
epolo. The stairs establish
e structure of the
rounding space and also
perception; the spaces
d the frescoes of the vault
pear in succession
cording to an architectural
ise en scene' especially
signed for the site.

**hloss Brühl,
gustusburg, stairway,
41–44**
any noble residences of
th-century Germany were
sed on a central body
asting a truly dramatic
irway – powerfully
namic, elegantly theatrical
he result of the fruitful
laboration of architect,
ulptor, and fresco painter.
e vestibule at Brühl
esents the skilled fusion
dynamic curving lines
unterbalanced by the
vere verticality of the
ired columns and the
rprising figural pillars.

### The Dientzenhofer family

The Bohemian late baroque was among the richest and most original artistic periods in the history of 18th-century Europe. The initial predominance of Italian taste, French stylistic elements, and the proximity of Vienna resulted in a harmonious and heterogeneous blend of forms that was unique in Europe. Prague again rose to rank among the most lively and dynamic cities, and its architectural verve was reflected in several important undertakings, from the domes of churches to new noble palaces and finally to major complexes, such as the sanctuary of Loreto.

The architectural face of the city and its region was in large measure a result of the work of a family of architects – the Dientzenhofers – whose creations are characterized by an insistent use of curving lines and complex plans composed of spatial cells derived from Guarini. Around 1700, they were responsible for the last great flowering of baroque ecclesiastical architecture.

Of particular importance were the churches of St Nicholas in the Little Quarter (Mala Strana) of Prague and St Margaret at Brevnov, near Prague, both works by Christoph Dientzenhofer. These two splendid churches present similar forms derived from the application of Borromini and Guarini principles, such as spatial juxtaposition and the large curved cornice on columns or pillars, also known as the 'Dientzenhoferian motif'. The churches by Dientzenhofer are composed of oval cells that interpenetrate following lines of expansion or contraction – a system called spatial syncopation or syncopated interpenetration – combined with the Central European system of mural pillars, which expresses the aspiration for strong plastic and spatial integration, while the external walls are generally treated as neutral surfaces. The space is presented as an 'open' system to which it is possible to add cells at will, following the principle of 'pulsating juxtapositions'.

**Our Lady of Loreto, Prague, begun 1721**
Nearer the forms of rococo, the façade of the sanctuary of Loreto – made beginning in 1721 on a design by Christoph Dientzenhofer and completed by his son Kilian – is especially wide and has austere architectural forms emphasized by the elegant colouring of the cornices, with subtly undulating movement only in the two higher side bodies and in the decorative bell tower.

**St Margaret, Brevnov, 1708–21**
The bi-axial interior of the small church of Brevnov is expressed on the exterior by the enveloping continuity of the walls. The interruption in the trabeation along the south side marks the unusual location of the entrance, establishing a convincing relationship between the interior and the exterior in which is recognized the same advance and withdrawal of the volumes and their oscillating movement.

*Left*
**Church of St Nicholas in the Little Quarter, Prague, 1703–11**
Modelled on the Borromini forms of S Carlo alle Quattro Fontane, the church of St Nicholas is striking for the supple play of its curving lines and for its monumental exterior prospects. Set on a high drum, the dome has a spectacular impact; it was designed to mark the centre of the city's Little Quarter (Mala Strana).

# Giovanni Santini

## St John Nepomuk, Z'dar

### 1719–22

The combination of a circular central space with ellipses inserted both externally and internally becomes an architectural reality in the votive chapel of the sanctuary of St John Nepomuk at Zelená Hora near Z'dar in the Czech Republic, made by Santini between 1719 and 1722.

Born to a family of Italian origin, Santini evolved a highly original style, the fruit of his varied training and his notable creativity. This style mixes baroque elements, such as stellar forms from Borromini, with elements drawn from Gothic architecture.

Drawing inspiration from the late-17th-century pilgrimage church of the Holy Trinity, known as the Kappel, designed by Georg Dientzenhofer, Santini worked out a complex plan with five ovals alternating with five triangular niches arranged around a circular centre. The result is a dynamic design that is most clearly stated in the cornice of the dome. Santini used the stellar plan and external convexity as visual echoes of a miraculous event that had occurred after the martyrdom of St John of Nepomuk: in the moment of his drowning in the Moldau River, five stars were said to have appeared around his head, forming a circle. The number five recurs in the design of the sanctuary, which has five entrances, five chapels, and five altars. Also related to the symbolism of the martyrdom of St John of Nepomuk – King Wenceslas IV had him thrown in the river when he refused to reveal what the king's wife had told in confession – is the elongated shape of the windows, which recalls the shape of a tongue.

Completely unique on the panorama of the European late baroque, St John Nepomuk is a Gothic-style church with a strongly nostalgic and irrational character. Santini's fondness for the Gothic probably resulted from his activity restoring the churches of Prague that had been destroyed by the Hussites. Around 1703 he had been commissioned to rebuild the great Cistercian church of Sedlec in the Gothic style to revive the medieval monastic tradition, and he designed a splendid system of interwoven ribs that were purely decorative, serving no structural function.

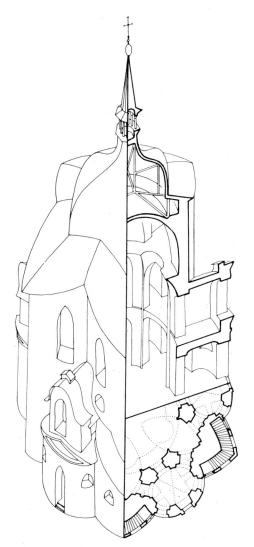

Santini's church is full of apparent contradictions. The use of a central plan without indication of the centripetal and centrifugal forces that compose it and the juxtaposition of volumes seem to symbolize the unreachable nature of the sky; the continuous walls make the spaces appear closed and inescapable. Perhaps Santini sensed in himself the contradictions of his age, the rift between thought and feelings, the disintegration of the European anthropomorphic tradition. Perhaps that is why he chose Gothic forms and, indeed, the most abstract Gothic forms from the medieval tradition, such as the play of intersecting lines that seem to have neither beginning nor end.

e centrality of the
nctuary is repeated in the
redible decagonal arcade
vered by a pointed vault,
which are ten Gothic-
le chapels. The diversity of
ntini's cultural repertory is
ade clear in the treatment
the internal surfaces
corated in stuccowork and
the pale tones of the
asterwork, derived from
rromini, connecting to a
stem of Gothic ribs. The
rangement of the windows
ovides abundant
umination.

### From Wunderkammer to cultural sanctuary

Assembling collections of 'wonders' – singular or rare objects, whether 'natural' or associated with works of art or gold working – was common in Europe by the late 16th century. As described by the Flemish writer Samuel von Quiccheberg in his popular book on collecting (1565), the model collection involved the union of a library and a *Wunderkammer* ('curiosity cabinet') in an encyclopaedic arrangement. The predilection for collecting precious objects and curious artefacts, natural specimens and artificial elements, scientific instruments and magical devices became intertwined with the first baroque libraries, where the growth of scientific knowledge blended with the strangest forms of nature, all of it tinged with the lingering speculations of medieval alchemists. These study-libraries, closely related to the *Wunderkammer* and *Kunstkammer* ('art chamber'), were not unusual throughout the 18th century. An outstanding example was the small library of

Frederick II, which he kept in Schloss Sanssouci at Potsdam in a small space shaped like a humanist's study. Over the course of the 18th century the leading courts of Europe began assembling monumental libraries. Most were housed in large rooms, often richly frescoed, with high ceilings and walls covered in shelves of books – quite often, however, with side rooms for the storage and display of exotic curios or precious objects. The Habsburg collection of books is preserved in a majestic hall designed by Fischer von Erlach and illuminated by large windows decorated with frescoes by Daniel Gran that celebrate Emperor Charles VI, portrayed as the protector of the arts and sciences. Emperors and princes were not the only possessors of book collections. In keeping with their age-old tradition of preserving knowledge, monasteries and abbeys had libraries, and over the course of the baroque age these began to acquire a monumental exuberance similar to that of their secular brethren.

**Library of the abbey, Melk, 1702–36**
The library of Melk stands out for the astonishing baroque qualities of its inla[...] and gilt shelves and the ceiling fresco by Paul Troge[...] made between 1731 and 1732, with an allegorical depiction of Faith protecti[...] earthly wisdom.

**Library of the abbey, Metten, 1722–29**
The frescoed ceiling, the stucco decoration by Franz Joseph Holzinger, and the extraordinary inlaid and gilt bookcases rank this highly evocative room among the most appealing of the European baroque.

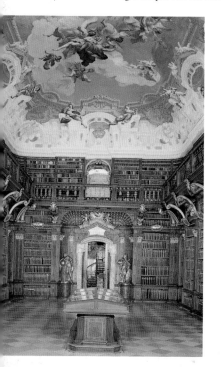

Library of the Clementinum
Jesuit college, Prague,
1721–27
'God is in one of the letters
on one of the pages of one of
the four hundred thousand
books in the Clementinum.'
says a character in a story
by Jorge Luis Borges,
speaking about the Czech
National Library, a symbol
of the old city.

*Opposite right*
**Hofbibliothek,
Vienna, 1721–35**
While the exterior speaks an
authentically French
classicism, the interior of the
Hofbibliothek by Fischer von
Erlach – a large oval setting,
domed, from which extend
the two wings of a
ponderous gallery marked
by the motif of twinned
columns – is packed full with
lively, elegantly luminous
material, the clarity of which
presents one of the most
extraordinary interiors of
the period.

# Bartolomeo Francesco Rastrelli
## 1742–62

### St Petersburg

Early in the 18th century Tsar Peter the Great founded the city of St Petersburg. Russia was beginning to open itself to Europe, and St Petersburg was the 'window' looking in that direction. The city took on a Western style, brought there and applied by Italian architects and an international collection of artists. Among the architects was Bartolomeo Rastrelli (*c.* 1700–71), the absolute leader of construction and urban planning under Tsarina Elizabeth. He created churches and imperial homes characterized by a singular version of the late baroque, fashioning hybrid but brilliant forms in which he adapted aspects of the local style to create variants that eventually composed a vast patrimony of forms. Rastrelli was of Italian origin but had grown up in France and had been living in Russia since the age of sixteen, so he can be considered a true Russian, and the style of his work became the style of Russian architecture in the middle of the 18th century. As court architect he designed the main palaces in the capital and outlying areas following an ideology that even in the late 18th century was characterized by the exaltation of the power of the state. So it was that while the rest of Europe marked the end of an epoch, Russia in the middle of the century was still at the height of its truly 'baroque' architecture.

His grand compositions are arranged along precise axes, like elegant proofs of geometric theorems, characterized by stylistic unity with a minimum of detail in the overall conception of the building. The strict hierarchy of the spaces and the obsessive repetition of architectural elements are accompanied by an uninterrupted variation in the profiles of the elements themselves. In his first mature work, the Strogonov Palace (1750–54), Rastrelli defined his personal style, presenting a giant order of strongly plastic engaged columns above a rusticated base mixed with curved cornices similar to those found on old Russian churches.

**Cathedral of the Smol'ny Convent, 1744–57**
Rastrelli's masterpiece is the cathedral of the Smol'ny convent. It has a central-plan layout with a high dome flanked by four domed towers that represent the most successful synthesis of a traditional Russian church with the motifs typical of baroque architecture. In keeping with the desires of the Tsarina Elizabeth, he inserted purely Russian elements in the articulation of the five onion domes.

**Bol'shoy Palace, Pushkin, 1752–56**
In the Bol'shoy Palace, Rastrelli multiplied to infinity the motifs earlier presented in the Strogonov Palace, creating a festive effect that is also, however, somewhat excessive. The long, narrow building has large projecting parts that alternate with stretches of wall, creating a framework marked off by the incessant rhythm of the colossal columns. The baroque aspects are dulled by Renaissance citations with extraordinary decorative effects, accentuated by the striking polychromy of the exterior.

**Winter Palace, St Petersburg, 1753–62**
The articulation of the four façades of this great block, with interior courtyard, seems to be yet another variation on the theme used on the Strogonov Palace. The face on the Neva River is dominated by giant columns, while the other façades present an alternation of plastic features and more neutral areas. The classical elements serve a purely decorative function; they add opulence but do so without significance, thus signalling the decadence of the great palaces of the absolute monarchies.

# Military architecture
## 17th–18th century

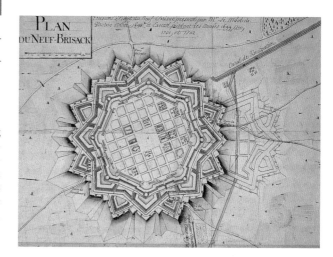

### The military geography of baroque Europe

The reworkings of urban areas that took place during the 17th century were almost always related to overall systems of defensive fortifications, and these systems evolved steadily in terms of form and type. In response to the increased power of artillery, bastions became lower and wider, and ditches and moats were introduced on such a scale that they represented an element of transition between the city and the surrounding countryside.

Military constructions, most of all fortifications, presented one of the major expenses faced by a baroque state in Europe, and the military geography of modern Europe came into being in part because of the varying ability of states to pay their bills. The more or less constant pressure of warfare between the emerging powers of the young modern Europe induced many cities to pay for avant-garde fortifications. Excellence in planning such fortifications was originally an Italian monopoly, but it shifted northward in the wake of the conflicts.

In 1667 King Louis XIV of France began a series of aggressive campaigns against the Spanish Netherlands and the Rhineland, thus providing the opportunity to make an ambitious programme of fortifications along France's northern and eastern borders. The pre-eminence of French military architecture results as much from the munificence of its sovereign as from the excellent qualities of its greatest military architect, Sébastien Leprestre de Vauban, who designed a series of revolutionary and ingenious fortifications, along with new cities, using ideas dictated by the pragmatic breaking of academic rules. He worked out an easy compromise between the 16th-century Italian obtuse-angle bastion and the 17th-century Dutch acute-angle bastion and reintroduced, in the Alps and the Pyrenees, the citadel, bastioned towers with blockhouses.

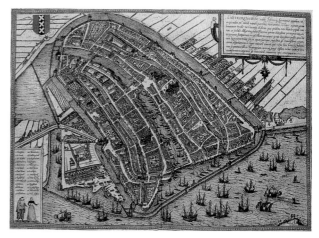

*Top*

**Sébastien Leprestre de Vauban, plan of Neuf-Brisach, 1698–1705, Paris, Direction de l'Architecture et du Patrimoine, Ministère de la Culture**
Neuf-Brisach has a regular octagonal layout, borrowed perhaps from the 16th-century geometric fortifications of the Venetian cities of Nicosia and Palmanova, with a right-angled street network. Here Vauban designs an 'ideal city' defended by monumental gates that combine the three typologies of bastion, ramparts, and deep moats.

**Georg Braun, plan of Amsterdam, engraving from *Civitates orbis terrarum*, 1582, Naval Museum, Genoa**
Being so often on the defensive, the Low Countries constituted such rich terrain for experimentation that they became the home to an important tradition of engineering, represented by the Dutch engineer Menno van Coehoorn. He gave a systematic arrangement to the northern tradition of moats filled with water, the use of low-profile ramparts, and brick bastions built at the water line and covered with earth.

*Opposite*

**Fortress of Saints Peter and Paul, St Petersburg, begun 1703**
Built for Peter the Great on small island in the Neva to protect the passage toward the Baltic, the fortress was transformed into one of the most impressive fortifications in Europe by Domenico Trezzini, completed in 1718. Its bric bastions, modelled on Dut and Swedish examples, enclose a true citadel: the fastest and least expensive way to defend the city.

# Luigi Vanvitelli

## Royal palace of Caserta

### 1751–73

Together with Juvarra, the other great interpreter of the late baroque in Italy was Luigi Vanvitelli; in 1751 Charles III entrusted him with the creation of what proved to be his most ambitious undertaking, the enormous complex of the royal palace at Caserta.

Vanvitelli's creation is an expression of the architectural culture of the Italian late baroque, along with enrichments from the French experiences of the Louvre and Versailles and the Spanish experience of El Escorial. The quality of Vanvitelli's language resides in the impeccable logic of its symmetries, in the precise geometry behind the arrangement of the many and various elements. The palace looks like an immense block. An internal gallery – the *'gran portico'* – runs along its longitudinal axis and leads to the garden. There is also a transverse axis, thus creating four equal-sized, symmetrical oblong courtyards; the octagonal junction of the vestibule at the crossing of the two axes is the structure's heart. The entire design of the building spreads outward from that point, an arrangement related to the 18th-century tradition of theatrical apparatuses. In fact, the imposing vistas offered in all directions and the arrangement of the courtyards on diagonal axes make reference to the 'angle style' of the Bibienas, an Emilian family of specialists in stage scenery and theatrical architecture. The vestibule is the site of the ceremonial staircase, which shows the clear influence of 17th-century staircases. Vanvitelli had learned much in Rome, from the worksite of St Peter's to the works of Borromini, and he was an attentive student of both ancient tradition and the baroque. At Caserta he surpassed the late baroque language in favour of a sober and rigorous architectural discipline. By way of his balanced language, he proved himself capable of interpreting the needs of his patron, which combined both the functional and the celebratory. The union of tasteful elegance and competency at monumental renderings permitted him to make the royal palace and its surrounding park into a complex of great solemnity and also of fascinating variety and grace.

The geometric regularity the building's layout belie the existence of various insertions of great artistic value: the chapel, which is quite similar to that of Versailles, the tribunal, th observatory, and most of the theatre.

Connected to Naples by means of a straight avenu on a direct axis to the pal and the park, Caserta was designed not only to hous the court but also as a decentralized seat of the administrative and governing offices of the kingdom. The creation of the palace had an enormo impact on the surroundin countryside, a reflection o the original intention to make the palace the centr a new urban and territori structure. The long telescopic view toward th basin of the Grande Casca cuts the hill and crosses t park thanks to a highly original scansion of plane

# The formal garden
## 17th–18th century

### The French garden

The so-called French garden came into being during the baroque period. This is an architectural garden that transforms the landscape into a balanced, controlled work of art, and as such is an expression of the total domination of nature. The French garden resulted from the transformation of the 16th-century Italian garden into a broader system of spaces, paths, and visual axes, with rippling bodies of water and long vistas. An important model in European garden design during the 17th and 18th centuries was the court of the Belvedere in the Vatican, one of the most successful examples of the use of architecture as the predominant feature in the construction of a garden. Italian models began exercising increased influence on French garden design during the reign of Henry IV, whose queen was Catherine de' Medici, but it was only during the reign of Louis XIV that the French garden was transformed into an impressive work of art, from the splendid gardens of Vaux-le-Vicomte to the Tuileries in Paris to the park of Versailles.

The figure responsible for these wonders was André Le Nôtre, who at Vaux (1656) arranged the various formal elements along a longitudinal axis, which passes through the palace to descend the long slope by way of terraces to lose itself in the infinite distance. It is a garden conceived on the basis of long-distance views enlivened by the insertion of rows of parterres. At Vaux, Le Nôtre drew on all the gardens of Europe, making use of such motifs as the canal, the pond, stairs, and ramps and combining them in absolutely novel ways. Those elements were to become the common language of the formal garden throughout Europe.

André Le Nôtre, park of the palace of Versailles, begun 1661
Designed along a perspective axis that leads off toward the distant horizon, Versailles was not created merely to serve as a refuge and place of amusement; its innovative organization of space was also meant to be symbolic of the new order of the state. The park's arrangement and its iconographic themes interpret the symbolic meaning of royal order in the world. The route, which includes various stops at special vantage points, crosses the Galerie des Glaces, exits the palace, and by way of the Parterre d'Eau moves along the central axis past the Bassin d'Apollon, a pond symbolic of universal harmony – to end in a view along the canal to the distant horizon. The world is thus given the semblance of an orderly space, full of both sunshine and light.

La Granja, San Ildefonso, Segovia, early 18th century
The architectural complex of San Ildefonso, located near Segovia, is based on the model of Versailles, but because of its topographical situation covers a smaller area. It makes up for this, however, by extraordinary waterworks and fountains. The perspective view as symbolic expression of a world order is here transmuted into a narrow panorama held within a closed space.

**xandre-Jean-Baptiste Le
nd, garden of Peterhof,
etersburg, 1723**
he 18th century, the new,
erging power of tsarist
sia inherited the baroque
cept of the landscape
ked tight with exquisitely
bolic meanings. The
len of the Peterhof palace
nects this small Versailles
he Baltic Sea by way of a
al and is organized
und a central longitudinal
s enlivened by
aordinary waterworks,
uding a series of falls
orated by monumental
ntains.

**Garden of the palace of
Herrenhausen, Hanover,
end 17th century**
The development of the
baroque garden in Germany
followed the authoritative
models of the French formal
garden, combining the
ornamentation with plant
parterres with woven and
spiralling motifs and with
parterres of water. The
garden of Herrenhausen,
constructed along the usual
central perspective axis that
runs from the residence to a
round body of water,
includes several features of
Dutch origin, such as the
canal that surrounds the
entire area, and an orchard,
destined to become the
typology of the garden on the
German plain. The symbolic
presence of the labyrinth
leads back instead to 15th-
century Italian gardens.

## Urban changes
## 17th–18th century

### City-planning in European capitals

The consolidation of Europe's great nation states with their centralized governments meant new roles and celebratory functions for their capital cities. Other factors affecting cities were increased populations and a denser network of roads, leading to the redefinition of cities in terms of their shapes, sizes, and functions. In the baroque age cities were given regular structures, as far as that was possible, with an internal grid of streets and major roadways laid out to connect a series of focal points, major portals, churches, and palaces, with the monumental buildings given integrated façades.

An early example of the transformation of the city was the Rome of Pope Sixtus V at the end of the 16th century, where Domenico Fontana created the straight streets that unite the seven principal Roman basilicas, with the explicit intention of developing depressed areas far from the centre of the city and with the symbolic intention of giving life to a true holy city.

Most of the leading European architects of the 17th and 18th centuries were involved in city planning, including designs that changed the urban layouts of Europe's main cities: in Paris Le Vau and Mansart redesigned the city as a true modern capital, and the old fortifications were replaced by concentric rings of boulevards beyond which, thanks to radial streets, the urban nucleus opened out to the surrounding countryside. Turin was expanded three times, redefining the city according to a rectangular grid borrowed from the ancient Roman *castrum*. The 1666 fire of London made way for the redesigning of that city; in Vienna, great palaces were built one after another around the historic centre; and in 1703 Tsar Peter the Great had his new capital, St Petersburg, built up from nothing. According to different modalities, 18th-century cities shared the desire to 'amaze': architects designed scenographic and theatrical façades for palaces, while splashing fountains blended architectural, sculptural, and natural elements in order to achieve surprising and delightful effects. Both the new European capital cities and the ceremonial aspects of the baroque court reflected the idealistic concept of the city as conceived long ago by Vitruvius, but that concept was now being draped in the robes of absolute monarchies, and it was becoming centred on the urban typology of the square, destined to become the theatre for the apotheosis of the king.

**Francesco de' Sanctis, Spanish Steps, Rome, 1723–26**
On the basis of the spirit of the *capriccioso* inventions of Borromini grafted onto the style of the rococo arose one of the most fascinating urban creations in Rome, carried out with a sure hand in terms of its scenographic effects and its surprising visual variety: the triumphal Spanish Steps in Piazza di Spagna. The complex play of ascending and descending rhythms, in perfect dynamic balance, is dominated by the axis of the church of the Trinità dei Monti and the obelisk, which marks the point where the two perspective lines meet.

**n Gómez de Mora,
za Mayor, Madrid,
npleted 1619**
a Mayor is the square in
heart of the city used for
emonies. This architectural
ology – rectangular,
rounded by homogeneous
ne-height buildings, and
sed to traffic – was based
the French model of the
ce des Vosges. This was the
major undertaking of
ular architecture in 17th-
tury Spain.

**Jules Hardouin Mansart,
Les Invalides, plan, Paris,
1675–1706**
Set along the central axis
of the Hôtel des Invalides –
the hospital-hospice for
veterans – Mansart's church
was made part of the urban
space, while its vertical
accentuation expresses its
role as a perspective focal
point. Mansart's plan called
for extended wings, much
like those in Bernini's plan
for St Peter's Square, but they
were never made; they would
have integrated the cathedral
to the square around it even
more solidly.

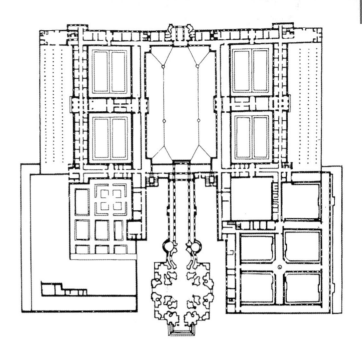

# The Palladian revival in England

## c. 1700–50

### Country houses

In opposition to the style of the Counter-Reformation and to the imposing vistas and axial arrangements of French state architecture, the English architecture of the first half of the 18th century remained substantially faithful to the classical style. Nobles and middle-class patrons were among the first to distance themselves from baroque rhetoric, turning instead to plainer and more elegant forms, imbued with dignity and decorum.

Once again, the basic reference model was the architecture of Palladio, based on rigorously symmetrical layouts whose simplicity and grandeur made it possible to adapt prototypes drawn from classical architecture.

The country houses inhabited by the majority of the aristocracy were composed of clearly defined geometric bodies, usually rectangles, with wings added to the sides, often composed of isolated buildings connected to the main body by galleries, with elegantly serene external decoration. The fronts were often preceded by a portico based on that of ancient classical temples, and a Ser-lian-motif window was often used on the *piano nobile*. There was no lack of strictly indigenous typologies, such as the combination of projecting windows called bow windows; these had been in use since the late Middle Ages, but beginning in the middle of the 18th century they became a constant feature of country houses.

The first leaders of this period of English architecture included Richard Boyle, Earl of Burlington, William Kent, Lancelot 'Capability' Brown, and John Wood, Jr; for them, the deliberate return to the ancient provided the source for an absolutely original indigenous architecture. The works of William Chambers and Robert Adam amplified this architectural vocabulary through a more liberal revisiting of the past that introduced suggestions drawn from Greek and Etruscan architecture. The energy that English architecture drew from classicism in the first half of the 18th century constituted a direct anticipation of the final overcoming of the baroque, which was to take place on the continent of Europe around the middle of the century.

**Lord Burlington and William Kent, Chiswick House, London, c. 1725**
The Palladian-style house, symbol in stone of the new 'enlightened' man, is set in front of the 'natural' world of a garden; Lord Burlington here gives a sample of the decomposition and recomposition of elements drawn from a variety of sources, but the original source for the whole is most certainly Palladio's Villa Rotonda of Vicenza.

**Lord Burlington and William Kent, Holkham Hall, Norfolk, vestibule, c. 1734**

In the ground plan and in the exteriors, Lord Burlington and Kent carefully distributed the volumes and the surfaces around the portico and the central body. The vestibule – one of the most spectacular interiors of the 18th century – is based on the theme of Palladio's Vitruvian hall, to which the architects added a great apse inspired by Roman baths. The pale tones of the alabaster, the Greek key frieze, and the volutes produce a fully classical effect in a setting that still reveals a dramatic character of baroque inspiration.

**Robert Adam, Kenwood House, London, library, 1767**

Robert Adam grafted a more knowing imitation of the Greek classical orders onto the rootstock of Palladianism. The combination of niches, apses, and areas of free-standing columns with pastel-colour walls and ceiling, pale stuccoes, and gold becomes the hallmark of the 'Adam style.' His decorative models were drawn from Herculaneum and Pompeii and from Renaissance grotesques. Pompeian-style painting invaded homes and became a true fad in England. Adam's interiors respond perfectly to the needs of comfort and intimacy and serene elegance of his English patrons.

**[Joh]n Wood, Jr, Royal [Cr]escent, Bath, 1767–74**

[Wi]th classicism, a true [nat]ional art began taking [for]m in England, translated [in] urban contexts into the [mo]numental arrangements [of] the 'circus' and the [cr]escent'. In these, the [lan]guage of the architecture [ser]ves the speculative ends [of] the entrepreneurial class. [Joh]n Wood presents in neo-[cla]ssical forms the baroque [ten]dency to integrate [bui]ldings and nature, in [thi]s case thirty houses [arr]anged in a crescent [aro]und a giant lawn.

# The Gothic revival in England

## c. 1750–1850

### Castellated Gothic

In England, in the second half of the 18th century, the term *Gothic* was freed of the negative connotations that had been attached to it by Renaissance art critics. This was a result of the early romantic infatuation with the Middle Ages, which saw medieval art as an expression of the national spirit; it was also a reaction to the Palladian officialism of Inigo Jones and the baroque classicism of Wren. Although it can be identified in other countries of Europe and also in the United States, this Gothic revival, as it came to be called, was strongest in England, where it was also associated with religious and national significance.

At the same time, the classical idea of beauty as harmony and balance was renounced by Edmund Burke in his *Philosophical Enquiry into the Origin of Our Ideas of the Sublime and the Beautiful* (1757), which laid the basis for an aesthetics of sentiment that distinguishes the beautiful from the sublime, the latter understood as the response to whatever is terrible and emotionally disturbing. This concept, together with that of the 'picturesque', drew attention to whatever was different, dangerous, surprising,

even decadent; the ideal of symmetry was abandoned in favour of asymmetry and irregularity. Ruins became a popular subject because of the emotions they inspire.

In this context, the asymmetrical layout of Strawberry Hill set in motion the so-called castellated Gothic, in which the country house is turned into a medieval castle placed in the midst of nature, if possible atop a rocky crag. Thanks to its association with the picturesque and the sublime, this strongly visionary style soon reached great popularity.

During the years 1810–20 the eccentric Gothic reveries, having reached a kind of culmination in the romantic concept of Fonthill Abbey, gave way to the demand for the accurate imitation of medieval forms combined with a return to medieval craftsmanship. The Gothic revival thus left the sphere of the country house and took its place as a style in competition with neo-classicism, and since Gothic was considered a Christian style by definition, it immediately conquered the sphere of church building, attaching itself directly to the late Perpendicular Gothic, considered a completely autonomous and original English creation.

**James Wyatt, Fonthill Abbey, 1795–1807**
Designed and built for the eccentric William Beckford Fonthill Abbey had an enormous cruciform plan with a panoramic gallery more than 100 metres long some of it presented in the state of ruin, the rest put to domestic uses. Wyatt created a visionary delirium that proved, however, to be structurally weak: the giant 84-metre-high tower ended up collapsing one night in 1825, destroying most of the romantic fantasy, leaving only the north wing.

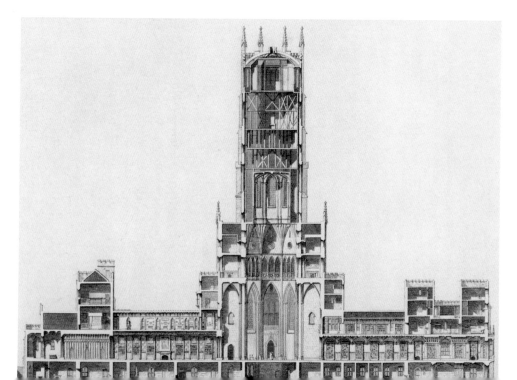

**Horace Walpole, Strawberry Hill, Twickenham, library, 1748–c. 1777**
In planning his country home of Strawberry Hill, the author Horace Walpole created a heterogeneous style, a kind of rococo dressed up in Gothic inserted in a typically picturesque setting. The architectural structures do not reflect actual historical sources and are instead scenographic inventions meant to awaken the imagination and to create a strong suggestion of times gone by.

**William Butterfield, Church of All Saints, Margaret Street, London, 1849–59**
Between 1850 and 1870 the neo-Gothic went through a period of unexpected vivacity characterized by extreme variety, from geometric shapes to structural polychromy to naturalism. Butterfield's original language represented a detailed declaration of the new Gothic: an architecture interpreted in terms of the chromatic variety of its structures, with eclectic forms drawn from the most massive modules of the Italian and Spanish 13th century with ahistorical additions from Butterfield himself.

# Charles Barry, Augustus Welby Pugin
## Houses of Parliament, London
### 1836–68

On 16 October 1834, a fire destroyed the Old Palace of Westminster; its reconstruction presented the opportunity to create a symbolic work that associated the renewed interest in Gothic art with an authentic national style, appropriate for churches and large-scale public buildings. Because of its ideological and moral associations, Gothic seemed the ideal choice for government and administrative buildings for it exalted their celebratory and noble character.

A competition was held for the best design for the new building, and in keeping with the sentimental and literary romanticism of this increasingly nationalistic period, the competition requested designs in the 'Gothic or Tudor' style, which was thought to be in harmony with the medieval origins of the English parliamentary system. Charles Barry won the competition, but the complex building he created, with an essentially classical arrangement despite the elaborate Gothic details added by Pugin, remains a unique work and did not influence later architecture. Even so, the event marks the first time neo-Gothic had been considered a suitable style for a public work. The Perpendicular style of the Houses of Parliament thus became symbolic of the political structure of England.

Unlike the visionary fantasies of much English Gothic revival architecture, the Houses of Parliament reflect the efforts Barry and Pugin made to reproduce medieval architecture with structural exactness and scrupulous accuracy. The very long river front, measured off regularly by a perpendicular grid, is enlivened by polygonal corner towers; the striking horizontality is attenuated by the rhythmic succession of buttresses. The dressing in brick and stone hides an interior with such 'modern' structural systems as columns and beams in fire-proof iron, an adaptation from industrial architecture. The entire structure is dressed in complex Gothic-style decoration that blends with the structure in a harmonious, well-balanced way. Leaving aside the individual late-Gothic forms, the exterior fits with the theories of neo-classical and picturesque architecture: the homogeneity of the surfaces and the articulation of the masses were designed on the basis of the front along the Thames and in keeping with the nearby medieval Westminster Cathedral.

The definition of the interior of the buildings – from the House of Lords to that of the Commons to more intimate areas, such as the library – reveals an almost fanatic attention to detail. Pugin's style employs Gothic shapes and ornamentations to exalt the stately, ceremonial aspects of the parliament. The precious materials, furnishings, and fittings rekindled the artisan tradition and also encouraged the experimentation with new techniques that is typical of the taste of the Victorian age.

# Landscapes and parks

## 18th century

### Nature 'rediscovered'

In opposition to the rigid geometries of the elegantly arti-ficial formal French garden, the English landscape garden sought to exploit the emotional aspects of the irregularity and variety of nature. The fascination of dense, wild nature was further enriched by scenographic elements, including ruins – at the time highly appreciated for their evocative effects – leading to the birth of a taste for ruins created on purpose in parks and gardens as part of the aesthetics of the picturesque.

The new concept of the landscape had begun in the first half of the 18th century thanks to the genius and originality of William Kent, who between 1730 and 1740 designed the gardens of Chiswick, Stowe, and Rousham, creations that fully abandoned Le Nôtre's symbolic geometries and sym-metrical divisions. Without doubt, the rolling hills of the English landscape were the departure point for this revo-lution, at the base of which is the desire to return to a pri-mal nature, eliminating all the artificial methods of the baroque age and their spatial manifestations. Thus Charles Bridgeman, who performed an important role in the tran-sition from French to English gardens, gave his own inter-pretation to the French 'ha-ha', the concealed ditch that divides a garden from the surrounding parkland. The architecture of baroque gardens was based on the spatial continuity between a building and its garden, with nature organized following a concept of the world; the new ideal of the English garden separated the building from its envi-ronment. Instead, a new symbolic fusion was achieved through the introduction of artificial ruins, which mani-fest the nostalgic desire for a 'return': fusion with nature becomes possible only through the 'death' of architecture.

*On this page*
**William Kent, park of Stowe, 18th century**
The new aesthetic concepts of the sublime and the picturesque increased the emotional impact of architecture in relation to i surrounding environment. 1748 Kent created the Elysi Fields at Stowe, a little valle offering a succession of views, including allegorical and patriotic constructions

'Capability' Brown,
Blenheim park, c. 1764
With Lancelot 'Capability'
Brown the art of the English
garden made a true
revolution. In his serene and
balanced compositions, the
nature of grassy slopes and
bodies of water concur in the
creation of an atmosphere of
quiet meditation. Works of
architecture do not serve as
mere 'belvederes' but are
imbued with a moral
significance.

Henry Flitcroft and Henry
Hoare, Stourhead park,
1744–65
Cultural references, often
drawn from contemporary
landscape painting, enrich
the English garden, with the
introduction of artificial
ruins, crags, waterfalls, and
classical-style or exotic
pavilions. The Pantheon set
on the banks of a lake is
similar in all respects to the
version by Claude Lorrain
*Landscape with Aeneas
at Delos* in London's
National Gallery.

### The antique style

In 1753 Marc-Antoine Laugier published his *Essai sur l'architecture* in which he postulated a return to original forms in the practice of architecture. This was a concept imbued with Enlightenment rationalism and closely related to the classical current never long dormant in French art, not even during the years of the regency and the rococo.

In France, the return to more classical forms confirmed the end of the baroque in the name of a single national style; rococo immoderation was rejected in the name of the 'beautiful simplicity' of antiquity. The current generation of architects, however, such as Pierre Contant d'Ivry and Jacques-Germain Soufflot, were still tied to the fantasy concepts of Roman ruins drawn from Piranesi, often expressed in the sharp contrast between decorative abundance and bare wall surfaces.

It was the court architect Ange-Jacques Gabriel who made the final, definitive break with rococo elements, entrusting himself instead to the reassuring solidity and purity of form, grace, and restraint. Both his urban undertakings (Place de la Concorde, 1743–54) and those more directly architectural aim at the restoration of an official and public architecture. Aligning the ideology of the French court with the positions taken by Enlightenment philosophers, Gabriel established the ground rules of the national official style, to which only later would it be possible to attach antique-style citations filtered in by way of engineering.

It was in the 1770s that French neo-classicism took hold with greater coherence, and it did so in buildings of a less traditional type than the palace and the church. Such was the case, for instance, in the public theatres, works unrelated to court patronage, such as the Grand Théâtre in Bordeaux, designed by Victor Louis, the splendid internal stairway of which became the model for that in the Paris Opéra.

**Jacques-Germain Soufflot, Panthéon (formerly Ste Geneviève), Paris, begun 1757**
Ste Geneviève can be considered the manifesto of the ideas postulated by Laugier in terms of sacred architecture. In place of powerful arcades on columns of the type of St Peter's or the Gesù in Rome, there are thin, free-standing columns and continuous trabeations; in place of a longitudinal nave with barrel vault, there is a central Greek cross plan with a dome. This masterful technical creation was achieved through the use of flying buttresses, rampant arches, and an iron framework. Setting a structure of Gothic wisdom within a classical shell, the extraordinary building is at once revolutionary and reassuring, a result of developments in engineering while still faithful to models from the past.

**Jacques Gondoin, Ecole de Chirurgie, Paris, 1769–75**
Strict in the application of neo-classical forms to architecture, Gondoin adopts in the School of Surgery the typology of the Parisian hôtels with their *corps-de-logis* located behind a *cour d'honneur*. He broke with tradition, however, with the insertion of a peristyle on columns with a continuous trabeation and an attic running above; the entrance is designed as a triumphal arch.

**Ange-Jacques Gabriel, garden of Versailles, Petit Trianon, 1762–64**
Located in a 'French-style' garden where the viewer can take advantage of the single-focus view of the whole, the volumetric clarity of the classical-Palladian forms of the Petit Trianon, made for Madame de Pompadour, is striking for its perfect balance and for the limpid uniformity of the symmetrical front façade, articulated on right angles to form a closed and autonomous rectangle. The garden front presents a Corinthian peristyle; the overall concept is closely related to the interpretation of Palladian villas by way of English Palladianism.

# Visionary neo-classicism and architectural utopias
## c. 1750–1800

### Etienne-Louis Boullée and Claude-Nicolas Ledoux

The architectural designs of Etienne-Louis Boullée and Claude-Nicolas Ledoux present the extreme forms of French neo-classical architecture. They follow a route that runs from its origins to embrace absolute forms – spheres, cubes, cylinders, pyramids – whose source, in keeping with Platonic ideals, resides in nature.

More active as a teacher of theory than as an architect, Boullée worked out visionary, even megalomaniacal projects – such as the utopian monument to knowledge in his *Design for a library* (1783–85) – in which he repeated past themes, bringing them to levels of abstraction and gigantism and thus rendering them impossible to create but also increasing their influence. He designed only public buildings, monuments to the republic erected in the name of reason in which he used the simple forms of geometric solids.

Ledoux designed, and in part made, the factory complex of Chaux at Arc-et-Senans, today one of the most admired monuments of industrial archaeology, in which he arrived at a radical simplification of forms and decorative apparatuses, reduced to a few neo-Greek citations. Ledoux made his last works – his so-called architecture of the Revolution – after the French Revolution, and their graphic structure and visionary character are attempts to give form to the theories and utopian ideals of the epoch.

It had to wait for Jean-Nicolas-Louis Durand to bring Boullée's and Ledoux's visions to a feasible design reality, reducing the fantastic emotional rhetoric to an economical and normative building type. With Durand, the Platonic simplicity of the volumes becomes a modular prototype with which to establish a universal building typology, which he theorized in his famous compendium *Précis des leçons d'architecture* (1802–5).

**Claude-Nicolas Ledoux, Barrière de la Villette, Paris, 1785–89**
Ledoux built several *barrières* ('toll-gates'), from this one at Villette to one at Monceau. They represent the kind of reworking of utilitarian constructions to which architects dedicated themselves with great frequency during the Enlightenment period. The monumental form of the building has been imaginatively reinterpreted in an attempt to overturn the form's meaning, following modalities that cannot help but recall Piranesi.

*Opposite*
**Claude-Nicolas Ledoux, Maison du Directeur, Saline de Chaux, Arc-et-Senans, 1775–79**
The design for a factory with associated living quarters at the salt mines at Arc-et-Senans became an early form of the 'architecture of the Revolution' in which Ledoux designed an ideal city with a semicircular plan that united ideas of absolutism – as in the perfect centrality of the director's house – with those of a moralistic utopia. The overall style of the complex is somewhat traditional, but in individual buildings – the salt storehouse decorated with stalactites and stalagmites, the workshop shaped like a grinding wheel with concentric rings, the salt-block colonnade of the director's house – Ledoux displayed great freedom in applying the formal reperto of history combined with h imagination in strongly expressive architecture.

Etienne-Louis Boullée, design for the cenotaph of Newton, 1784, Paris, Bibliothèque Nationale

Inventor of the 'architecture of shadows', as he himself defined it, Boullée here imagines the cenotaph of Newton – discoverer of an order within the infinite and thus a hero to neo-classicism – as a large cosmic globe brimming with light. Holes in the spherical shell bring luminous rays of light into the interior, creating – by way of the help of nature and not through a pictorial fiction – the impression of a starry sky. Although never made, the design testifies to the ambition of neo-classical architecture to take on grandiose projects, truly worthy of the memory of imperial Rome.

# German neo-classicism
## 1800–50

### Karl Friedrich Schinkel and Leo von Klenze

'Every age has left a sign of itself in an architectural style; why has ours not worked out its own style?' With these words in 1826 Karl Friedrich Schinkel, returning from a trip to England, stated his aim to make himself the bearer of a new national style, of an architectural culture destined to express itself in an original manner with a vocabulary and stylistic experimentation motivated by a profound ideology.

In the public buildings he made in Berlin between 1816 and 1822 Schinkel adopted a rigorous neo-Greek style involving a careful selection of certain Attic elements, with variations made in their syntactic compositions. Thus the severe colonnades – but quite often without the canonical tympanum – hide a compositional liberty that was based on functional requirements. Variations were made in the layouts of these buildings so as to better integrate the functionality of the internal spaces with those of the spaces around the building. In his designs for buildings, he was also attentive to how the building would be inserted in its urban context, while also creating a serene and controlled relationship with the natural elements. In these ways, Schinkel – without ever breaking free of stylistic codes drawn from antiquity – indicated the route to the development of modern building design through the synthetic overcoming of differences.

While Schinkel gave new identity to Berlin, Leo von Klenze, as the result of a fortunate encounter with Ludwig I of Bavaria, became the leader in the urban renewal of Munich. Klenze rigorously applied neo-classical forms to his buildings, beginning with their location in the most isolated position possible in order to best amplify their monumental nature. Along with the 'cult of the monument', dictated by the nationalistic elation of the wars of liberation, he gave free expression to his passion for antiquity and created monumental celebrative works. The impressive Walhalla was dedicated to the spirit of the German people.

**Leo von Klenze, Walhalla, near Regensburg, 1830–42**
Symbol of the concept both archaeological and romantic of Greek civilization, the Walhalla presents the ideal of a temple of Germanic heroes in rigorously Greek Doric forms: a peripteral temple, based on the model of the Parthenon, which is reached by climbing a monumental outdoor stairway on a peak above the Danube. The view of this temple set in a timeless landscape achieves the height of the neo-classical movement.

**o von Klenze,**
**opylaeum, Munich,**
**46–50**
he Greek revival, or more
ecifically the theme of the
henian Propylaeum,
ready inaugurated in the
andenburg Gate by Carl
otthard Langhans in
89–93, and symbolizing
e similarities between
cient Greeks and ancient
rmans, is brought to a
umphal and highly
iginal conclusion by
enze in the Propylaeum
Munich.

**Karl Friedrich Schinkel,**
**Schloss Charlottenhof,**
**Potsdam, 1826–36**
The desire to integrate the
functional aspects of internal
and external spaces, creating
a harmony of structure and
environment, found full
expression in the schloss of
Potsdam, where Schinkel
introduced interior
complexity behind a classical
involucrum. The pleasure
villa built for Prince Charles
strikes a perfect relationship
between the low 'Italian-
style' body of the building,
with its Doric portico, and
the garden, loggias, canals,
and pavilions in a pleasing
and sophisticated fusion of
nature and architecture.

# Neo-classical architecture in the United States 1770–1850

## The Federal style and Greek revival

In 1776 the Declaration of Independence was signed; the establishment of an architectural style suitable for the young nation was not long in coming. The premises of this style involved an elaboration of European classicism, and its role as the symbol of national pride was personified by the figure of the future president Thomas Jefferson. This was not an ideological classicism, however. Although a connoisseur of European history and culture, Jefferson seems to have been interested in those aspects of architecture specifically related to the definition of architectural forms and their technical creation. Thus the references to balance and symmetry, to the composite articulation of columns, tympana, and trabeations in Jefferson's home at Monticello became a reference point for the classical movement in America.

In North America, the last two decades of the 18th century and the early years of the 19th were dominated by two parallel approaches to classicism, the Federal style and the Greek revival. The Federal style is characterized by a sequence of heterogeneous forms enclosed by rectangles of various size that delimit and give form to harmoniously linked spaces; leading exponents of this style include Charles Bulfinch and William Thornton. The Greek revival involved closer adhesion to the values and expressive and stylistic models of the Greek civilization; it was stimulated by the important archaeological discoveries of the early years of that century and reached its greatest intensity around 1820.

In his work, Benjamin Henry Latrobe, a leading exponent of the American Greek revival, associated the idea of archaeological exactness with stylistic purity; in 1801 he designed the Bank of Pennsylvania in Philadelphia, an austere building modelled on a Greek Ionic temple with porticoes around a central domed space. Latrobe's creativity extended to the smallest details of such buildings; to give one example, in presenting Corinthian capitals he replaced the classical acanthus leaves with the more American tobacco or corn leaves.

*Opposite*

**Thomas Jefferson, Virginia State Capitol, Richmond, 1785–96**
In designing this prototype of the American public building, Jefferson used simplifications of French neo-classicism, replacing the original Corinthian style with the more sober Ionic order, a symbolic reference to the spirit of the ancient republics. In this building Jefferson gave a clear indication of the architectural signals the young American republic intended to send. From the Maison Carrée, the Roman temple at Nimes, he drew the ideal type for the new American architecture.

**Thomas Jefferson, University of Virginia, Charlottesville, 1817–26**
The design of the University of Virginia is one of the earliest examples of a university campus in which the constructions are inserted in a landscape and grouped and connected by way of a system of pavilions. Jefferson, using the model of England's Cambridge, gave a new and convincing definition of a centuries-old theme from ancient architecture, at the same time succeeding in making use of an array of motifs from classical architecture, from Palladio's Rotonda to the Pantheon of Rome to citations of the Baths of Diocletian.

William Thornton,
Benjamin Henry Latrobe,
Charles Bulfinch, Capitol
Building, Washington, DC,
1792–1827

The complicated design
history of the US Capitol
demonstrates how the
creation of a state
architecture still posed
problems that were difficult
to resolve. Thornton's
original design called for
a large neo-classical
construction with large
wings and a dominant dome;
when still uncompleted, it
was burned by the British
in 1814. Latrobe was hired
to restore it and in doing so
reworked it, most of all in
the interior.

# Thomas Jefferson

## Monticello

### 1769–1809

Jefferson designed his mansion himself, beginning work in 1769. By 1772 it was ready for occupancy, but Jefferson continued changing and adding to the building for many years, partly as a result of his years spent in Europe as US minister to France, where he came in contact with the new French and English architecture. Based on the central-plan buildings of Palladio, filtered through Jefferson's interpretation of English country homes, Monticello is a monumental and elegant building. It is not without a purely classical citation – drawn from the Vitruvian description of Pliny's villa – modified by being given greater depth so as to create two rooms off a central axis with a double series of rooms in the wings closed off by polygonal apses. The classical white portico with four Tuscan columns stands out sharply against the red fabric of brickwork of which the entire building is composed. A dome atop an octagonal drum indicates the heart of the building, an ample central hall illuminated from above by circular windows. Jefferson added functionality to this aesthetic creation, introducing numerous 'modern' technical innovations, such as service elevators for food and folding beds. Basing himself on classical architecture, variously reinterpreted through his wide-ranging originality, Jefferson created a work that speaks directly to the sensibilities of the observer, because of its elegance and even more because of the way in which it is inserted in the landscape. Built atop a hill and elevated on a high socle, the house at Monticello is perfectly fitted to its setting. The references to balance and symmetry and the composite articulations of columns, tympana, and trabeations skilfully emphasized by the use of the red/white colours were to become enduring terms of reference for the American classical movement.

In the long design evolution of his home at Monticello, Jefferson adapted a layout from *Select Architecture* by Robert Morris of 1775 to a façade for a two-storey building from Palladio's *Four Books*. Work on this well-thought-out building went ahead from 1769 to 1782; between 1793 and 18 the building, still incomple was transformed to have a single floor.

# The neo-classical in Italy

## c. 1750–1850

### The land of the 'thousand neo-classicisms'

What most distinguishes Italian neo-classicism is its lack of a unitary character, a result of Italy's political fragmentation, the absence of a central state, and its domination by foreign powers. Even so, all of the European neo-classical movements drew their inspiration from Italy. Its many works of classical Greek and Roman art – looked upon as surviving elements from a happy bygone era in which creativity and reason were fused, an idea presented in the works of Winckelmann and Mengs – made the Italian peninsula the primary stop on the Grand Tour, the educational trip for young gentlemen that included obligatory stops at Rome and the archaeological sites of Herculaneum and Pompeii.

Italy did not present a particularly creative panorama in terms of new ideas – indeed, French art exercised a great deal of influence there through a paradoxical kind of 'reverse' flow – until once again Rome and its monuments furnished the models for a new architecture. The circular temple derived from the Pantheon took on new meanings and was used in both religious and secular architecture; examples are the secular and celebrative temple by Canova at Possagno (1819–30) and the church of S Francesco di Paolo at Naples by Pietro Bianchi (1817–31). In the same way the villa was revived by way of the Palladian tradition, and the triumphal arch was rediscovered to celebrate Napoleonic pomp, such as the Arco della Pace by Luigi Cagnolo in Milan (1807–38). Thus the neo-classical involved no 'state architecture' in Italy. From the Venice of Gian Antonio Selva to the Rome of Piranesi, Marchionni, Stern, and Valadier, from the Borgo Teresiano, the grid-pattern neo-classical district of Trieste built under Empress Maria Theresa, to Austrian Milan – with Piermarini and Pollack – and then to Napoleonic Milan – with the wonderful city-planning of Cagnolo and Canonica – Italy was home to a thousand neo-classicisms, exactly as many as were the centres of artistic creativity.

**Giovanni Battista Piranesi, S Maria del Priorato, Rome, begun 1764**
In his only architectural work, Piranesi expressed the complexity of his perception of ancient Rome. The exuberant decoration of the wall around the church – with its apparently casual blend of motifs drawn from both imperial Rome and Christianity – contrasts with the distinct clarity of the façade, in which the choice of limpid geometric forms and the flat background surfaces indicate, in a neo-classical style, the overcoming of the predilection for the values of late baroque architecture.

**Giuseppe Piermarini, Villa Reale, Monza, 1777–80**
The constant presence of the Austrian archduke's court in Milan inspired the Milanese aristocracy to update their residences. Piermarini was a leading player in this neo-classical season, creating numerous palaces in which the taste for simple forms, defined by sharp surfaces and sober decoration, was associated with a preference for bare horizontal and vertical strips that take the place of the traditional architectural orders. Archduke Ferdinand's summer residence looks far more [l]ike a royal palace – with expli[cit] references to Versailles an[d] Caserta – than a suburba[n] villa. The U-shaped layou[t] with two projecting bodie[s] unites the typology of the 18th-century villa to that of the urban palace.

**...seppe Valadier, Casina ...adier, Rome, 1816–17**
...e extreme liberty with ...ch Valadier applied the ...ssical language is clearly ...icated by the coffee house ...the Pincian Hill, a small ...lding composed of a ...ual and ironic assembly ...lassical citations.

**...faele Stern, new wing of ...Chiaramonti Museum, ...ican, 1817–22**
...e return to Italy of ...works carted off to France ...Napoleon stimulated new ...rest in Rome's museums ...l in the care for Italy's ...stic patrimony. In Rome, ...passage from traditional ...ecting of the Villa Albani ...e to 'modern' and

'enlightened' museum organization is well represented by the new wing of the Chiaramonti Museum; a long, classical space with solemn lines, severe and rigorous, in which the wealth of marbles and mosaics creates a splendid frame to ancient statues. The enlargement of the Vatican museums was part of the papacy's attempt to achieve hegemony in cultural and antiquarian fields; it also represents an outstanding example of European museum architecture.

# The neo-classical city

## 1800–50

### Civil magnificence

The urbanistic transformations of Europe's cities were part of larger political strategies. The baroque approach to city planning, which involved selecting specific elements and reworking them to increase their scenic impact within the urban context, was abandoned, replaced by a concept of the city as a single organism distinguished by austere buildings and capable of providing a homogeneous visual experience. Thus architecture assimilated town planning in the name of a different relationship between form and function. Architecture also changed its subjects; the homes of the nobility gave way to the institutions and buildings housing the new functions of the state and its finances. At the same time, the classical look once reserved for buildings celebrating political power was now extended to the middle-class residence.

These two opposing movements are represented by two exemplary urban projects from the early years of the century. The first was in St Petersburg, where the traditional Byzantine-Russian forms were abandoned in favour of a city programme involving large public buildings arranged around an articulated system of squares, perfected by Carlo Rossi; the other was in London, where John Nash's arrangement of Regent Street and Regent's Park brought to completion the London policy of coordinated façades that already characterized the famous Bloomsbury squares. In 1767 Robert and James Adam designed the Adelphi, a unitary residential complex, sober and more or less free of decorative elements, with a front along the Thames (now destroyed).

In Italy, too, thought was given to creating a new image of the city, from projects formulated for Milan by Giovanni Antonio Antolini, Luigi Canonica, and Luigi Cagnola to new aspects for Naples by Enrico Alvino, to the arrangement of the 17th-century Piazza del Popolo in Rome by Valadier. On the other side of the Atlantic the young American nation was designing its capital, planned by Pierre-Charles l'Enfant, following a V-shaped scheme centred on the Capitol and the White House.

**Giuseppe Valadier, Piazza del Popolo, Rome, 1813–2** In Piazza del Popolo, Valadier took on the delica problem of working with historical fabric of Rome, and he did so without showing any inhibitions in terms of restructuring or even large-scale demolitio The elliptical square resolv the problem of connecting the baroque urban layout the system of stairs – later replaced by a skilful distribution of arcades an loggias – that climbs the Pincian Hill. The result is transformation of the 17t century 'trident' with the insertion of a transversal a defined by the large exedr on both sides, with the intention of harmoniously joining the square to the h on one side and to the Tib on the other.

**Carlo Rossi, Rossi Street, St Petersburg, 1828–34**
The triumphal affirmation of the neo-classical in Russia was expressed in large-scale urban complexes symbolic of the power of Tsar Alexander I. Carlo Rossi was made principal architect of St Petersburg in 1816. In his urbanistic vision, the idea of monumental grandeur was achieved successfully in the complex of the Alekandrinsky Theatre and in the street named for him. The sweeping arcades and colonnades lead back to imperial Rome and converge on the focal point of the rear façade of the theatre.

**John Nash, Regent Street and Regent's Park, London, 1812–30**
In the neo-classical remodelling of an entire residential zone of London following a scheme that involved the harmonious combination of streets and gardens, regularity and morphological uniformity make this an outstanding example of early 19th-century urban planning. The programme involved strictly coordinated design, but not without variety, as in the sinuous shape of the crescent, the intervals produced by squares, as well as the veritable villages of cottages and villas arranged around the park.

# Exoticisms
## *c.* 1750–1850

### Oriental suggestions

As historicist styles spread, European architecture began showing the tendency to employ decorative and structural elements drawn from the art and architecture of the East. In the period between the English expansion in India during the first half of the 18th century and the French conquest of Algeria in 1830, what had initially been idle curiosity about a different world turned into marked interest, becoming a style, and a trend in taste, that took off in a variety of different directions, from chinoiserie to the passion for Egyptian art, from the stylistic motifs of India to those of Arabian art.

The importation of such precious objects as lacquerware and porcelain during the early 18th century stimulated interest in Chinese art, but only in terms of its decorative qualities. Art from the Far East was filtered through Western taste and applied superficially to European models. It was initially expressed in the production of objects inspired by Oriental motifs, but then came the thoroughly rococo creation of small 'Chinese' arrangements in which the furnishings, tableware, and wall decorations created highly refined settings; it finally led to the almost literal replication of buildings, such as the Pagoda in London's Kew Gardens or the Tea Pavilion of the park of Schloss Sanssouci in Potsdam. This taste began to decline around 1770 but continued in further imitations during later years, such as Marvuglia's Chinese Palace at Palermo of 1799. At the same time, following the military and scientific expeditions to Egypt in 1769 and the Napoleonic campaign of 1798, the Egyptian style spread throughout Europe; once again, the initial taste for furnishings grew to take on a monumental scale, involving urban creations, with gardens strewn with pillars and obelisks and cemetery tombs shaped like pyramids.

European city squares filled more and more with souvenirs from the Orient, much like triumphal displays of conquests made in far-off exotic lands, often with eclectic styles generated by the confusion of archaeological references. Thus came into being those heterogeneous constructions in which Asian elements – the Royal Pavilion of Brighton – are joined to those neo-classical.

**William Chambers, Pagoda of Kew Gardens, London, 1757–62**
The English turned to Oriental models to replace the geometric gardens of French and Italian derivation; alongside neo-classical and Gothic buildings, the landscape garden came to be enriched by tea houses, pagodas, and small bridges. In this context the Pagoda at Kew Gardens exists between transgression and impulses, translating into architecture what Chambers had presented in his *Designs of Chinese Buildings, Furniture, Dresses, Machines and Utensils* (1757), a repertory of Oriental motifs based on designs made during a trip to China.

**anzio Marvuglia,
inese Palace in Favorita
rk, Palermo, 1799–1802**
his Chinese Palace
arvuglia prolongs into the
h century the style for
noiserie that was typical of
e rococo art of the first half
the 18th century, using his
ginal flair to blend
ssical and exotic motifs.

**Johann Peter Benkert
and Matthias Gottlieb
Heymüller, Tea Pavilion,
Schloss Sanssouci,
Potsdam, 1754**
The park of Potsdam, made
to satisfy the intellectual
interests of the king of
Prussia, Frederick the Great,
was up to date in terms of
the stylistic novelties of the

period, such as Oriental-
style buildings. Transformed
into a romantic landscape
garden, it makes use of such
ornamental constructions as
the Tea Pavilion, a curious
building decorated with gilt
statues of mandarins and
Chinese notables.

# John Nash

## Royal Pavilion, Brighton

### 1815–23

Within the sphere of historicist currents veined with exoticism, the British expansion in India was the determining factor for the affirmation of a neo-Indian style, the most felicitous result of which was the Royal Pavilion at Brighton.

Built for the amusements of the regent, the future King George IV, it can be taken as one of the closing chapters in the architecture of Europe's ancien régime. The creation of the pavilion involved turning an earlier, Palladian-style building made by Humphry Repton and James Wyatt into a flamboyant palace with the eclectic and fanciful flavour typical of the English 'picturesque'. The author of this transformation was John Nash, who joined an abundance of decoration to the most modern technical methods of the period. The main salon is in fact built around a framework of cast iron that supports the Oriental-style dome, leaving intact the original interior. In the same way, cast iron is used for some of the finishings, such as the highly original bamboo stairs and the palm-shaped columns. The Oriental style of Mogul Indian architecture used for the exterior and the chinoiserie used for the interiors completely cover the building, and although based on the profoundly Western concept of a 'pleasure palace', the building's appeal is greatly amplified by its sense of exotic notions made stylish by the works of romantic poets. The opulent dream world of the Royal Pavilion is made possible thanks to the use of elements skilfully kept hidden: iron for the construction, gas for the large lamps that provide illumination, and a primitive kind of concrete for the exterior dressing of the palace. The level of skill and artifice is extraordinary, the wealth of the variations seems infinite and is always surprising – from Gothic towers to Indian domes and onion domes, from the exterior neo-classical front to the pagoda over the music room to the minarets – with a fluid transition from architecture to landscape and a multiplicity of 'picturesque' vantage points that mask the underlying framework of the building.

The music room represents the culmination of Nash's decorative fantasy. Extraordinary lotus-shaped glass lamps illuminate a shining gilt cockleshell dome, the lower frieze is composed of panels of backlit glass, flying dragons support the silk wallpaper, gilt spheres and intertwined serpents decorate the cornices of Chinese scenes painted on mural panels – everything concurs in creating a sumptuous and refined setting.

# Eclecticism

## *c.* 1830–1920

### Urban styles and aesthetics

As its types became normalized, and the number of its forms reduced, neo-classicism gave way to a radical secularization of architecture; at the same time, however, it lost the ability to invent a new architectural language. To make up for this, recourse was made to a wider and wider range of historicist citations and to formal crossovers among the various styles of the past in the desire to break free of the compositional canons of the treatises of Vitruvius and the Renaissance. As early as the second half of the 18th century, the idea of a variegated and manifold past began to spread, a past that could not be recreated through the imitation of a restricted number of models. The taste for things medieval had never waned in Britain, and it now led to a precocious form of neo-Gothic architecture along with the poetics of the 'picturesque'. The idea soon spread across Europe of national patrimonies of historical-monumental architecture.

The interchangeability of decorative forms opened the way for forms resulting from the contamination among genres, and this took place along two basic lines: the revisiting of a single model selected from among the many that history offers, and the mixture of heterogeneous elements. So it was that alongside the neo-classical and the neo-Gothic there were also the neo-Romanesque, neo-Byzantine, neo-Egyptian, and neo-Renaissance, with all the possible intermediate variants. A variety of motivations led to these eclectic expressions. Some were political (the Gothic was seen as an English style, 17th-century French 'classicism' was an expression of national unity), some were religious (both the Romanesque and the Gothic were seen as emblems of the Catholic restoration in France), yet others were social (the 'bastions' of industry in Flanders, Holland, and Germany). However, since these notions did not rest on any basis that was not by nature rhetorical they were open to easy manipulation. Through the integration of neo-classical, neo-Gothic, exotic, and utopian elements, the new age made use of the entire patrimony of styles elaborated in the past, stripping them bare of any historical connotations and reducing them to mere forms.

**Imre Steindl, Parliament Budapest, 1882–1902**
Symbol of the Hungarian nation, this building was directly inspired by London Houses of Parliament, with monumental neo-Gothic façade imposed on a layout that respects baroque conventions. An impressive dome, internally ribbed and decorated with neo-Gothic gilt, marks the ideal as well as the visual centre of the building.

**[Ch]ristian Jank,**
**[Sc]hloss Neuschwanstein,**
**[Ba]varia, 1869–86**
[Th]e castles of Ludwig of
[Ba]varia revived the Gothic
[cul]ture of the great legends
[an]d myths as well as the
[cla]ssical style of Louis XIV as
[an] expression of royal power
[an]d a rejection of the outside
[wo]rld. Set atop a hill in the
[Ba]varian Alps, Schloss
[Ne]uschwanstein, entrusted
[to] the court scene painter
[Ch]ristian Jank for the design
[of] the exterior and the
[de]sign of the rooms inspired
[by] the works of Wagner,
[ref]lects Ludwig's passion for
[th]e Wagnerian world and
[re]peats the fairytale image
[of] the castle as the site par
[ex]cellence of fantasy.

**Paul Abadie, Sacré-Coeur,**
**Paris, 1874–1919**
At times, form and
programme seem to
coincide; in the Parisian
basilica of Sacré-Coeur,
located atop the hill of
Montmartre from which
it dominates the entire city,
Abadie – authoritative
exponent of the eclectic
taste and author of 'period',
restorations – combined
Byzantine modules with
romantic forms that recall
the domed church of St
Front in Périgueux.

## City-planning in the late 19th century
### Beginning 1850

**Urban expansion**

The 19th-century industrial city, as described by Baudelaire in *Les Fleurs du mal*, presented a misleading image. Beneath their magnificent surfaces, such cities hid far different realities, the grim and often repellent results of uncontrolled urban growth. In response to the changes made necessary by growing industrial and technological development, the European city expanded outward from its historical centre, forming rings of suburbs that then became part of the metropolis; the influx from the countryside of masses of peasants in search of work made necessary homes, services, and means of transportation integrated with the surrounding territory. Some sort of regulation was required to establish new hierarchies of values, functions, and images; not just urban growth but territorial growth had to be controlled, leading to the new discipline of urban planning, which sought to regulate expansion through the application of plans, and these changed the appearance of the most important cities of Europe. The plans put into practice around the middle of the 19th century, and carried out without losing sight of the baroque taste for urban scenography, were based on criteria drawn from studies of sanitation and functionality. The new means of urban transportation – with electric trolleys running above and, eventually, below ground – made possible new models – more theoretical than real – of linear urban growth, permitting urban development by way of ever-widening circles of residential suburbs around the historic centre.

Paris, Barcelona, and Vienna were among the first cities to adopt plans for urban renewal, and the undertakings are good illustrations of the complexity of carrying out operations designed to change an urban fabric. Although their plans involved different modalities, they share a vision of the physical reality of cities that gives value to position and function. Such large-scale urban plans are designed to involve the entire city and give buildings the role of establishing the identity of districts and locales. Within a city's flowing, abstract image, such monumental structures present themselves as references to past historical epochs and thus constitute a sort of museum that unites the obsession with the past with an awareness of the originality of the current reality.

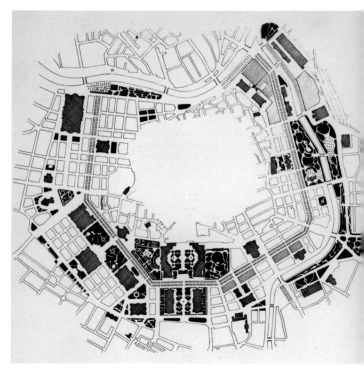

**Ludwig Förster, Ring plan, Vienna, 1859–72**
Perhaps more than any other European city, Vienna has preserved its single-centred urban appearance, with a hierarchical integration of districts and rings in which the template for aggregation has been repeated on an adequate scale. The oldest urban area was integrated with the modern city by way of the establishment of the Ring, an interesting device that makes possible the creation of a new street system without destroying the original fabric. The ring along which public buildings, monuments, squares, and gardens are located – in fact, the ring of the ancient fortifications – became the city's monumental centre, with new institutions and new civil and cultural functions. A street network arranged in rays spreads outward to the surrounding countryside, providing the framework for the future growth of city districts.

**orges Eugène
ussmann, plan of
ris, 1853–69**

e plan for Paris worked
t for Napoleon III by
ussmann, who was
pointed *préfet* of Paris in
53, established the image
a modern city in which
de, straight boulevards
n to form stellar *rond-
ints* to create visual axes
d evocative vantage points.
ussmann's objective was
confer a modern image on
e city while also making
e best use of monumental
uctures and also
proving the quality of the
ildings and the circulation
traffic. Considered the
ventor of the City of Light,
ussmann designed a
ssuring, middle-class city
ted out with all the extras

– services, buildings made
for community life, ample
green spaces – in which the
urban proletariat was
removed from the historical
centre.

**Ildefonso Cerdá, plan
of Barcelona, 1859**
One of the most important
urban plans of the 19th
century was made by Cerdà
for Barcelona: the integrated
expansion of the city was
regulated by a rectangular
grid about twenty-two blocks
wide that incorporates the
Gothic Barrio, the oldest
nucleus of the city, and is
crossed by two large diagonal
arteries. The enlargement
and his plan are illustrated
in his book *Teoría General
de la Urbanización*, published
in 1867.

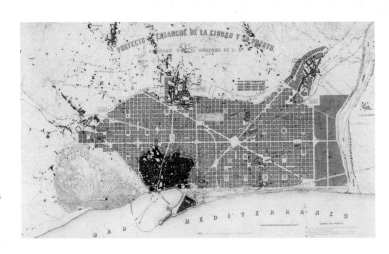

# From company towns
## to garden cities
### 1850–1918

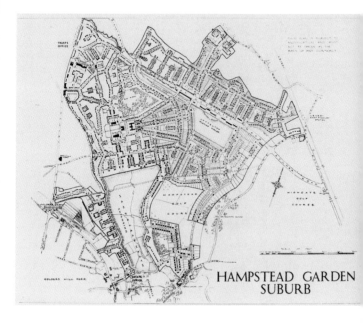

HAMPSTEAD GARDEN
SUBURB

## Housing types during the late 19th century

The population growth of Britain and its industrial development meant the movement of great numbers of people to cities, leading to the creation of workers' neighbourhoods with alarming, squalid living conditions. This reality, already described in the works of Dickens and condemned by Engels, obliged technicians, legislators, and intellectuals to think of a new arrangement for the country's cities, beginning with London and its outlying areas.

Urban congestion fuelled the demand for suitable housing, leading to an early reworking of housing typologies in order to meet the growing demand for low-cost homes for workers. Two basic routes were followed. On the one hand were the building campaigns sponsored by philanthropic organizations, which usually presented strongly ideological solutions involving large collective buildings integrated with a system of public services; on the other – and this occurred not only in Britain but in Germany, France, and the United States – there was the creation of company towns in which private companies offered homes to their employees. These homes were often summary reproductions of the typical middle-class home, although drastically reduced in size and in terms of available services. During the 1840s such company towns were only isolated experiments, but by the end of the century they had become widespread, with the addition of parks and social services.

The idea of an urban form that could efficiently integrate a town with its surrounding landscape led the debate toward the concept of the garden city – high-quality residences joined to form a settlement surrounded by common green spaces with elevated standards of services – as proposed by the English town planner Ebenezer Howard in his *To-morrow: a Peaceful Path to Real Reform* (1898). Howard proposed self-sustaining satellite towns with modern conveniences in agricultural locations, thus resolving the conflict between the city and the countryside. These theories were further elaborated early in the 20th century by the efforts of Raymond Unwin, who designed the first English garden city as well as the Hampstead Garden Suburb near London, and Barry Parker.

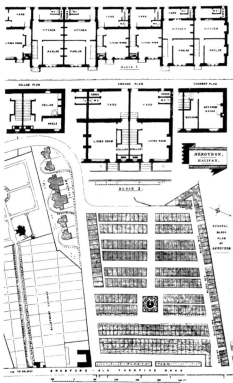

**Raymond Unwin and Barry Parker, plan of Hampstead, London, 1905**
The garden city employed the idea of the 'balanced territory': the metropolis, source of so much anguish to the 19th-century middle class, is broken up into acceptable-size towns without negating the structural base of the urban economy.

**George Gilbert Scott and William Henry Crossland, plan of Akroydon, 1861–63**
The first workers' towns were based on the paternalistic concept of the relationship between capital and work, favourable to a welfare policy designed to eliminate social unrest. Gothic-style forms were chosen as the best for insertion in a rural setting in an attempt to prove that industry did not bring the anonymity and inhuman dimensions of cities to outlying areas, but instead meant that housing would become more comfortable.

*On this page*
**Workers' town of Crespi d'Adda (Bergamo), 1878**
Based on similar English towns, and closely following their layout, the workers' town of Crespi d'Adda was given its precise urban shape by the different types of housing – single- and two-family homes, each with its own garden-vegetable patch – and by its layout. It is arranged along two perpendicular avenues that intersect at the entrance to the factory, marked by the tall smoke stack that becomes the geometric and symbolic reference point of the entire complex. The visual contrast between the humble modesty of the workers' homes and the ostentatious luxury of the owner's villa emphasizes the community's strict hierarchical structure. The peculiar aspect of Crespi d'Adda is that it was conceived from the outset as the site for an ideal life, a model of orderly and productive industrial society, an idea sprung from the 19th-century paternalist ideology in which utopia and philanthropy are interwoven to serve economic needs.

# New materials
## and urban typologies
## 19th century

**Iron, glass, and the arrival of the engineer**

The perfecting of new building materials and techniques, such as the industrial-scale manufacture of iron and steel alloys in Britain between the end of the 18th and the start of the 19th century, made possible experiments with new shapes and types of buildings.

The stylistic complexity of 19th-century architecture, with its mixture of classical forms, archaeological citations, and references to cultural models of the past, together with the aesthetics of the new building materials and their technical possibilities, presented a vast and diversified repertory which was used in the complex design operations undertaken to redefine new spaces and types to respond to the necessities of the new society. Certain architectural typologies appeared more congenial to the use of the new materials, among them the artificial world of the green house, the exhibition pavilion, and large commercial centres, which exalted the ductility of a metallic framework to form vast areas of glass. Very similar were the great train stations of the period, which were composed of two different but complementary structures: the architectural dimension of the building, in which citations from the past were blended with typological requirements, and the spectacular technological expressiveness of the great shed roofs over the tracks.

Shifting the focus of architecture from questions of display and celebration to those of physical construction led to the birth of a new professional figure in the world of buildings, the engineer, thus also causing a split in the field of architecture, a division destined to endure throughout the 20th century. The engineer sees structural precision as his major goal and transforms designs so as to achieve the greatest economy of materials, redesigning a building around a structural skeleton. In this way the terms of the theoretical debate also changed, no longer revolving around the classical orders and seeking instead to explore the expressive possibilities of different languages, thus prefiguring the overcoming of historicist models.

**Henri Labrouste, Bibliothèque Nationale, Paris, 1858–68**
Using the new materials and techniques to express Gothic morphologies can present, here, forms that are both functional and antiacademic. The roof supported by thin cast-iron columns presents synthesis between engineering and architecture.

**Joseph Paxton, Crystal Palace, London, 1850**
Crystal Palace inaugurated a new, highly functional architectural typology thanks to the use of prefabricated elements and particular technical measures. The vast transparent space was destined to be further developed by 20th-century architecture.

## Galleries

*A new urban typology that was defined by the use of new materials – iron and glass – is that of galleries: covered pedestrian passages lined with storefronts. Covered by glass panes set in metallic frameworks, galleries came into being in Paris through the initiative of various entrepreneurs during the first decades of the 19th century, changing the rules for commercial spaces. Not open to wheeled traffic and illuminated at night, galleries offered a kind of comfort that in certain senses anticipated that of the great department stores of the future, and they could reach monumental dimensions, such as the Galleria Vittorio Emanuele I in Milan (1865–67) or that of Umberto I in Naples (1887–90).*

**Gustave Eiffel, Eiffel Tower, Paris, 1889**
For the Paris Exposition Universelle of 1889 French engineer Gustave Eiffel designed a tower symbolic of the modern age, made of an iron framework supported on masonry piers, the iron framework perfectly visible, graceful, and essential to prove the expressive possibilities of the new material. The tower was the highpoint in the career of an ingenious engineer and builder in iron, and its efficiency legitimized the abandonment of traditional figurative schemes and brought a drastic increase in the height of buildings.

**Structural engineering put to public use**

Structural engineering applied to the making of bridges is one of the fields in which the application of the new construction technologies and materials introduced over the course of the 19th century produced significant changes.

The Coalbrookdale Bridge over the Severn River in England – built in 1779 to a design by Abraham Darby and John Wilkinson and made entirely in cast iron – can be taken as the first member of a vastly numerous family, which beginning at the end of the 18th century revolutionized landscapes and methods of transportation while also revealing the level of complexity already reached by engineering. In 1801 James Finlay patented a system of trusses to stiffen the decks of suspension bridges, a construction method of fundamental importance that was further developed with the introduction of cables and iron links. During the first half of the century, numerous bridges were built in England using this technique, from the Union Bridge at Tweed to the Clifton Bridge near Bristol.

The suspension bridge system was perfected by Josiah White and Erskine Hazard in crossing the Schuylkill River in Pennsylvania (1816) and by the Seguin brothers at Tournon-Tain over the Rhone (1825); both bridges were early uses of bundled wire in place of wrought-iron chains. Johann August Roebling – author of railroad bridges at Niagara Falls (1855) and over the Ohio at Cincinnati (1867) – brought about a significant technical improvement in suspension bridges thanks to the use of wire cables and stiffening trusses, which were more structurally solid than preceding versions. At the same time steel tended to replace iron, and designers concentrated on obtaining lighter structures using smaller quantities of material but guaranteeing greater tensile strength and elasticity. Gustave Eiffel was also a leader in bridge building. His bridge over the Douro River (1878) is composed of five piers and a central parabolic arch that supports a continuous girder, and his railway bridge over the Truyère at Garabit (1884), the quintessence of economy and elegance, uses tapering iron towers.

**Sir Benjamin Baker, Firth of Forth Bridge, Edinburgh, 1882–89**
The bridge is composed of three giant units supported by pylons over a total length of about 2,500 metres; it was perfectly suited to the many visionary works of the period and was immediately popular. Very few people criticized the bridge's appearance, but among them was William Morris, one of the fathers of modernism, who called it 'the supremest specimen of all ugliness'.

**John Wolfe-Barry and Horace Jones, Tower Bridge, London, 1886–94**
Movable bridges appeared at the end of the 19th century. Barry and Jones built Tower Bridge in London to resolve the problem of commercial traffic. The central structure is a movable roadway that can be raised or lowered to permit the passage of ships along the Thames.

*Opposite*
**Jules Röthlisberger, bridge at Paderno d'Adda, 1887–89**
The bridge at Paderno d'Adda, designed by the Swiss engineer Röthlisberger, who had already made numerous viaducts in the Alps, is striking for its daring construction in iron inspired by the arched bridges by Gustave Eiffel. It is composed of a rectilinear girder supported by a parabolic arch with a span of 150 metres.

# Art nouveau
## 1890–1914

### 'Line is a force'

During the second half of the 19th century critics like John Ruskin and artists like William Morris looked upon the Industrial Revolution as the cause of social, cultural, and artistic ills and promoted in its place a movement for revivifying the decorative arts and artisan crafts – the arts and crafts movement – but by the end of the century it was no longer possible to escape contact with the culture of modernity and assembly-line production. Until the outbreak of World War I the desire for the new resulted in a Europe-wide movement toward artistic change that was expressed using substantially similar formal elements and theoretical assumptions.

The optimistic faith in the progress of modern industrial civilization on the one hand and the rejection of all eclecticisms on the other caused the rise of a language drawn directly from nature, full of plant and animal references expressed with a dynamic line, decorative, agile, and flexible.

The adoption of this new language – based, according to the definition of the Belgian designer and architect Henri van del Velde, on the 'line as force' – permitted the confirmation of a basic concept of modernist theories: function, that is use, must be matched by form, and decoration – where there is decoration – should be natural and grow from the structure. The agreement of form and function is beauty.

The primary goal was the creation of a work of 'total art', an artistic design that overlooked no element but used all the elements to give the whole a harmonious effect. Hence the stringent relationship between exterior and interior and between an interior and its furnishings, down to the design of objects of daily use, including the most mundane household furnishings.

Horta and van de Velde in Belgium, Guimard in France, Mackintosh in Scotland, Gaudí in Spain, Wagner, Olbrich, and Hoffmann in Austria, and Basile in Italy used the new industrial technologies and materials to serve the expressive needs of a modern language – largely international and recognizable everywhere – and they did so without doing away with references to local traditions, from the Gothic to the rococo, from Celtic art to the Moresque.

*Above*
**Otto Wagner, Majolica House, Vienna, 1898–99**
The condominium on the Wienzeile is considered the first recognition of the right of a home made for ordinary people to aspire to artistic dignity. The extraordinary façade – decorated in Secession style and dressed in ceramic tiles designed by Klimt bearing ornamental floral motifs – accomplishes the goal of combining decoration and architecture. None of the floors was given special treatment, the decoration being equally divided among the apartments.

*Below*
**Ödön Lechner, Institute of Geology, Budapest, 1898–99**
The harmony of the colours and the use of light makes this an outstanding celebration of the splendour of the Hungarian Secession style. The fantastic tent-shaped roof dominates Pest with its blue glazed tiles and spires inspired by Indian temples; the yellow plaster of the walls, decorated with blue Zsolnay ceramics, contrasts with the toothing of the bricks and the cornices.

*Opposite*
**Hector Guimard, Métro Station, Paris, 1900–1**
Around 1900 Guimard designed the stations and entrances of the Parisian Métro, giving an urban dimension to floral decorations until then used only for interiors. Using iron and enamelled steel he designed signs, balustrades and lamp posts in organic forms with frameworks that support glass roofs.

# Brussels
## 1892–1910

**Victor Horta and Belgian art nouveau**

In 1892 the Belgian architect Victor Horta designed and built in Brussels the Tassel House, a building that enclosed a marvellous stairway held up by sinuous metal supports. Horta followed this first creation with many others over the coming years in which his language, strongly influenced by the writings of Viollet-le-Duc and by the creations made possible by developments in the field of engineering, made use of bare metal areas following a continuous line, fluid and curving. This line, further developed, gradually came to involve all of the architectural elements.

So delighted was the response to the Tassel House that within the span of a few years the face of the Belgian capital had been transformed, the style spreading to private homes as well as to commercial and social structures. Among these the Maison du Peuple – commissioned from Horta in 1895 – represents a sort of detailed manifesto for all of Belgian art nouveau: rising metallic lines that serve both support and decorative functions, large glass surfaces, a structural

framework in light, flexible steel. Horta gave artistic dignity to elements that had traditionally been left hidden, giving them an original character through the combination of soft materials like wood, hard ones like marble, and rough ones like iron, thus transforming them into fluid, plastic substances. He used this style in the floors and furniture he personally designed, just as he designed the extraordinary balustrades and handrails that mark the spatial passages among different rooms.

At the same time, Paul Hankar built in Brussels his house and that of the painter Ciamberlani; he too had been influenced by the writing of Viollet-le-Duc and the ideas of the arts and crafts movement. His primary goal was that of uniting the fine arts and the applied arts in a decorative synthesis, developing a highly personal style that showed a preference for the use of wrought iron. Indeed, since he worked for less wealthy clients he was forced to exploit less expensive materials. His early death deprived Belgian art nouveau of a major source of inspiration.

**Paul Hankar, Hankar House, 1893**
The façade of Hankar House echoes Italian Renaissance architecture and, together with the neo-15th-century Ciamberlani House, represents a highly original example of the art of Paul Hankar, a man of vast learning who was passionate about archaeology.

**Paul Cauchie, Cauchie House, window, 1905**
The face of Cauchie House represents a rare and delightful example of 'art on architecture'. The art nouveau fresco surrounds a singular thermal window rearranged through the insertion of ornamental elements.

**tor Horta, Tassel
use, 1892**
Tassel House Horta
vocatively leaves bare a
es of thin iron columns
t twist upward, almost
 vegetal branches to open
he top in leaves and buds.
s plant element reappears
l is amplified in the
ign of the floor mosaics,
he frescoed decoration,
he ornamental details in
nze, and in the iron of
 brackets and balustrade
he stairs. The use of the
ing, vibrant line, applied
oth decorative and
ctural uses, expresses the
ence of art nouveau.

*posite, far right*
**tor Horta, Baron von
velde House, 1895–97**
e octagonal centre of the
on von Eetvelde House is
nposed of thin cast-iron
mns that support the
ss covering from which
ndant light pours down,
ch changes according to
time of day, giving a
tering appearance to the
rflowing decoration. The
monious use of glass and
n marks a turn in Horta's
 toward a greater
nsparency and lightness,
ays maintaining his
ect control of support
ctures.

# The Viennese Secession
## 1897–1914

**'To every age its art, to every art its freedom'**

The motto inscribed over the entrance to the Secessionhaus designed by Joseph Maria Olbrich provides an emblematic summary of the programme of the Viennese Secession movement, founded in 1897 by a group of artists – among them the architects Olbrich, Josef Hoffmann, and Otto Wagner – with the aim of opposing official academic art in favour of an architecture and art suitable for the evolution of modern society. The shared goal was liberation from any historicist revival and the aspiration to create a work of 'total art'.

In terms of architecture, the members of the Viennese Secession sought to control decorative opulence and organicism in favour of more rigid designs through the use of cubic blocks and geometric decorations. In his *Moderne Architektur* of 1895, Wagner presented a new way of conceiving artistic creations based on reflection on the concept of 'style'. According to Wagner, style is closely connected to constructed form and should be thought of as an intrinsic derivation of modern progress. One result of this is the rejection of all Renaissance and baroque ornamentation in favour of decoration that serves to make the architectural theme more legible. Hence the outer shell of a building is not a bare surface to be clothed in decoration but an expression of the building's functional organization.

The works by Wagner, Olbrich, and Hoffmann renovated the appearance of the capital, especially in terms of its residences, which was the terrain on which they intended to demonstrate their modernity. Olbrich introduced an original architectural form in the exhibition pavilion of the Secession artists in 1897, and in 1899 gave the imprint of his style to the artists' quarter of Darmstadt, Germany. In 1903 Hoffmann and Kolo Moser founded the Wiener Werkstätte ('Vienna Workshop'), a society for the production of furnishings and art objects inspired by the ideas of William Morris. During the same period Hoffmann designed houses at the Hohe Warte, a district-garden where he experimented with the union of architecture and applied arts.

**Joseph Maria Olbrich, Secessionhaus, Vienna, 1897–98**
The Secession Pavilion was based on a square module with an atrium topped by a hemispherical dome of gilt-bronze laurel leaves and berries, framed by four towers. Contemporaries dubbed the dome the 'golden cabbage'. The pavilion was notable for its basic forms and balanced distribution. It teems with embellished decorations that make its 'architecture-painting' one of the most important moments in the passage from late-19th-century sensibilities to the modern movement.

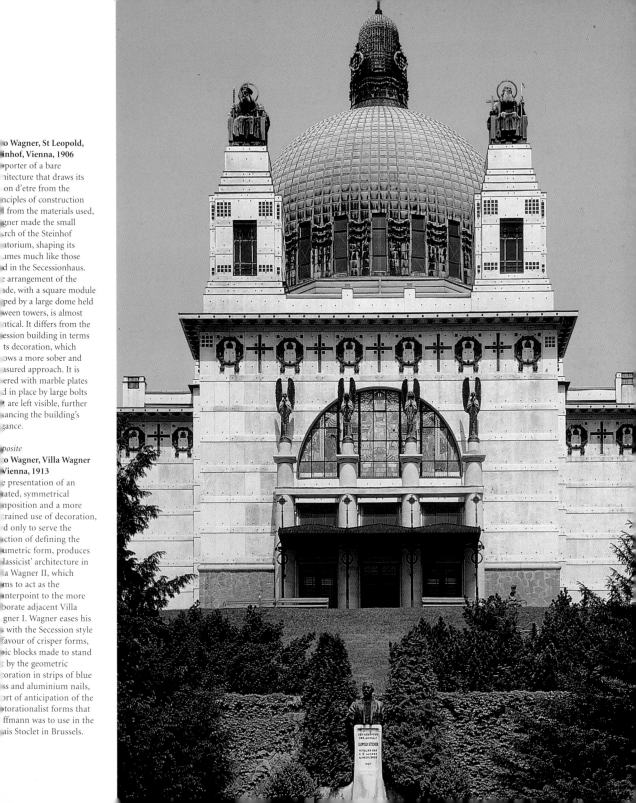

**...o Wagner, St Leopold,
...nhof, Vienna, 1906**

...porter of a bare
...nitecture that draws its
...on d'etre from the
...nciples of construction
... from the materials used,
...gner made the small
...rch of the Steinhof
...atorium, shaping its
...umes much like those
...d in the Secessionhaus.
...e arrangement of the
...ade, with a square module
...ped by a large dome held
...ween towers, is almost
...ntical. It differs from the
...ession building in terms
...ts decoration, which
...ows a more sober and
...asured approach. It is
...ered with marble plates
...d in place by large bolts
... are left visible, further
...ancing the building's
...gance.

*...posite*
**...o Wagner, Villa Wagner
...Vienna, 1913**

...e presentation of an
...ated, symmetrical
...nposition and a more
...trained use of decoration,
...d only to serve the
...ction of defining the
...umetric form, produces
...lassicist' architecture in
...a Wagner II, which
...ms to act as the
...nterpoint to the more
...borate adjacent Villa
...gner I. Wagner eases his
...s with the Secession style
...favour of crisper forms,
...ic blocks made to stand
...: by the geometric
...coration in strips of blue
...ss and aluminium nails,
...rt of anticipation of the
...torationalist forms that
...ffmann was to use in the
...ais Stoclet in Brussels.

# Josef Hoffmann

## Palais Stoclet, Brussels

### 1905–14

In the Palais Stoclet Hoffmann reached the height of simplicity and geometric abstraction, making use of elementary forms that are, however, enlivened by discreet decorative elements. Preliminary drawings reveal that Hoffmann intended to build a building with an almost perfect bilateral symmetry with its centre indicated by the large bow windows on the façade, with a forceful interaction of all the elements arranged in a regular way and constructed on a basic square/cube module, which Hoffmann chose because of its characteristic of being directionless and thus unable to produce even the most minimal dynamic effect. Located on the outer edge of the urbanized area of Brussels, Palais Stoclet is designed to combine the advantages of being near the urban centre with all the advantages of living in the country. The long façade along the street is not immediately visible in all its impressive extension to someone coming from the city; it is as though the main prospect were the western, stepped front, topped by the high telescope-shaped tower. The verticality of this front contrasts with the horizontal tendency of the projecting body that houses the entrance and reduces the volumetric importance of the polygonal bow window. Continuity is provided by the use of moulding in gilt bronze that emphasizes the external margins of the façade; the linear elements that these frames introduce have nothing to do with the 'force lines' that appear in Horta's works. The visual result is highly effective. Indeed, Palais Stoclet can be taken as the herald of a new deconstructivist spatial concept, one that would be employed by both the De Stijl movement and Mies van der Rohe in Barcelona. The surfaces are presented as defined spaces; by being framed, they have their own separate existence and do not emphasize the plasticity of the volume; the windows, also framed, also deny the plasticity.

Because of its high cost, the fact that it was built as the residence for a well-to-do industrialist, and its occasional concessions to decoration, this work reflects old ways. Because of its new spatial arrangement, its stylistic rigour, and the exceptional coherence of all its parts, it reflects many demands of the new architecture and can be considered a point of passage between the Secession and protorationalism.

During the opening years of the 20th century, Josef Hoffmann showed a marked tendency to lead the formal vocabulary of architecture to an extreme form of geometrics. This tendency grew only stronger after the foundation of the Wiener Werkstätte, when he extended his activity to all branches of artisan art. It was thus applied to the design of modern furnishings, elegant and stylized, with functional forms that are not ornamental, built in a simple way, well proportioned and coordinated through the moderate use of the square as a decorative element. As Hoffman himself said, 'The simple square and the use of black and white as dominant colours are especially interesting to me because never have these pure elements appeared in any preceding style.'

'Nature is the greatest architect that has ever existed.'
**Hector Guimard**

Art nouveau came to have a meaning in France that differed from its meaning in Belgium and Austria. France's academic conventionality and technical-engineering tradition had no intention of assimilating the new figurative culture whole, and instead it was accepted more as a decorative style than an architectural style. While proudly self-sufficient, France was open to a wide panorama of international architecture by way of the universal expositions. The 1889 exposition (with the Eiffel Tower) had been dedicated to the triumph of functionalism; the 1900 exposition, also in Paris, celebrated the arrival of the new century with unprecedented splendour. A ceremonial baroque architecture made its appearance; its bizarre forms and fantastic and illusionistic decorative motifs could not hide their historical sources.

In 1896 Adrien Bérnard, president of the French Métro, entrusted the design of the surface stations to Hector Guimard, a 'new artist' who had made his own interpretations of some of Horta's floral productions. In the wondrous metal works he created for the Métro he expressed the metamorphosis of architecture and nature and in so doing combined decoration and functionality. Like Horta, Guimard had been influenced by the theories of Viollet-le-Duc, and he looked upon iron as the material of the future. However, Guimard did not use iron as did the generation of structuralist engineers; for Guimard iron – while never losing its support functions – assumes elongated, sinuous forms that replicate the curving lines of nature, thus always avoiding any sense of symmetry or parallelism.

During a trip to Scotland and Belgium in 1894, Guimard had been drawn to the English country-house movement, according to which every house can rise to the status of a work of art in virtue of its beauty and harmony. Thus Guimard was not content to create pure and simple architecture, but wanted to become, in his own words, an *architecte d'art*, that is, an expert in the techniques of all the arts: the essence and end of a building are its 'decoration'. In the works Guimard made for the palaces of the Parisian middle class and the Métro stations, he presents an art understood as 'fashion' that uses the curved line and ornamental elements to delight the public.

**Jules Aimé Lavirotte, block of flats on Avenue Rapp, 1900–1**
In Lavirotte, architecture and decoration blend in an almost 'baroque' superabundance, as in the condominium in Avenue Rapp, in which he created a kind of stone symbolism. This architectural sculpture makes masterful use of ceramic tiles and is notable for its erotic overtones. Indeed, at various points of the building, the architect's obsessive and compulsive fetishism reaches provocative levels.

...or Guimard, Castel
...nger, main prospect,
...graph drawing from *Le
...el Béranger, 1894–98*
...wing his discovery of
...a's Tassel House
...nard made radical
...ges in his original
...Gothic plan for Castel
...nger – a residential
...plex with thirty-six
...ments – making it
...mic through the
...of projections and
...ntations. The structure
...bellished by the highly
...nal matching of such
...rials as hammered iron,
..., stone, and ceramics,
...e a refined naturalistic
...ration emphasizes the
...us elements, signalling
...xuberant triumph of
...t motifs.

*...site*
...tz Jourdain, The
...ritaine, 1902–5
...building housing the
...ritaine department
...seems to present a
...contrast; the façade,
...ugh up to date in style,
...ays its structuralist
...ix, leaving the
...ctural components
...sed. Even so, there are
...hes of decoration, and
...onvex shape of the
...onies gives the building
...se of dynamism.

1

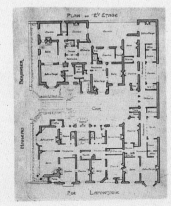

2

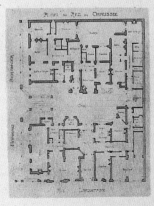

3

# Charles Rennie Mackintosh
## 1868–1928

### Glasgow

Because of the works of Charles Rennie Mackintosh, Glasgow ranks among the most important cities in the history of European art nouveau. The Scottish architect inherited the tradition of the arts and crafts movement and also worked out his own highly original contribution to the new style, giving life, in 1897, to the architectural design of the Glasgow School of Art, an austere and compact construction that assembles closed architectural bodies following a rhythm of 'disturbed symmetry', meaning disturbed by the carefully controlled presence of asymmetrical elements.

The same sense of rigorous simplicity that is expressed in his architectural language appears in his designs for furnishings, in which colour and decorative affectations are rejected in favour of the sharp contrasts of black and white, of lacquered wood, and the mat design – of clear Japanese derivation – of rectangular lattices. In the art school, in Windyhill, and in Hill House, in the furniture exhibited at the Secession in Vienna in 1900 and at the exposition in Turin in 1902,

Mackintosh elaborated a version of art nouveau clearly different from that of the Belgian version, consisting of the progressive reduction of supple curves in favour of geometry.

In fact, while his pictorial mural decorations, windows, and other minor architectural details are still informed by linearism – which although different from the concave-convex rhythms of Horta betrays a decorative character – as one moves on to Mackintosh's furniture and then to his architecture a taste for planes, volumes, and their geometric combinations comes to prevail. The interior spaces of Mackintosh's architecture and the objects contained within them belong to the domain of the line, colour, and the play of squares; his external spaces belong to the domain of volumetric rigour, of interlocking planes, of the geometry of slabs of stone, of the clear colouristic uniformity of plaster. Only in the disposition of the masses does the lean and controlled exterior covering reflect the wealth and variety within, and everything is presented with great coherence in a perfect synthesis of organicity and abstraction.

**School of Art, Glasgow, library, 1896–99, 1907**
The treatment of natural light is one of this buildi[ng] signs of 'modernity'. The space of the library lives the dialectic tension betw[een] interior and exterior in which the light plays a decisive role. Mackintosh uses the traditional Engl[ish] bow windows to spread [it] arranging them in vertic[al] lines and overturning an[d] doubling them to obtain prismatic forms that generate not planes but luminous volumes. The definition of the architectural space – a wood-lined narrow galle[ry] begins with the shapes o[f] objects and the furnishin[g] eventually expanding to [the] complex plastic structure the shelves.

**House, Helensburgh,**
**2–5**

ideal of a simple home
looks like a work of art,
osed by the English
ntry-house movement,
the architecture of
tish manor houses were
sources of inspiration
he design of Hill House,
nctional building
posed of solid, square
mes that fit together
in a scheme freed from
ical rules. The
dorned walls of rustic
plaster enclose an
rior characterized by the
roscuro juxtaposition of
rooms. Together with
s Stoclet, Hill House is
sidered a manifesto of
nouveau because of its
plex and variable masses
the perfect relationship
blished between the
rior and the interior. The
gn of the furniture with
rchitectural character
the careful application
ght represent the
evement of a complete
k of art.

**School of Art, Glasgow,**
**north front, 1896–99, 1907**
Composed as it is of
volumetric blocks, the
Glasgow School of Art is a
manifesto of simplicity; its
only art nouveau elements
are the wrought-iron
brackets of the windows
on the top floor. Despite its
apparent austerity, the
building has a very various
configuration: the north
front is a true repertory
of surprises that give the
structure an extreme
dynamism. The obligatory
point of observation, from
the side and from below
looking up, reveals the
variation in the depth of
the upper windows – more
than twice the height of
the others – and the heavy
sculptural articulation.

**Gaudí and architecture as a natural phenomenon**

Around the end of the 19th century Barcelona was one of the first cities to implement a version of urban planning based on a design procedure that comprised regulations to homologize types. This made it necessary to differentiate between one building and another, a distinction operated on the basis of decoration, most of all in terms of a building's 'public' parts – façade, entrance, stairs – meaning the zones of transition between the public spaces of the street and the private spaces of the home. In Barcelona this was made possible thanks to the great amount of decoration applied to buildings, a custom closely tied to local artisan tradition. This decoration often involves the structural parts of a building; thus the support framework can assume forms drawn from the natural world, and the relationship of these forms is separated from the divisions of building lots through the use of projections, indentations, and cornices that move according to the logic of living organisms. Catalan modernism has roots in the Spanish architectural tradition. In particular, the highly personal and eclectic language of Antoni Gaudí y Cornet blends decorative and structural elements from Flamboyant Gothic, from *plateresque*, from Mudejar art, as well as the use of *azulejo* tiles and original mosaics in bright colours that are in keeping with the Mediterranean tradition. His talent was supported by great building skills that led him to select Viollet-le-Duc as the primary source of his work. He had a strong sense of historical continuity and paid close attention to the use of materials and to the natural-artificial relationship, and he had an intuitive sense of certain morphological-constructive principles, such as the use of the parabolic arc that contributes to reinforce the dynamic-graphic sense of his lines. Faithful to the principle that being original means returning to origins, Gaudí revitalized not only styles of the past – which he blended with literary and visionary references – but also a concept of rupestrian architecture generated by the seismic movements that rend the earth. Taking the compositional freedom of eclecticism to its limits, Gaudí arrived at the plastic deformation of the physical plants of buildings, so that it became more or less impossible to separate the structure of the building from its decorations in iron, cement, and ceramic – thus anticipating expressionist themes.

**Antoni Gaudí, Güell Park, 1900–14**
Initially conceived as a garden city on the English model, Güell Park was remodelled to preserve the downward slope toward the sea. The great central terrace made of polychrome ceramics creates both an area of vibrant light and a square covered in shadow.

**Lluís Domènech i Montaner, Palau de la Música, 1905–8**
From its lights to its walls the interior of the Music Palace is completely immersed in a profusion of decorative details. The surreal atmosphere is accentuated by the jewel-coloured glass and the blazing illumination produced by the lamps located on the capitals of the columns.

**toni Gaudí, Casa
lló, 1905–7**

remodelling the Batlló
use Gaudí dressed the
ditional structure of the
lding in a mosaic of
eous paste in various
ours and at various angles
nake use of the iridescent
ections of sunlight. The
e in the ornamental details
he exterior – the wrought
n of the balconies, the
dow surrounds, the roof
h its polychrome majolica
s – and the interior
nishings, with special
ention given to materials
l colours, from intense
e to white, creates a
lding of an almost baroque
endour. The apartment
ses Gaudí designed are
npletely faithful to the
ic of exploiting their
lding lot as far as possible,
at the same time they
ow a distributive and
ctional logic that matches
ir physical images, making
analogy to the morphology
iving beings.

*posite*

**ep Puig i Cadafalch,
sa Ametller, 1898–1900**

luenced by the two great
alan architects, Gaudí
l Domènech, Puig united
itics and architecture in
career, making forms of
at balance, elegance, and
mopolitanism inspired
the local tradition, from
talan baroque to the
hitecture of the early
nish Renaissance to that
dieval. The result presents
armonious style of forms,
terials, and colours, with
ents of vague eclecticism
açades treated in
nochrome with
oration that dominates
amic and fluid spaces.

# Sagrada Familia, Barcelona

## Begun 1882

The Sagrada Familia involved Gaudí throughout his entire life, and in it he expressed his intellectual ideas as well as his religious beliefs, which became more and more mystical as he aged. At the same time, the Sagrada Familia represents the extreme result of an art nouveau interpretation of the Gothic style. Work began on the Sagrada Familia – still in large part unfinished today – in 1882 on a neo-Gothic design by the architect Del Villar; by 1893 only the area of the apse had been completed. Even so, and despite a sea of difficulties, not all of them financial, the project was in large part completed in 1906. 'The straight line belongs to man, the curved line belongs to God,' so affirmed Gaudí, who had become, around the end of the 19th century, the proclaimer of a new mystical-visionary architectural religion, arranged and supported by a geometry of parabolic curves, ellipses, hyperbolas. Gaudí's design follows a complex symbolic programme, expressed with an exuberant and imaginative vocabulary that innovates the structure and its decoration, no longer separate but fused. With a narration that unites popular figures, learned citations, and religious symbols, Gaudí presents realistic and allusive iconography at the same time. The decoration sprouts organically from the architecture, modifying and modelling the geometric structure of the fronts and the towers and transforming the vertical supports into a forest of arboreal shapes. The extraordinary organization of the nave and vaults, conceived on the basis of light and acoustics, or the articulation of the astonishing façade, inspired by the theme of the Nativity – with its incredible spiralling towers – communicate both dynamism and stability, stupor and reverence, religious piety and love for nature, all of it pervaded by a vague sense of suffering. The work proceeded at such a slow pace – Gaudí saw incompleteness and imperfection as necessities – that when the architect died, in 1928, only the first of the four towers of the Nativity façade had been completed; in 1976, the Passion façade was completed. Gaudí has thus left a very special legacy to Barcelona, and in the style of the great medieval cathedrals, the construction of this temple has become an undertaking for the city itself, coming to involve generations of architects and patrons.

Gaudí interpreted the artisan practices of his time through the elaboration of a new construction repertory, which in his hands as a modeller of complicated structures became an instrument for architectural expression. It involves a constant effort to achieve continuity among the parts of an organism understood in the natural sense. He constantly avoided the straight line and the angle, always opting for curving forms in movement; this effort led him to a reworki of the logic of constructior which he constantly studie through the use of models.

## Redundancy and architecture

Arriving late in Italy, modernist trends were first accepted only by the restricted group of decorative artists – designers, furniture manufacturers, ceramists – active within the orbit of the magazine *Emporium* or in the arts and crafts society Aemilia Ars.

The great exposition of decorative and modern art held in Turin in 1902 marked the consecration of the Italian 'Stile Liberty' (art nouveau), from the exotic furniture by Carlo Bugatti to the wrought iron by Alessandro Mazzucotelli, from the painted ceramics of Galileo Chini and the decorated glassware of Vittorio Zecchin to the lace by Michelangelo Jesurum. At the same time, the exposition also provided the stimulus for the application of the novelties of the new 'international style' to architecture. In fact, the festive, brightly coloured pavilions by Raimondo D'Aronco seem to demonstrate an awareness of the structural innovations of constructions in iron and glass, but they also seem to at least wink at the stylistic creations of Wagner and Olbrich.

With the support of the Turin exposition – which included architectural and furnishing designs by Behrens, Olbrich, and Horta – Italian Liberty architecture exploded in the figures of Pietro Fenoglio,

Giuseppe Sommaruga, Ernesto Basile, and Giuseppe Brega. After working on functional buildings and those made for public use, such as hotels, cemeteries, spas, and train stations, they turned to the design of private homes for the well-to-do middle class. The principal centres of the new style were Turin, Milan, and Palermo; indeed, the style was seen as a primarily urban phenomenon, with most of its application in cities experiencing major economic growth. This growth had little effect on the structure of the cities; those undertakings that were supposed to involve entire streets or city quarters were often reduced to mere surface operations involving the application of coloured ceramics, wrought iron, and decorative cement to buildings with a traditional layout. Cities with firmly established personalities rejected the Stile Liberty, relegating it to the periphery or permitting it only on such utilitarian structures as cafés, restaurants, and shops.

Even so, the Stile Liberty became widespread throughout Italy, most particularly as a result of certain notable applications, and it became the characteristic style for vacation spots or spas – for bungalows or large hotels – or for sites that symbolically welcomed and expressed the amusements and sophisticated rites of the middle class.

**Giuseppe Sommaruga, Palazzo Castiglioni, Milan 1900–3**
Many modernist architects reinterpreted the baroque legacy in the light of new building materials, introducing an opulent and overly decorative architectural style. The sumptuously theatrical Palazzo Castiglioni – decorated with provocative sculptured panels by Ernest Bazzaro, wrought iron by Alessandro Mazzucotelli, and carved woodwork by Eugenio Quarti – was daringly plopped down amid the stately series of classical buildings along Milan's Corso Venezia. The explosive plasticity of the rustication on the ground floor, the sculptural insert and the turgid wrought iron were the cause of scandal on its inauguration.

**Ernesto Basile, Hotel Villa Igiea, Palermo, 1898–1903**
An attentive early interpreter of Secessionist stylistic formulations, Basile designed some of the most beautiful villas in Palermo. Considered one of the most influential representatives of the 'Stile Liberty', he dedicated as much effort to the interiors of his building as to the exteriors. There are unequivocal French influences in Hotel Villa Igiea, in the softly elegant forms skilfully treated to form a perfect symbiosis of painting and decoration.

**Giuseppe Brega, Villa Ruggeri, Pesaro, 1902**
Even with its abundant, overgrown, and amorphous decoration, the façade of Villa Ruggeri cannot disguise the persistence of Italian tradition. Brega composes the eastern façade with eye-shaped windows, floral elements on the walls shaped like noses, and an entry that recalls a mouth, thus creating a sort of vegetal portrait not unlike those created by the painter Giuseppe Arcimboldo.

# Prague and Budapest

## *c.* 1898–1918

### The many souls of the secession

Early in the 20th century, the secession revolution invaded the city of Prague. In the Czech capital art nouveau did not inspire the kind of heated controversy and violent criticism it had elsewhere in Europe. This was partly because the provincial Bohemian city looked on the secession – soon enough folded into tradition – as an opening to modernity, and partly because, despite its debts to the Austrian Secession, the style made possible a detachment and a cultural autonomy from Vienna, thus giving it not negligible nationalistic values. Over the course of the first decade of the century Prague covered itself in hundreds of 'extravagant' buildings. The central train station, homes, banks, school, theatres, and most of all the magnificent Municipal House, the Obencí Dùm, were erected following the forms and aesthetic principles of the secession, an architecture characterized by a notable stylistic heterogeneity embellished – near the

far end of the movement – by the revivalism of the 1890s and the cubism of the 1910s. More than anywhere else, in Prague art nouveau took on the traits of an official language, the language of the reborn Bohemian society. As an artistic language, the way it united an unbridled spirit of state celebration with modern forms made an ideal expression of political power. While Josef Fanta followed the route of monumentalism, with an exaggerated faith in secession forms transformed into a personal eclecticism, the combined work of Osvald Polívka and Antonin Balsanek gave life – between anachronism and novelty, neo-baroque and secession – to the Obecní Dùm, an expression of the many souls of the official Prague Secession, from those more tied to tradition, revitalized by letting in new forms following a line of naturalistic development, to those more 'modern', who departed from the same historicist premises but evolved following the progressive application of geometry to forms.

**Ödön Lechner, Museum of Applied Arts, Budapest, 18** In the wake of the Jugendsti an eclectic and imaginative construction style flowered i Hungary, dominated by the figure of Ödön Lechner, for whom the search for maximum luminosity was the dominant idea in the arrangement of internal spa

**Josef Fanta, main railway station, Prague, 1901–9** Fanta's mature neo-Renaissance experience is cle in the shapes of the central body of the station, but it is inserted in a compositional scheme that leads back to contemporary English architecture.

**tonin Balsanek and
svald Polívka, Municipal
ouse, Prague, 1903–11**

is large building resulted
m a combination of
les, but they were kept
atially separate – Balsanek
d the exterior, Polívka did
e interior – in an unusual
ur-handed plan that went
ainst the spirit of
odernist criteria. A grand
mmary of Czech art of the
rly 1900s, the Obencí Dùm
ts side by side ostentation,
nament, the plant world,
d geometric symbols in
arch of an unattained
sion of nature and culture
a compound disunity in
nich the decorative wealth
d abundance of inventions
e amazing. The exterior is
a demonstration of how
an architect with a solid
historical base like Balsanek
could manage to interpret
tradition in a modernist
sense with only a minimum
updating in his decorative
vocabulary.

# Amsterdam and northern Europe

## c. 1890–1918

### Northern lights on new visions

Hendrik Petrus Berlage stands as a figure key in northern European architecture between the end of the 19th and beginning of the 20th centuries, important both because of his influence on Dutch architecture and because he formed a cultural link between the Untied States and Europe. Berlage believed that architecture served the political and cultural development of society, so the new architectural vocabulary had to fit modern life and its technological developments, and do so in all aspects of a construction, both in terms of the materials and their use. Berlage's works show a profound material clarity and a simplicity of form, which explains his disdain for everything that was 'stylish', meaning all decorative trends. The union of the close attention to physical realities – typical of a country locked in a perennial struggle with the elements and displayed in the development of urban policies closely tied to architectural designs – with the great ethical teachings of Berlage made possible the felicitous contributions of the group of designers commonly called the Amsterdam school. These artists operated primarily in Amsterdam between the first decade of the 20th century and the immediate postwar period, and their close attention to materials and to the wall exhibited in all its material concreteness left indelible signs on the appearance of the city.

On the other side of the Baltic, the architecture of Finland was presenting equally innovative ideas thanks to the highly original figure of Eliel Saarinen. Early in the 20th century the architectural tradition that had formed under the aegis of Karelianism – the use of local materials, granite and wood, bearers of particular symbolic values associated with the functionalism of popular architecture – was no longer sufficient to satisfy the needs of the new generation of architects, who began turning to the English arts and crafts movement, to the Darmstadt art colony, and to French and Belgian art nouveau. The GLS studio – Gesellius, Lindgren & Saarinen – developed an organic architecture dominated by plasticity and by natural harmony, as is made abundantly clear in the country home of Suur-Merijoki (destroyed). Built in 1903, it represented a kind of synthesis of all the contemporary trends in architecture, painting, and the applied arts, and as such was the ideal to which all Finnish architects until Alvar Aalto dedicated themselves: the dream of a 'total' work of art.

In the main hall of the stock exchange Berlage made clear his attention to the use of materials and to his conception of the wall, which he presents in all its concrete reality, not only to emphasize its size but to present a synthesis of the 'architecture of the wall', modelled and sculpted by decorative elements that amplify its serious and austere character, with a spatial concept that reaches great lightness in the roof in hammered iron and glass supported by iron trusses.

this page
ndrik Petrus Berlage,
ck exchange, Amsterdam,
96–1903

rlage, strongly influenced
the ideas of Viollet-le-
c on the supremacy of
hitectural construction,
ates a block that contains
e various components of
e building in a superficial
sion and also in a clear
d simple solidity visible
every detail. Both the
ck exchange and the
lsinki train station had
rner towers (not visible
the photographs). Both
esent a high level of
hitectural clarity. Such
wers were understood as
ymbolic gesture and were
ed by many exponents of
nouveau; in a sense they
re a foretelling of the
hitecture of the
erican skyscraper.

# The Chicago school
## 1870–1910

### The birth of the skyscraper

In 1871, in one of the most famous disasters in US history, the city of Chicago, at the time constructed almost exclusively of wood, was destroyed almost entirely by a great fire. The rebuilding of the city in stone and steel marked a revolutionary turning point in the history of architecture. The so-called Chicago school of architecture refers to the innovations worked out by the architects and engineers involved in the city's reconstruction. They faced certain very specific problems: the insertion of new buildings in what remained of the urban fabric; the design of structures that would be technologically trustworthy and resistant to fire; and the design of forms suitable for the functions of the new buildings, most of them for the use of service industries.

Among these architects was William Le Baron Jenney, who had studied at the Harvard Scientific School and the Ecole des Beaux Arts in Paris. He proposed a new, multistorey building – the skyscraper – in which vertical height, made possible by the invention of the elevator, increased exponentially the use of the building lot. The structure was made technically possible thanks to the use of a metal skeleton framework; the framework also determined the modulation of the exterior. His student Daniel Hudson Burnham worked out an expressive language to explore new possibilities in the design and composition of the large surfaces of the façades of commercial buildings, a category that included office buildings, company headquarters, department stores, and other similar large structures. Soon many architects were actively involved in the drive to establish a building model suitable for the evolution of the typology of the tall commercial building. Among the most important members of the Chicago school were Dankmar Adler and Louis Sullivan, and they soon became the leaders; in twelve years of activity they made numerous buildings in which the technical-constructive and typological demands were placed side by side with the constant effort to elaborate decorative and structural elements in a new language.

**Louis Sullivan, Schlesinger & Mayer Department Store Chicago, 1899–1904**
Advances in industrial technologies and the use of steel frameworks allowed Sullivan make the first skyscrapers in which the supporting skeleton was left visible; even so, he did not eliminate the decoration which he used to emphasize the vertical-support elements the entrances, and the outline of the lower floors of these otherwise spare and rational buildings.

**Dankmar Adler and Louis Sullivan, Guaranty Building Buffalo, New York, 1895**
Sullivan worked out a method for designing skyscrapers by dividing them into three functional areas: the large ground floor access area, the attic located atop the building and the shaft in between with an indeterminate number of floors. His buildings make plain the principles that were to revolutionize architecture, and not only American architecture during the 20th century.

**Daniel Hudson Burnham
and John Wellborn Root,
Reliance Building, Chicago,
1890–95**
Within the sphere of the
design programme for
commercial buildings, the
Reliance Building represents
the high point of the Chicago
School's 'structuralist'
current, which was led by
Baron. However, in their
close modulation of the
façade, Burnham and Root
asserted a new motif for
weather reflection.

**Daniel Hudson Burnham,
Flatiron Building, New
York, 1902**
Twenty-two floors high, the
Flatiron Building is notable
for its narrow, triangular
shape, a result of fitting it to
the shape of a building lot
on a busy street corner.

# Futurism

## 1909–16

### The new city

On 20 February 1909, the Italian poet Filippo Tommaso Marinetti published 'The Founding and Manifesto of Futurism' on the front page of *Le Figaro*. In it he delineated the principles of an avant-garde Italian movement that was meant to change all the arts. At the centre of futurist thought was the affirmation of modernity by way of the cult of industrialization, the machine, and speed. Futurism also called for the rejection of museums, academies, and anything else that represented traditional culture. The movement's first painters, Boccioni and Severini, expressed their futuristic zeal in their choice of subjects, which included speeding trains, worksites, and workers on strike. A subject of central importance to futurism was the modern city.

The same cultural viewpoint shaped the thinking of Antonio Sant'Elia, who in 1914 published, probably in collaboration with Marinetti, 'The Manifesto of Futurist Architecture'. This was originally a statement accompanying the exhibition of a series of his drawings entitled 'The New City': monumental electric power stations, railroad stations, futuristic skyscrapers, typologies adopted to new materials and construction methods. The manifesto makes clear his intention to break with historicism and with the traditional city: the 20th-century city must be 'like an immense and tumultuous shipyard, agile, mobile, and dynamic in every detail'. Following in the wake of Sant'Elia as futurist architects were his friend Mario Chiattone and, a little later, Virgilio Marchi, an architect and stage designer. Not one of the works designed by the futurist architects was ever made – Sant'Elia died during World War I, and at the end of the War both Marchi and Chiattone returned to a more traditional style – but the influence of futurist architecture shows up in nearly all of the avant-garde movements in Europe and North America between the two world wars.

Antonio Sant'Elia, study for the 'New City', 1914 This drawing, one of Sant'Elia's most famous, was published together with the 'Manifesto of Futurist Architecture'. It presents a multilevel urban complex of iron and concrete connected to the 'tumultuous' city around it by way of both horizontal and vertical routes. The image blends elements from the history of architecture with those from the city as imaged by Sant'Elia: high oblique volumes, iron bridges and walkways, buttresses, elevated towers, viaducts, highways.

**Antonio Sant'Elia, study for a power station, 1914**
Sant'Elia made many studies of electric power stations, regarding them as symbolic of the modernization taking place early in the century as well as the motive force of the 'New City.' As 'cathedrals of progress' the infrastructures imagined by Sant'Elia rise with towers and pinnacles to affirm the arrival of modernity.

*Opposite below*
**Mario Chiattone, design for a fashion palace**
Chiattone presents building types – monumental multistorey structures – and urban realities similar to the ideas expressed by his colleague Sant'Elia.

LA CENTRALE ELETTRIC

# The beginning of the modern movement
## Early 20th century

### Protorationalism

The architecture that came into being in Europe and the United States in the years between the two world wars is most often said to belong to the 'modern' movement. The term is applied to the collective efforts of various architects active during those years who distanced themselves from academic styles, made use of new materials and technologies, and sought to eliminate all useless or superfluous ornamentation. Other terms are sometimes used to express substantially the same concept, such as 'rationalism' or 'functionalism', but these refer to specific trends moving within the overall sphere of modernism.

The use of iron and glass spread during the early years of the 20th century, most of all in the construction of industrial buildings. A leading pioneer in the use of reinforced concrete and steel was Albert Kahn, who designed factory buildings for the Ford Motor Company, enormous concrete sheds illuminated by large windows without even a touch of superfluous decoration.

During those same years concrete came into use in Europe. Auguste Perret made the first use of reinforced concrete in a residential building, in Paris in 1902. Max Berg, acting as a senior building official in Breslau (now Wroclaw, Poland), explored the unexpected possibilities of reinforced concrete, using it to cover a space – the Jahrhunderthalle – three times larger than the dome of St Peter's with a large vault without supports.

The first applications of these new materials and technologies to architecture were attended by concern about the relationship between industrialization and the quality of the created product. To this end, artists, artisans, architects, and industrialists in Germany founded the Deutscher Werkbund.

**Auguste Perret, house in Rue Franklin, Paris, 1902–3**
The load-bearing structure is a framework of beams and pillars in reinforced concrete. This structural skeleton makes possible the use of large windows on the façade, which in turn folds in to form a recess. This recess makes it possible to increase the number of windows, adding more light to the interior. The framework of reinforced concrete and the surfaces of the curtain walls, dressed in Faenza marble, are easily legible on the façade.

**x Berg, Jahrhunderthalle, eslau, 1911–13**

e use of reinforced
crete made it possible
cover a single very
ge space. In the
rhunderthalle, a cupola
metres in diameter
ts on four arches; it is
nposed of 32 radial ribs
ned by four concentric
crete rings. The building
luminated naturally from
ve through windows.
e use of exposed concrete
icipates certain aesthetic
nds particularly
lespread during the
stwar period.

### Deutscher Werkbund

*The Deutscher Werkbund was founded in Munich in 1907. This association of designers, artists, architects, and industrialists was created to improve the aesthetic qualities of objects, favouring collaboration among the various professional fields and the correct use of the means of production. This climate led to the felicitous collaboration between the architect Peter Behrens and Emil Rathenau, the founder of AEG, one of the leading German industrial companies. One of the most important moments in the affirmation of the Werkbund was the Cologne exposition in 1914 in which various architects participated, proposing new typologies of industrial buildings. Among the most innovative constructions presented was the Glashaus ('Glass Pavilion') designed by Bruno Taut. This was composed of a circular concrete base upon which was set a polygonal body with walls made of thick glass slabs topped by a prismatic glass dome.*

# Peter Behrens

## AEG Turbine Factory, Berlin

### 1908–9

Between 1907 and 1914 Peter Behrens served as design consultant for AEG (Allgemeine Elektrizitäts-Gesellschaft), the German electricity-supply company. Behrens oversaw the design of a wide range of objects, from letterheads to lamps to factory buildings. The turbine factory, built in Berlin between 1908 and 1909, presents a paradigm of early 20th-century architecture, for Behrens succeeded in blending functionality and elegance, matching the use of modern materials and techniques to classical symbols and proportions.

AEG, founded in 1883, had built its first factory in an area to the north of Berlin in 1896. This complex was composed of several traditional-style buildings made of brick and iron with decorative inserts of medieval inspiration. By 1907, the time of Behrens's arrival, increased demand had made the large-scale production of turbines necessary, leading to the need for suitable space. Behrens, working in collaboration with the engineer Karl Bernard, was asked to design a space large enough for the steps in the assembly process, with enough room for cranes to lift and move component parts during the various phases of assembly and also giving access to railroad cars. Another basic requirement was that the area be illuminated with as much natural light as possible. Behrens was also asked to include a smaller body alongside the main shed to act as storeroom or for use in secondary operations. The result is a rectangular parallelepiped, 127 metres long and 25 wide, covered by a single jointed transparent span with a polygonal profile. It is flanked by a smaller building with a flat roof.

The façade of the iron-and-glass structure is given solidity by masonry pylons and by a polygonal tympanum above a large expanse of glass, bearing the company's name and logo. The image of the façade is reminiscent of a classical temple. The sides of the building are marked off by the regular spacing of steel columns that taper toward the ground and rest on exposed hinges. The long side of the building is thus composed of a continuous glass wall divided in spans and resting on a foundation of reinforced concrete.

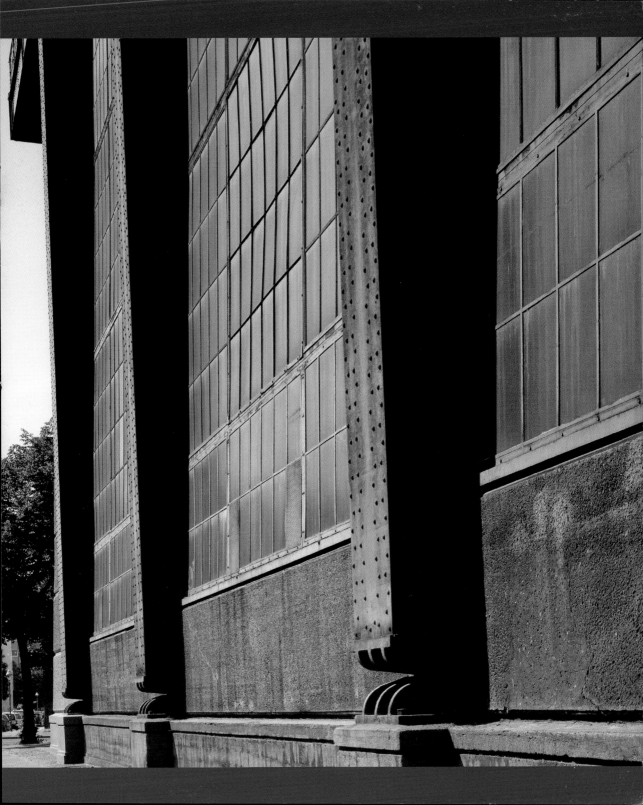

# Adolf Loos
## 1870–1933

### The crusade against decoration

Adolf Loos was one of the leading architects in Vienna at the beginning of the 20th century and was one of the most important precursors of modern architecture. Originally a member of the Viennese Secession movement, he later detached himself from it and became one of its fiercest critics.

Before dedicating himself completely to architecture, Loos wrote newspaper articles on architecture and art, and these essays were later collected and published in various languages. In his theoretical writing on architecture, in open polemic with 19th-century eclecticism and Jugendstil decoration, he carried on a determined crusade against every type of decoration in an effort to purify architecture and dedicate it to utility. The theories that he presented in his writings were given solid form in his buildings. In 1910 Loos built two of his most important buildings, both in Vienna: a multistorey office building for the men's clothiers Goldman & Salatsch on the Michaelerplatz and a single-family house for the Steiners. Both are excellent examples of how Loos worked to eliminate decoration from architecture.

Aside from the strict simplification of forms, Loos rejected the horizontal arrangement of rooms and sought to design interiors on the basis of the functional uses of spaces, beginning with the notion that the size of each room should be based on its function and importance. The basis of this arrangement is the *Raumplan*, according to which the height of a room is related to its function. Thus the interiors in homes designed by Loos are often composed of rooms that penetrate one another, that differ in height, or that extend over several floors, all of them connected to form fluid and open spaces. Examples are Scheu House (1912–13) and the Moller House (1927–28) in Vienna and the Müller House in Prague (1928–30).

**American Bar, Vienna, 19**
Also known as the Kärtne Bar, this is one of Loos's most elegant creations. Th interior is the result of the combination of multiple materials: brass, marble, mahogany, coloured glass and mirror glass.

**Michaelerplatz Building, Vienna, 1909–11**
This building stands in th historic centre of Vienna. very simple structure – th Viennese call it the 'Barn' it is dressed in white plast and its only decoration is the green marble of the lower floors. In fact, the differing treatment of the surfaces reflects the differe uses of the internal spaces commercial in the lower area and residential on the upper floors.

**Steiner House, Vienna, 1910**
The house that Loos built for Hugo and Lily Steiner can be taken as emblematic of his theories. It is an architectural body without ornament composed of symmetrical bodies that frame a central area. The different sizes of the windows reflect the different functions of the interior spaces.

**Moller House, Vienna, 1927–28**
The house designed for the Viennese textile magnate Hans Moller stands in a hilly residential area. The house's street face is marked off by windows arranged on a smooth surface; the part that projects outward is a kind of conversation nook that thus finds itself suspended between the interior and the exterior.

# Walter Gropius
## 1883–1969

### The Bauhaus

The masters of the modern movement in architecture are generally thought to have been Le Corbusier, Mies van der Rohe, Frank Lloyd Wright, and Walter Gropius.

Gropius's fundamental contribution consisted in having intuited the need and the importance of joining art and technological developments with the goal of creating architectural and industrial products suitable for the spirit of the 20th century. The outstanding expression of this idea was the foundation of the Bauhaus, the school of art and architecture in Weimar, which moved to Dessau in 1925. The school succeeded in uniting some of the most fecund artistic forces of the early 20th century in a common programme.

Gropius's first important building was the Fagus Works, a shoe-last factory built in Germany in 1911. It is a brick parallelepiped with enormous glass surfaces and a thin steel skeleton framework.

Large transparent surfaces are also a feature of the new Bauhaus building that Gropius designed for the school after its move to Dessau. Gropius also designed special buildings to house the various departments of the school. He also designed homes for the teachers, small, two-storey one- or two-family residences of a type that he later repeated in the homes he designed for an experimental quarter of Stuttgart in 1927. Gropius's interest in the creation of low-cost housing also shows up in the Törten district at Dessau (1926–28), where he designed lots made particularly economical through the use of prefabricated elements.

In 1928, after handing over direction of the school to Hannes Meyer, Gropius moved to Berlin, where he participated in the programme of urban renewal of the city that involved various German architects in the creation of workers' housing organized in districts (*Siedlungen*) built near large factories. In 1934, shortly after the Nazis took power, Gropius moved to Britain, then in 1937 he was called to the United States by Harvard University.

**Homes of Bauhaus teacher Moholy-Nagy House, Dessau, 1926**
The furniture was made in the school's workshops and reflects a way of conceiving domestic life in agreement with the school's goals of efficiency and functionalism. Tubular steel was first used to make furniture by Marcel Breuer who both studied and taught at the Bauhaus.

**Walter Gropius and Adolf Meyer, Fagus Works, Alfeld an-der-Leine, 1910**
This building is of importance because of its use of a new construction system, an internal framework in reinforced concrete that makes possible the three-storey-high glass outer shell that even turns the corners of the building thanks to its thin steel skeleton.

### The Bauhaus

*In 1919 Walter Gropius took over direction of both the Weimar School of Arts and Crafts, until then directed by Henri van de Velde, and of the Academy of Fine Arts in the same city. Gropius decided to unify the two schools to form a single institution, thus creating the Staatliches Bauhaus of Weimar, commonly known as the Bauhaus. As conceived by Gropius, the goal of the school was to combine the world of artistic production with that of modern industry. Doing so required solid training in functional craftsmanship as well as industrial methods. The result was a school devoted to all fields of art, in which practical teaching and theoretical teaching were given the same value and taught at the same time. The curriculum thus provided for artisan methods, theories, and lessons in all fields of the arts and sciences. The students worked in special laboratories, and their products were often manufactured by local industries. Gropius sought to provide the students with the best possible teachers, and the faculty included Paul Klee, Wassily Kandinsky, Theo van Doesburg, Lyonel Feininger, László Moholy-Nagy, Johannes Itten. For this reason the Bauhaus was not only an excellent school but also a centre of the artistic and intellectual avant-garde, a catalyst for ideas and personalities. In 1924, for political reasons, the school moved to Dessau, where Gropius designed its buildings. In 1933 the Nazis took power in Germany, and the Gestapo closed the school.*

*On this page*
**Bauhaus, Dessau, 1925–26**
Compositional clarity and the use of materials make the Bauhaus one of Gropius's finest achievements. The complex is composed of a series of buildings, each serving a different function and thus having a different arrangement on the façade of open spaces (glass areas) and full spaces (concrete dressed in white plaster). The glass body of the main building, which houses workshops and classrooms, is connected to a second building, housing laboratories and the dining hall, by an elevated passageway housing the administrative offices. The way the supporting structure is separated from the face of the building is clear in the laboratory classrooms, and in fact the glass walls are possible because they do not serve a support function.

# Le Corbusier
## 1887–1965

### Machines for living

Charles Edouard Jeanneret, known since 1920 as Le Corbusier, is one of the artists who most influenced the direction of 20th-century architecture.

He learned from the most important architects of his time – he trained and worked with both Behrens and Auguste Perret – was fascinated by the construction possibilities offered by such new materials as iron and reinforced concrete, and was inspired by classical architecture, which he studied during a long journey across Italy, Greece, and Asia Minor in search of the immutable values of architecture. Drawing on all this, Le Corbusier codified a new architectural language that blended the needs of modernization in the building process with adherence to the proportions of the classical world.

In 1923 Le Corbusier presented the key points of his architectural ideas in the book *Vers une architecture* (*Towards a New Architecture*, 1927). A collection of articles originally published in a magazine, his book became one of the most influential architecture texts of the 20th century. In it Le Corbusier expresses his reflections on architecture, extolling the vigour and functionality of the works of engineers (silos, ships, airplanes), the importance of mass production, and the use of new materials and calling on architects to abandon the slavish imitation of styles of the past and to adhere to the classical world as the means to produce beauty and awaken emotions.

During the mid-1920s, Le Corbusier applied his architectural ideas to the creation of urban villas in Paris and nearby, homes made for an elite and refined clientele. In these he made use of his studies of prototypes for homes that could be reproduced in series, which he called 'machines for living'. These were white boxes held off the ground on *pilotis* (columns or stilts), with flat roofs for gardens, free (open) interior plans, long, ribbon windows, and unbroken industrial-type façades.

Two of the most important works from this period are the Villa Stein-de-Monzie at Garches (1926–28) and the Villa Savoye at Poissy (1928–31). Le Corbusier explained the experimental language applied in these works in an essay written in 1926 entitled 'Five Points of a New Architecture'. It was published on the occasion of the 1927 Stuttgart exposition and did much to direct developments in modern architecture throughout the 20th century.

**House in the Weissenhof district, Stuttgart, 1927**
Le Corbusier designed two buildings for the exposition organized in Stuttgart by Mies van der Rohe, and in them he applied his 'five points' for the first time. Clearly visible are the horizontal ribbon windows, the *pilotis* that lift the building off the ground, and the flat roof-garden.

this page
a Savoye, Poissy,
8–31

s villa, which was
ently declared a national
nument, stands in the
dle of a clearing about
ty kilometres from Paris.
nsidered a paradigm of
onalism, the villa involves
application of Le
busier's 'Five Points of a
w Architecture': the *pilotis*
this case concrete pillars)
support the structure,
ing it off the ground and
s freeing space; the open
n made possible by the
ence of load-bearing

walls, replaced by the
structural framework; the
ribbon windows that run
along the outside of the
building; the façade, which
is free since it has no load-
bearing function; and the
flat roof-garden.

The fulcrum of the house
is a continuous path, which
Le Corbusier called the
*promenade architecturale*,
composed of an interior
stairway that joins the
ground floor to the second
floor and then leads up to the
roof by way of a ramp, thus
traversing the entire building.

# Ludwig Mies van der Rohe
## 1886–1969

### The precision of the modern

Mies van der Rohe, along with Wright, Gropius, and Le Corbusier, is considered one of the masters of 20th-century architecture.

Between 1908 and 1912 he worked as an assistant to Behrens, in whose studio he met Gropius and Le Corbusier. Those experiences, along with his study of Schinkel's work, constitute the primary elements on which he drew in the elaboration of his personal language, which was based on the study of proportion, the precision of forms, and the adoption of new technologies and materials.

In the 1920s he designed two skyscrapers – never built – in steel and glass, experimenting with the expressive qualities of transparent, reflecting surfaces of glass. During the same period he made several country houses in brick and reinforced concrete. In 1926 he made the monument in Berlin to the antiwar socialists Karl Liebknecht and Rosa Luxemburg using blocks of brickwork; it was later destroyed by the Nazis.

In 1927 he was made the first vice-president of the Deutscher Werkbund, for which he organized the 1927 housing exposition in Stuttgart. The leading exponents of modern architecture were invited to present their works on a hill near the city; his contribution was a residential complex with steel-framed row houses.

During these years he sought to reduce the amount of constructed mass in his architecture, preferring space to material and closely analysing the compositional elements of architecture. This approach is clear in the masterpieces he made during the 1930s: the German Pavilion for the international exhibition in Barcelona in 1929, the Tugendhat House at Brno of 1930, and the model house for the Berlin exposition of 1931. From 1930 to 1933 he replaced Gropius as director of the Bauhaus, but the climate imposed by the Nazis forced him to emigrate, first to Britain and then to the United States.

**Design for a skyscraper o[n] Friedrichstrasse, Berlin, 1921–22**
Between 1918 and 1922 Mies van der Rohe was pa[rt] of the Novembergruppe, a[n] association of artists tied t[o] expressionism. During tho[se] years Mies experimented with the expressive qualiti[es] of glass in two projects for office towers, never built: [a] skyscraper with acute-angl[ed] on Friedrichstrasse in Ber[lin] shown in the photograph, and a glass skyscraper wit[h] a curvilinear plan.

**Model house for the construction show in Berlin, plan, 1931**
The model house, demolished after the exposition, applied the compositional principles of the Barcelona Pavilion t[o] the private home: a regula[r] arrangement of pillars supports the roof and wal[l] slabs, which serve no supp[ort] function and only divide t[he] internal spaces without interrupting the continuity between one room and the next and then continue beyond the roof line.

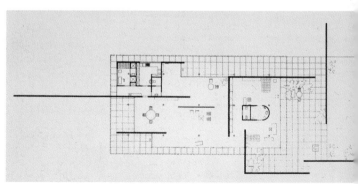

...sidential complex in ...e Weissenhof district, ...uttgart, 1927

...ery architect invited to ...rticipate in the Stuttgart ...osition was asked to ...esent a prototype for a ...idential building. The ...ilding designed by Mies ...a four-storey complex with ...enty-four apartments. The ...ndows form horizontal ...nds along the façades ...errupted by pillars flush ...th the façade. The steel ...mework permitted greater ...edom in the interior ...ganization of the individual ...artments.

**Tugendhat House, Brno, 1930**
The house is located on a hill just outside Brno, in the Czech Republic. A smooth white parallelepiped, it faces the city below with large terraces and windows. The bearing structure is composed of cruciform steel pillars, and the internal space is divided by walls that serve no support function. The patron's financial means made possible the use of precious materials, such as onyx for the flat wall that divides the living room and ebony for the curving wall that marks off the dining room. The broad, continuous windows provide light and also permeability between interior and exterior. Two of the long glass panes in the living room, by way of an electrical device, could be made to slide down vertically into the floor, much like automobile windows.

313

# Ludwig Mies van der Rohe

## German Pavilion, Barcelona

### 1929

The pavilion was constructed as a temporary structure for the international exposition in Barcelona in 1929. It was built to represent Germany and to host various official ceremonies, such as the meeting of the German delegation and the Spanish royal family. One year later it was demolished, as were all the ephemeral constructions made for the exposition, but it was reconstructed between 1981 and 1986 on the basis of the original designs and period photographs.

The pavilion is a complex of rectangular elements – two pools and two open structures – supported on a pedestal and arranged according to precise proportional and geometric relationships. The basic module for the project, for example, is based on the travertine slabs of the floor covering and is thus 1.09 x 1.09 metres; the larger pool and the perimeter of the main construction are rectangles sized in accordance

with the laws of the golden section. The main structure is composed of eight cruciform plated-steel columns which support thin roof planes that project past the walls. The interior is marked off by independent walls arranged at right angles to one another or in parallel, creating a fluid space. The exterior walls are composed entirely of transparent glass, adding to this fluidity.

The pavilion is a strikingly abstract and symbolic work, and the way it articulates space by way of rectangular planes and straight lines reflects the ideas of the avant-garde De Stijl group. The construction also reflects ideas of 'clarity, simplicity, and honesty', which in the words of the German commissar general Georg von Schnitzler, speaking at the official opening, composed the image that the Weimar Republic wanted to present to foreigners.

In creating the pavilion M van der Rohe distanced himself from the contemporary concerns fc economy of means in constructions. Indeed, the work is embellished by cos and refined materials: wall made with precious marbl and onyx, windows of spe tinted glass, vertical suppo in plated steel, the base in slabs of travertine. A sculpture by George Ko. *The Dancer*, stands in one of the pools of water. As the focal point of the arrangement, it alludes to the principles of classical order following which the building is arranged. Inter and exterior, opacity and transparency, alternate in a harmonic whole. The interior has neither doors nor windows; the ar of the rooms are indicated dividing walls. The main room is defined by a vertic partition wall in onyx, by a carpet in black velvet, and a red curtain, the colours thus alluding to the Spanis flag. The pieces of furnitur designed for the occasion, most especially the 'Barcelona' chair in plated steel and white leather, hav become famous and have been reproduced.

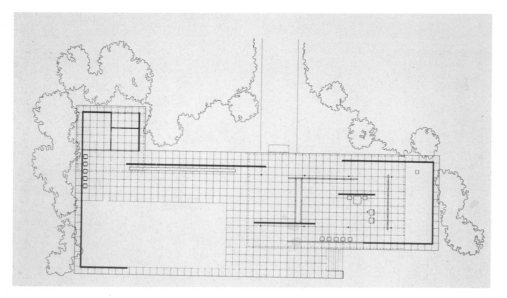

The plan shows the composition of the building: the covered areas, pools of water, wall sections, transparent walls, and cruciform columns. The extreme material essentiality of the work gives it an almost abstract appearance.

## Frank Lloyd Wright

### 1867–1959

### Organic architecture

At his birth, his mother was already convinced he would become 'the greatest American architect'. Frank Lloyd Wright was one of the most fecund and productive architects of the 20th century: when he died, aged ninety, he left more than 400 designs and constructed works, and with his ideas and creations he made a decisive contribution to the direction taken by architecture in North America and Europe.

His name is closely associated with the concept of 'organic architecture', essentially meaning an approach to architecture based on the creation of harmonic relationships among the parts of a building and between the parts and the whole that is expressed in fluid spaces in harmony with the surrounding environment and in the use of natural materials. During the first years of his career Wright worked on the theme of prairie houses: single-family dwellings designed in most cases for an educated and well-to-do elite in the suburbs of Chicago. These are notable for the articulation of long, horizontal volumes; they are most often built on level ground and are covered by large roofs that slope only slightly but that project. These houses are illuminated by continuous ribbons of windows. In 1910 Wright's language changed in response to a variety of influences, from Japanese culture to that of the traditions of pre-Columbian natives, as is evident in the block houses he built on the hills of Los Angeles over the course of the 1920s.

Before making his masterpiece of organic architecture, Fallingwater, at Bear Run, Pennsylvania, Wright worked on the elaboration of urban models, presenting alternatives to the traditional American metropolis, such as Broadacre City, designed in 1934, based on the idea that each family would be given a one-acre plot of land.

New archetypes began appearing in his designs around 1925, including the circle and the spiral, later destined to appear in his most famous works of the postwar period.

**Millard House, 'La Miniatura', Pasadena, 1922–23**
In this house Wright employed a new constructive system he called textile blocks: blocks of concrete decorated with geometric motifs, joined to one another using steel attachments. The warm, dry climate of California meant Wright had to apply different ideas from those he had used in the prairie houses of Illinois, and his California designs create block buildings that are we protected from the exterio with internal shaded patio and areas of water.

**lits House, Highland
k, Illinois, 1901–2**
e Willits House is an
mple of a prairie house.
e articulation of the
umes, parallelepipeds
tected by projecting
fs, repeats the cruciform
ign of the layout, which
rranged around the
mney, seen as the focal
nt of the house since it is
focal point of domestic
, Continuous expanses
glass put the domestic
rior in contact with the
rounding landscape.

**Robie House,
Chicago, 1906–9**
The patron, Frederick Robie,
had requested to be able to
'see his neighbours without
being seen' and at the same
time wanted to be able to
enjoy a view of a nearby
park. The high base wall and
the projection of the roof
contribute to the sense of
being protected, of the house
as a 'refuge'.

# Frank Lloyd Wright

## Fallingwater, Bear Run

### 1936–37

In 1936 the Pittsburgh department-store owner Edgar J. Kaufmann commissioned Wright to build a holiday home on his family's vast holdings in Pennsylvania. Wright chose a woody site crossed by a stream, the course of which runs over the irregular shape of large boulders. Wright decided to place what would become the masterpiece of his organic architecture alongside the stream, on a rocky ledge directly over the falling water.

The most striking aspect of this house is its close integration with the surrounding landscape. The plants, water, and rocks enter the rooms, becoming part of the domestic setting. The house is composed of horizontal planes, supported by four central stone pillars, that extend in every direction, ending in smooth concrete projecting terraces that resemble overlapping trays. The rooms are separated from the surrounding landscape by ribbons of continuous glass. A stairway in reinforced concrete leads from the living room to the stream; a pathway through the woods leads over a small bridge to the entrance of the house. The entryway opens directly onto the living room, which occupies the entire main floor, with one terrace located directly over the stream, and another facing the mountain behind. As is common in Wright's interiors, the centre of this space is the fireplace. The living-room floor is composed of irregularly shaped slabs of stone, the walls are dressed in stone, the furniture, designed by Wright himself, is made of walnut.

The bedrooms are on the second floor; all the rooms have terraces facing different directions. The final floor, smaller in size than the others, is a study and a bedroom, both of which also give onto a terrace.

The living room, arranged around the fireplace, is the central point of the house. Large expanses of glass put the interior in close contact with the exterior woodland. Nature is also present in the interior, in the stone flooring, the wooden furniture, the natural-fibre wall covering. Nature and artifice blend in an organic construction, with every material serving a function: stone for vertical supports, reinforced concrete for horizontal planes, glass and metal, painted red, framing the openings. Wright's original design called for the concrete overhangs painted yellow ochre to be dressed in gold leaf so as to shine in the sun and reflect in the water.

# Alvar Aalto
## 1898–1976

**Between functionalism and tradition**

The importance and the fascination of Alvar Aalto's architecture result from his ability to blend the language of Finnish tradition with Mittel-European rationalism, which he had come by during travels he undertook after earning his degree. In the buildings he designed beginning in 1927, the year in which he began his independent activity, Aalto combined abstraction and the functional rigour of the modern language with the attitude of an 'organic architect', which is expressed in the special attention he devoted to the well-being of the people destined to inhabit or use his structures. This attention shows up in the careful use of light, natural materials, colours, and the relationship the building has with the nature around it, almost always a Nordic landscape of woods and lakes. In fact, this aspect of his style shows up most of all in his most important works, all of which were made in Finland.

In the library of Viipuri (1927–35) he conceived a unitary spatial organism arranged on several levels: the spaces of the reading room, the loans desk, and the book deposit are arranged with a horizontal and vertical continuity.

The Paimio Sanatorium (1929–33) constitutes an eloquent example of the interplay between architecture and medical therapy. The complex is composed of three separate bodies arranged across the wooded landscape to form a single architectural organism. Various architectural and technological expedients are employed to make the life of the patients comfortable and to assist them in their stay in the sanatorium: the illumination is designed to exploit sunlight as much as possible, the walls and ceilings of the rooms are tinted with colours that favour repose, the walls are soundproofed.

In Villa Mairea (1938–39) the language of international modernism blends with local folk traditions: white rectangular volumes are placed together with structures in wood and stone, and large windows favour the relationship between interior and exterior.

**Villa Mairea, Noormarkku, 1938–39**
The villa was built for the Gullichsen family as a holiday home with rooms for guests. The L-shaped plan adds protection and privacy to a small interior court that includes a pool; the public front of the building is more formal. The layout alludes to the traditional Finnish house-farms, which have inner courts protected from cold winter winds. Aalto combined materials of modern architecture, such white painted concrete, with materials from the Nordic tradition, such as stone and wood, the wood also being used in the interiors, in the wall coverings, and in the thin support columns. Large windows put the interior o the rooms in contact with the Finnish landscape.

**...imio Sanatorium,
...29–33**

...cause of its skilled
...mbination of functional
...ments and measures
...signed to favour the
...ll-being – most of all
...ychological – of the
...tients, this building
...joyed great success and
...racted interest from
...road. The building is set
...a wooded landscape; all
...e areas designed for the
...e of the patients enjoy
...noramic views and face
...uth so as to be sunny. The
...tients' tranquillity is
...voured by precise technical
...easures taken in the design
...the interiors and the
...rnishings. The pale yellow
...our of the floors in the
...ain hall and the atrium
...okes the idea of the sun
...d warmth; a special system
...plumbing and taps
...luces the sound of water
...a minimum; and
...undproofing further
...luces disturbing noise.

**...brary, Viipuri, 1927–35**

...e various rooms of the
...rary are arranged on
...eral levels and connect
...form a continuous, fluid
...ole. The reading areas are
...uminated by conical
...lights specially designed
...that solar rays will not
...mage the books and the
...ders will not be disturbed
...sudden changes in levels
...luminosity.

# Expressionism

## c. 1910–25

### The eloquence of materials

In terms of the figurative arts and literature, the term *expressionism* usually refers to avant-garde movements that took place in Germany during the first years of the 20th century. In terms of architecture, the same word is used in reference to various artists active in the Low Countries and Germany during the period from around 1910 to 1925. What these artists have in common is the use of a language that was opposed to 19th-century eclecticism but was also against the rationalist-functionalist tendency of those years.

In the opinion of some architecture historians, the roots of expressionist architecture are to be found in the Deutscher Werkbund. In fact, industrial architecture, with its simple, essential forms and use of new materials, influenced the work of such rationalist architects as Gropius and Le Corbusier; the unusual volumes of industrial structures also favoured the evolution of an 'antirational' trend, as seen in works with strong expressive impact, with sinuous or highly articulated forms. The expressionist language was also manifested in the refashioning of forms from nature, such as spirals, curves, and crystals, and in works in which the expressive values of certain materials, such as brick or glass, are emphasized on exterior surfaces.

**Fritz Höger, Chilehaus, Hamburg, 1921–24**
Nicknamed 'ship's prow', this building was made to house a warehouse for merchandise imported from Chile. It is dressed in dark red klinker. Aside from recalling the shape of a ship, this construction drew inspiration from the brick constructions of the Gothic cathedrals of northern Germany.

**J. M. van der Meij, Michel de Klerk, Pieter Kramer, Scheepvaarthuis, Amsterdam, 1912–18**
The structure of the building – the administrative headquarters of several Amsterdam shipping companies – is made in reinforced concrete and is enclosed by a rich and imaginative façade composed of a variety of materials: terracotta, brick, concrete. The friezes and sculptures are inspired by navigation and maritime commerce.

**Hans Pölzig, Grosses Schauspielhaus, Berlin, 1919**
The auditorium of the 5,000-seat theatre is covered by a vast dome dripping with pendentives like stalactites, recalling the interior of a cave.

**Erich Mendelsohn, Einstein Tower, Potsdam, 1920–24**
The tower, built to house an observatory and a research centre on Einstein's theories of relativity, has a shape that makes it seem like the result of a lava flow. Despite their appearance, the outer walls were constructed in a traditional method using bricks that were then covered in a thick layer of plaster.

# De Stijl
## *c.* 1917–30

### The Dutch avant-garde

One of the avant-garde groups that had the greatest influence on the development of modern architecture in Europe was De Stijl, founded in Leiden in 1917, active in Holland, and named for the magazine *De Stijl*. The various artists who composed the group included the painter-architect Theo van Doesburg, the painter Piet Mondrian, and the architects Gerrit Rietveld, J. J. P. Oud, and Robert van 't Hoff.

The movement's primary objectives, strongly influenced by cubism, were the rejection of individualism in favour of an objective vision of reality and adherence to the principles of truth, order, clarity, and simplicity. The goal was the establishment of a coherent compositional methodology applicable to all the arts. These aims, derived from Mondrian's pictorial experiments, were expressed in the creations of the members of the group: rigorously geometric compositions based on the use of the right angle in primary colours that were developed on two or three dimensions.

One of the first architectural designs the magazine published was Oud's 1917 plan for a 'beach boulevard' on the seaside at Scheveningen: a row of apartment houses forming parallelepipeds of different heights aligned on a single front. Between 1920 and 1923 Theo van Doesburg made various studies for homes in which the dimensions were established by way of axonometric and three-dimensional models.

The most interesting finished building was the Schröder House, designed by Rietveld (1923–24) at the far end of a block of row houses in an Utrecht suburb. This was a parallelepiped with floors intersecting at right angles and an exterior of planar surfaces.

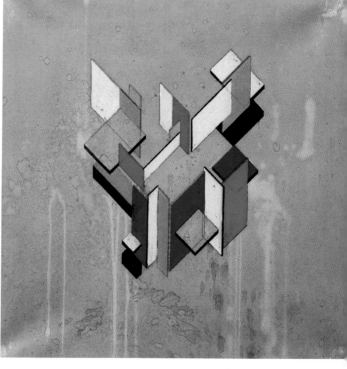

**Theo van Doesburg, design of the counter-construction of the private house, 1923**
This design was one of the series of works presented at the De Stijl exposition held in Paris in 1923. Van Doesburg made it together with his colleague van Eesteren. It was van Doesburg who came up with the idea of the counter-construction, an analytic method directed at demonstrating the construction of architecture by means of the decomposition and reaggregation of the planes of space following right angles and interpenetrations.

**J. J. P. Oud, design for workers' houses on a 'beac boulevard', Scheveningen, 1917**
Presented in the first issue the magazine *De Stijl*, the design presents several characteristics of Oud's activity within the group; absolute simplification of t design, the use of smooth surfaces, and the serial orde created by the repetition of modules, the symmetry, and the movement of the volumes along the compact front of the street.

**Gerrit Rietveld, Schröder House, Utrecht, exterior and interior, 1923–24**

This work is considered an emblem of De Stijl architecture. It results from an assembly of elements, including perpendiculars, that serve different functions and have different characteristics: the primary elements in white; connecting elements in masonry coloured grey and white; linear horizontal and vertical elements – beams, pillars, downspouts – in black, grey, red, yellow, blue; openings and exterior connections – doors, windows, railings, external stairs giving access to the roof – in blue or black. The structure is in masonry, wood, and iron. The projecting slabs of some of the balconies are in reinforced concrete. The interiors are also defined by different coloured lines and planes. The rooms can be separated by movable walls. These expedients respond to the patron's request for flexibility in the use of the spaces.

# Architecture and revolution

## in Russia

### c. 1917–30

**The Soviet avant-garde**

In Russia, the toppling of the old regime that took place with the Revolution of 1917 was followed by an artistic period of intense activity in formal experimentation directed at the establishment of a creative language capable of expressing the new ideals and aspirations of Soviet society. With the elimination of the beaux-arts educational system, the art schools in Russia encouraged use of a language based on abstract art that gave life to a style – also applied to architecture – based on elementary geometric forms and on symbolism drawn from the world of the factory and mass production. By the second half of the 1920s the Soviet economy had overcome the stagnation of the postrevolutionary period, and architects were making out ways to create new works that would respond to the models of life proposed by postrevolutionary socialism. At that time, the architects were united in two main associations, the OSA (Association of Contemporary Architects) and the ASNOVA (Association of New Architects), the first being more rationalist, the other with more expressive tendencies.

During those years a great number of designs were made for workers' clubs, public buildings, homes, and factories, only a small portion of which were ever built.

Among the Soviet architects who succeeded in achieving international fame was Konstantin Mel'nikov, creator of various workers' clubs in Moscow. He was known for the Soviet Pavilion at the 1925 Exposition Internationale des Arts Décoratifs et Industriels Modernes in Paris and for his house in Moscow, a singular building with a cylindrical structure and hexagonal windows.

With the ascent of Stalin in the 1930s, the Soviet authorities began using architecture as a vehicle for the expression of political power. As in all European totalitarian states, experimentation was replaced by an architecture meant to be inspiring, monumental, and triumphalist.

**Konstantin Mel'nikov, Mel'nikov House, Moscow, 1929**
Two different-height cylinders, the architect's home and his study, interlock to create a single building. The hexagonal openings – the windows – in the exterior of the building result from the division of the entire external surface into 200 hexagonal modules, 60 of which are open, thus forming the windows.

**[Ko]nstantin Mel'nikov, [Rus]akov Workers' Club, [Mo]scow, 1927–28**
[Th]e building, a culture [cen]tre for trolley workers, [ho]uses an auditorium for [13]00 people. The ground [flo]or is taken up by the large [ma]in auditorium with its [or]chestra area, over which [sta]nd the three small [au]ditoriums located in the [thr]ee projecting bodies; each [of] these can be divided off [fro]m the main auditorium [by] a system of movable [wa]lls. The reinforced-[co]ncrete construction was [cre]ated through the assembly [of] geometric volumes with [sh]arp angles and diagonal [lin]es that resemble an [en]ormous mechanical gear.

**Il'ya Aleksandrovich Golosov, Zuyev Club, Moscow, 1928**
This building, with its strong visual impact, is composed of the intersection-contraposition of two volumes: a transparent vertical glass cylinder that houses the staircase and a horizontal smooth-sided orthogonal volume.

# The international style

## *c.* 1920–32

### A common language

The expression 'international style' was first used, in 1932, by the American historian Henry-Russell Hitchcock, who together with Philip Johnson prepared the text to accompany the exhibition 'Modern Architecture: International Exhibition', held at the Museum of Modern Art, which included works from between 1922 and 1932.

Looking back over that decade of architecture it was possible to distinguish certain common traits that resulted from the overcoming of historical styles.

The leading exponents of this new language were Le Corbusier, Mies van der Rohe, Gropius, Wright, and Aalto, but a large number of architects, quite often students and followers of the 'masters', were drawn to the style, which provided an alternative to the eclectic tendencies dominant in Europe and North America.

In their text Hitchcock and Johnson identify the three stylistic principles behind international-style architecture: the effects of mass and solidity that had characterized the architecture of the past were replaced by a lightened sense of volume achieved by means of

planes supported by thin concrete or metal pillars; regularity and order were used to give clarity to architectural creations; and applied decoration was eliminated to avoid the arbitrary use of artificial elements.

Other recurrent elements of the international style, recognizable as elements from Le Corbusier's 'five points', are the use of continuous smooth or glass surfaces, flat roofs, and ribbon windows.

**Richard Neutra, Lovell House, Los Angeles, 1927–29**
The horizontal sense of the construction is emphasized by the lines of white concrete supported by a light steel framework.

**Rudolph Schindler, Lovell Beach House, Newport Beach, California, 1923–2**
The house is suspended on row of five open-form concrete piers. The detachment of the home from the ground, the use o white-plastered concrete, and the horizontality of the continuous windows show the building's relationship the designs by European masters. The internal articulation of the spaces into rooms of single or double height is legible on the side elevation.

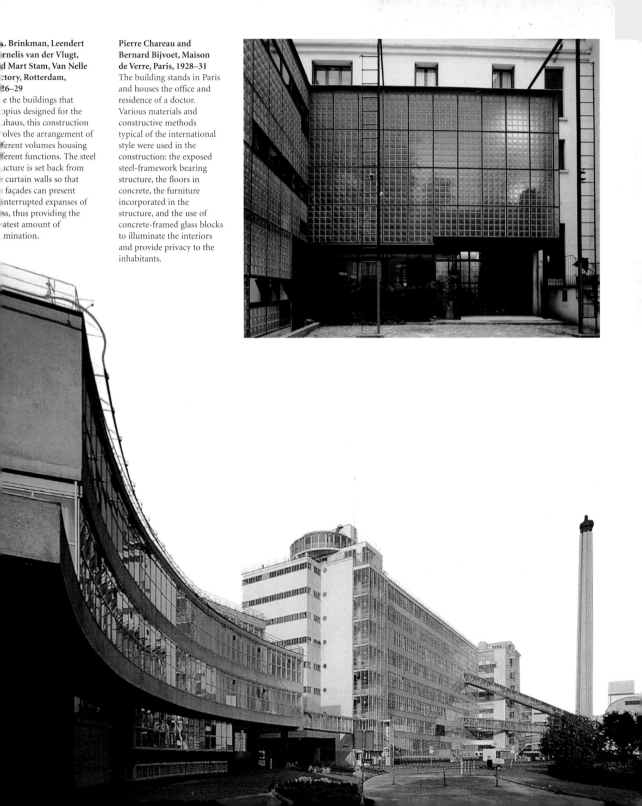

**A. Brinkman, Leendert [Co]rnelis van der Vlugt, [an]d Mart Stam, Van Nelle [Fac]tory, Rotterdam, [19]26–29**

[Lik]e the buildings that [Gr]opius designed for the [Ba]uhaus, this construction [inv]olves the arrangement of [dif]ferent volumes housing [dif]ferent functions. The steel [str]ucture is set back from [the] curtain walls so that [the] façades can present [un]interrupted expanses of [gla]ss, thus providing the [gre]atest amount of [illu]mination.

**Pierre Chareau and Bernard Bijvoet, Maison de Verre, Paris, 1928–31**

The building stands in Paris and houses the office and residence of a doctor. Various materials and constructive methods typical of the international style were used in the construction: the exposed steel-framework bearing structure, the floors in concrete, the furniture incorporated in the structure, and the use of concrete-framed glass blocks to illuminate the interiors and provide privacy to the inhabitants.

# Italian rationalism
## and Fascist architecture
### *c.* 1920–40

**Between classicism and rationalism**

The many architects active in Italy between the two world wars, and the various architectural movements they followed, present a panorama that is both highly complex and full of contradictions.

On the one hand were the architects who followed a sober and simplified classical language, quite often full of assonances with the creations of the Viennese Secession. This group included Ponti, Portaluppi, and De Finetti in Milan. At the same time, many other Italian architects were seeking ways to apply logical and rational criteria to their productions while also making reference to the classical roots of Italian culture. This was not an attempt to imitate the buildings of antiquity but rather to reappropriate an aesthetic based on proportion, rhythm, and the correct relationships between the parts and the whole, informed by mathematical regularity.

The birth of Italian rationalism is usually thought to coincide with the birth of Gruppo 7, a group composed of seven Lombard architects: Sebastiano Larco, Guido Frette, Carlo Enrico Rava, Luigi Figini, Gino Pollini, Giuseppe Terragni, and Adalberto Libera. Until the mid-1930s rationalism was in a certain sense seen as the official architecture of Fascism, based on the equation that modernization of the state entailed modernization of architecture. Rationalist architects made numerous buildings during those years. Post offices, train stations, urban renewal, and all those works that the Fascist regime distributed across the territory of Italy, such as the local Fascist headquarters (Casa del Fascio), Fascist Youth Movement buildings, and seaside holiday homes, became important opportunities for the affirmation of modern architecture.

Around the end of the 1930s the regime began to assume a style more in keeping with the affirmation of its imperialist aims, identifying itself in rhetorical architecture, academic and magniloquent.

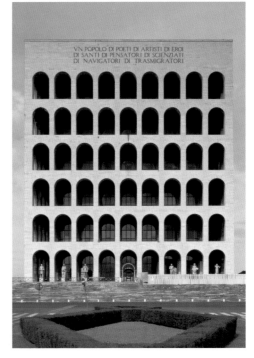

**Marcello Piacentini, Città Universitaria, Palazzo del Rettorato, Rome, 1932–35**
Public architecture in Italy during the 1930s employed language based on the basic myth of ancient Rome, hence monumental buildings in marble using traditional architectural elements. Columns, trabeations, pilaster strips, and Latin inscriptions were the fruit of the rhetoric imposed by the political climate of the time.

**Giovanni Guerrini, Ernesto La Padula, Mario Romano, Palace of the Italian Civilization, EUR, Rome, 1937–42**
With its strong visual impact, this building expressed rigor and monumentality. Its dominant position, the statues located along the perimeter, the dressing in smooth white travertine marble, the abstract forms, and the resemblance to the Colosseum increased its grandeur.

**seppe Terragni, House of Fascio, Como, 1932–36**
building, today the
mand post for the
binieri of Como, was the
Fascist party head-
rters. As a construction, it
ost clearly distinguished
e attention given to its
portions; it is a square
llelepiped, 33 metres per
, 16.5 metres high. Each
e building's four façades

is different, presenting four different modalities of rhythmically balancing the open and closed spaces. The building is composed of a skeleton framework in reinforced concrete dressed in white travertine marble. Inside it is a court surrounded by windows and illuminated from above by skylights in concrete-framed glass panels.

### Nazi architecture in Germany

*While in Italy, at least initially, modern architecture had the support of the regime, in Germany modern architecture was treated like a threat that had to be extirpated. This attitude resulted from several factors, including the socialist aspects of several undertakings involving workers' housing made by modern architects, the break with traditional German architecture, and the lack of faith in new building methods. Furthermore, the international style was poorly suited to Hitler's self-celebratory and omnipotent aspirations. Shortly after taking power Hitler named Paul Ludwig Troost as his principal consultant for architecture, and following Troost's death, in 1934, he was replaced by Albert Speer. Speer succeeded in interpreting Hitler's aspirations in his 1938 design for the new Berlin chancellery, characterized by giant halls dressed in marble with reliefs of Nazi emblems and coats of arms. His plan, never made, for the urban restructuring of Berlin dates to 1937. The centre of the new city was a 'North-South Axis', a long monumental avenue running between a triumphal arch in honour of Hitler to the 'Grosse Halle'.*

# Urban reform
## between the world wars

**Amsterdam, Rotterdam, Vienna**

In the years following World War I, industrial development and the enormous influx of workers to cities drew the attention of architects to the design of urban housing districts, in most cases concentrated near factories. The goal was to provide acceptable living conditions for the new masses of workers. In some cities, large residential complexes were designed, often extending over several city blocks, with community services, such as laundries, nursery schools, and libraries, located inside the complex or nearby. In Amsterdam, Michel de Klerk built the Eigen Haard residential complex, nicknamed *Het Scheep* ('The Ship') because of its shape. The buildings, all of them faced in brick, are organized around a courtyard. The differing geometric shapes of the buildings indicate their different functions. In the Kiefhoek district of Rotterdam, Oud designed a series of residential blocks; these are basic constructions, without decorative elements, composed of the repetition of cell-types.

Vienna presents an exemplary case for Europe during the first postwar period. A programme of municipal improvements and reforms to favour the less-well-to-do classes was expressed in terms of architecture in the construction of public housing, including about four hundred residential blocks, called *Höfe* because of the internal courtyards located along their perimeter. Special attention was devoted to the public spaces in these complexes: the laundries are often provided with modern equipment, the communal baths are sometimes equipped with pools and saunas. The expression 'Red Vienna' is often used in reference to the urban measures of these years because of the underlying political tilt of the movement. The principal function of the new undertakings was in fact that of providing homes for the poorest classes and making community services available: nursery schools, for example, were designed to serve as centres for children's health care.

One of the most famous blocks was the Karl Marx Hof, designed by Karl Ehn between 1926 and 1930.

**Michel de Klerk, Eigen Haard Housing Project, Amsterdam, 1917–21**
The obelisk-tower signalle the entrance to the intern courtyard and was origina meant to be topped by a cock, the symbol of the Dutch Social Democratic party. The steep roofs of t buildings protect them fr winter snow.

**...Ehn, Karl Marx Hof,**
**...na, 1926–30**
...building extends nearly
...ometre in length and
...designed to house 1,400
...tments. The entrance
...es and heavy towers
...en the front, which has
...ppearance of a fortress.
...was the site in 1934 of
...nt clashes between
...nese socialists and forces
...e extreme right.

**J. J. P. Oud, Kiefhoek**
**district, Rotterdam, 1925–29**
Each apartment is arranged
on two levels. On the ground
floor are the living room,
facing the street, and the
kitchen, which faces a small
rear garden; the second floor
is usually divided into three
bedrooms. The sparseness
of the construction is
emphasized by the uniform
use of white plaster, the total
absence of decorative
elements, and the continuous
ribbon of windows.

# The United States
## 1918–29

### Art deco and the skyscraper

The period between the end of World War I and the collapse of the New York Stock Exchange in 1929 was a period of great building development in the United States. The nation's road network and rail lines were increased, the outlying areas of urban centres grew, and skyscrapers rose to change the skylines of major cities. During these years, the European avant-garde movements used technological innovations and the new opportunities offered by new building materials in the search for suitable forms to express the spirit of the times; in the United States, however, the use of historical styles was still much in vogue. In 1922 the *Chicago Tribune* held a competition for the design of its new headquarters; the 263 designs submitted in response presented a wide range of styles. The first prize went to Raymond M. Hood and John Mead Howells for a neo-Gothic building with a structural framework dressed in stone and topped with a crown of spires.

The term *art deco* is often associated with the American architecture of this period. The name, derived from the name of the international exposition held in Paris in 1925 ('Exposition Internationale des Arts Décoratifs et Industriels Modernes'), referred to an architectural style that, ranging between avant-garde and tradition, made use of abstract ornamental motifs or those drawn from various stylistic or historical traditions. One of the most famous art deco buildings of these years was the Chrysler Building, designed by William van Alen at the end of the 1920s, which was the tallest building in the world – 319 metres – until the construction of the Empire State Building in 1931.

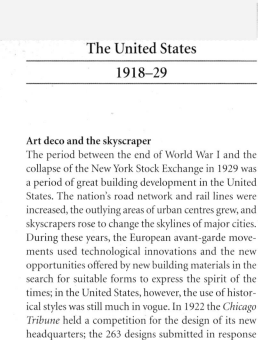

**Richmond Shreve, William Lamb, and Arthur Harmon, Empire State Building, New York, 1931**
The Empire State Building, with its high telecommunications tower that stands out against the New York skyline, was from the moment of its inauguration one of the best-loved buildings in the world. It owes some of its fame to the world of movies, for its panoramic terrace has served as a special setting in many film. The steel structure is dress in limestone and granite. The building reaches a height of 380 metres.

*Above*
**Rockefeller Center, New York, 1931–40**
Three architectural groups designed Rockefeller Cent Corbett, Harrison & MacMurry; Reinhard & Hofmeister; and Hood, Godley & Fouilhoux. The last-named were responsib for the RCA Building. The centre is composed of a group of buildings that ris gradually from the street, recalling an enormous Mayan temple. Steel structures are dressed in granite and marble.

mond M. Hood and
1 Mead Howells,
cago Tribune Building,
cago, 1922–25

verticality of the
ding is emphasized by
ndary pilasters that run
ig the façade, growing
ower at the top. This was
design that won the 1922
test; the winner was
sen by a jury and by the
ders of the paper.

William Van Alen, Chrysler
Building, New York,
1928–30

A shaft 170 metres high rests
on a 20-storey-tall base and
narrows upward to
culminate in a spire. Several
references to the famous
Chrysler automobile appear
along the surface of the
building, including a frieze
of hubcaps near a setback
and hood ornaments
fashioned as gargoyles. The
surface of the building is
given a modern, machinelike
polychromy through the use
of grey trim on the white
skin and stainless steel on
the spire. Four colossal
American eagles located
around the base project
toward the horizon. The
elegant lobby is dressed in
shiny metal and marble.

## The works of the masters
## in the postwar period

**Between continuity and renewal**

World War II was one of the most destabilizing events of the last century, with important consequences also in the field of architecture. The conditions that had caused the birth of modern architecture had lost force, and architects found themselves forced to seek new solutions while at the same time heeding the importance of the architectural revolution of the 1920s. This concerned most of all the 'masters', who reworked their language to avoid sterile imitation, but did so without betraying the principles they had matured in the prewar years. Gropius and Mies van der Rohe, having fled Nazi Germany during the 1930s, moved to the United States. The works Gropius made in the United States, primarily schools and single-family homes, do not share the expressive intensity of his prewar designs in Germany, but Mies van der Rohe seems to have found Chicago, birthplace of the skyscraper and the steel framework, a setting congenial to his style. On the banks of Lake Michigan he designed his first steel-and-glass skyscrapers. With the collaboration of Philip Johnson, Mies designed one of the most influential buildings of the postwar period, New York's Seagram Building (1954–58), an impressive skyscraper whose sharp glass-and-steel silhouette became a highly imitated prototype. Frank Lloyd Wright's language also changed as he adopted new models of reference, such as the circle and the spiral. In 1943 he began work on the design of the Guggenheim Museum in New York, inaugurated in 1959, a building organized around a spiral ramp that constitutes the arrangement of the museum's display as well as the generative element of its overall design. Unlike their German colleagues, Le Corbusier and Alvar Aalto had remained in Europe during the war. Between 1945 and his death, in 1965, Le Corbusier designed strikingly recognizable buildings that are unrelated to the *machines à habiter* of the earlier years; he introduced curvilinear forms and sculptural volumes to his language while showing a preference for exposed concrete. The postwar period found Aalto carrying ahead the organic architecture he had initiated in the prewar years. He came to the United States and made one of his most important works in Cambridge, Massachusetts: the Baker House Dormitory at Massachusetts Institute of Technology (1947–48).

**Mies van der Rohe and Philip Johnson, Seagram Building, New York, 1954–58**
The thirty-eight-floor building on Park Avenue was designed for the Canadian multinational Seagram & Sons. It has often served as a model because of its elegant simplicity and technical perfection. The curtain wall of bronze and glass forms a dense grid that accentuates the building's stark verticality. It is embellished by the grey-amber tint of window glass and the green travertine dressing of the columns of the base.

**nk Lloyd Wright, 
ggenheim Museum, New 
k, interior, 1943–59**

 building rises off Fifth 
nue like an upside-down 
al ivory box. On its 
rior an inclined ramp 
ows the perimeter of the 
side walls, leading the 
tor on a continuous 
te that leads from the 
und floor to the last 
r. A large central skylight 
 windows open in the 
er shell of the building 
vide most of the lighting.

**Le Corbusier, Notre-Dame 
du Haut, Ronchamp, 
1950–54**

Architecture and sculpture 
blend to give form to one of 
Le Corbusier's most famous 
buildings. The solid walls in 
concrete dressed in white 
cement lean in toward the 
interior; the concrete shell 
of the roof swirls skyward, 
lifting the building. The 
interior is illuminated by 
natural lighting that enters 
through narrow glassed 
openings; the floor, 
following the slope of the 
site, is slightly inclined 
toward the altar, focusing 
attention in that direction.

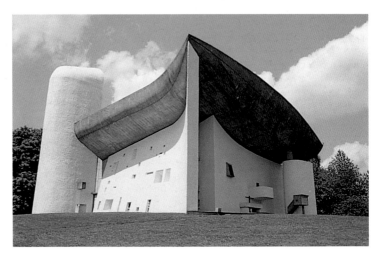

# Le Corbusier
## Unité d'Habitation, Marseilles
### 1945–52

Le Corbusier continued the architectural programme of the 'machines for living' in the postwar period in the *unités d'habitation*, housing projects that represent not just large-scale apartment houses but urban-planning schemes and social statements. The *unité* is a small, self-sufficient city that rises vertically to free the surrounding terrain – used for traffic and green spaces – and at the same time it is a large social 'container'. The building in Marseilles has space for about 1,600 residents who have available restaurants, stores, and even a hotel; various collective services are located on the roof terrace, including a pool and a playground for children. The enormous structure, which some have compared to a transatlantic liner, is about 140 metres long, 24 wide, and about 60 metres high; it is 18 storeys high and has 23 types of home destined for different users: single people, couples, larger families. Most of the apartments have two floors in an L-shaped plan. Every three floors there are two 'fit-together' apartments, each with a double-height living room. The apartments are arranged along internal halls that run the full length of the building longitudinally. Between 1945 and 1968 Le Corbusier designed six *unités d'habitation*, without ever improving on the quality he had achieved at Marseilles.

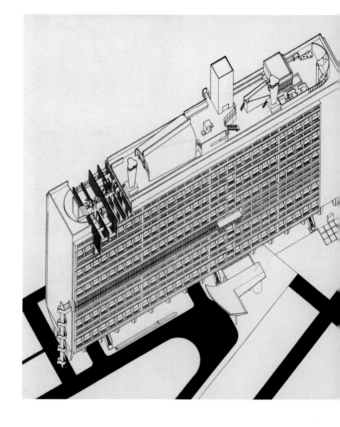

The structure is in exposed reinforced concrete. Only the *brise-soleils* ('sun shades') are painted – red, blue, green, and yellow. The arrangement of the internal apartments is visible on the façade: the height of the windows distinguishes the double-height apartments. The greater number of *brise-soleils* near the seventh floor indicates the location of the community services. The entire construction is raised off the ground on pillars – *pilotis* – in reinforced concrete that narrow downward.

All the apartments and ev[en] the building itself are size[d] on the basis of the Modul[or] which is symbolically sculpted on the façade. Th[is] is a measurement of scale devised by Le Corbusier a[nd] based on the proportions [of] the human body. Standing on the roof of the buildin[g] are the high chimneys and the various structures for community life, including [a] playground for children, a[n] outdoor track, a nursery school, a solarium, and a [...]

## North American trends:
## the 1950s and 1960s

### In the wake of the masters

In the United States, much as in Europe, the developments in modern architecture during the postwar period were not unrelated to the developments of the 1930s and the 'masters'. The work of Mies van der Rohe was of particular importance during this period, and his 'minimalist' simplicity and use of steel and glass were repeated by other architects, such as Philip Johnson, Charles Eames, and Eero Saarinen, whose language went through progressive evolutions. Philip Johnson became one of the leading exponents of postmodernism, while Saarinen abandoned his severe glass cubes around the 1960s and moved instead in the direction of plastic forms of an expressionist derivation. A primary example of this is the TWA terminal he designed at New York's John F. Kennedy Airport, a construction of reinforced concrete that recalls the wings of a bird.

Louis I. Kahn's career followed a different course from those of the architects just cited. His training had taken place before the international style had taken root in the United States. Kahn studied at the University of Pennsylvania, where he acquired the elements of classical definition following the academic tradition of the Ecole des Beaux-Arts: symmetries, axiality, proper proportions, the hierarchy of parts. Contact with rationalist architecture – in Rome, Egypt, and Greece – had led him to fashion a personal language that used modern materials and technologies to explore and present geometric forms, often monumental, that are related to history.

His most important works from this period include the Yale University Art Gallery at New Haven (1951–53), the Richards Medical Research Laboratories at the University of Pennsylvania in Philadelphia (1957–65), the Salk Institute for Biological Studies at La Jolla, in California (1959–65), and the Kimbell Art Museum in Fort Worth (1966–72), which some see as his masterpiece of those years.

**Louis I. Kahn, Salk Institute for Biological Studies, La Jolla, 1959–65**
The building resulted from the encounter between the aims of the scientist Jonas Salk – who wanted to establish a research centre California that would also a work community – and sensitivity of Louis I. Kahn Two parallel curtains, crea by the laboratory towers, mark off a courtyard. A th band of water forms the symmetrical axis of the complex and connects it to the ocean it overlooks.

o Saarinen, TWA
minal, John F. Kennedy
port, New York, 1956–62
r large vaults made of
nforced concrete rest on
haped supports. The
pty spaces generated by
structure are filled in
h glass. The building's
anic form almost
tainly alludes to birds
flight.

**Philip Johnson, Glass House, New Canaan, 1949**
Philip Johnson designed the Seagram Building, together with Mies van der Rohe. In the design of his home in Connecticut, he adopted the master's minimalist aesthetic, creating a transparent box whose steel structure is reduced to the bare essentials. The domestic space is in close relation with the surrounding landscape, which also gives the inhabitants some privacy.

# The assimilation of the modern

## 1950–60

**Latin America, Australia, Japan**

The modern movement in architecture originated in several countries of Western Europe, in the United States, and to a certain degree in the Soviet Union. By the end of the 1950s, however, this new architectural language had extended to other areas of the world. Its circulation was favoured by new means of communication and by the fact that many of the masters of modern architecture were active beyond their national borders – Le Corbusier, for example, made buildings in India during the postwar period. It is also true that architects from all over the world travelled to Europe or the United States for training.

The arrival of modern architecture in a new territory most often set in motion a process of assimilation between the 'new' and the 'traditional'. This happened in both Mexico and Australia, where the newly imported international style was blended with indigenous elements by way of the use of local materials and archetypes. Sometimes the adoption of new expressive forms was an aspect of a country's route toward independence, often following political movements that caused a break with the past, as happened in Brazil. During the late 1950s a group of modern architects, among them Oscar Niemeyer and Lucio Costa, were entrusted with the construction of Brasília, a symbol of national rebirth. They designed the Plaza of the Three Powers, including the administration building, a skyscraper of Le Corbusier inspiration, furnished with *brise-soleils* and dressed in the local granite. In the plan for Brasília, the country's new capital city from 1945, Niemeyer applied a modern language imbued with great monumentality.

Traditional Japanese architecture and modern architecture have many elements in common, such as the structural framework and the repetition of modular elements; even so, the arrival of the new expressive modalities in Japan brought about the reworking of local and traditional concepts. Kenzo Tange, one of the major Japanese architects of the postwar period, has been moving in that direction.

**Kenzo Tange, Peace Centre and Peace Memorial Museum, Hiroshima, 1949–55**
One of the first buildings by Tange in the postwar period, the Hiroshima Memorial Museum combines Le Corbusier's 'five points' with elements drawn from Japanese tradition, such as the light sun-screens and the modular arrangement of the façade.

*Opposite top*
**Luis Barragán, San Cristóbal estate and stables, Los Clubes, Mexico City, 1968**
Barragán is a leading Mexican architect who blends modern ideas with reflections of the local culture. Here he reinterprets the Mexican typology of the patio surrounded by smooth walls, creating a series of architectural spaces in which simple rectangular planes, most of them coloured, enclose, protect, and connect private spaces, gardens, and expanses of water.

*Opposite bottom*
**Oscar Niemeyer, Plaza of the Three Powers, Brasília, 1958**
The focal point of the design of the new capital is the square of the Three Powers. A building in the shape of a saucer houses the Chamber of Deputies; one in the shape of a dome houses the Senate. The pair of monumental glass skyscrapers house the administrative offices.

# Jørn Utzon

## Sydney Opera House

### 1953–73

The Sydney Opera House, which Utzon began designing in 1953, is today one of the best known buildings in the world, already emblematic of its city, perhaps even of its entire continent.

The drive to give the city of Sydney a cultural centre dedicated to music that would add prestige to the city dated to the end of the 1940s. In 1955 an international competition was held, calling for designs that would include two auditoriums, one with 3,500 seats, the other with 1,200, along with all the related scenery spaces, rehearsal rooms, a transmission centre, a restaurant seating 250 people, two meeting rooms, and a bar and foyer for each hall.

The first prize went to the thirty-eight-year-old Danish architect Jørn Utzon, at the time unknown. His design was astonishing: the two auditoriums are set side by side in a stone base; attached to this are the great compositions of the 'shells' of the roofs. The jury claimed it had made out in the winning plan the chance to make one of the most representative architectural works in the world. The international press reacted to Utzon's design with wonder, embarrassment, and disdain; the more farsighted and enlightened predicted a destiny as an iconic building. And so it was. Work began in 1957 and dragged on until 1973. Utzon was assisted by the London engineering company Ove Arup & Partners, one of the world's most prestigious. Many problems had to be solved, requiring continuous studies and research. Friction grew between Utzon and the public administration of Sydney, most of all when the costs exceeded the predicted amounts. In 1966 Utzon was forced to quit, leaving the work unfinished. The building was completed by others and opened in 1973, becoming, as predicted, one of the best-known and loved structures of the last century. From Bennelong Point, in the bay of Sydney, the twelve shells of the Opera House stand out, 60 metres high, similar to large sails, but also like towering waves heading out toward the ocean.

The Sydney Opera House owes much of its success to its location. The building stands on a promontory surrounded by water on three sides and is thus highly visible from both land and sea. The sensitivity that Utzon displayed in inserting the building in its context probably reflects the influence of northern European organic architecture.

is drawing shows the
mplexity of the roof
ults. Both the structure in
nforced concrete and the
verings are composed of
:fabricated elements
sembled on site. The
mplex is composed of a
se – the depth of which
houses the two auditoriums
along with their technical
and service rooms – and
over that the vault of the
coverings, the composition
of which is not determined
by the articulation of the
internal spaces.

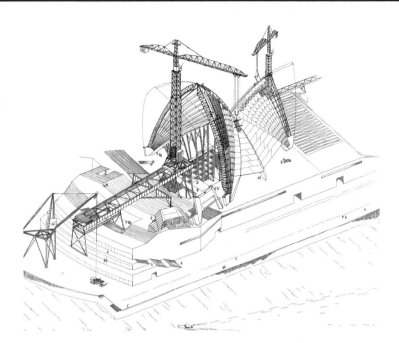

## European trends

### 1950–60

#### Postwar architecture

Modern architecture in Europe during the immediate postwar years was primarily a means for solving very real problems, from the reconstruction of cities ravaged by the War to the creation of functional and economical housing for the new masses of workers. In most cases, the results were impersonal modern buildings showing no relationship to their settings. In the midst of this, there were also, however, architects who sought to connect their creations with the ideas current in the 1920s and 1930s, achieving a critical revision valid for their own time.

One of the trends of those years was brutalism, which took Le Corbusier's *béton brut* ('raw concrete') and extrapolated it into the idea of leaving the physical plants and materials of buildings visible. Most of the architects involved in this were British, including Peter and Alison Smithson and James Stirling.

Another trend, this one more widespread on the Continent of Europe, involved bringing out the aesthetic qualities offered by engineering. One of the French exponents of this was Jean Prouvé, who made elegant buildings in metal and glass. In Italy, Pier Luigi Nervi designed public buildings,

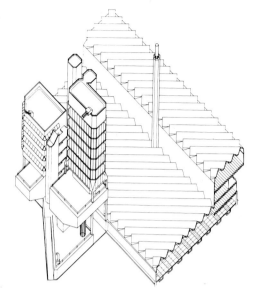
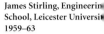

exhibition halls, and sports centres exalting the aesthetic qualities of structural elements in reinforced concrete. At the end of the 1950s, in collaboration with Gio Ponti, he made the Pirelli Tower in Milan. The reworking of the modern language also saw attention brought to a structure's relationship to the history and nature of a site by way of the revival of traditional typologies and the use of local building methods and materials.

**James Stirling, Engineering School, Leicester University, 1959–63**
Three distinct blocks make up the complex, an office tower, a four-storey building for laboratories, and an area for workshops. The patron requested that the building not be in exposed concrete, so Stirling used a dressing red brick and tile; the remaining structural elements are left exposed. There are various references to the architecture of the 'masters', such as the glass tower similar to Bauhaus architecture and the projecting volumes, reminiscent of Russian architecture of the 1920s. Other elements are drawn from the language of industrial architecture.

**Hans Scharoun, Philharmonic Concert Hall, Berlin, 1956–63**
In the wake of organic architecture and the expressionist architecture of the 1920s, some architects designed buildings with strong individual character. Such is the case with the Berlin Philharmonic, with its extremely complex geometry composed of curves, projections, and inclined planes.

**BPR, Velasca Tower,
ilan, 1956-58**
his is one of the most
cognizable architectural
orks of postwar Milan:
26-floor tower with a
ojecting upper body
pported by oblique
ttresses. The concrete
ructural framework is
sible in the shafts on
e façade, which also
centuates the verticality of
e building and puts it in a
lationship to the ribbing
the nearby cathedral. The
ape of the tower recalls
e medieval communal
laces and is related to the
earby Sforza Castle.

**Gio Ponti and Pier Luigi
Nervi, Pirelli Tower, Milan
1955–59**
This elegant 34-floor tower
is symbolic of the economic
growth of the city during
the postwar period. It stands
out against the Milan sky,
representing the prestige of
the Pirelli company, whose
main offices are located in
the tower. Ponti abandoned
the usual rectangular
ground plan of the tall
building imported from the
United States, adopting a
lozenge shape.

# High tech
## The late 20th century

### The aesthetics of technology

The second half of the 20th century saw the affirmation of what is usually called high-tech (high-technology) architecture, a style with roots leading back to the iron architecture designed by 19th-century engineers. In fact, many high-tech buildings can be said to descend from such structures as the Eiffel Tower and Crystal Palace.

High tech refers to an architectural concept that bases its aesthetic and its essence on the expressive qualities, sometimes exaggerated, of constructive elements derived from the worlds of engineering and technology: the architectural shape is determined by the shape of the structural components. Traditional building techniques, such as brickwork, are abandoned in favour of new structures and materials: steel, light metal panels, plastic materials.

Montreal's 'Expo '67' marked an important step in the affirmation of this approach to architectural design. The German Pavilion, designed by Frei Otto and Rolf Gutbrod, and the US Pavilion, designed by Buckminster Fuller, made use of advanced-technology structures to cover larges spaces with the smallest possible amount of materials. Frei Otto and Günter Behnisch repeated the technology used for the Montreal pavilion in the design of the Olympiapark built for Munich in 1972.

The iconic building of this trend is the Georges Pompidou Centre, built in Paris between 1971 and 1976 by Renzo Piano and Richard Rogers; here structure and physical plant become one and the same.

During the last twenty years of the 20th century many architects – chief among them Renzo Piano, Richard Rogers, Norman Foster, and Nicholas Grimshaw – used the language of high-tech architecture in the design of buildings, primarily public or commercial spaces or sports complexes.

**Foster and Partners, Hong Kong and Shanghai Bank, Hong Kong, 1979–86**
The steel skeleton that is the bearing structure of this 180-metre-high skyscraper is located on the exterior of the building. This expedient made it possible to 'empty' the inside of the building, leaving a vertical courtyard ten floors high, crossed by elevators and escalators. The bank's offices face onto this courtyard.

**inter Behnisch and
ei Otto, Olympiapark,
unich, 1968–72**
is type of cable-net roof,
rticularly well suited to
vering the large spaces
stadiums, provides both
nsparency and protection
m the elements. It creates
ort of tent composed of
veb of Plexiglas plates
pported by inclined
el pylons.

**Buckminster Fuller,
USA Pavilion, 'Expo '67',
Montreal, 1967**
This structure is an example
of the geodesic domes that
Buckminster Fuller designed
during the 1950s and 1960s.
These spherical construc-
tions, composed of modular
metallic elements in
hexahedral or octahedral
shapes, were able to cover
large spaces. The dome at
Montreal – which visitors
could see while crossing the
pavilion on a monorail –
measured 76 metres in
diameter and 41.5 in height.

# Renzo Piano and Richard Rogers
## Georges Pompidou Centre, Paris
### 1971–78

The Georges Pompidou Centre, one of the best-loved and most talked-about architectural structures of the last century, was the result of a competition held at the end of the 1960s by the Paris administration that reflected the ambitious aims of the French president Georges Pompidou; the building also displays the design sensibilities of Renzo Piano and Richard Rogers, along with collaboration from Ove Arup & Partners, one of London's leading studios of engineering consultation.

The goal of the competition was to give Paris a new multifunctional centre able to attract and host a large number of users – the contest guidelines called for a structure able to support 10,000 visitors daily. The activities to be housed included libraries, museums, temporary exhibitions, a cinema research centre, centres for specialized research, theatres, and conference rooms. The idea was that of a flexible,

polyvalent structure that could be transformed to meet the needs of the public and the city. Among the 684 designs submitted in the competition, the one chosen (and made with only a few modifications) was that of Renzo Piano and Richard Rogers. This called for a glass parallelepiped 140 metres long, 50 metres wide, and 50 high, held within the network of the coloured metallic tubes that compose the building's structural system as well as its physical plant.

This arrangement of the structural system made available about 7,500 square metres of open space on each floor, with no interior bearing walls or partitions, thus space that could be transformed or adapted as needed.

Over the years the Centre has become the iconic work of high-tech architecture: the structure of the building coincides with its essence, which effectively combines technology and decoration.

The Pompidou Centre is located on the edge of a va area in the centre of Paris, the Plateau Beaubourg, no far from the historic Les Halles market, which was destroyed shortly before construction began on the Centre. Some of the building's enormous popularity results from its 'playful' character. Its presence has given identity the square where it stands. While apparently extraneo to the setting, it is in reality profoundly tied to it: its terraces, windows, and transparent covered passag create a continuous relationship between the visitor and the city. The uneven line of the escalator is emblematic of the building, making it instantl recognizable. At the same time it offers an understanding of the arrangement of the buildin which is not really a rando heap of tubes but a carefull arranged system of module that repeat following a determined rhythm.

ch colour corresponds to
ifferent function. White
sed for the bearing
ucture and the air intakes;
l is for the platforms and
 elevator cages; blue is the
-conditioning system;
low is the electrical
tem; green is for the water
es. The primary load-
aring structure is
nposed of steel and cast-
n tubes and beams, with
 Gerber girders that
pport the main structure
ible on the façade.

# Postmodernism
## Second half 20th century

### Overcoming the modern

The term *postmodern* was coined by the American theorist Charles Jencks in his 1977 book *The Language of Post-Modern Architecture* to describe certain architectural tendencies that sprang up in the 1960s in opposition to the dictates of rationalism. In its search for an authentic and essential style, the modern movement had excluded traditional historic forms as well as decorative elements from its repertory. In contrast to this, the postmodern expresses itself, generally, through mixtures of styles, citations of classical elements in an ironic or playful way, along with references to popular culture. Basic elements of architecture, such as columns, arches, and tympana, often lose their original meaning when used as ornamental elements. The sober tones and desire for logic that are characteristic of international rationalism gave way to a language based on chromatic and material combinations that are often provocatively absurd or 'wrong'. The best-known architects to have adopted this type of expression, at least in certain phases of their career, include the Americans Robert Venturi, Charles Moore, and Philip Johnson, the Spaniard Ricardo Bofill, the Britain James Stirling, and the Italian Aldo Rossi.

The affirmation of the postmodern took place in Italy at the first international architecture show at the Venice Biennale (1980), directed by Paolo Portoghesi, in the 'Strada Novissima', a sequence of façades from the past fashioned with abundant historical citations.

**Philip Johnson, American Telephone and Telegraph Building, New York, 1982**
An enormous pierced tympanum crowns the summit of this skyscraper, completely dressed in pink granite, making it recognizable on the New York skyline.

**Charles Moore, Piazza d'Italia, New Orleans, 197?**
Made for the Italian community of New Orleans this construction is composed of ironic citations of Roman and Renaissance elements assembled in a semicircular space and reproduced with unusual materials in vivacious colours.

**[Ald]o Rossi, Residential [blo]ck on Kochstrasse, [Ber]lin, 1984–87**
[Ro]ssi is the author of [nu]merous works in which [rig]our and purity are [ass]ociated with explicit [cita]tions of evocative or [sym]bolic elements drawn [fro]m classical archetypes of [arc]hitecture. The regularity [of t]he composition of this [res]idential block is [int]errupted at the street [cor]ner, where an opening is [ma]de and filled by an [ove]rsize column.

**Robert Venturi, Vanna Venturi House, Chestnut Hill, Philadelphia, 1962–64**
Apparently similar to the American vernacular single-family house, the house that Venturi designed for his mother presents various elements and citations that make it contrary and disproportionate, such as the broken tympanum and round arch and the asymmetrical arrangement of the windows and doors.

# James Stirling and Michael Wilford

## Neue Staatsgalerie, Stuttgart

### 1977–84

In 1977, after a national contest gave only unsatisfactory results, the government of Baden-Württemberg announced an international contest for the enlargement of the State Gallery of Stuttgart, a late classical building from 1842.

James Stirling and Michael Wilford won the contest and were entrusted with the construction of the work. The complex design is based on a U-shaped layout into which a circular courtyard is inserted; both open spaces are crossed by a series of ramps and pedestrian pathways that make them visible but not accessible, except from the museum. Despite the apparent simplicity of the layout, the organism presents itself as a complicated series of volumes, inclined surfaces, and routes; a tortuous ramp connects the city to the museum entrance, signalled by an undulating glass wall at the entrance foyer. The U-shaped block includes the museum galleries: a series of communicating rooms that extend along the external walls and are connected to the 19th-century museum by way of a covered bridge. The work is a collage of historical citations and 'postmodern' creations, such that its playful appearance makes it attractive, but its complexity makes it baffling. In 1995 the gallery was enlarged with the addition of a building that houses the music school and the academy of dramatic arts of Stuttgart.

The heart of the complex is an internal rotunda, which includes many classical citations – a short trabeation supported by a pair of Doric columns, a series of round arches, classically inspired statues – making it also a homage to Schinkel's neo-classical architecture.

materials are assembled
sort of collage, but the
they are used provides
ethod of reading the
position of the building.
pathways are indicated
andrails in pink and
; access areas are
alled by metallic awnings;
ntrance is indicated by
undulating glass wall;
colour stone walls
stitute the continuous
sing of the building and
e same time connect it to
older buildings.

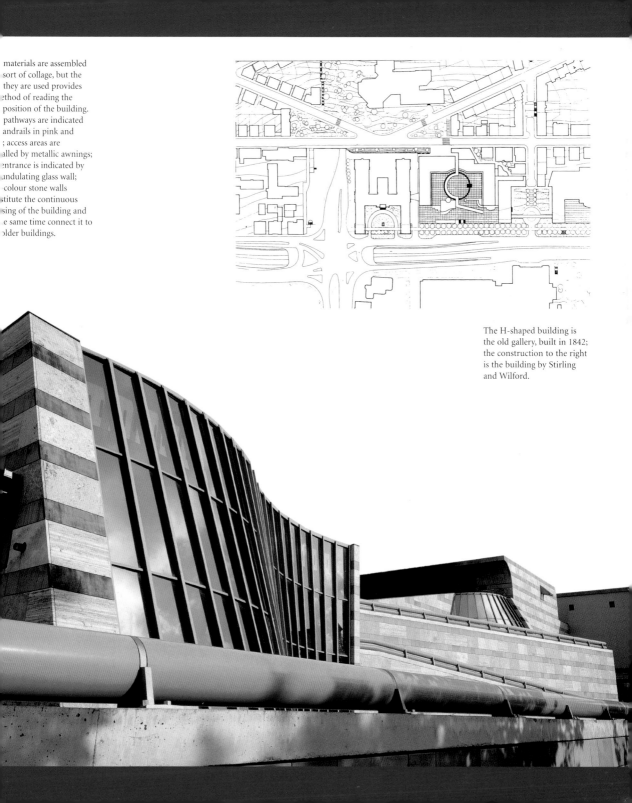

The H-shaped building is
the old gallery, built in 1842;
the construction to the right
is the building by Stirling
and Wilford.

# Deconstructivism

## End 20th century

### Precariousness at the end of the millennium

The term *deconstructivism* refers to an architectural style, often associated with postmodernism, that was developed in Europe and the United States during the last two decades of the 20th century. It can be defined as a design attitude involving a marked deformation of Euclidean geometry that gives little weight to the previously standard canons of proportion and construction of classical and modern architecture and rejects all rules of coherence and rigour. The recurrent traits of this architecture are obliqueness, precariousness, disharmony in the matching of forms and materials, and irregularity.

The conventional traits of architecture are decomposed and recomposed to make apparently incoherent forms that often challenge the laws of gravity.

Before being applied to architecture, the term *deconstructivism* had been used by the philosopher Jacques Derrida at the end of the 1960s to indicate the multiplicity of meanings and readings that can be given to any one text. The concept was introduced to architecture in 1988 by a show at the Museum of Modern Art in New York entitled Deconstructive Architecture that had been organized – just like the 1930s show at the same museum that introduced the international style – by Philip Johnson. The show presented the works of seven architects identified as the leading exponents of the new style: Frank O. Gehry, Daniel Libeskind, Rem Koolhaas, Peter Eisenman, Zaha Hadid, the Co-op Himmelblau group, and Bernard Tschumi.

The true pioneer of this 'trend', however, was Frank O. Gehry, who performed the first experiments in deconstructive architecture in California around the end of the 1970s, in particular a series of buildings in which he combined unusual materials in apparently unstable and precarious structures. His language, like that of many of his contemporaries, modified over the course of the 1990s, acquiring a special expressiveness through the use of computers in design.

**Co-op Himmelblau, UFA Multiplex Cinema, Dresden, 1993–98**
Often, as in this building, high technology is not used to optimize the qualitative rendering of materials but rather to achieve an image of precarious instability.

**ak O. Gehry, California ospace Museum, Los eles, 1982–84**
structed on the occasion e 1984 Olympic Games, building is composed ctangular volumes, ections, oblique planes, the apparently random ication of opaque and sparent walls. A full-scale 4 fighter jet is suspended the entrance.

**Günter Behnisch, Hysolar Research Building, Stuttgart Technical University, 1986–87**
This research institute's building is composed of a chaotic assembly of steel beams that extend outward, tilting uprights, odd inclines, projections, and a general mixture of materials.

*Right*
**Frank O. Gehry, Nationale-Nederlanden Building, Prague, 1992–97**
The citizens of Prague have nicknamed the pair of corner towers 'Ginger and Fred'. Like a pair of dancers the buildings seem to lean against each other for support or affection or both.

## Great works of the early 2000s

Of all the many architectural typologies, that of the museum seems to have attracted the most attention from institutions and organizations, both public and private, during the early years of the 21st century. In a certain sense the museum has come to occupy the place formerly occupied by the cathedral. The museum has become the new citizen monument; in many cases, museums have been the essential element in revivifying urban areas (the Georges Pompidou Centre in Paris); in some cases museums have been used to commemorate (the Jewish Museum in Berlin). At the same time, as a result of the social and cultural changes of the early 2000s, the museum itself has undergone a process of revision and modernization. One of the principal changes regards the users of museums, for museums are no longer designed to serve the needs of an elite group of scholars and have become spaces visited by everyone, intellectuals, tourists, enthusiasts, children, the disabled, the merely curious. A visit to a museum is no longer limited to the

opportunity to see at first hand relics or works of art and has become an itinerary through a microcosm of various activities related to culture and entertainment. People go to observe, learn, participate in events, meet, play, make purchases, amuse themselves, eat, and drink. Architecture thus has a function of representation: it must attract the attention of the public and the media, call attention to itself as a statement, an immediately recognizable structure. At the same time it must meet the needs of a heterogeneous and demanding public and must therefore provide a diversified set of services within a comfortable and well-serviced setting. As a result, many older museums have been enlarged.

The museums that opened during the first years of the 21st century present a vast panorama. This 'museu-mification' involves many fields of interest: the various forms of art and science, the cultures of peoples and nations, the celebration of particular consumer goods. The broad range of works made represents the multiple languages of contemporary architecture.

**Mario Botta, MART, Museum of Modern and Contemporary Art, Rovereto, 1988–93**
The exhibition halls and other services of Botta's museum are arranged around a large central courtyard that is the heart of the museum. A large transparent dome covers and illuminates this large internal space – which makes up for the lack of a true city square near the museum – in which the public is welcomed and gains access to the galleries and assorted cultural services.

**Hans Hollein, Vulcania Museum, Saint-Ours les Roches, 2002**
The 'Parc Européen du Volcanisme', designed by Hollein near an inactive volcano in the Auvergne, hosts exhibition halls of popular science on volcanic phenomena and earth sciences. The main structure is a 22-metre-high cone dressed in dark basalt on the exterior and in gilt metal on the interior. Local volcanic stone was used in the dressing of the other buildings.

**a Hadid, Contemporary
s Centre, Cincinnati,
3**
e urban network of
ares and streets
tinues into the museum
tortuous up-and-down
e along a ramp that
tes the six floors of the
ding, crossing the large
ces of the exhibition
s, which face onto the
e of the ramp.

**Peter Zumthor, Kunsthaus,
Bregenz, 1997**
A simple concrete cube
dressed in panes of glass
constitutes a presence at
once discreet and easily
recognizable in the centre of
the city on Lake Constance.

# The preservation
## of culture
## 20th–21st century

### Cultural centres, libraries, schools

Cultural centres, libraries, and schools, much like museums, went through a process of revision during the opening decades of the 21st century that included basic reconsideration of their architectural design. Cultural centres – polyvalent spaces designed to appeal to people of different interests and to involve them in a variety of activities, often directed at the celebration of the cultural traditions of an area or of a country – have been created all over the world. A well-known example is the Parisian Institut du Monde Arabe, designed by Jean Nouvel, which houses an exhibition space and a museum of the art and history of Islamic civilization; there is also the Tjibaou Cultural Centre designed by Renzo Piano in New Caledonia dedicated to the native Kanak culture of the territory of the French colony.

Like museums, libraries are breaking free of their one-time reputation as gloomy, dusty repositories and are changing to serve the new modalities of preservation, cataloguing, and consultation; there is also the fact that paper is progressively being replaced by other methods of information storage, requiring luminous, comfortable spaces furnished with areas suitable to meeting the demand for new services.

The world of instruction, meaning schools at all levels, also finds itself at the centre of important changes and is fertile terrain for the design of new didactic spaces and the use of innovative technologies.

**Jean Nouvel, Institut du Monde Arabe, Paris, 1981–87**
The building, another rectangular structure that faces a lower, curving structure, blends Western elements and Islamic symbolism. The façade is composed of glass panels decorated with geometric arabesques that also serve function since photoelectr cells that direct the flow o daylight into the building inserted in the grids betwe the glass panels.

**Renzo Piano Building Workshop, Jean-Marie Tjibaou Cultural Centre, Nouméa, 1991–98**
A series of curved structu designed to provide an efficient system of natural ventilation, built of wood and steel and similar in shape to seashells, constit the main spaces of the cer in New Caledonia, dedica to the culture of the nativ Kanak. The centre is composed of various exhibition spaces, teachin laboratories, an auditoriu study and research centre with space for dance and other traditional expressiv forms. The activities are distributed along a route immersed in the nature o the setting.

**Richard Meier, Getty Center, Los Angeles, 1985–97**
The Getty Center was the largest architectural undertaking by a single designer in the 20th century. It covers an area of 440,000 square metres with 88,200 square metres covered that include a museum complex, an auditorium, centres for humanistic studies and the study of art history, a library, and an institute for the preservation of artworks. It is a true city of art, laid out along pathways, gardens, and areas of water.

**Snøhetta, Alexandria Library, Alexandria, 1996–2000**
The site of the new library includes the area once occupied by the historical library of Alexandria, founded *c.* 288 BC by Ptolemy I. The building is a section of cylinder 160 metres in diameter, with an inclined roof between 20 and 30 metres high. Engraved on the exterior wall are characters from all the world's alphabets.

## Sports complexes

## 20th–21st century

### Sports as spectacle

During the first decade of the 21st century the burgeoning importance of sports events made necessary the construction of new structures adapted to the presentation of true spectacles with an increasingly large – indeed an international – public. Olympic games, world championship games in a variety of sports, and winter sports presented many designers with the opportunity to take on a particular challenge, the creation of a complex in which the aesthetic, functional, normative, and security aspects cannot be separated. The language of the individual architect must confront the rigid rules imposed by the requisites of high-level competitions along with the structural requisites involved in the creation of these highly particular spaces. The creation of these stadiums and sports centres involves the covering and illumination of vast spaces along with the control and movement of enormous numbers of people. The application of complex and innovative technologies and the collaboration between architects and engineers have resulted in highly functional buildings that are at the same time elegant, such as the ski jump designed by Zaha Hadid on Bergisel Mountain, which stands out against the sky much like the athletes who jumped off of it.

**Santiago Calatrava, Olympic Stadium, Athens 2004, detail of the roof**
The work by Calatrava was directed at improving the existing Olympic complex of Athens. A new polycarbonate roof was set over the original structure by tubular steel arches suspended by cables.

Eduardo Souto de Moura, Municipal Stadium, Braga, 2002–3

The stadium was built to host the European football championship games of 2004 and is located on the slope of Monte Castro in Portugal. Only the long sides of the football field are flanked by stands, and one side is set against the side of the mountain. The roof is composed of cables and is designed to look like the suspension bridges built in the Andes by Peru's Incas.

**Zaha Hadid, Bergisel Ski Jump, Innsbruck, 2002**
The ski jump is composed not just of the jump itself but also of a café and viewing terrace located near the top of the concrete tower. The jump is 90 metres long and nearly 50 high. Continuous cladding in metal strips contributes to making the structure fluidly elegant.

# Performance spaces

## 20th–21st century

### The quality of a space

The design of performance spaces has always involved leading architects. In the early years of the 21st century the growing needs of theatrical companies and of the public led to the design of new spaces as well as to undertakings to adapt existing spaces, in both cases involving increasingly complex requirements. The desire to provide the public with large-scale diversified entertainment has led to the increase in size of theatrical halls, the structural and technical characteristics of which must respond to the demands for versatility dictated, for the most part, by financial needs. It is often the case that the same site is used for different kinds of events: concerts, dance performances, conferences, plays. Ancillary spaces are also required (rehearsal spaces, dressing rooms) as well as the areas made necessary by scenery and acoustical activities, which have become increasingly complex and elabo-

rate, which is the primary reason so many historical theatres have been enlarged or restructured. The achievement of excellent acoustical qualities has been of paramount importance in the design of spaces for musical performances. Acoustics usually involve the shape of the hall and the materials used in wall coverings, for such factors affect reverberations and the spread of sound waves; in fact, different materials absorb sounds in different ways. In such undertakings the collaboration between the architect and specialized technicians is of great importance. To all this must be added the direction of crowds of people through public spaces and a variety of related services and implementations to provide security (escape routes, proper ventilation, fireproofing). Architects are also called on to design buildings that, whether through discretion or through high visibility, are inserted in the surrounding environment in an intelligent manner.

**Mario Botta, enlargement of the Teatro alla Scala, Milan, 2002–4**
Aside from performing restoration work designed to preserve the hall and the façade by Giuseppe Piermarini, Botta built two new volumes in the rear area of the theatre complex, a scenic tower shaped like a cube housing the new rehearsal halls and an elliptical body to house dressing rooms and various service spaces. The two bodies are dressed in marble

**nk O. Gehry, Walt Disney
acert Hall, Los Angeles,
9–2003**
ry began making the
 for the building in
; construction began
999. It can be seen as
key element in the
orking of central Los
eles. The exterior is
sed in plates of titanium,
interior in panels of
glas pine, which
vides excellent acoustics.

**Renzo Piano Building
Workshop, Parco della
Musica, Rome, 2002**
The complex is composed
of three separate halls, with
700, 1,200, and 2,800 seats,
that are identifiable from the
exterior. These three bodies,
ironically nicknamed
Crickets, are soundproof
structures. Their cladding
in lead plates alludes to the
domes of Rome.

### The aesthetics of company logos

It was often the case during the 20th century that a company's public image came to be associated with the name of an architect or with a building designed by a famous architect. The relationship between AEG and Behrens stands as an early example of this phenomenon; later examples include a forest of American skyscrapers – the Seagram Building, Chrysler Building, AT&T Building – designed as physical manifestations of major companies.

The trend continued into the 21st century; it seems more than ever true that being recognizable is an essential aspect of advertising, a necessary factor for any company that hopes to make itself distinguishable. This applies both to industries and to companies in the service sector; the exterior image of a site of production or a headquarters building is taken to reflect a company's spirit and style. Nor is interior design overlooked, for its purpose is to welcome the public and to establish a workplace environment congruent with the work being performed. Today as in the past, collaboration between the architect and the patron is essential to identify the functional and communicative needs of the building, the aim of which is also to attract new clients. There is then the architect's creativity, for great results are often obtained through the skilled use of innovative technologies and materials.

**Herzog & de Mueron, production facility of Ricola, Mulhouse-Brunstatt, France, 1992–93**
Ricola specializes in herb-based products. The glass, concrete, and steel structure of this building includes such evocative details as polycarbonate dressing of the front of the building with plant motifs that allude to the aromas used in the products.

**Renzo Piano Building Workshop, Maison Hermès, Tokyo, 2001**
This building stands in an elegant commercial zone of Tokyo and is distinguished, paradoxically, by its discretion in an area full of highly visual, ostentatious constructions. The 11 floors are dressed in earthquake-resistant glass bricks; illuminated at night, the building becomes a large and luminous 'magic lantern'.

*Opposite*
**Frank O. Gehry, DG Bank Berlin, 1995–2000**
In accordance with building code restrictions, the exterior of the building presents a sober parallelepiped dress in stone, with its windows regularly arranged. The interior atrium, however, presents quite unexpected spaces. An undulating transparent skylight provides natural light from above, the conference room is located within a structure shaped like an enormous horse's head.

# Ecclesiastical buildings
## 20th–21st century

### Places for spirituality

Numerous contemporary architects have confronted the demanding assignment of designing 'places for spirituality'; modern-style buildings – since it would make little sense today to build 'old-style' churches – designed to perform functions whose roots are in the past. Today's churches must be large enough to hold large assemblies of the faithful, but at the same time be places used for prayer. The most important examples are probably those in which essentiality and lyricism are blended in an architectural form that is simple and at the same time full of symbolic references, without glitter and superfluous decorations but with such important measures as attention to detail and the use of light. This can be seen in both the church designed by Siza at Marco de Canaveses, Portugal, and in the Church of the Light designed by Tadao Ando at Osaka. In some cases the sensitivity of the designer results in a work of great actuality despite the more or less explicit allusions to the architecture of the past, such as in the chapel designed by Botta on Monte Tamarao in the Ticino Canton. The fact that large numbers of people move from country to country, bringing their religion with them, has led to novel expressions of religious buildings, such as the mosque in Rome designed by Paolo Portoghesi, which is one of the first examples in which Islamic symbolism is set within Western realities.

# Transportation and infrastructure
## 20th–21st century

### Interconnections in the new millennium

The economic growth of the early part of the new millennium, the increase in tourist routes, the increasingly less settled styles of life, and the reduction in travel costs have contributed to a general increase in movement. The intensification of traffic and the birth of new airline companies have made necessary the enlargement of existing airports and the creation of new ones. Rail transport has become more efficient through the introduction of new high-speed lines, and the expansion of urban areas has increased the number of new train stations and underground lines. The modernization and enlargement of streets has encouraged the construction of new infrastructures and routes of connection. Undertakings once delegated exclusively to engineers have been capably handled by contemporary architects who, collaborating with technical studios, have been able to confront highly complicated undertakings, joining functional needs and elegance in the resolution of complex logistical and structural problems.

**Renzo Piano Building Workshop, Kansai International Airport Terminal, Osaka, 1988–94**
The airport is located on an artificial island, 1.7 kilometres long, created to avoid noise pollution in a densely populated area. The roof of the terminal is made of stainless-steel panels and is earthquake-resistant.

**Nicholas Grimshaw, Waterloo International Terminal, London, 1993**
The Waterloo Terminal is one of the key stations on the high-velocity rail line between Britain and France. Its most distinctive feature, a 400-metre-long curved glass roof supported by a metal structure – an allusion to Britain's 19th-century iron-and-glass stations – follows the curving shape of the railway tracks.

tiago Calatrava,
t de l'Europe,
éans, 1996–2000
realization of this design
made possible thanks to
ly advanced building
nology. A single curving
resting on two three-
ed concrete pylons
redibly supports a 470-
re-long bridge. The arch
the bridge are in steel.

Zaha Hadid, Car Park and
Terminus, Hoenheim-Nord,
Strasbourg, 2002
A thin continuous band of
reinforced concrete and a
dense series of variously
inclined pillars configure
this transportation hub on
the outskirts of the city
where drivers leave their
cars and take trains. This
is part of the Strasbourg
authorities' efforts to limit
congestion in the city by
instituting new lines of rail
transport.

### 'Grands projets' at the end of the millennium

The architectural creations in Paris during the last years of the 20th century seemed to result from the determination of French presidents to hold fast to the policy of *grands projets* of the rulers of the 18th and 19th centuries. They thus promoted important architectural and urbanistic initiatives. President Pompidou promoted the construction of the cultural centre that today bears his name; his successor, Valéry Giscard d'Estaing, began the project of reuse of the Gare d'Orsay and other important undertakings, such as the construction of the Défense district, a new administrative-financial centre of the city, as well as the Parc de la Villette. President Mitterrand, in office from 1981 to 1995, announced as early as his first public appearance the desire to complete the works begun by his predecessor and the intention to begin new public works, encouraging the work of young architects. Between the end of the 1980s and the early 1990s important constructions were concluded, such as the new Opéra at the Bastille, the functional adjustment of the Louvre, the construction of the new Bibliothèque Nationale, and the Institut du Monde Arabe.

The building that is iconic of the new Paris is, however, La Grande Arche of the Défense, a headquarters of public and private offices designed by the Dane Otto von Spreckelsen. It stands on an axis with the Napoleonic Arc de Triomphe and was inaugurated on the occasion of the bicentennial of the French Revolution.

**Gae Aulenti, Musée d'Orsay, 1980–86**
The museum came into [being?] with the functional conversion of the Orsay station, built in 1900. Th[e] route of the new museum follows the main axis of [the] original building.

**Dominique Perrault, Bibliothèque Nationale, 1989–97**
The 'Très Grande Bibliothèque' is composed of four crystal towers at t[he] corners of a rectangular platform at the centre of which is a court-garden. [The] reading rooms look out o[n] this green space. The entir[e] complex has room for ab[out] 4,000 readers.

**Johann Otto von Spreckelsen, La Grande Arche, 1982–8[9]**
The construction, a symb[olic] entrance to the city, is th[e] western end of a line that[] runs through the Louvre[,] Arc de Triomphe, and the Place de la Défense. It is a hollow cube, 110 metres [high,] dressed in white marble.

*Opposite*
**Ieoh Ming Pei, Grand Louvre, Pyramid, 1983–9[?]**
The pyramid is the most recognizable of the undertakings in the functional readjustment [that] has involved various area[s of] the palace of the Louvre. [The] pyramidal roof of metal a[nd] glass, 21 metres high, ma[rks] the new entrance to the museum and houses vari[ous] underground spaces and public services.

# Berlin

## Late 20th century

### The worksite of German unification

Berlin experienced profound changes during the last years of the 20th century. Most of the restyling of the city was a result of the reunification of Germany in 1989, but as early as the 1970s a serious debate had been going on between city administrators and architects concerning possible solutions to the progressive degradation of vast areas of the western zone of the city. The damage from World War II, the disorganized demolitions and reconstruction projects of the postwar period, and the erection of the Berlin Wall in 1961 had had a profound impact on the urbanistic well-being of Berlin, causing a progressive loss of identity. An intense programme of urban renewal – known as IBA, for Internationale Bauaustellung ('International Exposition of Architecture') – was set in motion in 1979 and concluded around the end of the 1980s. The activities of the architects involved constituted an important moment of reflection on the essential elements of the city. With the fall of the wall and the institution of a single German capital, the city was transformed into a large 'urban laboratory'. Beginning in 1993 architects from throughout the world were called to make their contribution to the revitalization of the city, with the creation of new infrastructures and the construction of works designed to fill the great 'voids' created by the elimination of the wall.

**Aldo Rossi, Quartier Schützenstrasse, 1992–98**
The undertaking is based on the wish to reconnect the city with its history. The block is structured around the original internal courtyard, a traditional element of 19th-century Berlin architecture. The individual houses on the front present a collage of different building archetypes assembled as though fragments of previous buildings.

**Foster and Partners, restoration of the Reichstag, 1995–99**
One of the symbols of the new Germany is the parliament building, which was constructed in 1894, destroyed by fire in 1933, and bombed during World War II. The undertaking involved the restoration of the existing building and the construction of a glass dome crossed on its interior by a helicoidal ramp.

**...mut Jahn, Sony ...re, 1995–2000**

...complex stands on
...rea adjacent to the
...damerplatz, centre of
...isticated life in Berlin
...ng the 1920s, bombed
...orld War II, and
...doned following the
...truction of the nearby
... Beginning in 1995 the
...e area was involved in
...mbitious reconstruction
...ct financed by three
...cinational corporations
...involving the work of
...ral internationally
...ous architects, among
... Renzo Piano, Arata
...ki, and Helmut Jahn.
... was responsible for
...creation of the Sony
...plex, including the
...pean offices of the
...cinational and a
...mercial square open to
...oublic. This square has a
...sparent roof.

*...osite*

**...iel Libeskind, Jewish
...eum, 1988–99**

...building, an urban-scale
...ument to the Holocaust,
...ll of symbolic values. A
...ng wall runs across the
...like a deep tear in relief.
...walls dressed in sheets
...nc are in turn rent and
...ollowing an apparently
...rary logic, much like
...arbitrary sense behind
...actions of the murderers
...e Holocaust.

# London

## 20th–21st century

### The conversion of Docklands

Like many other European cities, London experienced large changes during the closing years of the 20th and opening years of the 21st century. The passage from an economy based on industrial production to a postindustrial reality had its part in the transformation of Europe's cities, making necessary the conversion of vast unused spaces and supporting the growth in the service sector with new applicable structures: banks, offices, and cultural complexes in response to growing tourism.

At the centre of the urban-renewal processes of London was the area of Docklands, the docks, landing stages, and storehouses along the Thames related to the activity of the port of London, which closed in 1972. The most important undertakings involved in the conversion of Docklands were concentrated in the area of Canary Wharf on the Isle of Dogs, which the Thatcher government declared an 'Enterprise zone'. Direction of the development of this area was entrusted to the London Docklands Development Corporation, charged with transforming the zone occupied by the docks and warehouses into a new economic-financial pole of the city. The undertaking began at the end of the 1980s with the construction of high office buildings around a central square. Outstanding among these was the symbolic building at Canary Wharf designed by Cesar Pelli, a tower distinguished by its pyramidal top. Most of the architects involved in this one particular undertaking were American, such as Pelli and Skidmore, Owings & Merrill, but two of the main architects in the transformation of the city were the Londoners Richard Rogers and Norman Foster. Together with the contributions of their European colleagues, such as the Swiss Herzog & de Meuron, they are changing the face of the city with buildings distinguished by continuous experimentation and advanced technology.

**Foster and Partners, Swiss Re Tower (The Gherkin), 2003**
The tower, with its immediately recognizable shape, stands in the heart of the city of London and houses the new headquarters of the Swiss Re insurance company. The site of the building was previously occupied by a Victorian building damaged by an IRA bomb and later demolished. The circular plan narrows upward. The glass covering reduces the force of wind on the facade and provides natural illumination to the interior spaces.

**r Pelli, One Canada
re, 1991**
uilding designed by
on Canary Wharf is
on of the conversion
ocklands: a tower 236
es high topped by a
mid dressed in steel. It
es the headquarters of
ewspapers, *The Daily
raph* and *The
endent*.

**Herzog & de Meuron, Tate
Modern, 1994–2000**
The new exhibition space on
the banks of the Thames,
facing St Paul's Cathedral, is
an efficient example of the
reuse of an existing
structure. The gallery
occupies the space of the
former Bankside Power
Station, designed by Giles
Gilbert Scott after World
War II. The heart of the
building is the former
turbine hall, which houses
the entrance atrium, more
than 30 metres high.

# Barcelona
## 20th–21st century

### The modern face of Spanish democracy

After the end of the dictatorship with the death of Franco in 1975 and the first democratic elections in 1979, Spain began a period of great building activity, most of it designed to give the nation a new, modern face and to meet the needs for new infrastructure and public institutions. Before the 1992 Olympic Games the city of Barcelona undertook a large-scale urban renewal process that involved the activity of more than 150 architects in the designing of more than 300 new buildings. A key role in this phase was played by Oriol Bohigas, superintendent of urbanistic services of Barcelona. His role was that of coordinating the various projects within an overall organic plan. The process of restyling Barcelona was not limited to the construction of new offices and involved the redesign of the city through the restructuring of public spaces, the rehabilitation of badly rundown buildings, and the reorganization of pedestrian and automobile thoroughfares, most of all in the coastal area.

Indeed, most of the undertakings designed to give the city a new outward appearance were concentrated in the coastal area. Decaying districts, abandoned factory buildings, and buildings related to the city's former activity as a port were cleared away. Their place was taken by seaside installations, hotels, shops, restaurants, and night spots.

The Universal Forum of Cultures held in Barcelona in 2004 became the primary reason to reclaim the vast area between the Port Olímpic and the Besòs River, with the construction of new residential areas and a seaside area of gardens and tourist attractions.

**Herzog & de Meuron, Forum Building, 2000–4**
Designed to house the various events related to 2004 Universal Forum of Cultures held in Barcelon this building was the cen of the urban-renewal programme in the area between Port Olímpic an the mouth of the Besòs River. A large blue triang overlooking the sea, it is rent by openings and transparencies as though flowing with water. It ho an auditorium for 3,200 people. Around it are walkways and covered squares with restaurants, exhibition spaces, offices and vantage points.

**Arata Isozaki, San Jordi Sports Palace, 1983–92**
The palace by Isozaki was conceived as a multisport facility for use in the 199. Olympic Games with application afterward to a variety of events. The building's outstanding fea is its large central dome.

el Moneo, Auditori
ic Centre, 1999
eo's auditorium is one
e most important
ral centres in the new
elona and also one of
most important centres
lassical music in Spain.
ipying an entire lot in
Eixample district, it has
hall for chamber music

and another for symphonic
museum. Its façade is
measured off by vertical
concrete pillars. Its elegantly
simple appearance is
accentuated by its cladding
in steel panels.

**Frank O. Gehry, *Peix* ('Fish')
sculpture for the Vila
Olímpica, 1992**
The enormous fish shape
designed by Gehry using
Catia software – also used
for the design of the
Guggenheim Museum in
Bilbao – dominates the area
of Port Olímpic. This long
stretch of coastline,

reconstructed for the 1992
Olympic Games, is located
to the northeast of Port Vell,
the old port of Barcelona,
transformed in the 1980s.

# Frank O. Gehry

## Guggenheim Museum, Bilbao

### 1991–97

The museum in Bilbao came into being from the encounter between the administration of the Basque provinces and the Solomon R. Guggenheim Foundation. The project was part of a vast programme of urban renewal and development of service industries in response to the crisis of the 1980s, a result of the collapse of the maritime transportation industry, which had been the backbone of the local economy. The new museum was designed to form the major element in the process of the economic rebirth of the city, becoming an attraction for tourists and thus generating income.

A suitable site was chosen for the new museum, an abandoned area on the banks of the Nervión River, and a competition was held for the design. The architects asked to participate were the Japanese Arata Isozaki, the Austrian Co-op Himmelblau group, and the American Frank O. Gehry. The guidelines for the structure, as presented by Thomas Krens, director of the Guggenheim Foundation, called for an attractive and easily recognizable building that would be related to the existing urban and environmental setting, including the hill along the river and the adjacent Puente de la Salve, and that could display large-size works of modern art.

On 21 July 1991 the design by Gehry was chosen. In October 1993 the first stone was laid for the new museum, and it opened on 9 October 1997. The ingenuity of Frank O. Gehry, the use of advanced software made by the French aerospace company Dassault – capable of transforming utopian designs into reality by supplanting the right angles of Euclidean geometry – and the assistance of Skidmore, Owings & Merrill of Chicago generated a building that is an exceptional work of architecture, striking because of its series of concave and convex surfaces, dressed in stone and titanium plates that change colour according to the amount of sunlight and reflect in the waters of the Nervión.

The entrance is reached by way of a foot bridge that connects the museum to the old city. A stairway descends into the heart of the building, a multifloor gallery 50 metres high illuminated by large expanses of glass, which visitors enter by elevators and walkways. The structure is made of galvanized steel and reinforced concrete. The exterior dressing is in limestone, whitewashed masonry, and thin titanium plates. These plates – only 0.3 mm thick – are one of the most interesting aspects of the building. Titanium is both flexible and strong and takes on different colours according to the angle of the sun.

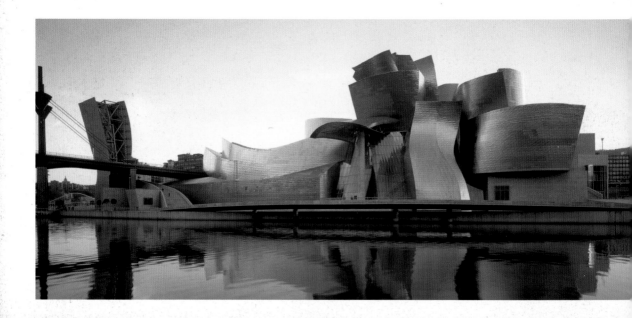

# Future prospects

## 21st century

### Between technology and ecology

In 1956 Frank Lloyd Wright made a futuristic design for a mile-high skyscraper, a construction with 528 floors inhabited by 130,000 people. Many such projects were dreamed up during the 20th century, architects letting loose their imaginations and coming up with urban arrangements that were quite impossible to build because they would have cost too much and because the technology necessary to make them feasible did not exist.

Today the most advanced architectural studios on the planet are taking on ambitious technological challenges, step by step bringing Wright's dream closer to reality. Work on the construction of the London Bridge Tower, designed by Renzo Piano and, at 306 metres, the tallest skyscraper in Europe, is scheduled to conclude in 2009; meanwhile, the tallest skyscrapers in the world are rising in South-East Asia. In 1998 at Kuala Lumpur in Malaysia the Petronas Towers went up, designed by Cesar Pelli and 452 metres high, thus much less than the 800 metres of the Millennium Tower, designed by Norman Foster, scheduled to be built in Tokyo Bay in the coming decade.

At the same time that technological experimentation makes possible the creation of works that until recently could only be imagined, architecture is investigating new ways to make responsible use of natural resources so as to help reduce the progressive ecological alteration of our planet. The design of new technologies and physical plants that will reduce or prevent the waste of energy, such as thermal insulation, and the use of new sources of energy, such as solar energy, will be only some of the most important challenges of the third millennium.

**Renzo Piano Building Workshop, London Bridge Tower, London, 2009**
The tower will rise beside London Bridge station in the centre of London near the Thames. An upward-narrowing blade, it will rise 306 metres into the sky of London. Its 66 floors will be used for shops, hotels, apartments, and a museum.

**Cesar Pelli, Petronas Towers, Kuala Lumpur, 1998**
These are the tallest structures in the world, rising from a common base to stand side by side in the Malaysian sky at 452 metres in height. The two towers are joined at the forty-first floor by a hallway. The plan, based on the intersection of two squares connected by circular segments, recalls the symbolism of Islamic tradition.

**geru Ban and Frei Otto,
anese Pavilion, 'Expo
0', Hanover**
theme of the exposition
'humanity, nature, and
nology'. The Japanese
sented this experimental
ding, made exclusively
cological, recyclable
erials, primarily wood and
er. The roof was made
-retardant through the use
olyesters treated with
cially designed polymers.

**Nicholas Grimshaw, Eden
Project, St Austell, Great
Britain, 2001**
The project was designed in
response to the principles
announced during the 1992
United Nations Conference
on Environment and
Development held to promote
the responsible use of the
planet's resources so as to
create a sustainable future for
all living things. The eight
biospheres of the Eden
Project reproduce subtropical
and desert environments and
offer the visitor the
opportunity to come into
contact with thousands of
plants from different natural
habitats: the largest
greenhouse in the world.

**to, Alvar Hugo Henrik**
**kortane, 1898–Helsinki, 1976)**
er studies at the Helsinki Polytechnic
16–21) Aalto earned his diploma in archi-
ture. Following travels in Scandinavia, cen-
. Europe, and Italy, he made his professional
ut in 1922 and opened his first studio, in
äskylä. He moved to Turku in 1927 and
ndoned the neo-classical style of his early
rks to approach European functionalism,
iving at the formulation of a highly personal
e, a synthesis of abstraction and natural-
. In the mid-1930s he founded the ARTEK
oden furniture company. In 1940 he came to
USA and taught at MIT. On his return to
land he settled in Helsinki, where he began
most original and expressive period of his
eer. He also did work outside Finland,
luding urban projects.

**am, Robert**
**irkcaldy, 1728–London, 1792)**
er training in Rome on the works of Piranesi
d Raphael and the classical ruins of Hercu-
eum, Pompeii, and Split, Adam worked
h his brother James on the design of numer-
s country houses and private residences in
ndon (Kedleston Hall, 1761; Osterley Park,
51), in many of them also making the deco-
ions and furnishings, skilfully alternating
numental, archaeological spaces (Syon
use, 1762), with those more intimate and
er. Having become famous, he dedicated
nself to large-scale urban projects, most espe-
lly the Adelphi residential complex on the
ames in London (1768; destroyed). Adam's
le blended neo-Palladian elements with a
te for archaeology and Renaissance-flavour
coration, setting the style for an elegant and
ined 'domestic' neo-classicism.

**berti, Leon Battista**
**enoa, 1404–Rome, 1472)**
chitect, musician, painter, writer, and man
eclectic taste, Alberti is an emblematic figure
within the artistic-intellectual sphere of 15th-
century humanism. After early studies at the
universities of Padua and Bologna, he moved to
Rome in 1432. Passionate scholar of antiquity,
he studied the architectural typologies of the
classical world and undertook their 'updating'
to a modern level. He did this through the treatises he wrote, the buildings he designed and
built, and the monuments he restored and rein-
tegrated. In Florence he designed Palazzo Rucellai, a historical prototype of the noble residence
of the Renaissance period; in the Tempietto of
S Sepolcro annexed to the palace he presented
a jewel of measurement and decoration. Even
more complex is his design (left partially unfinished) for the Tempio Malatestiano in Rimini
(1450), a combination of classical architectural
motifs applied freely to a sacred structure. In
1459 he moved to the Gonzaga court in Mantua, where he built the churches of S Sebastiano
and S Andrea.

## Ammannati, Bartolomeo
**(Settignano, Florence, 1511–Florence, 1592)**
Italian architect and sculptor, a leading figure of
Florentine mannerism, Ammannati worked in
and further developed the stylistic themes of
the late Renaissance and then, having grown
especially pious in his later life, in part as a result
of contact with the Jesuits, he ended his career
with a 'recantation' of the most declaredly secular and intellectual of his works. He got his
training around 1540 as collaborator of Jacopo
Sansovino in Venice and made an important
trip to Rome (1550–55), during which he
worked on marble monuments and the arrangement of the grotto of Villa Giulia, prototype of
the mannerist garden. On his return to Florence
he was commissioned to complete important
Renaissance buildings, such as the Laurentian
Library, the Salone dei Cinquecento in Palazzo
Vecchio, and most of all Palazzo Pitti, for which
he designed the majestic courtyard facing Boboli
Gardens. The work seen as symbolic of his art
is the vast complex of the Fountain of Neptune
(1563–77) in Piazza della Signoria, in which
elegant sections, agile and leaping, alternate with
areas that are more serious and rhetorical.

## Ando, Tadao
**(Osaka, 1941)**
Before opening his first studio, in 1969, Ando
made many trips to Europe, America, and
Africa, and the impressions he collected during
these travels helped him in the formation of the
synthesis of Orient and Occident that distinguishes his architectural production. The outstanding traits of his earliest creations were
introspective minimalism and geometric simplicity; he passed from there to increasingly
complex and articulated buildings, although
fundamental aspects of his work remain his
elegant and abstract use of simple materials
and his desire to integrate and complete his
architectural forms with natural elements, such
as water, light, and wind, as revealed in the
Japanese Pavilion for the World Exposition in
Seville (1990–92), which earned Ando international fame.

## Arnolfo di Cambio
**(Colle di Val d'Elsa, c. 1245–Florence, 1302)**
Arnolfo di Cambio was an architect and sculptor with a solid classical training. Following
the example of his master, Nicola Pisano, he
drew inspiration from the monumental stateliness of ancient Rome, as in the bronze figure
of St Peter in the Vatican basilica, but his style
was also open to the linear values of the French
Gothic. In the later years of his life his artistic
personality became more complex through the
increase in architectural interest, expressed by
the two great Roman ciboria he designed, one
in S Paolo fuori le Mura (1285) and one in S
Cecilia (1293) in which architectural schemes
blend with sculptural parts in an original way.
He designed and directed the construction and
decoration of S Maria del Fiore in Florence
(1296–1302) and was responsible for the design
of Palazzo Vecchio.

## Asam, Cosmas Damian
(Benediktbeuren, 1686–Munich, 1739)
## Asam, Egid Quirin
(Tegernsee, 1692–Mannheim, 1750)

The Asam brothers are emblematic of the high season of rococo decoration in southern Germany. Architects, painters, and decorators, the Asams translated the theatrical aspects of the late baroque into exuberant, dramatic forms. Egid Quirin, primarily a sculptor and stuccoist, made altars, statuary groups, and ornamental stuccoes; Cosmas Damian was a painter, his style reflecting his studies in Rome but freely developed with forms, colours, and perspective views that lead into endless skies. Among their most important works are the churches of Andernach, Rohr, Weingarten, Weltenburg, and Straubing. In 1733 the Asam brothers became involved in the construction and decoration of the church of St Johann Nepomuk in Munich, which was arranged as a bright theatrical scene.

## Aulenti, Gae
(Palazzolo della Stella, Udine, 1927)

Aulenti got her degree from the Milan Polytechnic in 1954 and opened her studio two years later, performing design activity in the fields of architecture, interior design, industrial design, and theatrical scenery. She worked on the project for the renovation and conversion of the Gare d'Orsay in Paris (1980–86), making it the Musée d'Orsay museum of impressionist art. She oversaw the restructuring of Palazzo Grassi in Venice (1986) and the National Museum of Catalan Art in Barcelona (1987–2004). In 1996 she won the competition for the new Asian Art Museum in San Francisco, which opened to the public in 2003.

## Barragán, Luis
(Guadalajara, Mexico, 1902–Mexico City, 1988)

Barragán earned a degree in engineering in 1923 and began a career as a self-taught architect. The formulation of his personal style was deeply influenced by two trips to Europe, in 1924 and 1931; of the first remained the strong impressions made by Arabian architecture and the Mediterranean gardens of Spain and the ideas of the landscape architect

Ferdinand Bac, whom he met in France. The second trip was important for the encounter with Le Corbusier and contacts made with new European movements. Several private homes he made after his return to Guadalajara in 1926 already revealed the highly original and sensitive blend of these European experiences with the forms and materials of Mexican architecture, a blend that would come to distinguish his style. His language gained increased precision through the combined use of plant and water forms along with simple volumes, a style that characterized the works he began making in Mexico City in 1936.

## Barry, Charles
(London, 1795–1860)

Important exponent of the Victorian eclecticism of the Gothic revival, as in St Matthew's in Manchester (1822–25; destroyed), St Peter's in Brighton (1825–26), and St Peter's in London (1830–32), Barry preferred Renaissance forms in the houses and public buildings he made. In 1836 he began collaborating with Pugin on the reconstruction of the Houses of Parliament in London, a substantially classical building set within a Perpendicular Gothic frame.

## Basile, Ernesto
(Palermo, 1857–1932)

Having earned his degree at Palermo Basile dedicated himself initially to the study of Sicilian Arab-Norman architecture. Basile's historicist background is clearly expressed in his few works, from the design for Palazzo Montecitorio in Rome to the buildings for the universal exposition held at Palermo in 1898. Around the turn of the century he moved away from the eclecticism of his first period as he developed a more personal language, one that revealed his version of art nouveau. The works he made during this second period include the Hotel Villa Igiea in Palermo (1898) and many small villas in which the shape of the structure and the decoration achieve a pleasant balance, resulting in some of the outstanding examples of the Italian Stile Liberty.

## BBPR
(Gian Luigi Banfi, 1910–45; Lodovico Barbiano di Belgioioso, 1909–2004; Enrico

Peressutti, 1908–76; Ernesto Nathan Roge 1910–68)

In 1932, having just earned their degrees fro the Milan Polytechnic, the four architects set a studio in Milan. The studio was soon part the lively debate of modern architecture, revealed by its architectural creations, its p ticipation in the 1935 CIAM (Congrés Inte nationaux d'Architecture Moderne), and theoretical activity of some of its members. stance attracted many international contac and its activity was varied, ranging from arc tecture to urbanistics to industrial design. T studio's postwar creations showed a progress movement away from the rationalistic towa expressive values more attentive to enviro mental problems and traditional values, as w as concern for the insertion of architectu within a pre-existing historical context. T Torre Velasca in Milan, a typical example this period, is considered by many to be the st dio's outstanding creation. During the sam period the studio was also involved in t rearrangement of Milan's Sforza Castle.

## Behnisch, Günter
(Lockwitz, Dresden, 1922)

Having received his diploma in 1951 from t Technische Hochschule, Stuttgart, Behnis opened a studio with Bruno Lambart in 195 in 1979 the studio became Behnisch & Partne During the early part of his activity he work primarily on schools using standardized cor ponent parts. He collaborated with Frei Otto the design of the Olympiapark stadium Munich (1972). Behnisch & Partners design the Hysolar Research Building in Stuttga (1986–87), and their other projects includ the Deutsches Postmuseum in Frankfurt (199 and the Bundestag in Bonn (1992).

## Berg, Max
(Stettino, 1870–Baden-Baden, 1947)

After studies at the Technische Hochschu Charlottenburg in Berlin, in 1909 Berg becar a senior building official in Breslau, a post held until 1925. Between 1912 and 1913 built the Jahrhunderthalle in Breslau, a stru ture famous for its roof, a dome 65 metres diameter supported by ribs in exposed rei forced cement. He was involved in city-pla ning projects in Breslau between 1919 a

21; in that city he made the Nord-Oder and ⁓d-Oder hydroelectric stations (1920–25) and ⁓ pavilion for the 1925 exhibition.

**⁓rlage, Hendrik Petrus**
**⁓msterdam, 1856–The Hague, 1934)**
⁓ter earning his degree at the Zurich Poly-
⁓hnic, Berlage travelled to Italy, Austria, and
⁓rmany. Returning to Amsterdam in 1881
⁓ began work under the engineer Theodorus
⁓nders. His professional activity along with
⁓ theoretical works earned him a place
⁓ong the founders of modern Dutch archi-
⁓ture. His activity can be divided into three
⁓riods. From 1881 to 1902 he made a series
⁓ buildings, including the Amsterdam
⁓change, in which he demonstrated the desire
⁓ return to authentic forms in opposition to
⁓ reigning eclecticism. In the following years
⁓ worked in urbanistics, presenting a series of
⁓ans marked by forceful unitary designs in
⁓position to the tendency toward decentral-
⁓tion; the creation of these projects led to the
⁓rmation of the Amsterdam school of archi-
⁓cture. In the last period of his activity he
⁓ve form to several works in a language sim-
⁓r to that of Frank Lloyd Wright, whom he
⁓d met during a trip to the United States in
⁓11; these works contributed to the spread of
⁓right's language and style in Europe.

**⁓rnini, Gian Lorenzo**
**⁓aples, 1598–Rome, 1680)**
⁓rnini is symbolic of an entire epoch and
⁓le, the baroque, of which he was the physi-
⁓l incarnation. He dominated the Roman
⁓tistic scene for more than six decades, inter-
⁓eting the most vital aspirations of the cen-
⁓ry. Dynamism, inventive fantasy, the ability
⁓ mould materials: all these revolutionary ele-
⁓ents were present even in his early sculptural
⁓oups in the Borghese Gallery. In 1624 he was
⁓t in charge of St Peter's, where he made the
⁓ldacchino on the tomb of the apostle, with its
⁓ebrated twisted columns; the tomb of Urban
⁓III, an ideal model for legions of later artists;
⁓e phantasmagorical Cathedra Petri; the tomb
⁓ Alexander VII; the elliptical St Peter's Square,
⁓th the embracing arms of its colonnades;
⁓d the Scala Regia. There were countless other
⁓mmissions in baroque Rome, all of them
⁓asterpieces of ingenuity and theatricality: the

Cornaro Chapel in S Maria della Vittoria (with the sculptural group *Ecstasy of St Theresa*), the Four Rivers Fountain in Piazza Navona, the monument to the Blessed Ludovica Albertoni in S Francesco a Ripa, and Palazzo Montecito-rio (begun 1650).

**Borromini, Francesco (Francesco Castelli)**
**(Bissone, 1599–Rome, 1667)**
Borromini's famous disputes with his colleague and rival Bernini resulted primarily from rea-sons of personal temperament and artistic sen-sibility. Borromini achieved his success only with difficulty, and it never seemed definitive; he committed suicide. The work that proved decisive in his affirmation was the church of S Carlo alle Quattro Fontane, with its revolu-tionary interior spatial solution. The Oratory of S Filippo Neri makes clear his break with the Renaissance language in its revival of individ-ual structural and decorative elements. The masterpiece in this regard is the church of S Ivo alla Sapienza, with its complex ground plan. His other important commissions include the renovation of St John Lateran, the church of S Agnese in Piazza Navona, and the celebrated false-perspective colonnade in Palazzo Spada.

**Botta, Mario**
**(Mendrisio, Canton Ticino, 1943)**
After several years of apprenticeship to a tech-nical draughtsman, Botta studied at the Istituto Universitario di Architettura in Venice between 1964 and 1969, graduating with Carlo Scarpa. During those same years he worked as an assis-tant to Le Corbusier and Louis I. Kahn. In 1969 he moved to Lugano and opened his own studio. The guidelines of his language have been recognizable from his very first creations: respect for the external landscape, orderly geo-metric shapes, and abundant recourse to craft-work. Various combinations of these elements are clearly visible in the single-family dwellings he made during the 1970s and 1980s, and they are still part of his work, along with an increas-ing decomposition of the building into its component parts, as evidenced by the large-scale international commissions of the last years. Such formal experimentation is also characteristic of his activity as a designer. Since 1996 he has taught at the Academy of Archi-tecture in Mendrisio, which he founded.

**Boullée, Etienne-Louis**
**(Paris, 1728–99)**
Boullée was both a theoretician and architect and indeed was distinguished more for his theories than his creations. The fundamental part of his architectural work is composed of a series of fantastic monumental designs made as illustrations for his *Architecture, essai sur l'art*, preserved in the Bibliothèque Nationale, Paris, and not published until 1953. In these designs for immense public buildings, he experimented with a new architecture based on simple geometric forms with symbolic and celebratory functions.

**Bramante (Donato di Pascuccio)**
**(Fermignano, Urbino, 1444–Rome, 1514)**
A most excellent architect and artist, Bra-mante was a splendid interpreter of the clas-sical in forms that grew increasingly monu-mental and audacious, from the Milan of the Sforzas to the Rome of Pope Julius II. Bra-mante arrived in Milan around 1480. Aside from important works of architecture (S Maria presso S Satiro, S Maria delle Grazie, the cloisters of S Ambrogio), he made paintings with rigorously monumental figures in stately spatial settings that influenced the Lombard school. After the fall of Ludovico Sforza he left Milan and moved to Rome in 1499, where he began an extraordinary reworking of classical architecture (the Tempietto built beside S Pietro in Montorio left a profound impression on the artists of the period, among them Raphael), such that in the span of only a few years he became the most important architect at the papal court. For Julius II he designed the overall rearrangement of the Vatican palaces around the Belvedere courtyard, and begin-ning in 1506 he laid the basis of the recon-struction of the basilica of St Peter's, later car-ried forward by Michelangelo.

**Brega, Giuseppe**
**(Urbino, 1877–1929)**
Brega studied architecture at the University of Urbino and worked as an architect and as a designer in the experimental laboratories in the manufacture of Ruggeri ceramics. In 1902 he built the Villa Ruggeri at Pesaro, considered one of the outstanding examples of the Italian Stile Liberty.

## Brosse, Salomon de
### (Verneuil-sur-Oise, c. 1571–Paris, 1626)

De Brosse, who was active during the reign of Henri IV and Marie de' Medici, designed in the span of only a few years many important châteaux and royal buildings, including the châteaux of Coulommiers and Blérancourt and the Palais du Luxembourg in Paris (1619–24), drawing inspiration for its U-shaped layout and corner pavilions from Florence's Palazzo Pitti. De Brosse's works reinforced the classical orientation of the French architectural culture of his time.

## Brown, Lancelot 'Capability'
### (Kirkharle, 1716–London, 1783)

Nicknamed 'Capability' because of his extraordinary versatility, Brown was the most important English garden architect of the 18th century. He introduced broad expanses of grass to gardens, along with carefully composed stands of trees and bodies of water with multiple inlets crossed by small bridges. Such extremely natural motifs attracted an enormous response across Europe, leading to a true revolution in the art of garden design. This classical landscapist conception was derived from the picturesque settings in the landscape paintings by Claude, Poussin, and Dughet, acquired by English collectors during their trips to Italy. Brown was active in various English parks, but his masterpiece is Blenheim Park near Woodstock, built around Blenheim Palace, the residence of the duke of Marlborough, apogee of the English baroque. In 1764 King George III nominated Brown master gardener for Richmond, Surrey, and Hampton Court Palace

## Brunelleschi, Filippo
### (Florence, 1377–1446)

Trained as a goldsmith and skilled in the techniques of metalworking (the silver figures on the altar of S Jacopo in Pistoia Cathedral) and wood carving (the Crucifix in S Maria Novella, Florence), Filippo Brunelleschi 'discovered' his true calling for architecture as the result of a series of trips to Rome, the first and most important of which he made in the company of Donatello (1402). A leader of Florentine cultural life, in 1409 he began his involvement in the worksite of the cathedral of S Maria del Fiore, and beginning in 1418 he undertook the creation of the cathedral's enormous dome, designed in accordance with absolutely new technical and aesthetic criteria. A scholar of applied mathematics, Brunelleschi inaugurated the period of 'scientific' perspective in order to conceive and rationally construct measured spaces; it is with Brunelleschi that humanism in art comes into being. The buildings he made in Florence present a series of prestigious prototypes in a wide variety of styles, from majestic basilicas to centrally planned chapels, from private palaces to hospitals, from urban layouts to military and mechanical designs. Everything he did was dominated by the constant sense of a marvellous calculated rhythm, such that every part of a structure has a striking relationship to the proportions of the whole.

## Burnham, Daniel Hudson
### (Henderson, 1846–Heidelberg, 1912)

Burnham received his training in the discipline from the Chicago engineer William Le Baron Jenney and because of his contacts and talents was soon receiving important commissions. In 1873 he went into partnership with John W. Root. Being a practical and excellent administrator, Burnham made the perfect partner to the versatile and imaginative Root. Both men performed important roles in the evolution of the Chicago school of architecture, making several important works that were daring experiments in the use of new building technologies. Worthy of note was the Flatiron Building in New York (1901–3), for a time the tallest skyscraper in the world. After Root's death, in 1891, Burnham also dedicated himself to urban planning, adhering to the neo-classical style of the European Ecole des Beaux-Arts and becoming one of the leading exponents of the City Beautiful Movement with his 1907 plan for Chicago.

## Calatrava, Santiago
### (Benimamet, Valencia, 1951)

Calatrava studied at the art school of Valencia from 1968 to 1969 and at the Escuela Técnica Superior de Arquitectura from 1969 to 1973, earning his degree in architecture in 1974. From 1975 to 1979 he studied civil engineering at the Zurich Polytechnic, and in 1981, writing a thesis on reticular foldable structures, he obtained his doctorate in technical scienc In that same year he opened a studio of arc tecture and engineering in Zurich, and in 19 he opened a second studio in Paris. Calatra is one of the most interesting figures on t panorama of contemporary architecture a engineering; his recent works include brid in Barcelona, Valencia, Mérida, Seville, a Paris; the glass gallery in Toronto, the Montj Tower in Barcelona, several large-scale ro (such as those for the station in Lyons), a designs for a cultural centre in Valencia, t airport of Bilbao, and the new station in Lisb

## Cauchie, Paul
### (Ath, 1875–Etterbeek, 1952)

Belgian painter and architect, Cauchie stu ied at the Ecole des Arts Décoratifs of t Académie des Beaux-Arts in Brussels from 18 to 1898. In 1896 he founded a mural-painti company and enjoyed great and immedia success. A self-taught architect, he built own home in Brussels (1905) and in 19 opened a company for prefabricated wood houses in The Hague.

## Chambers, William
### (Gothenburg, 1723–London, 1796)

English architect and essayist, Chambers spe much time in France, Italy, and the Orie before establishing himself in London, whe he supported the foundation of the Roy Academy of Arts in 1798. Author of seve works of French and Palladian derivation which he contributed to the spread of the tas for exoticism in architectural and garden de oration, including *Design of Chinese Buildin* (1757), he designed the Pagoda in Kew ga dens, London (1757–63).

## Chareau, Pierre
### (Bordeaux, 1883–East Hampton, 1950)

After studies at the Ecole des Beaux-Arts Paris and a period of apprenticeship in a fu niture company, Chareau undertook his ov career as a designer and architect, opening studio in 1918. In 1919 he exhibited the furn ture designs he had made for the Dalsace apa ment at the Parisian Salon d'Automne. In 19 he took part in the Parisian exposition of de orative arts with the design for an office libra His first work of architecture was the Cl ouse of Beauvallon (1927); his most important was the Maison de Verre in Rue St Guilume, Paris. In 1940 he emigrated to the nited States; one of his last works was a stuo made for the painter Robert Motherwell at ast Hampton, New York (1948; destroyed).

## hiattone, Mario
### ergamo, 1891–Lugano, 1957)

hiattone studied at the Brera Academy in lilan and in 1915 earned a diploma in archicture at the institute of fine arts in Bologna. 1913 he joined the Nuove Tendenze group d in 1914, with Antonio Sant'Elia, exhibed futurist studies on the theme of the modrn city. In those years he also designed furnire and decorative art objects. After World ar I he moved to Lugano and developed a esign language more directed toward the clascal tradition, with a neo-medievalist derivaon. His architectural works include a counry house at Condra (1934) and a covered narket at Mendrisio (1945).

## o-op Himmelblau

he Co-op Himmelblau group was founded in ienna in 1968 by Wolf D. Priz (Vienna, 1942), lelmut Swiczinsky (Poznan, 1944), and Rainer Michael Holzer, who left the group in 1971; in 989 Frank Stepper (Stuttgart, 1955) joined he group. During its first years of activity the roup made various projects in the field of xperimental architecture in opposition to the sual urban design. Their most recent works nclude the enlargement of the Ronacher Theatre at Vienna, the east pavilion of the Groninen Museum, and the UFA Cinema at Dresden.

## ietro da Cortona (Pietro Berrettini)
### Cortona, Arezzo, 1596–Rome, 1669)

eading architect of baroque Rome as well as maginative painter, Pietro da Cortona xpressed the most theatrical pictorial style of he European 17th century in a brilliant and umptuous way. He was trained in Tuscany ut by sixteen was in Rome, where he came into ssociation with Bernini, with whom, under he aegis of Pope Urban VIII, he worked in the arberini family palace. On the basis of a classical Emilian layout, he made scenes that were icher, more coloured, and more moving: the ighest expression of this was his decoration of the main hall of Palazzo Barberini, with a vast and luminous allegorical composition packed with swirling clouds, symbolic figures, and illusionistic views. In Florence he painted the reception rooms of Palazzo Pitti. During his last years in Rome, he dedicated himself to frescoes (Palazzo Doria Pamphili, Chiesa Nuova), even though by then he was entrusting much of the actual execution of the painting to students. Among his architectural works is the arrangement of S Maria della Pace with a semicircular portico on the façade, inserted in an urban context that was especially remodelled for it.

## Cuvilliés, François de
### (Soignies, 1695–Munich, 1768)

Leading exponent of the Bavarian rococo, Cuvilliés, who trained in Paris, became court architect in 1724, involving himself in stucco and gilt decoration. He made his major works in Munich and in the immediate area, including the reworking of the Residenz, where he built the wonderful theatre, and the pavilion in the park of Nymphenburg. His most complete work is the Amalienburg hunting palace. Cuvilliés made an important collection of prints and decorative models that became widespread in Europe.

## D'Aronco, Raimondo
### (Gemona, Udine, 1857–San Remo, 1932)

In 1877 D'Aronco began studies at the Accademia delle Belle Arti in Venice and from an early age took part in many competitions, always with great success. Aside from his activity in Italy, D'Aronco worked as an architect in Turkey, where he oversaw the restoration of the Hagia Sofia and the palace at Yildiz. He was commissioned to design the main building and the entrance pavilions for the 1902 Turin exposition. His style revealed the influence of the Viennese school of Otto Wagner and the work of Joseph Maria Olbrich. Together with Ernesto Basile and Giuseppe Sommaruga, he is considered one of the leading exponents of Italian art nouveau.

## Dientzenhofer, Christoph
### (Sankt Margarethen, 1655–Prague, 1722)

Important member of a prolific family of architects of German origin, together with his two brothers Georg and Johann and his son Kilian Dientzenhofer defined the baroque style in Bohemia, introducing the taste for the curved line and the elliptical layout, derived from studies conducted in Italy on Guarini and Borromini, in many churches built in Prague and other centres. Characteristic of his style are slender and capricious bell towers ending in small domes. The emblematic work of his career is the dome of St Nicholas in the Little Quarter in Prague, which he began but which was completed by his son Kilian.

## Doesburg, Theo van
### (Utrecht, 1883–Davos, 1931)

After his debut in a fauvist style Doesburg, under the influence of Kandinsky, turned to a form of geometric abstraction that soon came to involve the examination of vertical and horizontal relationships while colour slowly gave way to the prevalently constructive values of whites, blacks, greys, and flat primary colours. This stylistic evolution was greatly affected by his meeting in 1916 with Mondrian and the architect Oud, with whom he founded the magazine De Stijl in 1917 and gave life to the neo-plasticism movement. Painter, architect, and art theorist, Doesburg successfully proselytized for the aesthetic in the leading artistic centres of the period, Paris and Berlin. His influence was felt most of all in the sphere of the Bauhaus in Weimar and on Gropius; Doesburg taught at the Bauhaus and in Berlin (1921–23), having an effect on many aspects of the fields of graphics, typography, and architecture. His break with Mondrian, caused by his manifesto of elementarism, which appeared in 1926, accentuated his idea of the artistic product as an autonomous reality, determined by mathematical and optical laws; this became the central motif of the magazine Art Concret, which he founded in Paris in 1930 and which became a crucial reference point for the abstract artists of the 1930s.

## Domènech i Montaner, Lluis
### (Barcelona, 1850–1923)

After completing architecture studies in Madrid in 1873, Montaner quickly made himself known with his successes in a series of competitions. In 1875 he became a teacher at the Barcelona school of architecture; in 1910 he became that school's director. He designed the

Hotel Internacional (destroyed) and the Café-Restaurante del Parque for the 1888 universal exposition in Barcelona, but most of his career was dedicated to private homes. His style was strongly affected by the Catalan Gothic, to which he added elements drawn from classical and Renaissance art as well as Japanese art.

## Ehn, Karl
### (Vienna, 1884–1957)

Ehn attended the Akademie der Bildenden Künste in Vienna as a student of Otto Wagner. Between 1908 and 1950 he worked for the city administration, becoming a director in the field of residential housing. The various residential complexes based on English and Dutch models that he worked on during the 1920s and 1930s reflect the evolution of his highly original style. From an early language influenced by the Biedermeier style, as shown by the Hermeswiese Siedlung (1923), he moved to the monumental expressionism of the Karl Marx Hof (1927), finally adopting strongly geometric forms in the Adelheid Popp Hof (1932). The end, in 1934, of Vienna's Social Democratic administration brought an end to Ehn's professional career, and after that date he made only small homes.

## Eiffel, Gustave
### (Dijon, 1832–Paris, 1923)

A French engineer who became a builder, Eiffel experimented with new methods and materials and applied them in a variety of fields. His company, founded in 1866, made bridges, viaducts, locks, and metallic structures used in buildings throughout the world, always uniting formal style to matters of structure. This tireless activity led to many important large-scale works, among them the viaduct over the Douro (1977), that of Garabit (1880–84), and most of all the Eiffel Tower, made for the 1889 Paris world exhibition. Never dismantled, it has become the symbol of Paris and is also the symbol of the new 19th-century architecture, which was born of the conjunction of engineering science and architectural form.

## Filarete (Antonio Averulino)
### (Florence, c. 1400–Rome? 1469)

Trained in the humanistic climate of Florence, Filarete spent the first period of his career in Rome as a sculptor, making the bronze door of St Peter's (1433–45) for Pope Eugenius IV. Called to Milan by Francesco Sforza, he turned from sculpture to architecture and participated in the major worksites in the city, from the cathedral to the Sforza Castle (1451–55). During this period he made his most important work, the Ospedale Maggiore (1456), which until the 18th century was the unchallenged model for hospital design because of its layout – including symmetrical cross-shaped wards – and technical solutions. He also wrote his treatise on architecture, the first such theoretical work in Italian, in which he presented the theme of the ideal city, which he called Sforzinda, with its star-shaped layout, and made designs for the cathedral of Bergamo (1457). By bringing the new Renaissance lexicon to Lombardy, Filarete performed a very important cultural act, also succeeding in reviving the local tradition of Gothic decoration.

## Fischer, Johann Michael
### (Burglengenfeld, 1692–Munich, 1766)

Fischer, who moved to Bavaria in 1718, was an architect specialized in the construction of churches. The evolution of his style followed that of late baroque religious architecture up to the threshold of neo-classicism. Thus the works of his youth, built in the region around Munich, show the curving dynamic lines typical of such works in the early 18th century, but these progressively gave way to a more controlled and tightly organized style, one more suitable to the application of heavy ornamentation, such as the parish church of Rott-am-Inn (made unforgettable by the sculpture by Ignas Günther on the altars) and in his masterpiece, the abbey church of Ottobeuren.

## Fischer von Erlach, Johann Bernhard
### (Graz, 1656–Vienna, 1723)

The principal Austrian architect on the threshold of the 18th century, Fischer von Erlach trained in Italy as a sculptor, working in Rome and Naples, and when still young became involved at the highest levels in the efforts related to religious expression on behalf of Catholic patronage, in association with Bernini and Queen Cristina of Sweden. The high level of his classical training was reflected in his dedication to experiments and intellectual endeav-ours, including the writing of an important historical treatise, Fundamentals of the History of Architecture (1721). In 1705 he assumed the post of court architect and superintendent of imperial constructions under Emperor Charles VI. This official post did not prevent him from working on numerous ecclesiastic and private buildings that spread his style over a vast area between Austria and Bohemia. His most famous works include spectacular buildings in Vienna such as the Karlskirche and the court library. His highly interesting plan for the Schloss Schönbrunn was not made. Some of his principal works, including the large undertaking of the Karlskirche, were completed by his son Joseph Emmanuel Fischer von Erlach.

## Foster, Norman
### (Manchester, 1935)

After studies at the University of Manchester (1956–61), Foster obtained his master's degree at Yale University (1961–62). Together with Richard and Su Rogers and his future wife Wendy Ann Cheesman, Foster founded Team 4 Architects in London in 1963. In 1967 he and Wendy Foster founded Foster Associates, today Foster and Partners, with offices in London, Berlin, Frankfurt, Paris, Hong Kong, Singapore, and Tokyo. Among their most important works are the new headquarters for the Hong Kong and Shanghai Bank in Hong Kong, the Sackler Gallery in London, and the new Reichstag in Berlin.

## Francesco di Giorgio Martini
### (Siena, 1439–1501)

Architect, sculptor, military engineer, inventor, painter, and technologist, Martini played a central role in the development of art as well as in the development of the figure of the artist-intellectual of the late 15th century. He got his training and made his debut as a painter, a student of Vecchietta and colleague of Neroccio. In 1477 he was called to Urbino to act as the principal architect in the court of Federico da Montefeltro. Aside from works in the Ducal Palace in Urbino, he designed and constructed important forts and fortifications. Other masterpieces of architecture, datable to the 1480s, include the church of S Maria del Calcinaio near Cortona and the Ducal Palace in Gubbio. In 1489 he returned to Siena to sculpt the bronze angels in

e apse of the cathedral and to make a few
intings, but he left immediately, first for Milan
nd then Naples, eventually returning to Siena,
here he ended his eclectic career painting.

## ller, (Richard) Buckminster
## (Milton, 1895–Los Angeles, 1983)

fter attending Harvard and Cambridge
913–15) and serving in the navy during
orld War I, Fuller set up the Stockade Build-
g System with James Monroe Hewlett. Ded-
ated to solving modern problems with revo-
tionary ideas, he designed the self-contained
-D' house (1928) followed by the Dymaxion
ouse (1944–45), its name being an expres-
on of Fuller's principle of deriving 'maximum
itput from a minimum input of material and
ergy'. The Dymaxion was easy to assemble,
sassemble, and transport, with a hexagonal
an composed of six triangular rooms around
entral space for the building plant. Between
)48 and 1959 he made several examples of
odesic domes in metal, plastic, wood, and
rdboard. Easy to assemble and transport,
ese sturdy structures saw much military and
dustrial use. The most famous was the dome
ade for the Montreal 'Expo '67'.

## abriel, Ange-Jacques
## aris, 1698–1782)

piritual heir of Jules Hardouin Mansart, in
742 Gabriel succeeded his father, Jacques
abriel, as first architect to the French king. His
ther had continued and further developed
e elegant style created at the beginning of
e century by Mansart, and Gabriel completed
e works he left unfinished. He was distin-
ished for the purity and elegant repose of his
rsion of French classical architecture; like
e other French architects of the period he
nored the baroque, which was applied only in
e rocaille version in interior furnishings. His
assical style dominated French 18th-century
chitecture; it was a style based more on pro-
ortions than on structure and was thus a pre-
de to the later Louis XVI style and the Empire
yle. Between 1750 and 1755 he completed
e so-called Gros Pavilion at Fontainebleau
d designed Place Louis XVI (now Place de la
oncorde) in Paris, one of his most famous
orks, with its extraordinary scenographic
fect. In 1762 the king entrusted him with the

great project of the arrangement of the palace
of Versailles, but the work began only in 1772
and was interrupted by the king's death.

## Gagliardi, Rosario
## (*c.* 1690–1762)

Leading exponent of 18th-century Sicilian
baroque, Gagliardi was active in numerous
areas of eastern Sicily following the 1693 earthquake. His architecture displays a skilled synthesis between the architectural elements and
the decoration, with particular attention to
stuccowork. His principal works include the
church of S Domenico (1746–58) and the
monastery of S Chiara (1717–58), both at Noto;
the church of S Giorgio at Modica; and the
church of S Giorgio at Ragusa Ibla (1738–75).

## Gaudí y Cornet, Antoni
## (Reus, 1852–Barcelona, 1926)

Gaudí completed his studies at the Escuela
Provincial de Arquitectura in Barcelona, the
city destined to be the principal theatre of his
professional activity. He initially followed the
return to medieval forms proposed by the Catalan movement as the most genuine expression
of vernacular Spanish tradition. Early on he
met the wealthy industrialist Güell, destined to
be his most important patron, for whom he
made the first works characterized by a sensitive combination of Gothic and Moresque elements. Such experimentation later led him to
achieve a highly personal language freed from
every reference to the past and full of formal,
structural, and decorative inventions that surpassed every traditional compositional scheme.
Busy until the last days of his life with the creation of the Sagrada Familia, he was long
undervalued by official critics, and only recently
have the greatness and the prophetic qualities
of this isolated genius of architectural creativity been recognized.

## Gehry, Frank O.
## (Toronto, 1929)

Gehry studied at the University of Southern
California and at Harvard and in 1954 began
working for several architects. He opened his
first studio, in California, in 1962, and his first
works were influenced by the vernacular architecture of California and the work of Neutra
and Wright. A series of residential buildings

that he made during the 1970s, including his
own home in Santa Monica, built between 1977
and 1979, revealed his growing tendency to
dissolve the conventional compositional and
structural elements of architecture, leading to
a sort of architecture of programmatic deconstructivism. His creations became increasingly
sculptural during the 1980s and brought him
worldwide fame. Created with the help of computers, his works of the 1990s took on even
more irrational and plastic forms to the point
of rejecting traditional perspective and perspective values. In 1990 he received the Pritzker
Architecture Prize.

## Giulio Romano (Giulio Pippi)
## (Rome, 1492/99–Mantua, 1546)

A prestigious architect and master at organizing and directing decorative undertakings,
Giulio Romano got his training and was
involved in his first artistic projects through the
workshop of Raphael, becoming that artist's
most trusted assistant in the creation of major
cycles, such as the rooms and loggias in the
Vatican, La Farnesina, and the Villa Madama.
With the death of Raphael (1520) he took over
direction of the workshop, completing works of
great importance (Sala di Constantino in the
Vatican). In 1524 he moved to Mantua and
became the director of the last great artistic
season of an Italian Renaissance court. For the
Gonzagas he designed cycles of frescoes and
ambitious constructions (Palazzo del Te, Mantua Cathedral, the abbey of S Benedetto Po),
and he also made cartoons for tapestries and
designs for jewelry, taking care in all his works
to give the public image of the court of Isabella
and Federico Gonzaga the proper look. The
dispersion and destruction of the Gonzaga residence resulted in the loss of much of these
works. Giulio Romano's most complex operation remains the design and decoration of the
Palazzo del Te, in which every room presents
new and more enthralling ornamental devices.

## Golosov, Il'ya Aleksandrovich
## (Moscow, 1883–1945)

After earning his diploma in 1912 from the
Moscow School of Painting, Sculpture, and
Architecture, Golosov dedicated himself to
teaching at the Moscow Polytechnical Institute and in Vkhutemas, artistic and technical

workshop schools similar to the Bauhaus. Early in the 1920s he was one of the most important exponents of constructivism. Between 1925 and 1932 he was a member of SASS (Section of Architects in Socialist Construction), paying special attention to Western rationalism. By the 1930s he had returned to a more classical traditional language. His works include the Zuyev Club (1928) and the home in Pokrovskij Bullvar in Moscow (1936).

## Gondoin, Jacques
### (St Ouen, 1737–Paris, 1818)

Gondoin trained at the French Academy in Rome between 1759 and 1763, where he met Piranesi; on his return to Paris he was nominated architect to the king. His most important work, the Ecole de Chirurgie (1769–76), presents pure neo-classical forms. After the Revolution he redesigned Place Vendôme for Napoleon, replacing the statue of Louis XV with the bronze Vendôme Column (1806–11).

## Grimshaw, Nicholas
### (London, 1939)

In 1965, after studies at the Edinburgh College of Art and the Architectural Association in London, Grimshaw founded Farrell-Grimshaw together with Terry Farrell; the association ended in 1980, the year in which he founded Grimshaw & Partners. Along with Norman Foster and Richard Rogers, Grimshaw is considered one of the most important high-tech architects. Important among his early works is the apartment building in Park Road, London (1968). His evolution toward architecture based on the use of advanced technology and the visibility of the support structure include the Herman Miller Factory in Bath (1976), the commercial-residential centre in Camden Town, London (1989–90), the British Pavilion at the Seville exposition in 1992, and the Waterloo International Terminal in London (1993).

## Gropius, Walter
### (Berlin, 1883–Boston, 1969)

After studies in Munich (1903–4) and Berlin (1905–7), Gropius joined the office of Peter Behrens, from whom he learned the celebration of industrial development as a manifestation of a new culture. From 1910 to 1925 he worked with Adolf Meyer. The outstanding work of these years was the Fagus Works, a milestone in the modern movement. In 1919 he founded the Bauhaus in Weimar, the crowning achievement of his teaching efforts to blend artistic creativity with the requirements of industrial production. The school's relocation to Dessau, in 1925, began the technological era of modern architecture, influenced by contemporary Dutch architects and leading to a series of works of international importance. Gropius left the Bauhaus in 1928 and began a period of experimentation in urbanistics and the typology of the home. With the advent of Nazism he moved to England and then, in 1937, to Boston, where he taught at Harvard and continued his professional activity, first alongside Marcel Breuer and then with the TAC group.

## Guarini, Guarino
### (Modena, 1624–Turin, 1683)

Professor of philosophy and mathematics, Guarini trained in Rome on the works of Borromini. He was interested in the dialectic relationships between concave and convex architectural parts, thus elaborating a complex articulation that goes beyond the original Borromini style. A member of the Theatine order, Guarini moved the principle of the curving wall, which Borromini had applied to churches, to the façades of palaces: the front of Palazzo Carignano in Turin (1679), one of the heights of Italian baroque secular architecture, undulates along a concave-convex-concave curve; the principal area is oval, and between this and the convex part of the façade Guarini located two separate flights of stairs. Guarini was called to Turin in 1666 and remained there until 1681 as engineer and mathematician to Charles Emmanuel of Savoy. During these years he completed the chapel of the Holy Shroud (begun 1668) in Turin Cathedral, its dome an extraordinary example of the fusion of many models drawn from the Gothic and the Hispano-Arabic (a complex system of black marble ribbing extends from a twelve-pointed star, and thirty-six segmented arches symmetrically overlap, making this chapel the most original and evocative work of the Italian baroque), and made the church of S Lorenzo (1668–87). The chapel of the Holy Shroud was damaged by fire in 1997 and has been subject to slow reconstruction work and careful restoration.

## Guas, Juan
### (Saint Pol de Léon, Finistère, c. 1430–Toled[o] 1496)

The work of this Spanish architect is notab[le] for its inventive blending of stylistic mot[ifs] from Arabic art and from the Flamboya[nt] Gothic. His best-known works are the chur[ch] of S Juan de los Reyes in Toledo (c. 1479–8[0]) and the Palacio del Infatado at Guadalaja[ra] (1480).

## Guimard, Hector
### (Paris, 1867–New York, 1942)

One of the outstanding exponents of Fren[ch] art nouveau, Guimard made works that a[re] known for the application of modern co[n]structive techniques as well as innovative ma[te]rials. An outstanding work is the Cast[el] Béranger (1897–98) in Paris, a complex wi[th] 36 apartments that was an early example [of] quality construction in rental properties (t[he] most original aspect is the interiors, whi[ch] approach the style of Horta but with a mo[re] exuberant decoration). Other works from th[e] period are the Humbert de Romans audit[o]rium (1902; destroyed), which had a meta[l] framework roof. Guimard is best known for h[is] work for the Paris Métro, for which h[e] designed entrances with flowing art nouve[au] forms that replicate plant and animal for[m] perfectly interwoven in the structures.

## Hadid, Zaha
### (Baghdad, 1950)

Having completed her studies in mathema[t]ics at the American University in Beiru[t] Hadid moved to the Architectural Associatio[n] in London (1972–77), where she was dee[ply] influenced by the teachers Rem Koolhaas an[d] Elia Zenghelis. In 1977 she joined with the[m] to become a member of the neo-supremati[st] group OMA (Office for Metropolitan Arch[i]tecture). In 1979 she began work on her ow[n] taking part in numerous competitions an[d] winning world fame for her design of th[e] Hong Kong Peak (1983). She built the Vit[ra] fire station at Weil am Rhein, German[y] (1989). Her most recent works include th[e] Bergisel Ski Jump at Innsbruck (2002) and t[he] Contemporary Arts Centre in Cincinna[ti] (2003). In 2004 she was awarded the Pritzk[er] Architecture Prize.

## Hankar, Paul
### (Frameries, 1859–Brussels, 1901)

Together with Van de Velde and Horta, Hankar was an outstanding figure within the sphere of the art nouveau style, his influence extending outside Belgium. Hankar achieved a sort of constructive rationalism that rejected historicist eclecticism in favour of freer and more imaginative decorations, often based on Oriental motifs. His close study of the works of Viollet-le-Duc led him toward a free use of materials both in decoration and structure, displayed in refined polychromy, structural clarity, and the accuracy of details. His most famous works in Brussels are his own house (1893) and the Ciamberlani House (1897), with sumptuously decorated façades, walls in brick with coloured stone dressings, wrought-iron work, and finely moulded windows.

## Haussmann, Georges Eugène
### (Paris, 1809–91)

Serving Napoleon III as *préfet* of Paris from 1853 to 1869, the French city-planner Haussmann designed a plan for the restructuring of Paris dictated by needs of a political nature and by the economic-social realities resulting from the city's urban expansion. Haussmann reworked and amplified the city's street network, in some cases demolishing medieval quarters, opening wide avenues, and constructing peripheral districts, carrying out the first instance of large-scale urban planning. The arrangement of the city of Paris today, with is boulevards and centre free of residential congestion, is in large part a result of the 19th-century project.

## Herrera, Juan de
### (Mobellán, c. 1530–Madrid, 1597)

Military engineer in the service of Emperor Charles V, Herrera was chosen in 1569 by Philip II to take over construction of the monastery of the Escorial after the death of the first designer, Juan Bautista de Toledo. Laid out with a severe, monumental style, up-to-date in terms of Michelangelo's constructions in Rome, and also in keeping with the guidelines of the Council of Trent on religious art, the Escorial became the symbolic monument of its period. After the construction of the church (completed 1582), Herrera worked on other official buildings in Seville (the Lonja de la Mercaderes) and in Valladolid (the cathedral).

## Herzog & de Meuron
### (Jacques Herzog, Basel, 1950; Pierre de Meuron, Basel, 1950)

After studying under Aldo Rossi at the Technische Hochschule in Zurich, Herzog and De Meuron opened a studio in Basel in 1978. Their works immediately attracted great interest, leading to many large-scale international commissions. Among the most recent of these was the transformation of a power station on the banks of the Thames into exhibition space for London's Tate Gallery. Their extremely varied projects make clear an ongoing process of experimentation with new materials and new building systems, including the progressive detachment of the external shell from the internal spaces. A singular aspect of their style is the use of traditional building materials and methods; these are employed to create the expressive results of each project, so that structures in reinforced concrete give order to buildings but at the same time make them abstract.

## Hildebrandt, Johann Lukas von
### (Genoa, 1668–Vienna, 1745)

Son of a career soldier, Hildebrandt was born and educated in Italy, following the movements of the Austrian army and coming in contact with Prince Eugene of Savoy when still young. His Italian experience, most of all his studies with Carlo Fontana (c. 1690) gave him a taste for sculptural decoration, which he applied in many of the buildings he later designed. He settled in Vienna and in 1701 was named court architect to the Habsburgs. His activity included both religious and secular works, with churches, palaces, and villas spread from Bohemia to Austria to Franconia in which he applied rich plastic articulation to buildings with French-inspired layouts. Among his many works are the Schloss Mirabell of Salzburg (1721) and the palace at Pommersfelden (1713–16). His masterpiece, as well as a summary of his style, is the Belvedere complex at Vienna, composed of two palaces built for Prince Eugene, connected by a terraced French-style garden (1714–16 and 1721–22).

## Hoffmann, Josef
### (Pirnitz, Moravia, now Brtnice, Czech Republic, 1870–Vienna, 1956)

Hoffmann studied in Brno and then at the Academy of Fine Arts in Vienna, where he was a student of Otto Wagner. In 1895 he won the Prix de Rome and went to Italy to study ancient architecture. Although strongly influenced by Wagner's teachings and by contact with art nouveau, he did not remain indifferent to the Mediterranean tradition and the products of England's arts and crafts movement, aspects of which can be recognized in his first commissions, a series of villas in Vienna. In 1903 he helped found the Wiener Werkstätte, an association of artisans that was active until 1932 and that created the furnishings for a series of highly elegant works characterized by the simplification of the formal elements and the refinement of the decorative and chromatic details. Hoffmann's production after 1905 saw the blending of different linguistic styles, running from classicism to expressionism. During the last period of his career he was busy in a creative competition with the modern movement and most of all with the work of the young Le Corbusier, who was active in his workshop for a certain period. The Purkeersdorf sanatorium (1904–8) and the famous Palais Stoclet in Brussels (1905–11) present Hoffmann's elegance and grace, as in the smooth white surfaces and the graphic design of the windows.

## Höger, Fritz
### (Beckenreihe, 1877–Bad Segeberg, 1949)

Höger earned his diploma in 1907 from the Baugewerkschule in Hamburg and opened his studio in the same year. After making a series of small-size residential buildings, he turned to the design of commercial buildings characterized by the use of brick as dressing of the façades. His best-known work was the Chilehaus (1922–23), one of the masterpieces of German expressionism, the outline of which resembles the prow of a large ship. It is one of Hamburg's best-known architectural landmarks. Other notable works by Höger are the nine-storey Hannoverscher Anzeiger building in Hanover (1928) and the town hall of Rüstringen (1929).

## Horta, Victor
### (Ghent, 1861–Brussels, 1947)

After his studies and a period of apprenticeship in the studio of Alphonse Balat, Horta debuted in 1885 with a series of small works that immediately displayed his talent. The Tassel House in Brussels (1893) was a manifesto of art nouveau thanks to the introduction of revolutionary artistic, technological, and compositional elements. The use of iron as a material for both construction and decoration as part of an architectural programme based on the open plan and the three-dimensional articulation of space – elements that also show up in his later works – represent Horta's original contribution to the development of the modern movement in architecture. After a stay in the United States between 1916 and 1919, he fell back on a more traditional and severe style based on the classical.

## Isozaki, Arata
### (Oita, Kyushu, Japan, 1931)

Isozaki studied at the University of Tokyo as student of Kenzo Tange and then worked with Tange until 1963. During the 1960s Isozaki's work went through a mannerist period, displaying a strong orientation to abstract forms composed of cubic and semicylindrical elements in a clear break with the rationalist principles of modern architecture. In the 1970s his works showed an increasing move toward historicism, with fragments drawn from the Western architecture of the past inserted in a contemporary language. This trend toward eclecticism increased in the late 1980s. His alternations of high-tech language with a severely classical style made it difficult to identify a coherent line of development. Isozaki's works from the 1990s achieved a balanced synthesis of the earlier stylistic tendencies with a return to elementary geometric shapes, as for example in the Museum of Contemporary Art in Nagi (1991–94).

## Jahn, Helmut
### (Zindorf, Nuremberg, 1940)

After earning his degree from the Munich Polytechnic, Jahn moved to Chicago in 1965 to complete his studies at the Illinois Institute of Technology. In Chicago he worked as a teacher and joined one of the city's most respected studios, that of C.F. Murphy Associates. In 1973 he became design director, and since 1981 he has

been an associate of the studio, now renamed Murphy/Jahn. Among his most important works are the Crosby Kemper Memorial Arena in Kansas City (1975), the Michigan City Public Library in Indiana (1977), the State of Illinois Centre at Chicago (1979–85), the skyscraper at One South Wacker Drive in Chicago (1980), the office tower at Johannesburg (1981–85), the United Airlines Terminal at Chicago International Airport (1980–82), and the Sony Centre in Berlin (1995).

## Jefferson, Thomas
### (Shadwell, Virginia, 1743– Monticello, Virginia, 1826)

Third president of the United States and author of the Declaration of Independence, Jefferson was also an architect and made an important contribution to the style of American architecture in his design for his home at Monticello (begun 1769). With that work he introduced a more 'learned' style, based on Palladian ideas. He applied such ideas as well as notions drawn from his study of Roman architecture to other public buildings, such as the Virginia State Capitol Building (1785–96), making such sober and serene lines symbolic of the virtues of the young republic.

## Johnson, Philip
### (Cleveland, 1906–New Canaan, 2005)

As director of the Department of Architecture of the Museum of Modern Art in New York (1930–36), Johnson became interested in European avant-garde architecture, promoting the first trips to the United States of Mies van der Rohe and Le Corbusier and publishing, together with Hitchcock, *The International Style: Architecture since 1922* (1932) in conjunction with an exhibit of modern architecture held at the museum. Johnson's activity as an architect began in the 1940s with a series of works clearly influenced by rationalism. His language grew in complexity, involving the refined and open-minded use of classical elements inserted in up-to-date technical solutions, making him a precursor of postmodernism. He reached the height of his career in the 1980s with the AT&T Building in New York. The arrival of deconstructionism in the 1990s marked the conclusion of the architectural experiments of his long professional career.

## Jones, Inigo
### (London, 1573–1652)

Jones trained in Italy on Palladio and Scamoz and in the middle of the baroque age becam the leading interpreter of late Renaissance Eng lish classicism, leaving an indelible mark wit his works and influencing 18th-century arch tecture in the United States. Standing ou among his most important works are suc country houses as Queen's House at Gree wich (1616–35) and Wilton House (1633–40 the London Banqueting House (1619–22), an the restoration and enlargement of St Paul Cathedral in London. Also important wa Jones's activity as a stage designer, working i collaboration with Ben Jonson and other poet and his drawings, which are of great interes including designs for the palace at Whitehall

## Juvarra, Filippo
### (Messina, 1678–Madrid, 1736)

Architect and stage designer, Juvarra made h debut in Messina, where he worked makin stage and ceremonial apparatus, ephemera architecture that already revealed solutions h would further develop in his first works i Rome. In Rome he completed his training an combined his activity as a stage designer fo Cardinal Pietro Ottoboni's theatre group wit work as an architect, entering the Academy o St Luke when only twenty-eight. Success arriv in 1714 with his nomination as first architec to Victor Amadeus II of Savoy, king of Sicil whom he followed first to Messina and then t Turin, where he spent twenty years creatin more than thirty works. The masterpieces h made during this period of intense activity i Turin include the basilica of Superg (1715–18), Palazzo Madama (1718–21), an the Stupinigi hunting palace (1729–31), extra ordinary examples of classicism in which h daringly blended Italian and French tradition Called to Madrid in 1735 by Philip V, he mad several important projects, including the roy palace, completed after his death by his Turi student Giovanni Battista Sacchetti.

## Kahn, Louis I.
### (Oesel Island, now Saaremaa Island Estonia, 1901–New York, 1974)

Kahn emigrated to the United States in 190 and graduated from the University of Pennsy

nia in 1924. During the 1930s his interest in
e living conditions in Pennsylvania led him to
ake numerous housing projects. His works
⊃m the 1940s make reference to the stylistic
⊃dules of the modern movement, but in the
xt decade he arrived at an original brutalism,
e outstanding example of which is the enlarge-
ent of the Yale Art Gallery in New Haven. This
d his later works display all the characteristic
⊃tifs of his architectural language: a preference
r elementary geometric forms and composi-
⊃ns, the hierarchical separation of spaces, the
⊃phasis on secondary elements, and citations
⊃m the past. From 1962 to his death he applied
s urbanistic and architectural ideas to pro-
ts in India and Bangladesh.

## nt, William
## ridlington, Yorkshire, 1685–London, 1748)
mous as a landscape artist – many believe the
glish garden began with him – Kent was also
architect and painter. Painting, in fact, took
the early part of his career, and his involve-
ent in architecture began with a meeting with
rd Burlington in Rome. He returned to Eng-
ıd in 1719 and became one of the leaders in
e early 18th-century architectural culture of
gland, employing a style that joined Palla-
ın motifs to a lively flair for interior decora-
ıns. Among his most important works as an
chitect are Holkham Hall in Norfolk (c. 1734)
d the Horse Guards building in London
750–58; erected posthumously). In his
signs for parks and gardens he abandoned
e formal and artificial symmetry of the
ench garden in favour of a style based more
⊃sely on nature at its most picturesque.
mous among his garden designs are the park
Stowe in Buckinghamshire and that of
ısham Hall in Oxfordshire (1730–40).

## enze, Leo von
## ⊃ckenem, 1784–Munich, 1864)
student of David Gilly, and having trained on
e rationalist theories of Jean-Nicolas-Louis
ırand, Klenze became the leader in the urban
tructuring of Munich following a fortunate
counter with Ludwig I of Bavaria, who
ıred his passion for antiquity. Klenze's works
:lude the installation of Ludwigstrasse
317), the Königsplatz with the neo-Hellenic
ıldings of the Glyptothek (1816–30) and the

Propylaeum (1846–60), the south façade of the
Residenz, inspired by Palazzo Pitti (1826–35),
and the building, in a neo-Renaissance style, of
the Alte Pinakothek (1826–36). There is then
also the Walhalla (1830–42), the temple dedicated to the heroes of Germany, with its romantic blend of archaeological motifs.

## Klerk, Michel de
## (Amsterdam, 1884–1923)
The twenty-fifth son of a diamond cutter, De
Klerk attended evening school and worked for
Eduard Cuypers, becoming one of the leading
exponents of the Amsterdam school, the Dutch
avant-garde movement that took shape around
the magazine *Wendingen*. His first notable work
was the block of flats on the Johannes Ver-
meerplein in Amsterdam (1911–12). He took
part with J. M. van der Meij in the Scheepvaarthuis in Amsterdam (1912–16). He also
participated in the creation of the Amsterdam
Sud district, designed by Berlage (1921–23)
and several working-class housing developments, the Spaarndammerplantsoen (1917–21)
and the Eigen Haard (1921). Before his pre-
mature death he also made the flower cooper-
ative at Aalsmeer (1922) and the De Hoop row-
ing club on the Amstel (1923).

## Knobelsdorff, Georg Wenceslaus von
## (Kuckädel, 1699–Berlin, 1753)
Court architect to Frederick the Great of Prussia, Knobelsdorff took on the difficult task of
transforming Berlin from a small provincial
city into one of the major capitals of the new
Europe, making it a suitable monumental setting for its ruler. In achieving this goal he combined two very different traditions, the Palladian for the exteriors, with delicate raised
colonnades in keeping with the rules of the
classical orders, and the more recent French
rococo for the interiors, a style at once comfortable and decorative. His Berlin works
include the Schloss Charlottenburg (1740–43),
the court theatre (1741), the opera house
(1741–43), and most of all the residence of
Schloss Sanssouci at Potsdam (1745–47).

## Labrouste, Henri
## (Paris, 1801–Fontainebleau, 1875)
Outstanding member of the rationalist movement in 19th-century France, Labrouste was

both architect and engineer and intuited the
importance of iron as an architectural material. A former student at the Ecole des Beaux-
Arts, he awakened scandal and critical reac-
tions with his anti-academic ideas. In his very
first professional undertaking, the Bibliothèque
Ste Geneviève in Paris (1843–50), he made the
first use in a public building of an exposed-iron
structural framework. His masterpiece was the
reading room in the Bibliothèque Nationale
in Paris (begun 1868), in which ceiling domes
are supported by thin columns of exposed iron,
a solution both functional and extremely light.

## Latrobe, Benjamin Henry
## (Fulneck, Yorkshire, 1764–New Orleans, 1820)
Latrobe was born in England where he received
neo-classical training; he moved to the United
States in 1795 and is today considered that
country's first professional architect. He collaborated with Jefferson on construction of the
Capitol in Richmond and was made surveyor of
public buildings in 1803. His monumental
buildings, which did much to introduce neo-
Greek forms to American architecture, include
the Capitol (begun 1801), the Bank of Pennsylvania in Philadelphia (1799), and the Roman
Catholic cathedral in Baltimore (1805–18), the
first cathedral in the United States.

## Laurana, Luciano
## (Zara, c. 1420–Pesaro, 1479)
Example of a late-15th-century Italian 'court'
architect, Luciano Laurana was probably in
Naples at the end of the 1450s; in 1465 he was
in Mantua, where he came in contact with Leon
Battista Alberti. His absorption of central Italian humanistic culture showed up the next
year, when he moved to Urbino. Luciano Laurana became the principal designer of the
Ducal Palace, where he worked until 1472, following the instructions of his patron, Federico
da Montefeltro, while developing his own independent and ingenious style based on the application of mathematical ideas introduced by
Piero della Francesca.

## Lavirotte, Jules Aimé
## (Paris, 1864–1928)
Student of Antoni Gaudí, French architect
Lavirotte finished his façades with ceramic
decorations designed for him by Alexandre

Bigot. Around 1900 his architecture earned him great renown in Paris. In his two most famous buildings, the block of flats on Avenue Rapp (1900–1) and the Hôtel Céramique (1904), Lavirotte used art nouveau floral motifs with great skill. His powerfully symbolic ornamentation drew inspiration from the plant and animal worlds.

## Lechner, Ödön
### (Budapest, 1845–1914)
Exponent of Hungarian art nouveau, Lechner originally employed a historicist style, applying an eclectic style to his first works, such as the School of Applied Arts in Budapest (1893–97). In his later works, which show the influence of Gaudí, he showed a preference for the use of polychrome materials, most of all in the Institute of Geology (1898–99) and the headquarters of the Post Office Savings Bank (1899–1902), both in Budapest.

## Le Corbusier (Charles-Edouard Jeanneret)
### (La Chaux-de-Fonds, 1887–Cap-Martin, 1965)
After studying engraving at the school of applied arts in his native city, between 1906 and 1914 he travelled in Europe and the Middle East, studying on his own the architectural culture of Europe and coming in contact with the most important architects of the epoch. In 1907 he met Hoffmann in Vienna, in 1908 he worked in Paris for the Perret brothers, in 1910 he was in Berlin in the office of Behrens. In 1917 he moved to Paris, where he opened a studio with his cousin Pierre Jeanneret. The following years were full of urbanistic projects, architectural creations, and theoretical writings. The use of reinforced concrete and primary materials like iron and glass, industrialization of the worksite, the codification of certain technical prefabricated elements, and the use of pure colours are the distinctive traits of their new technical, typological, and formal language, represented in an emblematic way by the Villa Savoye (1928–31), which had a profound influence on entire generations of architects.

## Ledoux, Claude-Nicolas
### (Dormans-sur-Marne, 1736–Paris, 1806)
Principal protagonist of the French architectural revolution of the Enlightenment, Ledoux made projects based on the combination of geometric and elementary forms, from Parisian customs houses to the salt-works industrial city of Chaux at Arc-et-Senans (1775–79), a very early example of city-planning conceived in terms of industrial production.

## Le Nôtre, André
### (Paris, 1613–1700)
The first great garden architect, Le Nôtre was the creator of the so-called French garden, characterized by axial arrangements leading to unbroken vistas with the space of the garden geometrically defined by parterres of flowers and hedges, bodies of water, canals, and fountains. His most famous works are the park of the royal palace of Versailles (begun 1661), that of Vaux-le-Vicomte (1655–61), and that of château of Chantilly (1661–83).

## Leonardo da Vinci
### (Vinci, Florence, 1452–Amboise, 1519)
Leonardo's artistic training took place in Florence, in the multifaceted workshop of Verrocchio; this youthful experience would help determine his many interests in various artistic and technical applications, each of which involved the exercise of design. After his debut as a collaborator of Verrocchio, Leonardo began his own independent activity, early on showing his predisposition for portraiture and the investigation of nature. At thirty, in 1482, he left Florence for the court of Ludovico Sforza in Milan, where he spent much of his career. Painting and writing notebooks (the 'codices') were two different but complementary aspects of Leonardo's creativity, for he was open to the most diverse fields of interest. *The Virgin of the Rocks* (begun in 1483, today in the Louvre) and the *Last Supper* (1494–98) date to his early period in Milan. With the arrival of the French, he left Milan for Mantua and then Venice. On his return to Florence he began work on the *Mona Lisa* and continued the technological, geographical, and scientific studies he had started in Milan. He returned to Milan in 1506 and completed the *Virgin and Child with St Anne*, today in the Louvre. In 1513 he accepted the invitation of French King Francis I and moved to Amboise, bringing with him several paintings, thousands of pages of drawings and notes, and a crowd of students.

## Le Pautre, Antoine
### (Paris, 1621–91)
Student of Le Vau, Le Pautre further elaborated Le Vau's style in a series of works characterized by a classical style combined with lively dynamism, expressed most of all in the plans for buildings. His most successful work was the Hôtel de Beauvais in Paris (1654–56).

## Le Vau, Louis
### (Paris, 1612–70)
First architect to King Louis XIV and superintendent of royal constructions, Le Vau performed an important role in the evolution of 17th-century French architecture. His training period included an important trip to Italy, with visits to Genoa and Rome; in 1650 he began working for the French crown, building the pavilions of the king and queen at Vincennes, enlarging the church of St Sulpice, and participating in the completion of the Louvre. One of his major works was the château of Vaux-le-Vicomte, constructed in only five years (1656–61) for the finance minister Nicolas Fouquet. He then began work on the royal palace of Versailles, where he designed an enlargement of the original structure built in 1623 by Louis XIII, working together with Le Brun and Le Nôtre, who had worked with him at Vaux-le-Vicomte.

## Libeskind, Daniel
### (Lodz, Poland, 1946)
After studying music in Israel, in 1960 Libeskind moved to the United States. He obtained citizenship in 1965 and began studying architecture at the Cooper Union School in New York, later specializing at the University of Essex in England. He made a name for himself in 1985 at the International Garden Exhibition in Osaka when he and various other young architects were invited by Isozaki to design a pavilion. He later became known on the international scene, participating in numerous competitions and making exhibitions and installations. His work, which fully reflect the theories elaborated and expressed within the sphere of his teaching activity, can be traced to the contemporary architectural theories of deconstructionism. One of Libeskind's most important projects so far was the Jewish Museum, an annex to the Berlin Museum (1989–99).

## gorio, Pirro
**(Naples, c. 1510–Ferrara, 1583)**

Architect, painter, and antiquarian, Pirro Ligorio initially dedicated himself to painting and the archaeological excavations of Hadrian's Villa at Tivoli (begun 1549) directed by Cardinal Ippolito II d'Este of Ferrara, for whom Ligorio designed the Villa d'Este (1550–72), also at Tivoli, the garden of which, with its fountains, pavilions, and stairs, is one of the first and most famous examples of the 'Italian-style' garden. His mannerist taste was expressed in the scenographic decoration of the casino of Pius IV in Rome (1559–62).

## onghena, Baldassare
**(Venice, 1598–1682)**

Pupil of the architect and essayist Vincenzo Scamozzi of Vicenza, Longhena reached back to the roots of Renaissance Venetian architecture (Palladio and Sansovino) and worked out a personal language of unchecked inventiveness and imagination. His long career involved him in major undertakings that made him the absolute leader of Venetian architecture during the 17th century. His masterpiece is S Maria della Salute, designed in 1631, in which his pictorial taste found a truly original expression, exploiting natural light and the surface reflections on the water in canals to create theatrical chiaroscuro effects. The churches of the Scalzi (c. 1660) and the Ospedaletto are typically baroque architecture of extraordinary imagination; Longhena's civil architecture displays similar innovations, such as the Ca' Pesaro (c. 1660) and Ca' Rezzonico (c. 1667), both of them monumental presences on the Grand Canal in which Palladian models and those from Sanmicheli are interpreted with a sensibility that makes them seem as though sculpted from light and air.

## oos, Adolf
**(Brno, Moravia, 1870–Vienna, 1933)**

After courses at the Dresden Polytechnic, in 1893 Loos took a long trip to the United States, where he saw works by the Chicago school as well as expressions of the arts and crafts movement. Back in Europe he began his professional activity in Vienna, creating works that were direct physical expressions of the theories presented in his writings. In open opposition to the Jugendstil, the homes he built in the first two decades of the 20th century were concrete manifestations of his theoretical visions as expressed in the essay 'Architektur' (1910). Refined interiors of wood and marble contrasted with cubic exteriors with plastered surfaces left free of any ornamentation. In the 1920s he was made chief architect for the city, a position that permitted him to become involved in public housing. Isolated from the architectural culture of his time, he was closer to the protagonists of the European avant-garde. The revolutionary Tristan Tzara House (1926), which he made in Paris, shows the influence of the Dadaists.

## L'Orme, Philibert de (Delorme)
**(Lyons, c. 1510–Paris, 1570)**

French architect of the High Renaissance, leader during the central years of the 16th century and the period of the 'châteaux of the Loire', Philibert de L'Orme had an important period of training in Rome between 1533 and 1536. He thus acquired a solid sense of classical proportions, but he did not give up a subtle, elegantly decorative vein, which he expressed most of all during the years of the reign of Henry II (1547–59). He worked on the châteaux of Anet, Chennonceaux, and Fontainebleau, and designed the monumental tomb of Francis I in St Denis. During the 1560s he wrote treatises that served as true manuals during the long period of classical French architecture.

## Mackintosh, Charles Rennie
**(Glasgow, 1868–London, 1928)**

Mackintosh began his career working in the studio of John Hutchinson while attending evening courses at the Glasgow School of Applied Arts. In 1889 he was taken on as designer by the Honeyman & Keppie construction company, staying there until 1913. There he met Herbert McNair and the two McDonald sisters, with whom he formed The Four, a group of artists active in the fields of graphics and engraving. Thanks to the elegance and originality of their designs, the works of what would become the Glasgow school became well known at the international level. Meanwhile, Mackintosh had been busy since 1897 as an architect on his major commission, the Glasgow School of Art, where the geometric abstraction of the forms, united to the elegant combination of Gothic, Celtic, and Japanese decorative motifs presented an excellent synthesis of the elements of his artistic language. His fame is also tied to the many furniture designs he exhibited in 1900 at the Vienna Secession. Problems with alcoholism forced him to move first to Suffolk, then to London, and finally to France, where he dedicated himself to painting.

## Maderno, Carlo
**(Capolago, Ticino Canton, 1556–Rome, 1629)**

The revolutionary aspect of Maderno's architecture was essentially its implementation of a strong and vigorous style in place of the refined classicism still in use in Rome at the end of the 16th century. He studied with his uncle, Domenico Fontana, and after Fontana's departure received the important nomination to architect of St Peter's and completed the façade of S Susanna, his capital work, the intense energy of which meant the definitive overcoming of mannerism. Most of his activity was involved in the worksite of St Peter's on the design of the nave and the façade, his activity influenced by the inheritance of Michelangelo. He designed Palazzo Mattei (1598–1616) and Palazzo Barberini. By the time of his death, Roman architecture had been freed of academic mannerism and was to prove more readily accessible to the revolutionary work of Bernini and Borromini.

## Mansart, Jules Hardouin
**(Paris, 1646–Marly, 1708)**

Nephew of François Mansart, Louis XIII's famous architect, with whom a new classical period began in France, Jules Hardouin was the favourite of Louis XIV, who named him superintendent of royal constructions. He had been a pupil of his uncle, from whom he derived the sobriety of external decoration and the correctness of proportions. His major work was the royal palace at Versailles, in which he brought to conclusion the design by Le Vau to rework the small existing structure and to enlarge the palace with later structures, including most especially the Galerie des Glaces, the Grand Trianon, and the chapel. Architect and urban planner, Mansart designed Place Vendôme, formerly Place Louis-le-Grand, but his greatest work was the Dôme des Invalides, a church with a Greek-cross layout crowned by a dome connected to the façade, in which he did away with excesses of decoration, preferring combinations of volumes and lines.

## Meier, Richard
### (Newark, New Jersey, 1934)

After studies at Cornell University in Ithaca, New York, he trained in the New York office of Skidmore, Owings and Merrill and with Marcel Breuer. In 1963 he opened his own studio in New York. His first works were single-family homes and residential buildings that clearly showed the influence of Breuer along with an interest in the purism of Le Corbusier. Meier achieved fame with the 1969 exhibition of the New York Five, of which he was a member; in fact, the group was also known as the White architects because of his preference for that colour. He was soon working on a series of important international commissions. In these buildings he freely combined his repertoire of geometric forms, within which he articulated complex spaces influenced by the compositions of the avant-gardes of the 1920s. Having become one of the most sought-after architects in the world, he reached the apex of his career in the creation of the buildings for the Getty Centre in Los Angeles (1985–97).

## Mel'nikov, Konstantin
### (Moscow, 1890–1974)

After earning his degree from the Moscow Academy in 1917, he was drawn to constructivism, becoming a key figure within that movement and participating in the foundation of ASNOVA (Association of New Architects). From his first works, including his home in Moscow, one of the most singular buildings of the 1920s in Russia, he displayed the movement's expressive tendencies, captured in a dynamic form. He acquired international fame with his pavilion for the exhibition of constructivist objects with which he won the grand prix at the decorative arts exposition in Paris in 1925. He then worked on a series of projects emblematic of his original version of the constructivist language, including the five workers' clubs he made in Moscow (1927–29), which were characterized by the interpenetration of articulated volumes mixed with symbolic and fantasy elements. Having become the target of

Stalinist critics, he ended his career on the outer margins of public architecture.

## Mendelsohn, Erich
### (Allenstein, now Olsztyn, Poland, 1887–San Francisco, 1953)

Mendelsohn studied architecture in Berlin and Munich. The drawings he made between 1914 and 1918, which show how profoundly influenced he was by expressionism, earned him European fame at the show held in Berlin in 1919. The highly symbolic force of these drawings appears in his expressionist masterpiece, the Einstein Tower in Potsdam (1920–24). He then began a period of great professional success during which he developed a personal style characterized by forceful plasticity in the composition of volumes, supported by his extensive knowledge of the technical aspects of construction. He left Germany in 1933, moving to England and then to Palestine. In 1941 he emigrated to the United States.

## Michelangelo Buonarroti
### (Caprese, Arezzo, 1475–Rome, 1564)

The greatest marble sculptor of all time, as well as a painter and an architect, Michelangelo was the critical conscience of the Renaissance at the moment of its apogee and was thus an attentive witness of its crisis; he dominated the 16th century in Europe and has become its emblematic figure. Involved from his youth in the exciting artistic climate in Florence during the period of Lorenzo the Magnificent, with the rediscovery of the classical past, Michelangelo created the *Pietà* in St Peter's in Rome before the year 1500, and shortly after made the *David* in the Accademia in Florence. During the first decade of the 16th century he dedicated himself repeatedly to painting, first in Florence, where he competed with Leonardo in the decoration (lost) of Palazzo Vecchio and made the *Doni Tondo*, and then in Rome, where at the request of Pope Julius II he began the undertaking of the vault of the Sistine Chapel, a dramatic synthesis of the history of man and also a celebration of the beauty and wonder of creation. After this undertaking, which he worked on almost without interruption from 1508 to 1512, Michelangelo abandoned painting for more than twenty years, dedicating himself to sculpture and architecture (the New Sacristy of

S Lorenzo in Florence, then in Rome with the dome of St Peter's and the Square of the Campidoglio). He returned to his brushes in the 1530s for the long creation of the *Last Judgment* in the Sistine Chapel. In his old age he followed this 'awesome' masterpiece with two more marble versions of the *Pietà* (Museo dell'Opera del Duomo, Florence, and Sforza Castle, Milan).

## Michelozzi, Michelozzo di Bartolomeo
### (Florence, 1396–1472)

Having studied with Ghiberti and collaborated with Donatello, Michelozzo revealed his talents as an architect in the creation of the complex of the convent of S Marco in Florence (1436–44), in which the library expresses his efforts to achieve a balanced rhythmic and chromatic scansion of the rooms. In the Palazzo Medici-Riccardi in Florence (1444–59) he established the typology of the Florentine palace that architects would use until the 16th century. In a similar way, in the Medici villas of Careggi (c. 1435–40) and Cafaggiolo (c. 1450) he reinterpreted the medieval castle in a Renaissance style, opening the way to a new type of country house. In his works Michelozzo reconciles the measured style of the Florentine Gothic with new classical ideas.

## Mies van der Rohe, Ludwig
### (Aachen, 1886–Chicago, 1969)

Mies van der Rohe did not study architecture but trained in the offices of Bruno Paul and Peter Behrens. From the latter he drew the classical severity of means, purity of forms, the elegance of proportions, and the taste for detail that, combined with the use of modern industrial materials, characterized all his later work. He branched out on his own in 1912, opening an office in Berlin. Affected by the sense of renewal following the end of World War I, he designed a series of revolutionary buildings that constitute a decisive contribution to 20th-century architecture in which he delineated the tendency to reduce the structure to a technological essential that could be freely organized within the architectural space. His undisputed masterpiece is the German Pavilion for the 1929 international exposition in Barcelona, in which he achieved a spatial continuum, coordinating internal and exte l space. After directing the Bauhaus (1930–33), he moved to the United States in 1938, where he applied his principle of 'Less is more' to a few fundamental types, well suited to serve a variety of functions.

## Moneo, Rafael
## (Tudela, Spain, 1937)
After studies at the Escuela de Arquitectura of Madrid and a stay in Denmark at the studio of Jørn Utzon, Moneo returned to Madrid in 1965 and began his professional career, designing while also teaching and carrying on intense work as an essayist and critic. The characteristic elements of his style were clear from his very first works: severity of language, classical forms, particular attention to building materials, most of all brick, and rejection of the typological element as the point of departure for a design project. In the Bankinter (bank office building) in Madrid (1973–76), with which he gained great international recognition, he introduced the tendency to closely value the urban context while elaborating the enclosure elements, thus giving architects the new task of building for the city by abandoning the notion of the building as container. Results of this were international design projects, such as the new museum of modern art in Stockholm (1997).

## Morris, William
## (Walthamstow, London, 1834–London, 1896)
English poet, artist, craftsman, designer, painter, writer, social reformer, politician, and printer, Morris studied church history and medieval literature at Exeter College, Oxford; while there he also made friends with Edward Burne-Jones. He began his career as an apprentice to the Gothic-revival architect G. E. Street in 1856 and subsidized the *Oxford and Cambridge Magazine*. Through the encouragement of Dante Gabriel Rossetti and John Ruskin, he soon turned to painting and writing. In 1861 he opened a firm for artisan production called Morris, Marshall, Faulkner and Company, with Burne-Jones, Rossetti, and Philip Webb among the associates. Morris sought a revitalization of the splendour of medieval arts and crafts as an alternative to mass-produced goods; the firm made furniture, glassware, wool products, wallpaper, embroidery, painted and coloured glass,

all in austere forms with the linear treatment typical of Gothic art. In 1891 Morris started the Kelmscott Press, whose works were to be of great importance to the development of the art of the book. Firm in his opinions, much like his spiritual father, John Ruskin, Morris was against industrial society and became involved in politics during the 1880s. In 1883 he joined the socialist Democratic Federation; in 1884 he formed the Socialist League and began publishing the newspaper *Commonweal*. His reform and social ideals and his sharp refusal to use machines in the manufacture of objects made Morris one of the originators of the arts and crafts movement. He expressed his theories in many speeches and several books and essays, including *The Decorative Arts* (1878) and his collected works (24 volumes, 1910–15).

## Nash, John
## (London, 1752–East Cowes, Isle of Wight, 1835)
Highly original and prolific designer, the English architect Nash made use of the widest variety of styles and urbanistic ideas, building country houses and castellated villas, or 'castles', in a vaguely Renaissance style (Cronkhill, 1802) and cottages with a picturesque flavour. In the Royal Pavilion in Brighton he made a fantastic version of the Indian style, associating it with neo-Gothic, Chinese, and Moresque elements. He is perhaps best known for his development of the Marylebone region of London, most of all Regent's Park (1812–27), an impressive complex of rigorously classical buildings. Although working within the sphere of English neo-classicism he was among the initiators of the taste for historicist revival that became typical of English architectural culture.

## Neumann, Balthasar
## (Eger in Bohemia, 1687–Würzburg, 1753)
Perhaps the most talented protagonist of European rococo architecture, Neumann was active in both religious and civil architecture. Working on commissions from the prince-bishops of Würzburg, Neumann proved himself the most characteristic interpreter of the celebratory ambitions of the local German powers, from Cologne to Stuttgart, from Karlsruhe to Brühl to Vienna (he worked on the Hofburg). One of the basic characteristics of his work is the rejec-

tion of fantasy for its own sake; despite their continuous variety, Neumann's buildings also present a sense of architectural composure and reveal a close relationship between architecture and decoration. The sculptors of the Wessobrunn school translated in plastic forms the highly original idea of the altar of the fourteen elder saints of the pilgrimage church of Vierzehnheiligen, while the frescoes of Giambattista Tiepolo are perfectly inserted in the hall of the Residenz of Würzburg, Neumann's masterpiece, completed shortly after 1750 following decades of work.

## Niemeyer, Oscar
## (Rio de Janeiro, 1907)
After studies at the Escola Nacional de Belas Artes of Rio de Janeiro, he worked in the studio of Lúcio Costa in 1935 and for Le Corbusier in Paris in 1936, the influence of whom is clearly visible in his first works. He went on to develop a personal style in which his original plastic organization of volumes and the introduction of curved lines alongside a rational grid, derived from Spanish baroque forms and from the natural landscape of Brazil, permitted him to overcome the teaching of Le Corbusier and to make buildings of great effect. His extremely expressive and antirational language earned him the position of chief government architect during construction of the country's new capital. Between 1956 and 1961 he designed all the most important buildings, the figurative elements of which – rendered enormous to fit the giant urban space – give the entire structure an unreal appearance. During the military regime, between 1964 and 1985, he emigrated to Paris, where he worked on many international projects. His last works indicated that his formal repertory was not yet exhausted.

## Nouvel, Jean
## (Fumel, France, 1945)
By the time he graduated from the Ecole Nationale Supérieure des Beaux-Arts of Paris, in 1971, Nouvel had already worked for the architect Claude Parent and had opened his first studio, in 1970. In 1976 he was co-founder of the MARS group, and in 1980 he planned and directed the Paris biennial of architecture. In 1988 he opened Jean Nouvel, Emmanuel Cattani et Associés, quickly reaching interna-

tional fame thanks to an architectural approach critical of traditional models and solutions and instead rich with metaphors and surprising, provocative images, made using light materials with colours drawn from the daily life of the city and the periphery. The construction of the Institute du Monde Arabe (1981–87), a successful combination of the potentials offered by advanced technology and the possibilities of bioecological architecture, marked a fundamental point in his career and earned him many important commissions, making him one of the best-known French architects in the world.

## Olbrich, Joseph Maria
### (Troppau, Silesia, 1867–Düsseldorf, 1908)
After studies at the Vienna Academy, in 1893 Olbrich won the Prix de Rome, which also led to his being taken into Otto Wagner's studio, where he worked for five years. In 1897 he was among the young avant-garde Austrian artists who founded the Vienna Secession, for which he designed the Secessionhaus (1898), which earned him immediate notoriety and numerous commissions between 1898 and 1900. He was soon recognized as the most gifted and inventive of the Secession architects. In 1899 he went to Darmstadt to help create the Mathildenhöhe artist colony, of which he assumed direction and for which he designed the buildings and the exhibition pavilion with a panoramic tower that became famous. His work placed him within the climate of figurative renewal promoted by art nouveau, but he succeeded in overcoming the limitations and weaknesses of that style by combining its fantasy appearance with spatial and distributive concreteness, thus anticipating the later formulations of the modern movement.

## Otto, Frei
### (Siegmar, Saxony, 1925)
In 1947 he enrolled in the Technishe Hochschule in Berlin. A scholarship made it possible for him to spend time in Charlottesville, Virginia, after which he graduated and opened his own studio in Berlin. All of his activity has involved the design and creation of lightweight structures, including pneumatic membranes, most especially in roofs and tents. His most important works include pavilions for floral exhibitions in Kassel (1955) and Cologne (1957), the roof for the open-air shows at Cannes (1965), the West German Pavilion at the Montreal 'Expo '67', and, in collaboration with Günter Behnisch, the Olympiapark stadium in Munich (1968–72). Since the late 1960s he has been involved in the design of 'ecological architecture', architectural structures made with extreme attention to nature and natural resources.

## Oud, J. J. P.
### (Purmerend, 1980–Wassenaar, 1963)
After studies in Amsterdam and later at Delft, Oud worked for Joseph Cuypers, the first Dutch 'rationalist', and then for Theodor Fischer in Munich. His 1915 meeting with the painter Theo van Doesburg led to the founding of the magazine De Stijl and to a series of architectural creations profoundly influenced by abstract cubism, in contrast with the expressionistic compositions of the imaginative Amsterdam school. Between 1918 and 1933, in his position as Rotterdam city architect, Oud made several working-class city complexes distinguished by the harmonic compositions of the volumes and by white plaster surfaces that contrast with openings painted in the pure colours of Mondrian. In 1933 he returned to private practice, and his subsequent works show a softened style along with stylistic revisions that earned him criticism from several architects of the modern movement.

## Palladio, Andrea (Andrea di Pietro della Gondola)
### (Padua, 1508–Maser, 1580)
After learning the rudiments of sculpture in Padua, in 1523 Andrea moved to Vicenza, which became his adopted city. In 1537, nearly thirty years old, he was noted by Giangiorgio Trissino, an alert intellectual, very much aware of current literary, philological, and architectural matters, who gave him the classical-style name Palladio and opened the way for his astonishing career. Between 1538 and 1543 Trissino and Palladio took part in archaeological campaigns, first in the Veneto and then in Rome, on the Latium hills, in the Phlegraean Fields, The most typical period of Palladio's production began in 1542–43 with the solid Villa Godi-Malinverni at Lonedo di Lugo, north of Vicenza. Palladio became the symbolic architect of the Vicenza aristocracy, the absolu[te] leader of the renewal of the city in its priva[te] palaces and public buildings, including, begin[n]ning in 1546, the reworking of the façade of th[e] Palazzo della Ragione. In 1556 he took part [in] the foundation of the Accademia Olimpica [in] Vicenza, and in the same period on the ou[t]skirts of the city he designed Villa Almeric[o] Valmarana, the much imitated 'Rotonda', fo[l]lowed by, among others, the Villa Pisani [at] Mira and the Villa Barbaro in Maser. In 157[?] with the death of Jacopo Sansovino, Pallad[io] assumed the role of official architect for Veni[ce] and moved to that city. In November of th[at] year he published his Four Books of Architectur[e] the fundamental text for the spread of Pallad[i]anism. In Venice he was kept busy primari[ly] with church architecture (S Giorgio Maggio[re] Il Redentore). His last work was the Teat[ro] Olimpico in Vicenza. The work was still [in] progress when Palladio died, on 19 Augu[st] 1580; the theatre opened five years later than[ks] to the efforts of Vincenzo Scamozzi.

## Parler, Peter
### (Schwäbisch Gmünd, 1330–Prague, 1399)
A leading architect and sculptor of 14th-centu[ry] Prague, Parler changed the face of the Bohemia[n] capital during the reign of Charles IV, rewor[k]ing Mathias of Arras's original design for th[e] cathedral of St Vitus (begun 1353), designin[g] the Charles Bridge (begun 1357), and buildin[g] the castle of Karlstein for the emperor. H[is] highly original style had a great influence on th[e] late Gothic style of central Europe.

## Paxton, Joseph
### (Milton Bryant, Bedfordshire, 180[?]–Sydenham, London, 1865)
Famous for his proto-modern use of glass an[d] iron, Paxton built two greenhouses for the du[ke] of Devonshire at Chatsworth, Derbyshire, a[nd] then used this experience in his design for th[e] structure that earned him fame and also g[ot] him knighted, the Crystal Palace at the Gre[at] Exhibition in 1851. Built of prefabricated glas[s] and-iron modules, this structure was of a si[ze] unknown in its time; the enormous structu[re] was dismantled after the exhibition and rebu[ilt] at Sydenham. It was damaged by fire in 19[??] and demolished in 1941.

**i, Ieoh Ming**
**anton, 1917)**

i emigrated to the United States in 1935, at e age of seventeen. After studies at MIT and rvard he went to work in 1948 for the New rk builder William Zeckendorf. In 1955 he ened IM Pei and Associates, still ranked ong the best in the United States, and hieved immediate international fame, build-g a large number of public and commercial ildings of great effect throughout the world. cause of the stylistic diversity among the sociates and the long period of time over ich the office has been active, the projects ade have been very various, but they have vays been distinguished by extremely refined d skilled designs that range from rationalism postmodernism. Pei's best-known creations clude his design for the Grand Louvre 983–93), with its underground entry through enormous glass pyramid located in the urtyard, one of the most disputed architec-ral creations in Europe at its time.

**lli, Cesar**
**an Miguel de Tucumán, Argentina, 1926)**

ter studies at the National University of cumán and the University of Illinois at bana-Champaign, Pelli spent a period of prenticeship in the studio of Eero Saari-n, with whom he collaborated for ten years 954–64). From 1968 to 1977 he worked at ctor Gruen Associates in Los Angeles, mak-g one of his best-known works, the Pacific sign Centre in Los Angeles (1971–76). He rmed his own studio in New Haven in 1977 d became involved in the creation of pub-and commercial buildings, becoming one the best-known designers of skyscrapers. s most important works include the largement of the Museum of Modern Art in w York (1977), the Canary Wharf Tower d railway station in London (1986–90), and e Petronas Towers of Kuala Lumpur, laysia (1992–96), composed of twin 85-rey towers that are currently the tallest ildings in the world.

**rrault, Dominique**
**lermont-Ferrand, France, 1953)**

1978 Perrault graduated from the Ecole tionale Supérieure des Beaux-Arts in Paris,

and in 1981 he opened his own office in that city. His competition-winning design for the university buildings for electronic engineers and technicians in Marne-la-Vallée in the 1980s earned him attention and important commis-sions. Among these, the best known was with-out doubt his design for the Bibliothéque Nationale de France in Paris (1989–97), with its four large towers marking off a natural garden. His architecture has always been distinguished by strongly abstract and minimalist technical works and volumes, enriched and embellished by the high quality of the industrial-made con-struction materials used.

**Perret, Auguste**
**(Brussels, 1874–Paris, 1954)**

Perret began studies at the Ecole des Beaux-Arts in Paris but quit, completing his training by joining, along with his two brothers, his father's construction firm, known from 1905 on as Per-ret Frères. His theoretical and business training led him to work out a synthesis between the ideals of classical harmony and the financial demands of the construction industry. He achieved this through the use of reinforced concrete and the exploitation of its technical and expressive possibilities. These linguistic efforts reached a particular lyricism in the basil-ica of Notre-Dame, Le Raincy, near Paris (1923), in which the bearing structure in rein-forced concrete is also the building's decoration. After World War II Perret and his brothers made several large works, including the 1948 reconstruction of the city of Le Havre, the first official recognition of Perret's long and distin-guished carer as a builder, a career that puts him among the pioneers of modern architecture.

**Peruzzi, Baldassare**
**(Siena, 1481–Rome, 1536)**

Peruzzi trained as a painter in the circle of Pin-turicchio and as architect in the sphere of Francesco di Giorgio Martini. He moved to Rome c. 1503, where contact with Raphael moved his style closer to the classical. His first work, La Farnesina (begun 1506), has a clear, geometric structure and is still within the Tus-can tradition. Peruzzi was involved in the work on St Peter's, and following Raphael's death, in 1520, he was made the lead architect. During these years he produced a great quantity of

architectural drawings, views of buildings, and designs destined to have an important influence on later treatise writers (first among them Ser-lio). These works are notable for their experi-mental approaches and restless reworking of themes from Bramante. The result was Palazzo Massimo alle Colonne (begun 1532), remark-able for the interplay between the fragmentary structure of the internal spaces on the asym-metrical shape of the façade and the courtyard. Following the Sack of Rome (1527) Peruzzi returned to Siena, where he contributed to the reworking of that city's fortifications. Peruzzi's work presents a paradigm of that restless period, with its search for formal solutions that went against the classicism of the Renaissance.

**Piacentini, Marcello**
**(Rome, 1881–1960)**

Piacentini got his training in his father's office and at the College of Fine Arts in Rome. He ini-tially revealed his talent in a series of ephemeral works of clear eclectic inspiration and in var-ious urbanistic designs of a Mittel-European and North American style. His Roman designs of the 1920s, made for wealthy private patrons, show that he was up to date on stylistic trends in Vienna. His position against the young archi-tects of the rationalist movement and in favour of an architecture suited to contemporary life but also respectful of tradition soon made him one of the Fascist regime's official architects. His many public commissions during the 1930s included the 'E 42' Exhibition in Rome (1936–42), of which he designed the general layout with its evocation of the pomp of the ancient Roman Empire, also visible in the Palace of Italian Civilization designed by Guer-rini, La Padula, and Romano. The War brought an end to the many large worksites he was involved in, along with his professional career.

**Piermarini, Giuseppe**
**(Foligno, 1734–1808)**

Piermarini studied with Vanvitelli in Rome and then collaborated with him on the royal palace at Caserta. In 1769 he accompanied Van-vitelli to Milan, and it was in that city that he performed most of his activity. His conversion of the old Ducal Palace (1770–80) marked the beginning of a period of fecund activity span-ning a period of thirty years and making Piermarini one of the most important personalities on the panorama of Lombard architecture and earning him the chair of architecture at the Brera Academy in 1776. Considered one of the most authoritative representatives of Italian neo-classicism, Piermarini owed his fame to his great talent at adapting himself to existing architectural and urban settings and to the clarity of the spatial layouts of his works, which, even when works of great prestige, have a sense of extreme sobriety in their structure and decorative elements. His works in Milan include the Teatro alla Scala (1776–78), the library of the Brera and the botanical garden (1779), Palazzo Greppi (1772–78), and Palazzo Belgioioso (1772–81); there was also the royal villa of Monza (1780) and the Villa Borromeo at Cassano d'Adda (c. 1780–85).

## Piranesi, Giovanni Battista
### (Maiano di Mestre, 1720–Venice, 1778)
Italian architect and engraver, after a period of training in Venice he went to Rome, in 1740, and spent the rest of his life there, only making short trips to Naples, Pompeii, Herculaneum, and Paestum. He is best known for his engravings, in which his architectural imagination is joined to images of contemporary French models and the direct study of classical antiquity and the principal monuments of Rome, along with fanciful reconstructions and romanticized dreams. As an architect, he made the Aventine complex including the church of S Maria del Priorato, the square near it, and the villa, expressing all his decorative skill in these works. With his extreme interests in topography and the ancient world, Piranesi became an important stimulus for the evolution of Italian neo-classicism.

## Ponti, Gio
### (Milan, 1891–1979)
Having earned his degree in 1921 from the Milan Polytechnic, Ponti worked in the design of furnishings and decorative arts, becoming artistic director of the Richard-Ginori porcelain factory. Between the 1920s and 1930s he took part in the Novecento stylistic movement and made several houses, such as that in Via Randaccio (1925), designed together with Emilio Lancia. In 1928 he founded the architectural and design magazine *Domus*, which he directed

until 1940 and then from 1948 to 1978. In the 1930s he approached the style of Italian rationalism. Among the works of those years are the faculty of physics of the city university in Rome (1935) and the Palazzo of Montecatini in Milan (1938–39). His best-known work of the postwar period is the Pirelli Tower (1957–59). His works include buildings outside Italy, in Europe and South America.

## Pöppelmann, Matthäus Daniel
### (Hereford, 1662–Dresden, 1736)
Thanks to the architect Pöppelmann, Dresden earned the nickname 'Florence on the Elbe'. Augustus II, king of Saxony, entrusted him with the most important constructions in the capital of Saxony at its moment of greatest glory, along with the important 'adjunct' of Warsaw (Augustus was also king of Poland). Pöppelmann was an architect of vast culture: aware of the relative isolation of Dresden, he travelled extensively in Italy, France, and Austria, and kept himself up to date through personal contacts with numerous colleagues. Aside from enlargement of the royal palace and construction of the two enchanting castles outside the city for hunting and amusements, at Moritzburg and Pillnitz, Pöppelmann made one of the great masterpieces of 18th-century baroque architecture, the Zwinger, the vast porticoed enclosure surrounded by pavilions splendidly decorated by sculptures by Balthasar Permoser.

## Portoghesi, Paolo
### (Rome, 1931)
After graduating from the University of Rome in 1957, Portoghesi began intense activity involving historical research, teaching, and professional work destined to make him a key figure within the postmodern debate. By the end of the 1950s, his close study of the architecture of the past had led him to align himself against functionalist rationalism in favour of an historical orientation for the new architectural culture. Joined to his theoretical works were original and unmistakable creations, generated by the synthesis of notions drawn from Oriental architecture, the Gothic, baroque, Jugenstil, and from eclecticism, with compositional and formal elements from modern architecture. The apex of his work was the Mosque and Islamic Culture Centre in Rome (1975–93).

## Prandtauer, Jakob
### (Stanz, Tyrol, 1660–St Pölten, 1726)
A prolific Austrian architect, in 1708 Prandtauer received the official post of director construction in Upper Austria, a region that had been greatly damaged by raiding Turks. He perfected an efficient and innovative architectural model for the reconstruction of the large Benedictine and Augustinian abbeys, making them serve as centres of control over the surrounding territory and also comfortable and elegant residences, sometimes with apartments reserved for the emperor, in addition to their normal religious functions. Eloquent masterpiece in this regard is the abbey of Melk, created by exploiting a granite outcrop above the Danube (1702–38).

## Pugin, A.W.N.
### (London, 1812–Ramsgate, Kent, 1852)
English architect and writer, known for his prominent role in creating the Gothic revival seen as a return to aesthetic truths and constructive values. Numerous buildings were designed in this style, including the House of Parliament, which Pugin made with Charles Barry. Pugin's designs for homes (such as his own house, the Grange, on a cliff at Ramsgate, 1835) were of great importance and made way for the revival of residential architecture continued by Philip Speakman Webb. More important, however, were his writings, such as *Contrasts* (1836).

## Puig i Cadafalch, Josep
### (Mataró, 1869–Barcelona, 1956)
Representative of Catalan modernism, Puig created a personal interpretation of the style, connecting it both to the local folklore tradition and to ideas drawn from contemporary European architecture. His most famous works in Barcelona include the Casa Ametller, Casa Macaya, and Palau Quadras (1906). He has published works of art history and essays on the Catalan Romanesque.

## Raphael (Raffaello Sanzio)
### (Urbino, 1483–Rome, 1520)
Raphael, son of the portraitist and painter Giovanni Santi, while still an adolescent drew attention to his father's workshop because of his talents; at sixteen he was already an inde-

endent master. He began his career in the rtistic culture of Urbino in the wake of Piero ella Francesca, and around 1500 he joined erugino in a close and critical collaboration. is Florentine period (1504–8) was also disnguished by his ability to absorb and rework leas from other artists. In dialogue with ichelangelo and Leonardo, the still young tist achieved a supreme balance between the orrect application of the rules of Renaissance t, the imitation of nature, and the sweetness f expression. In 1508 Pope Julius II called him o Rome and entrusted him with the fresco ecoration of the rooms of his private apartent in the Vatican. The cycle began with the anza della Segnatura (1508–11) and continad with that of Eliodoro (1511–13), with a rogressive passage from harmonically nposed scenes within symmetrical backounds to more dramatic episodes, with plays f evocative light. Raphael also made altareces, portraits, and frescoes. During the apacy of Leo X he was kept busy with decotive works (the Vatican Loggias, La Farsina), and he once again changed his style, nticipating the themes and solutions of comg mannerism.

## ainaldi, Carlo
## Rome, 1611–91)

arlo was the son of the architect Girolamo, om whom he learned an original mixture of annerist and baroque stylistic elements from hich he never succeeded in freeing himself, en though he went on to develop a typically oman style. Rainaldi represents a phase of oman baroque slightly later than that reprented by the three great masters (Bernini, Bormini, and Pietro da Cortona). His name is sociated with three great works: S Maria in ampitelli, the façade of S Andrea della Valle, d the churches in Piazza del Popolo (S Maria Monte Santo and S Maria dei Miracoli). me of his constructions show architectural aracteristics typical of northern Italy and a enic layout that anticipates developments of e late baroque.

## aspall, Manuel Joaquim
## arcelona, 1877–La Garriga, 1937)

inter and watercolourist, Raspall earned his ploma in architecture in Barcelona in 1905 and began working primarily on the design of private homes. He was active in the city of Vallée, where he was responsible for renovation works. His works show the strong influence of the local culture and the Catalan version of art nouveau, known as *modernisme*; his watercolours were exhibited in Barcelona in 1896.

## Rastrelli, Bartolomeo Francesco
## (Paris, *c.* 1700–St Petersburg, 1771)

Having become Russian court artist under Peter the Great, Rastrelli directed the campaign of architectural renovation and construction carried on during the reigns of Elizabeth, Catherine the Great, and Alexander I, creating an unmistakable style that blends Russian typologies with Western ideas from the Renaissance and mannerism. He achieved extraordinary decorative effects in the lively polychromy of the exterior of the Summer Palace (1740–44; destroyed), the Smol'ny monastery (1748–55), the palace of Tsarkoye Selo (1752–56), and the Winter Palace (1753–62).

## Rogers, Richard
## (Florence, 1933)

Rogers studied at the Architectural Association of London and then specialized at Yale in New Haven. His first professional experiences took place between 1963 and 1967 when he was a member of Team 4 Architects, together with his wife, Su, and the Fosters. His tendency to insert formalist and constructivist motifs in his projects, already visible in his last works with the group, became even more marked after his separation from the group and culminated in the project with which he acquired international fame, the Georges Pompidou Centre in Paris (1971–78), made in collaboration with Renzo Piano. In 1977 he opened an office in London, where he continued to work out his personal language, distinguished by the overt display of the structural and operatingplant elements of buildings, negating all traditional sense of a façade, which has made him one of the emblematic exponents of high-tech architecture.

## Rossellino, Bernardo
## (Settignano, Florence, 1409–Florence, 1464)

Student and collaborator of Leon Battista Alberti, Rossellino was active in Tuscany and Rome, and was commissioned by Pope Nicholas V to enlarge the transept and apse of the basilica of St Peter's. His fame is tied to the arrangement of Corsignano (modern-day Pienza), the birthplace of Pope Pius II, to which he applied the Renaissance principles of urbanistics and architecture, making Albertistyle buildings around a trapezoidal square. By way of the fusion of architecture and sculpture he also created a new style of funeral monument that had a large following in Florence.

## Rossi, Aldo
## (Milan, 1931–97)

The fundamental elements in Rossi's formation, aside from his studies at the Milan Polytechnic, from which he graduated in 1959, were his editing of the magazine *Casabella-continuità* between 1955 and 1964 and his studies of Adolf Loos and Etienne-Louis Boullée, which influenced his first works. In the 1960s he began a series of studies on the relationships between architectural typology and urban morphology, collected in the book *L'Architettura della Città* (1966), a text destined to have a great deal of influence on later generations of architects. His theory of the presence of primary elements in the processes of construction of the city with which he affirmed the objective and impersonal character of architecture became a reference point for neo-rationalism. The methodology of his theoretical efforts found fruitful confirmation in the poetic dimension of his design practice, based on always new combinations of traditional and autobiographical architectural elements, earning him numerous commissions and international recognitions.

## Rossi, Carlo
## (Naples, 1775–St Petersburg, 1849)

Born in Italy, Rossi moved to Russia when still very young; he spent most of his working life in St Petersburg. Working in the wake of Giacomo Quarenghi, he modelled the panorama of the new Tsarist capital following the forms of a monumental neo-classicism of a Roman inspiration. Among the most important works he designed are the palace of the General Staff (1819–25), the Alekandrinksy Theatre (1827–32), the Senate house (1824–34), and the Mikhailovsky Palace (1819–23).

## Saarinen, Eliel
### (Rantasalmi, Finland, 1873–Bloomfield, Michigan, 1950)

Eliel Saarinen studied painting and architecture in Helsinki, where he was active as an architect from 1896 to 1923, the year in which he moved to the United States. His youthful works, made in collaboration with the architects Herman Gesellius and Armas Lindgren, show signs of the National Romantic style that, influenced by English models, was presented as an alternative to the dominant classicism. The collaboration among the three architects ended in 1904 when Saarinen won the competition for the main train station of Helsinki (1904–14) on the basis of a design he created personally on a rationalist base influenced by German models and destined to become a primary model for railroad architecture in that period. During those same years he became greatly interested in urban planning, which from then on was an inseparable part of his architectural projects, as in the complex of the Cranbrook Academy of Art (1926–41), a synthesis of his romantic naturalism and the American pioneering tradition. His son Eero trained in his Ann Arbor studio and continued his activity.

## Sacchetti, Giovanni Battista
### (Turin, 1690–Madrid, 1764)

Student and follower of Filippo Juvarra, Sacchetti made the royal palace of Madrid (1738–64), reducing the dimensions of Juvarra's original design and drawing inspiration from Bernini's designs for the Louvre. Sacchetti also made the garden façade of the palace of S Ildefonso, called La Granja, near Segovia, based on a design by Juvarra.

## Sagrera, Guillem
### (Felanitx, Mallorca?–Naples, 1454)

Catalan architect and sculptor active in the sphere of the Catalan Gothic tradition, although blended with influences from Burgundy, Sagrera worked in the Palma de Mallorca Cathedral (1420–47) and in the Llotja (market exchange; 1445). Documents indicate his presence from 1449 at the court of Alfonso of Aragon in Naples, where he directed work on the Castel Nuovo, designing the towers and the great hall.

## Salvi, Nicola
### (Rome, 1697–1751)

Salvi participated with Fuga, De' Sanctis, and other architects in the urbanistic reworking of Rome in the first half of the 18th century. His major undertaking, on which he worked from 1732 until his death, was the Trevi Fountain. That exuberant expression of Bernini-type theatricality, composed of crags, statues, and marine divinities, has come to be associated with the façades of Palladian-style palaces.

## Sanctis, Francesco de'
### (Rome, 1693–1740)

Architect of a certain importance, De' Sanctis was part of the rebirth of Rome in the first half of the 18th century, making the façade of SS Trinità dei Pellegrini (1723). His name is most closely associated with the Spanish Steps (1723–26), an impressive and aristocratic architectural undertaking with great scenic effects.

## Sangallo, Antonio da, the younger
### (Florence, 1484–Rome, 1546)

Nephew of Giuliano Sangallo and of Antonio the elder, he went to Rome in 1503, where he studied the models of antiquity while visiting the worksites of Bramante. Dating from this period are the church of S Maria di Loreto (after 1507) and Palazzo Baldassini (1510–15). With the patronage of the Farnese family he began his independent activity in 1523, working on the family's Rome palace (completed by Michelangelo) and the villas of Capodimonte and Caprarola (1515), the latter reworked later by Vignola. Well known and admired in Rome, he directed the worksite of St Peter's on the death of Raphael (1520), making a model severely criticized by Michelangelo. He was equally well known for his activity as a military engineer, inspecting the castles of the Papal States and working in particular on S Patrizio in Orvieto (1527–37) and the Fortezza da Basso in Florence (1534–37).

## Sangallo, Antonio da, the elder
### (Florence, c. 1455–1534)

Antonio collaborated with his brother Giuliano until Giuliano's death (1516). He also had the opportunity to express his own original ideas, which he did in ponderous masses of buildings that show the heavy influence of Bra-

mante. He was also known as a military engineer. His most important work was the dome Church of the Madonna di S Biagio at Montepulciano, a Greek-cross building that among the most original experiments with the theme of the central-planned building from the early 16th century.

## Sangallo, Giuliano da
### (Florence, c. 1445–1516)

Outstanding architect within the sphere of Renaissance culture, military engineer, and sculptor, Giuliano da Sangallo proved himself one of the most creative and original personalities of his time, both as heir to the tradition of Brunelleschi and as creator of innovative architectural forms. A stay in Rome in 1465 offered him the opportunity to study the buildings of the ancient city, of which he made detailed sketches in his *Notebooks*. He used this learning in the fecund and heterogeneous activity he began in 1480 and applied it to a variety of forms. As military engineer he worked on the fortification of Colle Val d'Elsa and on the fortresses of Ostia, Arezzo, and Sansepolcro his designs for the sacristy of Santo Spirito (begun 1489) and the Palazzo Gondi in Florence (begun 1490) lead back instead to the Brunelleschi tradition. In the Medici Villa Poggio a Caiano (after 1480) he created the architectural epitome of the Renaissance villa both in terms of its citations of ancient culture and in its layout and structure, which reflect the humanist yearning for a synthesis between architecture and surrounding space. His plan for the church of S Maria delle Carceri at Prato (begun 1485) shows he was involved in the theme of the central-planned building.

## Sanmicheli, Michele
### (Verona, 1484–1559)

Veronese architect and urban planner, Sanmicheli trained in Rome and was named master builder of the cathedral of Orvieto in 1509. He returned to Verona after the Sack of Rome (1527) and began working for the Republic of Venice, coming to represent, together with Falconetto and Sansovino, that movement toward the renewal of Veneto architecture that was open to Roman influence and thus introduced classical motifs with a mannerist interpretation. In the aristocratic palaces he made r leading Veronese families, he altered the proportional schemes of Bramante in favour of a greater exaltation of chromatic-luministic values. At the same time he performed fecund activity for Venice as a military architect, designing fortifications from the area of Padua to Dalmatia. Outstanding among all his works are the gates he designed for the new circle of walls around Verona (begun 1530), which blended defensive exigencies with stately elegance.

## Sansovino, Jacopo (Jacopo Tatti)
### (Florence, 1486–Venice, 1570)
One of the leaders in sculpture and architecture in Venice for many decades, Sansovino was among the greatest interpreters of the broad, serene, and solid classicism of the High Renaissance. Most of his early works in Florence were marble sculptures, comparable to the model of Andrea Sansovino, from whom he took his name, and related to the youthful works of Michelangelo. It was during the course of a long stay in Rome (1516–27) that he moved more decidedly toward architecture. He fled Rome after the sack of the city (1527), planning to go to France, but almost by accident he stopped in Venice, which became his adopted city. Involved in the renovation of the city promoted by Doge Gritti, he soon became the city's official architect and as such the author of buildings of great symbolic value, in the most important sites of the city (Procuratie, Loggetta del Campanile, Libreria Marciana, the interior of the Doge's Palace, the Mint). Although most of his activity was as a designer, Sansovino also worked as a sculptor in Venice, showing a preference for bronze with creations that anticipated the meticulous works of mannerism.

## Sant'Elia, Antonio
### (Como, 1888–Monfalcone, 1916)
After technical studies in Como and a period working as a master builder in Milan, Sant'Elia took courses at the Brera Academy and earned a degree as professor of architectural design at the Bologna Academy of Fine Arts in 1912. He opened his own studio in Milan and in 1914 joined the futurist movement, for which he wrote the text of the 'Manifesto of Futurist Architecture'. From a formal matrix still tied to

models from the Vienna Secession, as in the Elisi Villa (1931) at San Maurizio, near Como, the only work Sant'Elia made, he later developed a volumetric and spatial style at the theoretical-design level that was a precursor of the later constructivist movement as well as some lines of development of the modern movement. The more than three hundred designs he made, most of them between 1913 and 1914, give visionary form and image to a utopian metropolis of the future, with terraced skyscrapers, large multilevel arteries for vehicular traffic, and daring monumental buildings that could never have been constructed.

## Santini, Giovanni
### (Prague, 1667–1723)
Member of a family of artists of Italian origin, Santini elaborated a highly personal style that blended baroque elements with the lexicon of Gothic architecture, a result of his training as a restorer of medieval monasteries destroyed by the Hussites. In the construction of new buildings he presented highly original forms, from the triangular layout of Panenské Brezenay (1706–7) to the castle at Chlumec nad Cidlinou in eastern Bohemia (1721–23) to his masterpiece, the sanctuary of St John Nepomuk at Zeléna Hora near Z'dar (1720–22).

## Schindler, Rudolph
### (Vienna, 1887–Los Angeles, 1953)
In 1911 Schindler got his diploma from the Imperial Institute of Engineering in Vienna. During that period he also attended the architecture school of Adolf Loos and the art school directed by Otto Wagner. While following the European avant-garde movements he also studied the Chicago school and the works of Frank Lloyd Wright, which had been presented in the so-called Wasmuth portfolio, published in Germany in 1910. Schindler spent a brief period in the firm of Ottenheimer, Stern and Reichert before going to work, in 1917, in Wright's studio, first at Oak Park and then at Taliesin. In 1922 he opened his own studio in Los Angeles. One of his most important works was the Lovell Beach House at Newport Beach (1925–26). Other important works by Schindler include the Kallis House in Hollywood (1945), the Presburger House in Studio City (1945), and the Tilscher House in Bel Air (1949).

## Schinkel, Karl Friedrich
### (Neuruppin, 1781–Berlin, 1841)
A student of David Gilly, Schinkel worked first in painting and then stage design. Following a trip to Italy in 1803 he was drawn to classical, especially Hellenic, architecture. His first important architectural work was the Royal Guardhouse in Berlin (1816–17) with its severe Doric colonnade in front of a cubic mass derived from the rationalism of Ledoux. The rationalistic treatment of elements drawn from Greek art was the defining trait of his next two works, the Royal Theatre (1812–21) and the Museum of Berlin (1822). In 1826 he entered the service of the future king William IV, for whom he made the Charlottenhof residence at Potsdam in a neo-Doric style influenced by the aesthetics of the English picturesque movement, which Schinkel translated in the asymmetry of the composition and its relationship to the natural setting.

## Serlio, Sebastiano
### (Bologna, 1475–Fontainebleau, 1554/55)
Better known as a theoretician than as an architect, Serlio moved to Rome in 1515, where he worked under Peruzzi and came in contact with the architectural culture of Bramante and Raphael. He left Rome following the sack (1527) and moved to Venice, staying there until 1539 and publishing part of his treatise on architecture (eight volumes, 1537–75). Invited to France by Francis I, he was at Fontainebleau in 1541, where he assumed the title of chief architect of one of the most celebrated architectural undertakings in France. He spent the rest of his life there, publishing the other parts of his treatise, which had an enormous influence throughout Europe, presenting the classical Roman tradition, the 'pictoricism' of the Veneto region, and the decorative style of France. A true repertory of architectural forms and typologies, it served as an inexhaustible source for mannerist architects.

## Siza, Alvaro
### (Matozinhos, Portugal, 1933)
After architecture studies at the Escola Superior de Belas Artes in Porto and a period of apprenticeship with Fernando Tàvora, Siza opened his own studio in 1958, on the occasion of his first professional commissions. His very first

creations made immediately clear that his was an aesthetic-critical attitude far too original to be fit into any paradigm of reference. His language employs formal elements drawn from a wide variety of very different sources, all of which, however, lead back to the period of the flowering of modern architecture, combined with a close attention to topography and an effort to match architecture to environment. This has earned him world fame and increasingly important commissions, often outside Portugal. His most important recent work was the Portuguese Pavilion for the 1998 Lisbon exhibition. Together with his intense professional activity, Siza is also an active critic and theoretician and has presented his ideas in many essays and interviews.

## Sommaruga, Giuseppe
### (Milan, 1869–1917)

Sommaruga was a student of Camillo Boito at the Brera Academy and responded to Boito's historicist position by following an architectural theory directed toward the most innovative solutions of the period, related to the poetics of art nouveau. Sommaruga's work has been compared to that of the Viennese artists of the period, but it was distinguished by a greater material sensibility to surfaces, with abundant and rigorous decoration. Although it has a 19th-century layout, Palazzo Castiglioni in Milan (1901–4) achieved notable expressive results in its alternation of the traditional relationships between full and empty spaces. Sommaruga made many works for the Milan middle class, from the Villa Romeo to the Grand Hotel Tre Croci at Campo dei Fiori near Varese (1908–12) to the works made for the Sacconi family at Sarnico (1907–12).

## Soufflot, Jacques-Germain
### (Irancy, Yonne, 1713–Paris, 1780)

Having trained principally in Rome (1731–38), Soufflot moved to Lyons, where he made numerous buildings and, having been admitted to the academy, contributed to the increased attention being given to the constructive and technical solutions of the Gothic. In 1749 he returned to Italy in the retinue of the brother of Madame de Pompadour and sketched the temples of Paestum, beginning the critical revision of the architectural orders as they had

been established by Vitruvius. In 1755, having been put in charge of the *Bâtiments du Roi* and made director of work on the Louvre, he designed the church of Ste Geneviève (today's Pantheon), which constituted the manifesto of the new archaeological and technical classicism, thus favouring the development of new French architectural theories.

## Souto de Moura, Eduardo
### (Porto, Portugal, 1952)

Between 1974 and 1979 Souto de Moura studied architecture at the Escola Superior de Belas Artes in Porto, while at the same time working with Alvaro Siza. He began his professional career on his own in 1980 with the design of the covered market in Braga, the language of which revealed the brutalist teaching of his master, Fernando Tàvora. In later works he abandoned brutalism in favour of an original purism, a synthesis of regional building traditions and abstract elements drawn from the works of Mies van der Rohe and Barragán. This language, which he applied to various luxurious residential buildings made in Porto in the 1980s, helped him win many national and international competitions. In addition to his activity as an architect, Souto de Moura is also an active designer, with furniture designs in Portugal and elsewhere, and is also a teacher, first at the Escola Superior de Belas Artes and more recently in the architecture faculty of the University of Porto.

## Stirling, James
### (Glasgow, 1926–London, 1992)

After studies at the University of Liverpool and a period of apprenticeship in the London office of Lyons, Israel and Ellis, Stirling began his professional activity, which can be divided into three main periods. During the first, which covers the years 1956 to 1963, he worked in collaboration with James Gowan on a series of buildings with an unmistakable brutalist language. He began a period working alone in 1964, making large university buildings and taking part in several competitions with designs that reveal a receptive dialogue with the context. In 1970 he began his third period, working in collaboration with Michael Wilford, which led to the commission for the Neue Staatsgalerie of Stuttgart (1977–84). One of

the architect's most important and controversial projects, it introduced the version of design based on a strong expressive language and eclectic experimentation, that he was to apply in later projects.

## Sullivan, Louis
### (Boston, 1856–Chicago, 1924)

After a brief period of studies, first at Massachusetts Institute of Technology and then the Ecole des Beaux-Arts in Paris, Sullivan joined the office of Dankmar Adler in 1879, becoming a full partner in 1883. In 1886 he began work on the Auditorium Building in Chicago. Although the synthesis between structure and decorations was not completely successful, Sullivan's philosophy was made clear, most of all his desire to make the architectural form result from the harmonic and organic growth of its various parts. In later buildings the expressive unity that was lacking in the façade of the Auditorium Building was achieved through the rhythmic arrangement of equal stories, accentuated by vertical openings and minimal decoration. After Adler's retirement, in 1895, Sullivan received fewer commissions. Even so, he made the great Schlesinger and Meyer warehouse in Chicago (today Carson Pirie Scott & Co.), the work in which his style, synthesized in the famous statement 'Form should follow function', finds its fulfilment in the use of the support skeleton as the basis of the composition.

## Tange, Kenzo
### (Imabari, Japan, 1913)

After earning an engineering degree from the University of Tokyo in 1938 Tange began working in the office of Kunio Mayekawa, a former collaborator of Le Corbusier. He branched out on his own in 1946, making a series of important projects destined to bring about a renewal of Japanese architecture by freeing it from Western models. The works he made during the 1950s were distinguished by a symbolic rereading of the Japanese architectural tradition joined to an open-minded application of the modern language. With the increase in interest in urbanistic problems in the 1960s, Tange made several large-scale projects, including the plan for the city of Tokyo (1960) – perhaps his most important work – and buildings with

ng urban impact that made clear his
roach to the style of the Metabolism Group.
gained fame in 1964 for the arenas he made
the Olympic Games in Tokyo, leading to
missions from throughout the world. The
e of these later works has been less charac-
stic and more international.

## t, Bruno
(nigsberg, 1880–Istanbul, 1938)
t trained at the construction school in
nigsberg and opened his own studio in
lin in 1909. He immediately attracted great
ntion with his Monument of Steel Pavilion
he Leipzig exhibition in 1913 and with the
shaus (1914) at the first exhibition of the
utscher Werkbund in Cologne. The latter
rk brought him into contact with the poet
utopian Paul Scheerbart, whose ideas for
sarchitektur greatly influenced Taut, so
ch that they led, during World War I, to the
ef but intense phase of his theoretical
earch, destined to be the guiding light to
more radical avant-garde wing of German
ressionism. In 1920 he moved closer to
onalism and in later years was kept busy
igning large works of public housing to
ch he applied his Tayloristic theories of
ctional and economic architecture, theo-
s that led to the realization of some of the
st interesting works of 20th-century archi-
ure, such as the *Siedlungen* of Britz and of
ilendorf. He carried on intense teaching
vity between 1930 and 1933, when for polit-
l reasons he emigrated first to Japan and
n to Turkey.

## ragni, Giuseppe
(eda, Italy, 1904–Como, 1943)
1929 Terragni earned his diploma from the
an Polytechnic and while still very young
ame a member of both Gruppo 7 and
AR (Movimento Italiano per l'Architettura
ionale), immediately adhering to rational-
and, thanks to his strongly classical bent,
tributing to freeing it from the dictates of
European modern movement. Terragni's
disputed masterpiece is the Casa del Fascio
Como (1932–36), in which he made clear
independent abstract style that distin-
shed his personal language. His highly orig-
l adhesion to classical modernity, halfway

between academic classicism and orthodox
rationalism, based on an astute elaboration of
the best aspects of Italian 20th-century poetics and the painting of Giorgio de Chirico,
was destined in the 1960s to influence the
rational architecture of Aldo Rossi and the
New York Five.

## Toledo, Juan Bautista de
(Madrid, *c.* 1515–67)
Trained in Rome, Toledo worked in Naples,
making the church of S Giacomo degli Spagnoli
for the Spanish viceroy. Called back to Spain in
1599 by Philip II, he worked on his most
important work, the monastery-palace of the
Escorial (1563–67), completed after his death
by Juan de Herrera. Despite later changes, he
was responsible for the original layout of the
grandiose complex, which was made using
severe Renaissance forms. An example of the
so-called austere style, it became a symbol of
the Counter-Reformation rigour of the Spanish monarchy.

## Tomé, Narciso de
(Toro ? 1694–Toledo, 1742)
Member of a family of Spanish baroque architects and sculptors, Narciso de Tomé joined
his father and brothers in 1715 in work on the
façade of the university of Valladolid. He is
remembered most of all for the so-called El
Transparente in the cathedral of Toledo
(1721–32), the most astonishing work of the
Spanish baroque. It can be seen as a chapel
without walls installed within the Gothic interior by means of theatrical artifice: a phantasmagorical work of spatial illusionism, its many
layers of imagery illuminated by a metaphysi-
cal light, the whole populated by angels.

## Utzon, Jørn
(Copenhagen, 1918)
Utzon studied at the Copenhagen Academy of
Arts. Influenced by the ideas of Alvar Aalto
and Gunnar Asplund, in whose offices he
worked for a certain period, as well as by those
of Frank Lloyd Wright, whom he met during a
stay in the United States in 1949, he was soon
drawn to an organic conception of architecture.
In 1950 he opened a studio in Copenhagen
and put into practice his ideas for a progressive
architecture that takes its teaching from nature

and makes use of new materials suitable for
specific demands. He applied these ideas to a
series of very different projects, all distinguished by imagination, vitality, and technical
expertise. In 1957 he won the first prize in the
competition for the Sydney Opera House,
which became his unquestioned masterpiece,
the work responsible for his world fame. To
work on it he moved to Australia in 1962; in
1966 he returned to Denmark, leaving completion of the work to other architects. He has
since made many works inspired by the construction methods he first applied in Sydney.

## Valadier, Giuseppe
(Rome, 1762–1839)
Architect, archaeologist, and urban planner,
Valadier was one of the leading exponents of
Italian neo-classicism. Active in Rome and in
the Papal States, Valadier's adhesion to the
classical revival went beyond erudite ambitions in the will to recuperate the artistic
splendour and vitality of the Roman baroque.
He designed urbanistic projects, some of
which remained on paper, that had an important impact on the city, from the general plan
for the public walkway through the ancient
forums (1811) to the arrangement of the
square at St John Lateran (1822). His most
important project was the reworking of Piazza
del Popolo, in which he made use of neo-classical elements but did not overlook the
baroque scenographic tradition in the stairs
that climb the Pincian Hill.

## Van de Velde, Henry
(Antwerp, 1863–Zurich, 1957)
Van de Velde studied painting at the Academy
of Fine Arts in Antwerp and then in Paris,
where he met impressionist and symbolist
artists whose vision of space seemed to indicate new routes for architecture. The writings
of Ruskin and Morris directed him toward a
social vision of the work of art and led him to
abandon painting in favour of furniture
design. In 1896 he made his first work of architecture, Bloemenwerf, a house in the Brussels
suburb of Uccle, in which he displayed the
primary characteristics of his artistic thinking: awareness of the functions of constructions and of the value of use, along with the
rejection of naturalistic ornaments or stylistic

elements from the past. The fluent forms and curving lines of his furnishings and his architecture, appreciated most highly in Germany, made Van de Velde one of the primary exponents of art nouveau.

## Vanvitelli, Luigi
### (Naples, 1700–Caserta, 1773)

Architect, engineer, painter, and stage designer, son of the famous Dutch landscape artist Gaspar van Wittel, Vanvitelli got his training in Rome, where he made both artistic and scientific studies. Under the influence of Juvarra, he assimilated the classical style, the late baroque tradition, as well as the Roman baroque, thus evolving the theatrical style typical of his mature works. He was active in Rome, in the Marches, and in Naples; he was summoned to Naples in 1751 by Charles II and worked on the design of the royal palace at Caserta, his true masterpiece, marking the passage from the late baroque language to forms that were more sober, rigorous, and balanced.

## Vasari, Giorgio
### (Arezzo, 1511–Florence, 1574)

Painter, architect, and writer – author of the *Vite de' più eccellenti architetti, pittori e scultori italiani* ('Lives of the Most Excellent Italian Architects, Painters, and Sculptors') – Vasari is an outstanding figure on the panorama of Italian late mannerism. His training, based on early Florentine mannerism and the works of Raphael and Michelangelo with notions drawn from the Venetian setting, gave him an eclectic and erudite background that found fertile terrain in Rome (pictorial cycle in the Palazzo della Cancelleria) and led him to write the first edition (1550) of his *Lives*. In the service of Cosimo I de' Medici in Florence he became the primary creator of the celebratory exterior of the duchy, which by then was in a period of decline, by reworking the Uffizi, with its scenographic attachment between Piazza della Signoria and Palazzo Pitti; restructuring and decorating Palazzo Vecchio (1563–72); and most of all giving to the press the second edition of his *Lives* (1568), a milestone in art history and biography in which it is not difficult to make out the loss of energy and sense of decline in Florentine art in the period after Michelangelo.

## Vauban, Sébastien Lepestre de
### (St-Léger-de Foucheret, 1633–Paris, 1707)

Architect and writer in the service of Louis XIV, from 1653 on he was dedicated to the creation of fortresses and strongholds in defence of the French state, works in which the art of the fortification reached a high level of technical and artistic perfection. Among his most interesting works are the fortifications of Neuf-Brisach (1698–1705 ) and the defensive walls of Arras, La Rochelle, and St Malo.

## Venturi, Robert
### (Philadelphia, 1925)

Venturi studied at Princeton University in New Jersey and worked in the studios of Eero Saarinen and Louis I. Kahn before setting up an office, together with several associates, in 1958. In 1967 his wife, Denise Scott-Brown, joined the studio, from then on working together with Venturi on many projects and on the theoretical writing to which he owes much of his world fame. The studio, known as Venturi, Scott-Brown and Associates since 1989, has created many very different structures over the course of the years, but all have had in common the attempt to translate motifs from the psychology of perception into an autonomous and deeply American architectural language. This led to the intriguing and polemical invitation to consider commercial architecture, with its elements of advertising and neon, as a source to draw from in the design of contemporary architecture, a notion that became a key concept within postmodernism.

## Vignola, Jacopo (Giacomo Barozzi)
### (Vignola, 1507–Rome, 1573)

Trained in Emilia as a perspective painter, Vignola turned to architecture early on, influenced by Serlio's treatise and Renaissance works. He settled in Rome and became the favourite architect of the Farnese family, making for them the family palace and the villa at Caprarola (begun 1559). For Pope Julius III he worked on the Villa Giulia (begun 1550) in which the articulation of the architectural organism is sensitive to the surrounding natural space. He made the Italian-style garden and park of Villa Lante at Bagnaia (begun 1556) as well as numerous religious buildings,

of which the most important is the late chu of S Anna dei Palafrenieri (*c.* 1570) at the V ican. His masterpiece was the Church of Gesù (begun 1568), which inaugurated single-hall church made to serve the Coun Reformation's special needs in terms of prea ing and the liturgy.

## Viollet-le-Duc, Eugène Emmanuel
### (Paris, 1814–Lausanne, 1879)

When only twenty-four Viollet-le-Duc v given the important task of restoring Madeleine at Vézelay, an undertaking so followed by restoration work in Ste Chape and Notre-Dame in Paris, the cathedral Narbonne and St Denis. In 1853 he was ma inspector general of diocesan monuments a began work on his most important restorati the historical city of Carcassonne. In this followed two fundamental ideas, the desire bring to light the authentic monument a the conviction that the aesthetic value medieval art, and most especially Gothic is a matter of its technical value and archit tural inventiveness. He was the most prom nent exponent of the Gothic revival in Fran thus going against the reigning academic cl sicism, and he saw French Gothic architect as the model for a national style, emphasiz its constructional rationalism and in so do for the first time formulating the equati between aesthetics and technique that wo be fundamental to modern architecture.

## Vitruvius (Marcus Vitruvius Pollio)
### (1st century BC)

Roman architect and treatise writer, Vitruv is the author of *De architectura*, the only su treatise to survive from antiquity. In the volumes of that work he analyses the ent subject of architecture, from city planning the Greek orders to waterworks and build materials. Following the work's rediscov during the Renaissance the text by Vitruv constituted the model for the treatises writt during that period, from Alberti to Palladi

## Wagner, Otto
### (Penzing, Vienna, 1841–Vienna, 1918)

After studies at the Technische Hochschule Vienna and at the Bauakademie in Berl Wagner completed his training at the Acade

Fine Arts in Vienna (1861–63). He made
merous works in Vienna using a robust,
trained classical style, soon becoming one of
best-known professional architects in the
y and receiving many public and academic
mmissions. He expressed his ideas in *Mod-
e Architektur* (1896), calling for the need
a new approach to architecture and for-
lating the principles of an architecture gen-
ted by functional aims and expressed by
ing attention to building principles and to
materials used. He put these theories to
in the Post Office Savings Bank in Vienna
04). Wagner's teaching, writing, and build-
s had a strong influence on much of Euro-
n avant-garde architecture.

## bb, Philip Speakman
## xford, 1831–Worth, 1915)

chitect, interior designer, and artisan-artist,
bb served an apprenticeship in an adver-
ng agency before being hired by the archi-
t G. E. Street, through whom he met his
ure friend and employer William Morris. In
56 he began work as an independent archi-
t in London and later designed Red House
Morris at Bexley Heath, Kent (1859–60). In
52 he became an associate of the recently
nded Morris, Marshall, Faulkner and Com-
ny, for which he made interior designs,
luding furniture, tiles, and stained glass,
activity he carried on even after leaving
company, in 1875. He was then active in
preservation of historical buildings, per-
ting a technique for preventing the aging of
ls by replacing old materials with new con-
uction materials. Webb was one of the most
portant members of the Domestic revival in
gland. In his residences and country houses
sought to achieve a similarity to the late
dieval style, and did so without falling into
re historicism. He designed furniture, jew-
y, glassware, carpets, and furnishings. Most
the wallpaper and fabric designs sold by
lliam Morris were done by Webb.

## od, John, Jr
## ath, 1728–82)

ving worked with his father, John (known as
od of Bath), on the London Circus (begun
4), John Wood, Jr, is known for the creation
he Royal Crescent (1767–75), a residential

complex shaped much like a curving amphithe-
atre around a large lawn, with a giant order of
Ionic columns. The complex had a great deal of
influence on developments in English picturesque architecture.

## Wren, Christopher
## (East Knoyle, Wiltshire, 1632–Hampton Court, 1723)

The most important and famous English
architect of his time, Wren had a scientific
background, which, as he himself stated, was
reflected in his architectural work. Named in
1657 professor of astronomy of London, Wren
carried on activity that ranged from astronomy to physics to engineering, with inventions, theories, and experiments in a period
when science was affirming itself across
Europe. Among the founders of the Royal
Society, Wren decided, following the Great
Fire of London (1666), to specialize in architecture. Member of the royal commission for
the reconstruction of the city, he was named
superintendent general by the king and created plans for the rebuilding of many
churches, outstanding among them St Paul's
Cathedral (1675–1710). Aside from their
mathematical proportions, the hallmark of
Wren's work is a profound and measured
rationality that draws inspiration from both
the classical and French neo-classical, pro-
ducing original monuments that created the
standard model for a formal language that is
associated with the British aristocracy.

## Wright, Frank Lloyd
## (Richland Center, Wisconsin, 1867–Phoenix, Arizona, 1959)

After a short period studying engineering at
the University of Wisconsin, Wright entered
the Adler and Sullivan studio in 1888, collaborating with them for six years. During that
period he completed his training, which came
to blend the individualistic ideology of the
American frontier with a love of nature and
notions from the shingle style as well as Japanese architecture. All this contributed to the
development of an 'organic' ideal, anticlassical
and anti-European, leading him to seek out a
form of architectural expression with genuine
American bases. The professional career he
began in 1893 was destined to last more than

seventy years, during which the incessant
changes of forms and the development of an
endless variety of ideas evoked the myth of
the American pioneer forever looking for
something new to conquer. Wright's individualistic language did not generate students,
but he did have many imitators, and he influenced the most disparate forms of architecture. The results of his continuous experimentation are, among many others, the series
of prairie houses, the later Usonian houses,
and finally the spatial continuum he created by
the union of the spiral and the circle in the
Guggenheim Museum, New York (1943–59).

## Wyatt, James
## (Burton Constable, Staffordshire, 1747–Marlborough, Wiltshire, 1813)

An English architect, Wyatt trained in Italy and
rose to fame for his design of the Pantheon in
Oxford Street, London, becoming a popular
architect. He made classical-style buildings on
the model of those by the Adam brothers
(Heaton Hall near Manchester, 1772) and
purely neo-classical residences, such as Castle-
coole at Fermanagh (1790–98), reaching the
apex of his inventive originality in the extraordinary neo-Gothic country home of Fonthill
Abbey (1795–1807), built for William Beckford and partially destroyed.

## Zumthor, Peter
## (Basel, 1943)

After apprenticeship as a carpenter-cabinet-
maker, Zumthor studied interior architecture
at the Schule für Gestaltung in Basel and furniture design at the Pratt Institute in New
York. Back in Switzerland he worked as a consultant for the office overseeing the preservation of monuments in the Graubünden Canton. In 1979 he opened his own studio in
Haldenstein. His first works showed an affin-
ity with Italian rational architecture. With
time he developed his own, thoroughly original style, in which the controlled use of materials, building elements, light, and space permitted him to create works of high quality
and sensitivity. He has attracted much interest at the international level. His more important works include the exhibition space
'Topographie des Terrors' in Berlin (1993) and
the thermal baths at Vals (1991–96).

# Glossary

**Abacus:** uppermost part or division of the capital of a column, usually shaped like a parallelepiped; the architrave rests on it.

**Abbey:** collection of buildings, such as a church, cloisters, and guest rooms, that compose a monastery complex ruled by an abbot.

**Abutment:** the part of an architectural structure, as an arch, that directly receives the thrust or pressure of weight.

**Aisle:** corridor or passageway. In a church, the aisles run parallel to the nave.

**Ajimez:** architectural form created by two horseshoe arches paired at the sides of a central column.

**Alfiz:** rectangular panel that frames an arch, usually horseshoe-shaped.

**Altar:** in antiquity, a raised structure composed of a wooden plank or stone on which sacrifices were offered. In Christian religion, the altar is used for the celebration of the Mass; initially made of wood, altars were later made of stone, marble, or other materials.

**Ambo:** raised platform used by the reader in a church, later replaced by a pulpit.

**Ambulatory:** a walkway, usually covered, in a church; the passage around the apse in a basilican church; the space behind the choir in a Gothic church.

**Apse:** an architectural structure, semicircular or polygonal in plan, covered by a vault. In Christian churches it is usually located at the end of a central nave and sometimes also of aisles.

**Arcade:** a series of arches, often supporting a wall, with their columns or piers. A *blind*

*arcade* is an arcade set against a wall without openings in the arches.

**Arch:** usually curved architectural member spanning an opening and serving as support. According to the shape of the curve, arches are identified by a variety of names, including round arches, pointed or ogee arches, trefoil, lancet, basket-handle, or Tudor arches, or horseshoe arches, typical of Arab architecture. A *rampant arch* is an arch in which one abutment is higher than the other. *Hanging arches* are tall blind arches, often reaching the roofline.

**Architrave:** the lowest division of an entablature; a horizontal beam supported by columns.

**Archivolt:** moulding or cornice, bare or decorated, that follows the contour of an arch, whether on the outside face (lintel) or on the inside (intrados).

**Ashlar:** squared, even-faced block of stone.

**Attic:** in classical architecture, the part of a building above the main order on a façade. This area can often become a separate storey of the building.

**Azulejo:** terracotta or majolica glazed tiles in bright colours, used for floors and both interior and exterior wall dressings. Of Arabic origin, their use spread in Spain beginning in the 13th century.

**Baptistery:** a part of a church or a separate building near a church in which baptismal rites are performed.

**Barbican:** from the Arabic Persian *bahhana* (a fortified gallery), a defensive structure in front of a gate, such as a tower, an outer defensive work, a reinforced area on the

internal part of a wall, most of all in medie[val] and Renaissance fortresses.

**Barchessa:** a covered storage space attach[ed] to a farm house; the word is used for t[he] bodies forming the wings of Palladian vill[as] which usually function as service areas.

**Basilica:** Roman building with a rectangu[lar] layout made to serve a public function. T[he] Roman building was the source of the Chr[is]tian basilica, which is divided lengthwise [by] columns or piers into a nave and aisles, t[he] nave usually being higher than the aisl[es] The nave in a basilica terminates in a rou[nd] area called the apse.

**Bay:** a unit of space established by archite[c]tural members, such as the space betwe[en] two support elements (columns, pillars). [In] Romanesque and Gothic churches, a bay [is] the space delimited by four columns or p[il]lars supporting a vault.

**Benedictine, or stepped, choir:** choir flank[ed] by rectangular areas of decreasing size.

**'Bernadine' plan:** cruciform basilican p[lan] with a nave and two aisles, projecti[ng] transept, choir, and flat-ended side chape[ls]

**Bow window (also bay window):** a wind[ow] forming a recess in a room while also p[ro]jecting beyond the exterior wall, in so do[ing] increasing the amount of light.

**Brise-soleil:** shutter to block sunlight.

**Buttress:** a support element designed [to] strengthen a wall by countering the thrust [of] a vault or arch.

**Capital:** architectural element that crown[s a] vertical support element (column, pilaster, [or] pier) and is thus located beneath a horiz[ontal] lintel, entablature, or arcade. It is composed of a lower part (echinus), often decorated, and a simpler upper part (abacus). The basic types of capitals are the Doric, composed of a square abacus resting on a circular echinus; Ionic, with a generally ornate echinus ending in spiral volutes and a somewhat flat abacus; Corinthian, a bell-shaped one decorated by flowers and leaves; Tuscan, similar to the Doric, with wider and lower echinus; and composite, made up of Ionic elements (volutes) and Corinthian (leaves). There are also crocket, or hooked, capitals, Gothic capitals decorated with stylized leaves.

**Cathedra:** seat or throne made of wood, marble, or ivory, often decorated with inlays and bas-relief, located behind the altar at the end of the apse and used by the bishop during religious functions. Its presence creates a cathedral.

**Cathedral:** from the presence of the bishop's throne, or *cathedra*; the principal church of a diocese, the church where a bishop officiates.

**Cell:** a compartment, most especially one of the four triangular divisions of a vault.

**Cenotaph:** a sepulchral monument.

**Centring:** the temporary wooden structure built to support an arch or vault during construction.

**Chancel:** the part of the church with the altar and with spaces reserved for the clergy and the singers in the choir.

**Chapel:** a small room used for worship. A chapel can be isolated or included within a larger architectural complex. In most cases numerous chapels, each with an altar, are arranged along the length of a nave or aisle or around the transept.

**Chapter house:** the large room in a convent, monastery, or cathedral in which the chapter meets (the canons or members of the religious order); in monasteries and convents it usually faces a large cloister.

**Chevet:** the far end of a church, beyond the transept and including the choir, apse, and ambulatory. It can have a variety of plans and in Gothic architecture often includes radiating chapels.

**Choir:** term taken from ancient Greek drama (*chorus*); in a Christian church it is the area reserved for cantors and the clergy, usually composed of wooden stalls often carved or inlaid with a reading stand for the choristers. Today the term indicates the area included between the transept and the apse or the zone of the church located behind the main altar. According to its shape it can be ambulatory, stepped or Benedictine, or triconch.

**Ciborium:** a canopy located over the altar in Christian basilicas supported by four columns or pillars; a vessel used to hold the host.

**Cimborio:** Spanish word for the cylindrical or octagonal bodies used as the base of a dome.

**Circus:** in British usage, an open area at a street junction or intersection or a group of buildings arranged around such a space, which may then serve as a public garden.

**Clerestory:** the 'clear storey' in a church, the upper storey of a church with walls pierced by windows.

**Cloister:** an area in a monastery or convent restricted to the religious; a covered passage on the side of an open court, often with an open arcade or colonnade.

**Colonette:** a small or narrow column.

**Colonnade:** a series of columns inside or outside a building usually serving a support function.

**Column:** vertical architectural element with support function, usually cylindrical and composed of a base, shaft, and capital. The lower third of a column is often thicker (entasis) and then tapers slightly upward. Columns can be arranged in groups or can be free-standing. They can also be engaged, meaning set into a wall.

**Corbel:** architectural element that projects from a wall, often shaped like a capital, and serves as a support or bracket.

**Cornice:** a moulded and projecting horizontal decoration forming a band across a front or around a building.

**Corps-de-logis:** the principal section or block of a large building, such as a palace or mansion, containing the entrance and main rooms.

**Cosmati work, Cosmatesque:** a type of inlaid marble mosaic practised by Roman marble workers in the 12th and 13th centuries, so-named from the mistaken belief that all the city's leading marble workers came from the same family.

**Coupled:** architectural term for elements used in pairs, as in coupled columns.

**Crescent:** in British usage, a group of buildings arranged along a curving street or terrace.

**Crocket:** from the French *croquet*, 'hook', decorative device attached to a capital or gable, to an arch, to a curve of foliage.

413

**Crossing:** bay or other area of a church defined by the crossing of the main nave and the transept. According to how the two bodies intersect, the crossing can be *isolated*, in which the nave and transept are the same height and the square bay is defined by four equal and opposing arches, or *suppressed*, in which the bay is defined by lower and narrower arches that clearly separate the crossing from the transept, from the nave and from the choir.

**Crypt:** an area composed of one or more chambers located beneath the presbytery in a church. The crypt originated in the apostolic tombs made in Roman basilicas during the age of Constantine; beginning in the 7th century it assumed the function of housing the relics of the martyr saint to whom the church was dedicated. An *annular crypt* is surrounded by a semicircular ambulatory that follows the shape of the apse above; if other aisles and rooms are located off the crypt it is called a *hall crypt*. Beginning in the 10th–11th centuries the crypt took the shape of a nave and was enlarged, almost becoming a second, underground, church. Another name for the crypt is lower church.

**Cusp:** in Gothic tracery, a pointed projection formed by the intersection of two arcs or foils.

**Dome:** hemispherical architectural structure; as a roof, a dome is usually placed over a circular or square structure. The complete covering is composed of a pendentive, drum, dome, and lantern.

**Donjon:** also called the keep, the principal stronghold in a medieval castle, also used as a residence.

**Drum:** the cylindrical or polygonal wall supporting a dome.

**Echinus:** architectural element of the capital located beneath the abacus; in the Doric order, it has a convex shape without decoration; in the Ionic it is decorated with moulding.

**Elevation:** the side view of an architectural structure; a geometrical projection on a vertical plane.

**Enfilade:** distributional arrangement as though threaded on a string, in particular a series of rooms arranged so their doors form a continuous passage.

**Exedra:** an open or columned recess, often semicircular, with seats.

**Extrados:** the exterior curve of an arch.

**Façade:** the front exterior prospect of a building, usually with the main entrance (although transepts can have façades).

**Finial:** ornamental device at the top of a gable or spire.

**Foil:** in Gothic tracery, a small arc or lobe formed by cusps, making a leaflike design. The number of foils reflects the shape of a figure, as in trefoil, quatrefoil, cinquefoil.

**Framework:** element or arrangement of elements that form a structural or decorative whole.

**Gable:** the end wall of a building or part of a building; a high and narrow triangular structure typical of Gothic architecture.

**Galerie des rois:** carved band with the effigies of the kings of France located along the façade of a Gothic cathedral.

**Groin:** the projecting curving edge along which two intersecting vaults meet; a groin vault is created when two arches cross one another at right angles.

**Grotesque:** a style of decoration used in the 16th century adopting the fanciful or fantastic forms found on Roman wall decorations, most especially in grottoes.

**Ha-ha:** a ditch or other vertical drop separating a garden from the surrounding nature, thus forming a barrier without interrupting the view.

**Hall church:** a church with a nave and aisle of equal or almost equal height; Germ. *Hallenkirche*.

**Harmonic façade:** a façade framed by two towers.

**Iconostasis:** a screen separating the chancel (or bema) from the nave in a Byzantine church, often with doors and tiers of icons.

**Imafronte:** the central part of the façade of a church.

**Intrados:** the interior curve of an arch.

**Isabelline style:** named after Queen Isabella of Castile, Spanish style of architecture noted for its extraordinary flair and Flamboyant Gothic elements; often called Hispano-Flemish as being more accurate and to avoid confusion with Spain's Queen Isabella II.

**Keep:** the principal tower in a castle or bastion; the donjon.

**Keystone:** the wedge-shaped central piece of an arch or vault.

**Lancet:** tall, pointed window without tracery.

**Langchor:** choir style used in the churches of German mendicant orders, separated from the nave by a screen.

**Lantern:** a drum with windows above a dome.

**Layout:** *See* plan

**Lierne:** from the French, a cross rib or branch rib; a rib that runs from one rib to another to decorate a vault and thus does not spring from a main springer or a central boss.

**Loggia:** architectural structure, a roofed gallery open on one or more sides.

**Lunette:** a crescent-shaped opening above a door or in a vault.

**ihrab:** in a mosque, a niche indicating the ...ection of Mecca.

**...odule:** a size taken as the unit of measure ... establishing the proportions of an archi-...tural structure.

**...oulding:** in architecture, a decorative ...essed or relieved element.

**...ozarabic art:** art made in Spain during ...e Islamic domination by Christians ...ose work revealed the influence of Islam; ...m *Mozarab*, from *Mustarib*, meaning ...abicized'.

**...dejar:** name given to Moors who remained ...Spain after the Christian reconquest but did ...t convert to Christianity; the term is applied ...particular to their style of architecture; ...m *mudajjan*, 'allowed to remain'.

**...llion window:** a window divided in two ... more sections by slender vertical mem-...rs.

**...r épais:** a gallery built within the thick-...ss of a wall at the height of the windows.

**...rthex:** the portico of an ancient church, ...ecially with columns or pillars; the ...tibule of a church leading to the nave. ...e narthex is an *endonarthex* if it occupies ...part of the nave of the church; an ...narthex if it is located on the exterior of ...façade with an open portico.

**...ve:** the longitudinal area of a church lead-..., from the entrance to the altar, usually ...ked by rows of columns or piers. The ...e is usually flanked by aisles that run par-...l to it but are shorter than it. A nave with-...t illumination is a *blind nave*.

**...che:** a recess in a wall, usually semicircu-...usually used to hold a statue.

**...rman gallery:** gallery running in front of ...windows, typical of Anglo-Norman ...hitecture.

**...lus:** a small round window.

**Ogive, ogival:** diagonal or pointed, most especially in terms of an arch.

**Open plan:** building plan that is unencumbered by vertical support structures.

**Opus reticulatum:** Roman masonry of lozenge-shaped stones forming a net pattern.

**Opus sectile:** Roman wall or floor decoration composed of marble or stone pieces arranged to create geometric motifs.

**Order:** in terms of classical architecture, the order is the style of a building determined by its style and structure; *classical orders* are the columns used in classical architecture: Doric, Ionic, and Corinthian.

**Pendentive:** one of the concave triangular members that supports a dome; a spherical triangular section of masonry making a transition from a square to a circular surface.

**Peripteral temple:** a classical temple surrounded by columns on all sides.

**Pier:** vertical architectural element that supports an arch as in an arcade or a vault. There are two principal types, the compound, which has an engaged column on each side, and bundled or clustered, meaning composed of several columns joined to form a single element.

**Pilaster:** architectural structure usually rectangular and structurally a pier but treated as a column, sometimes projecting from the wall.

**Pilier cantonné:** a pier composed of a core to which are attached four shafts projecting in the cardinal directions.

**Pilotis:** French term meaning 'pile', as in 'foundation pile', used for the elements, usually made in reinforced concrete, that lift a building off the ground, creating a covered space without walls and thus in direct contact with the exterior nature.

**Pinnacle:** upright architectural element, usually ending in a spire, used to add weight to a buttress.

**Plan:** design of an architectural complex, building, or part of a building in a horizontal projection, as though seen from above. A central-planned building is organized symmetrically around a geometric centre. The same term is applied to a Greek-cross plan, so-called when its four arms are of the same length. In the Latin-cross plan, the long arm is cut by the short arm at about a third of its length. In the Tau plan, the transept is located at the far end of the longitudinal nave.

**Plateresque:** architectural style that flourished in Spain during the 16th century distinguished by its rich decorations ('silversmith', from the Spanish *plata*, 'silver').

**Portal:** monumental entrance to a civil or religious building given architectural emphasis.

**Portico:** an open gallery or colonnade, usually on the exterior ground floor.

**Presbytery:** in churches, the area around the altar reserved for the clergy, separated from the faithful by a screen. It may be elevated if above a crypt.

**Pronaos:** in Greek temples, the area between the colonnade and the area in front of the cell (temple); later, an architectural element to itself, composed of columns and piers outside or inside the façade of a building.

**Propylaeum:** in classical architecture, a colonnade located at the top of a flight of stairs, forming an interior or exterior portico through which one enters a monumental building, hence a monumental entranceway.

**Puteal:** well head.

**Quadripartite vault:** vault divided in four cells.

**Quoin:** the keystone or voussoir of an arch; a solid exterior corner of a building.

**Radiating chapels:** chapels located on the exterior side of the ambulatory of a Romanesque or Gothic church.

**Retable/Retablo:** both from the Spanish word *retablo*, meaning 'tablet', in reference to a frame for decorative panels at the back of an altar. Retables, which became widespread in Europe in the 14th century, most of all in Spain, can be richly decorated with painting or sculpture, and can include several compartments. There is also the similar *reredos*.

**Rib:** a support element, usually a moulded band, used in Romanesque and Gothic architecture to support the cells of a vault or a dome.

**Ribbon windows:** same-size windows arranged to form long bands or ribbons along the façade of a building.

**Rose window:** large circular window filled with ornamental tracery, usually located at the centre of the façade of a Romanesque or Gothic church.

**Rustication:** the working of a stone surface to make it rough.

**Sacellum:** from the Latin *sacrum*, 'sacred enclosure', a small votive chapel, thus any small structure made for worship, such as an oratory, chapel, small temple, or sepulchre.

**Sacristy:** room in a church where sacred vessels and vestments are kept.

**Schola cantorum:** area of the presbytery reserved for the singers, separated by a screen.

**Serlian motif:** a three-part window, in which the central, larger part is a round arch that rests on a trabeation supported by columns that form the two side parts of the window. It is named after Sebastiano Serlio, who illustrated such a window in his treatise on architecture (1551).

**Slab:** flat, rectangular architectural element, usually formed of a single piece, as in a concrete slab used to make floors and projecting or cantilevered parts.

**Socle:** architectural member that projects at the foot of a wall or pier or beneath the base of a column or structure.

**Span:** the distance between abutments or supports in a bridge or arch.

**Spandrel:** the triangular space formed by the curve of arches in an arcade.

**Spire:** a tall, tapering element, usually rising over a tower.

**Splaying:** spread outward, as the bevelling of a door jamb.

**Springers:** the stones supporting the arc of an arch.

**Squinch:** an arch or niche set across the corner of a square bay to convert the space into an octagon on which a round dome or vault can rest.

**Stavkirke:** 'stave church', a type of timber church found in northern Europe, most of all Scandinavia.

**Strapwork:** ornament composed of bands with the appearance of leather or metal twisted and rolled into fantastic shapes.

**Stylobate:** a continuous flat structure on which a row of architectural columns is supported.

**Tabernacle:** small receptacle, often shaped like a small temple, located at the centre of the altar and used to hold the holy sacrament, the host, or relics; a niche or chapel with a sacred image.

**Taper:** to grow thinner, as a column.

**Tiercerone:** secondary, accessory rib without support function that springs from the intersection of two other ribs.

**Topiary:** the art of training, cutting, and trimming trees or shrubs into ornamen[t] shapes.

**Trabeation:** in classical architecture, the ho[r]izontal elements resting on columns; in ge[n]eral, a horizontal beam or lintel supported [by] vertical elements and contributing to t[he] support of architectural elements.

**Tracery:** ornamental openwork in Got[h]ic architecture, as in stone work applied to w[all] surfaces or the upper part of windows.

**Transept:** the transverse element of a basil[ic]an church that intersects the nave to fo[rm] a cross shape; it is often as high or higher a[nd] as wide as the nave.

**Tribune:** in Roman basilicas the area us[ed] for the exercise of justice; in early Chri[st]ian churches, the seats in the presbyte[ry] reserved for the bishop and the clergy d[ur]ing ceremonies; thus the space of the pre[s]bytery and the apse, including radiati[ng] chapels; more in general, an arcaded galle[ry] above the aisle and open to the nave of t[he] church or any loggia or gallery inside [or] outside the building.

**Triconch choir:** choir structure with th[ree] semicircular areas of the same size formi[ng] a trefoil.

**Triforium:** in the elevation of a Romanes[que] or Gothic basilican church, the galle[ry] located at the height of the aisle ro[of] between the nave arcade and the clerest[ory] (sometimes found in the transept and cho[ir]).

**Trumeau:** the central post of a portal s[up]porting a lintel and tympanum, often be[ar]ing sculptural decoration in medie[val] churches.

**Truss:** timber framework forming triang[les] to support the roof.

**Tympanum:** the recessed, usually triangu[lar] face of a pediment within the frame of [the] upper and lower cornices; the area betw[een] the lintel and arch of a portal.

**Vault:** architectural covering based on the principle of the arch. Numerous types of vault exist. The simplest is the barrel vault, a tunnellike extension of an arch with its weight resting on side walls. A groin vault is composed of the intersection of two barrel vaults of the same size. A cross vault is the intersection of two barrel vaults crossing in a right angle. The domical or cloister vault is a domelike vault with a square or polygonal base from which curved segments rise to a central point. A ribbed vault has masonry ribs that concentrate the thrust.

**Voussoir:** a wedge-shaped piece, as of stone, used in the construction of an arch or vault; the central voussoir is the keystone.

**Watch tower:** in medieval fortifications, a powerful tower used for observation or as a final refuge for the inhabitants, although unlike a donjon it was not normally equipped with living quarters.

**Westbau:** evolution of the Carolingian westwork, a result of the loss of the political and civil uses of Ottonian churches. It is a large turreted body on the western side of the church; it later assumed the form of the harmonic façade.

**Westwork:** large structure with several floors built on the western end of the church, typical of Carolingian church architecture, serving political and civil functions. It is shaped like a tower and is usually framed by a pair of stair turrets; internally it is composed of a vestibule beneath an open tribune wrapped by a two-storey ambulatory. During the Ottonian age it evolved into the *Westbau*.

# Index of names, places, and works

# Photographic sources

AKG-Images, Berlin, 11, 39 above, 90 above, 273 below, 274 below, 281, 312 above, 323 above, 324 above; 163 above left, 372 above (Archives CDA/Guillot); 191 below (CDA/St. Genès); 210 above (Orsi-Battaglini); 4, 13, 16, 27 above, 19, 23, 32, 34, 36, 36 below, 37 below, 39 below, 41, 42, 43, 50, 56 right, 57, 59 below, 69, 71 below, 73 right, 74 right, 75, 77, 78 above, 79, 80 right, 81, 82, 87, 88, 89, 90 below, 91, 92, 93 above, 94 above, 95, 97, 98, 99 above, 104, 105 right, 106, 108 below, 109 above, 110 left, 119, 119 right, 120, 124 above, 125, 154 below, 155 below, 166, 168, 173 below, 187, 190, 205 right, 206 below, 211, 213 above, 216, 217, 218, 219, 220 right, 222, 223, 225 left, 228 right, 236 above, 238, 239 below, 243 above, 246, 253 above, 262, 263 above, 265, 297 below, 380 (Bildarchiv Monheim); 58 below (Henning Bock); 302 (Florence Delva); 255 right, 266, 335 above (Keith Collie); 229, 230, 231 above (Jerome Da Cunha); 63 above (Elisabeth Disney); 18 below, 20, 24 above, 38 below, 54 below, 55 above, 58 above, 73 centre, 76, 80 left, 84 left, 215 above, 248, 350, 360 above, 372 below right (Stefan Drechsel); 30 above (Hedda Heid); 12, 83, 96 below, 221 above, 252, 267 above, 278 right, 278 left, 288 right, 288 left, 308 below, 322 left, 349 below (Hilbich); 377 above (Dieter E. Hoppe); 30 below, 36 above, 44 below, 204 above, 291 (Andrea Jemolo); 280 below (Jànos Kolmar); 122 above (Francoise Kuntz); 6 (Tristan Lafranchis); 55 below, 105 above, 221 below (Paul M.R. Maeyaert); 85, 179 below, 184 right, 194 below, 277, 289, 373 (Joseph Martin); 73 above (Gilles Mermet); 198 below, 206 above (Robert O'Dea); 7, 259 below (Pirozzi); 284–85 (Florian Profitlich); 49 (Rabatti-Dominigie); 351 (Jurgen Raible); 170 below, 237 above (Jost Schilgen); 17 below, 21, 22 above, 24 below, 54 above, 59 above, 70, 117, 163 below, 203 above, 220 left (Schutze/Rodermann); 107 (Von Linden); 357 below (Irmgard Wagner); 374 centre (Reimer Wulf).

© Archipress/Artur, 361.

Alinari Archives, Florence, 71 above

Archivio Fotografico Associazione Cultur-ale Crespi D'Adda, 271.

Archivio Fotografico MART, 355 below.

Mondadori Electa Archives, Milan, 10, 22, 28 below, 37 above, 48 below, 60, 67, 100 above, 103 above, 109 right, 111 above, 129 above, 135 below, 136 right, 137 above, 138 below, 139, 144 above, 145, 146 below, 150, 151, 167 above, 173 above, 175 above, 193 above, 195, 210 above, 225 right, 241 above right, 259 above, 268, 272 left, 273 above, 275, 300 above, 301, 304 above, 307 above, 333 below / Sergio Anelli, Milan, 134, 152 below, 154 above, 245, 270 above, 347 above / Graziano Arici, Venice, 152 above, 153 above, 176 left, 243 below / Balestrini, Milan, 52, 53 below / Fabrizio Carraro, Turin, 276 above, 280 above, 306 below, 307 below, 310, 311, 313 below, 331 above, 333 above, 354 / Daniele De Lonte, 161 below, 240, 247 below, 261 below, 337, 338 below / Roberto Gargiani, 339 / Roland Halbe, Stuttgart, 364 / Andrea Jemolo, Rome, 144 below, 178, 179 above, 184 left / Diego Motto, Milan, 292 left / Paolo Perina, 188, 189 below / Marco Ravenna, 129 below, 135 above, 181 above / Arnaldo Vescovo, Rome, 8, 142 left, 176 centre, 185 left, 202.

Archivio Mondadori Electa, Milan, with permission of the Ministero of Cultural Activities, 66 above, 131.

© Scala Archives, Florence, 51, 53 above, 143, 235.

© Madijd Asghari/Artur, 347.

Achim Bednorz, Cologne, 9, 18 above, 25, 31, 33, 38 above, 40, 44 above, 56, 63 below, 64, 65 right, 86 right, 86 left, 110 right, 111 right, 112 below, 113, 115 above, 121 above, 163 above right, 164 below, 171, 172, 204 below, 205 above, 212, 213 below, 251 below.

Bibliothèque Nationale de France, Paris, 251 above.

© Luc Boegly/Archipress/Artur, 371 above

Bridgeman/Alinari Archives, Florence, 16, 255, 256.

Bridgeman Art Library, London, 283.

Cameraphoto, Venice, 28 above.

Fabrizio Carraro, Turin, 61 above, 35 above, 374 above.

© Corbis/Contrasto, Milan, 26, 45 below, 65 left, 66 below, 68, 101 right, 115 below, 119 left, 122 below, 123, 126, 165 above, 16 below, 169, 174, 175 below, 182, 193 below, 198 above, 199 above, 200, 201, 241 below, 244, 252, 255 above, 263 below, 267 below, 285, 286, 287 above, 290, 293, 296 right, 298, 316, 317 below, 319, 328 above, 33 right, 336, 341 above, 344, 348, 349 above, 352 left, 357 above left, 362, 368 below right.

Piero De Martini, Milan, 317 above.

© Michel Denancé/Archipress/Artur, 36 below, 366 above.

© Frank Eustache/Archipress/Artur, 37 below left.

© Klaus Frahm/Artur, 322 right.

Gérald Halary/Artedia, Paris, 269 below.

© Roland Halbe, Stuttgart, 299 right, 30 below, 304 below, 305, 309, 313 above, 31 323 below, 327 below, 334 below, 34 below, 355, 356, 357 above right, 359 abov 363 below, 365 above, 367, 370, 371 belo 374 below, 375, 376, 379 above, 383 below

© Jochen Helle/Artur, 330 below

© Werner Huthmacher/Arthur, 342 above

© Wolfram Janzen/Artur, 359 below.

Andrea Jemolo, Rome, 100 below, 159, 26 327 above.

© Reiner Lautwein/Artur, 279.

© Leemage, Paris, 191 above, 284 below.

© Erich Lessing/Contrasto, 96 above, 12 306 above.

© Magnum/Contrasto, Milan, 162 above.

© Dieter Leistner/Artur, 377 below.

© Duccio Malagamba, 369, 381.